CRITTERS

Of The

Little Spokane Watershed

A Guide And Photographic Tour Of

Native Plants, Fungi, Insects, Wildlife, Habitats

And Their

Inter-Relationships

CRITTERS

Of The

Little Spokane Watershed

A Guide And Photographic Tour Of

Native Plants, Fungi, Insects, Wildlife, Habitats

And Their

Inter-Relationships

Edited by Easy

Little Spokane Watershed Council

Published by Adventure Trail

for the

Little Spokane Watershed Council
P.O. Box 413, Spokane, WA 99210
Phone. (509) 747-5738, Fax: (509) 838-5155
Internet: Easy@ieplc.desktop.org

© 1996 by Easy

♻ Printed on recycled paper

This is ECF paper, elemental chlorine free,
and is acid free, for a shelf life of 200 years

Publisher's Cataloging-in-Publication Data
Easy
   Critters of the Little Spokane Watershed: a guide and photographic tour of native plants,
fungi, insects, wildlife, habitats and their inter-relationships / Edited by Easy.
   Includes index, references, photographs and illustrations. 320 pages.
ISBN 0-9653619-0-X
Library of Congress Catalog Card Number: 96-86697

"Healthy life is completeness
of relation
of organism, function, and environment,
and all at their best."

Patrick Geddes (1853-1932)

Contents

Acknowledgments

*C*RITTERS was composed from an ongoing collaborative work. The cooperative research, field work and shared knowledge of individuals who have studied the Little Spokane Watershed and the surrounding region for many years have provided a wealth of information about the watershed's critters, habitats and their inter-relationships.

Jean Gauthier, a naturalist, and Lori Lewis, a biologist, contributed many hours identifying and categorizing many of the critters that live in the watershed. Lori Lewis also contributed most of the critter descriptions. Rick Ward, a biologist, contributed the initial text for each of the habitats. Tom Rogers, one of this region's eminent naturalists, provided initial critter lists including a special focus on butterflies and insects, and several reviews of the material as it was being assembled. David H. Chance, a noted historian of the Columbia River Region, provided an initial outline for historic research related to the natural history of the Little Spokane Watershed. Barbara Johnson contributed data and text entry along with the numerous edits and adjustments to the materials. JoAn Henricks contributed copy editing suggestions.

Jan Reynolds, with an incredible knowledge and love of nature, provided the initial list of birds, adjusted from the Spokane Audubon Society's *Birds of the Inland Empire*. Dale Gill, one of this region's experts on lichens, contributed the list of lichens and mosses. Gary Blevins, Spokane Falls Community College biology instructor, provided many of the scientific names for the birds and other useful suggestions, edits and encouragement. Kelly Chadwick, with some initial lists of mushrooms from the Mushroom Club and a comprehensive knowledge of mushrooms, made significant contributions to the mushroom list. Ron Dexter, who lives in the watershed, contributed reviews and significant edits of the bird list.

Joe Guarisco, one of Spokane's fine graphic artists, contributed graphics including the habitat heading graphics and the graphic side of the Little Spokane Watershed poster. Maurice Vial suggested much needed additions and corrections on birds and mammals and painted the illustration that is on the cover and is on one side of the Little Spokane Watershed poster.

John S. Lewis, Patricia Vandenhoy, and Trish Bravo contributed many hours and hundreds of photographs from their exploration of the Little Spokane Watershed. Pam Kriscunus's journey by canoe and walking added to the photo collection. Ron Dexter and Pat Dexter contributed photos from their many years of photography.

Finally, and no less important, the critters and habitats of the Little Spokane Watershed contribute their timeless patience, as the people of the watershed become better stewards of the wealth of nature that is too often taken for granted.

Introduction

A viable quality of life, for people and nature living in and near the Little Spokane Watershed, depends on a watershed that is healthy, thriving, and restorative. Knowledge of the critters, their habitats and their inter-relationships with the watershed is one tool that can be used to work towards better qualities of life for everyone who lives in or near or passes through this magnificent watershed.

By realizing what the Little Spokane Watershed can be over the next one hundred years or so, fresh choices can be made to take advantage of once in a life time opportunities, insights and intuitions to allow the watershed to be more sustainable. This is not a small task. However the alternatives can be less than beneficial for people and nature in the watershed.

The Little Spokane Watershed is a fascinating place of intriguing complexity. It is almost unthinkable that anyone could exhaust the possible areas of study and understanding the watershed has to offer. *CRITTERS of the Little Spokane Watershed* is a guide and photographic tour that can be used to explore what the Little Spokane Watershed is and what the watershed can be. An intention to explore the watershed may provide a spark of insight that leads to a better quality of life.

Flora

Critters – Another Name For Species

The word 'critters' is used here as a non-technical term for species. These species can be native plants, fungi, wildlife and other species. Derived from the word creatures, the word 'critters' can be a friendly way to talk of particular species in the Little Spokane Watershed.

Diversity And Inter-relationships

The diversity of critters, their habitats and their inter-relationships are keys to how healthy the Little Spokane Watershed is and can be. By only looking at native plants and wildlife, without examining their inter-relationships, vital perspectives may be left out.

Fungus

Fauna

Northern Pygmy Owl

CRITTERS of the Little Spokane Watershed is intended to encourage the reader to explore the inter-relationships among the critters and the habitats; to notice how the diversity of critters, the diversity of habitats and the diversity of inter-relationships gives the Little Spokane Watershed its life blood; and to notice how fragile and how strong the inter-relationships and diversity can be.

Interrupting a single thread of this tapestry of life can have unintentional consequences far into the future. With patient stewardship, essential inter-relationships and diversity can be nurtured.

Looking At The Whole Watershed

The intent of *CRITTERS* is not to study a particular aspect of the watershed, without keeping the whole watershed in mind. Not only can the habitats, critters and their very many inter-relationships be examined, but how these all work together as a whole watershed can be explored. The whole watershed has rhythms and cycles that are influenced by the drum beat of the seasons and other drums of nature. A thriving, healthy and restorative watershed depends on many less than well studied inter-relationships of the whole watershed. By paying more attention to the native plants, fungi, wildlife, habitats and their inter-relationships, the quality of life in the whole watershed can be significantly improved.

Photographic Tour and Guide

The many photographs showing the watershed's breathtaking beauty and other qualities provide a tour of some of what can be found in the watershed. The habitats,

Slug in moss

their critters and their inter-relationships are the lens used to explore the Little Spokane Watershed. A more traditional field guide approach is to focus on a category of life, like birds or wildflowers. *CRITTERS of the Little Spokane Watershed*, however, guides the reader to look for inter-relationships and encourages the reader to explore how these relationships create this magnificent treasure of nature.

For those interested in a more in depth examination of the watershed, field guides and other reference material can be invaluable. The reference section lists a good number of resources that can be used to explore aspects of the Little Spokane Watershed in greater detail.

CRITTERS is intended to be readable by anyone who is interested in the critters of the Little Spokane Watershed in particular, and the critters of the upper Columbia River region in general. By exploring the photographs and their captions alone much can be learned about the watershed. When a photo or drawing of a particular critter is available, it is placed near a critter's description. Photos and drawings of critters not described are also placed throughout the text for a fuller feeling of the watershed.

Common Names

Common names for the critters are used throughout this book. A particular critter, like ponderosa pine, may have more than one common name; bull pine, blackjack pine, p pine, pondosa pine and western yellow pine are a few of the names. For this book a primary common name is used.

Bird common names and species separation are done according to the American Ornithological Union listing, current at the time of publication.

Moose in woods

For the critters with descriptions in the habitat sections, other common names are listed. The scientific name, which is usually Latin, follows the primary common name in these critter descriptions.

Aquifer water rushing from a hillside brings an ever present spray to the river birch limbs

Red squirrel ready to run

Critter And Habitat Lists

Without the ability to sort and sift through the watershed information by computer, it would be difficult and take considerable time to assemble even one ordered list of the watershed's critters. A computer database of the watershed's critters was used to make the various lists found in this book.

Each habitat section of this book includes a list of the habitat's more common critters. The appendix contains a full list of the more than 1,700 critters, listed by their primary common name. Along with the primary common name, this 'Critter List' shows how abundant each critter is in each of the habitat types. Not only can the list be used to find particular critters, it can be used to explore which critters can be found in a particular habitat.

Additional critter lists, with various selections and sortings of critters and habitats, are available from the Little Spokane Watershed Council. These additional reports include the other common names and the scientific names. There is additional information available, including the seasonal abundance for birds and if the bird species breeds in the watershed.

Helping To Make This Information More Accurate

As with most projects there are oversights, entry errors, omissions and other inaccuracies. Fresh eyes looking at these materials for the first time can catch these much more easily than eyes that have looked at the same pages many times. Thoughts, comments, suggestions, and corrections are most welcome. They can be phoned, mailed or emailed to the Little Spokane Watershed Council. Please see the back of the book for the address. From these corrections and additional research, the critter information in the Little Spokane Watershed database is to be periodically updated. New reports will include these updates.

A wealth of pine cones

Critter Overview

Over 1,700 critters have been identified that live in the Little Spokane Watershed. Not counting the smaller forms of life - protists, bacteria and virus - there are almost 500 plants, over 400 fungi and lichens, and over 700 animals. Among the plants there are almost 100 critters in the rose class and over 100 in the sunflower class. The fungi have more than 300 mushrooms. The animals have over 300 insects and more than 200 birds.

Critters Not In The Little Spokane Watershed

Another way to view the Little Spokane Watershed's critters is to explore which critters do not live in the watershed. Lions, giraffes, pythons and palm trees, obviously, do not live in the watershed. Neither do oak trees that can be found near Yakima, nor critters in the category that include avocado, pepper, tea, cotton and pineapple.

Ocean critters, from whales to brown algae, are not in the waterways of the Little Spokane. While there are fourteen different cone bearing trees, conifers, in the watershed, the cone-bearing podocarps that live in New Zealand are not to be found in the Little Spokane Watershed. There are no elephants or tigers, although less than 50,000 years ago the woolly mammoth and saber tooth tiger probably lived quite well in the Little Spokane Watershed.

Nor are there any of the great apes, only one primate is found in the Little Spokane Watershed – humans. This one species, by their humane choices, can have profound affects on how healthy, thriving and restorative the Little Spokane Watershed is for people and nature.

Ferns overhanging water

A World Comparison

The World Comparison Table is another way of viewing what species are or are not in the watershed. This table lists some of the many categories used to classify the critters of the world. Not all of these categories are found in the Little Spokane Watershed. This table shows a current arrangement of how the world's critters are organized. Most of the critters are organized in the order that they are thought to have evolved. This ordering provides insights about individual species and common relationships that they may share with other closely related species.

A World Comparison

Category	Little Spokane	World
PLANT	477	300,000
MOSS	29	10,000
Liverwort	4	6,500
Club Moss	1	1,000
Horsetail	3	15
Fern	9	12,000
Pine	13	777
Cedar	3	140
Pine	9	250
Flower	418	235,000
Dicot	-	170,000
Aspen	44	25,000
Mustard	11	-
Rose	95	60,000
Rose	43	-
Sunflower	140	-
Phlox	23	-
Phlox	11	-
Monocot	-	65,000
Grass	42	15,000
Grass	32	-
Rush	3	-
Sedge	5	-
Lily	32	25,000
Lily	25	8,000
Orchid	7	15,000

Category	Little Spokane	World
ANIMAL	753	1,400,000
FLATWORM	2	15,000
MOLLUSK	6	110,000
EARTHWORM	6	9,000
JOINT-LEG INVRT.	381	1,300,000
Crustacean	17	40,000
Spider	4	65,000
Millipede	1	8,000
Insect	358	1,000,000
Dragonfly	8	5,000
Grasshopper	19	1,000
True Bug	21	55,000
Beetle	44	500,000
Butterfly	79	140,000
Swallowtail	4	-
Skipper	11	-
Fly	61	80,000
Ant & Bee	27	90,000
Vertebrate	355	45,000
Lamprey	2	100
Fish	46	30,000
Amphibian	10	4,500
Salamander	2	450
Frog	8	3,800
Reptile	14	6,500
Snake	11	-
Bird	215	8,700
Waterfowl	26	-
Hawk	15	-
Hawk	10	-
Woodpecker	8	-
Thrush	104	5,274
Warbler	34	-
Mammal	68	4,060
Rodent	24	-
Squirrel	8	1,685
Beaver	1	2
Primate	1	197
Human	1	1
Carnivore	16	-
Deer	5	-

Category	Little Spokane	World
FUNGUS	451	70,000
Mushroom	342	100,000
Brittle	33	-
Gill, White Spore	81	-
Puffball	22	-
Ascomycetes	38	30,000
True Morel	3	-
Cup Fungus	14	-
LICHEN	31	-

Category	Little Spokane	World
PROTIST	17	60,000
PROTOZOA	6	-
ALGAE	7	10,000
MOLD	4	-

Category	Little Spokane	World
BACTERIA & VIRUS	7	2,800
BACTERIA	3	1,000
VIRUS	4	1,800

Type face indicates category: **KINGDOM,** *DIVISION/PHYLUM,* Class, *Order,* Family, *Subfamily*

Nature Categories For Critters – Taxonomy

Identifying and classifying critters have not been the easiest of tasks for biologists. With each new understanding about how critters can be classified, whole categories can be shifted. Fungi have been considered plants. With new understandings they are now in their own category.

For this book, one of the more recent taxonomies has been used to categorize the Little Spokane Watershed critters. The Lichens are treated as a category of fungi, even though they technically are a combination of fungus and algae. Six standard categories are used: Kingdom, Division/Phylum, Class, Order, Family and Subfamily. For other more detailed studies, each of these categories can have other divisions: e.g. sub-class.

The five major categories of life, Kingdoms, used in this book are: Plant, Fungus, Animal, Protist, and Bacteria and Virus. The primary focus of this book is on the Plant, Fungus and Animal species.

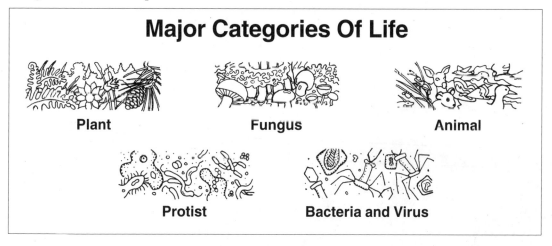

Major Categories Of Life

Plant   **Fungus**   **Animal**

Protist   **Bacteria and Virus**

Plants are the primary energy source for life on earth, converting sunlight into energy. Fungus are the earth's recyclers, returning many of the decaying species to the earth. Animals are the more mobile species, moving throughout the thin sliver of life on earth, the biosphere. These three main categories and the Protists, single cell species, and Bacteria and Virus are the essence of the earth's biodiversity. They form the essential inter-relationships of life on earth.

Of the more than 1,700 critters, there are two groupings of critters that deserve additional attention. They are the critters that are 'at risk' and the introduced critters. The critters 'at risk' are critters that could all to easily be decimated. The introduced critters are critters that have been recently, within the about last 100 years, brought into the watershed and the region. The 'at risk' critters have shown significant signs of decline while the introduced critters have increased rapidly, displacing native critters.

Critters At Risk

Forty one critters are considered at risk. Six of these have been missing from the watershed for a long time, but they can once again live in the watershed when barriers to their return are removed. The Wolf, Grizzly and Buffalo once made their home in the Little Spokane Watershed. Less than one hundred years ago, great salmon runs flourished in the Little Spokane. Today there are some land-locked Kokanee that have been seen in the Little Spokane, but the Coho Salmon and Chinook Salmon have yet to return home. The Bald Eagle, which is considered a threatened species, has been making solid progress in establishing new homes in the watershed.

Nine critters are considered candidate species as their species have dwindled over the past years. They are the Spotted Frog, Pacific Tree Frog, Loon, Golden Eagle, Vaux's Swift, White Throated Swift, Pileated Woodpecker, Western Bluebird, and Pigmy Shrew. These critters can benefit from a bit more care to better insure their homes in the watershed become more viable.

Seven birds are being monitored so that proactive measures can be taken if their numbers continue to decline. Two birds have protected breeding areas to encourage their populations to become more viable. There are eleven critters that are regulated game animals and four critters that are regulated as non-game animals. One species is considered rare.

Canada thistle, an introduced noxious weed

Here are the codes used in the critter lists for critters at risk: **MS** Missing, **ED** Endangered, **TH** Threatened, **CD** Candidate, **MN** Monitor, **RGM** Regulated Game, **RNG** Regulated Nongame, **RA** Rare, **PB** Protected Breeding Areas.

Introduced Critters - Noxious And Other

Eighty four critters have been introduced into the Little Spokane Watershed. Most, if not all, were introduced through human activities within the last 100 years. If introduced species do nothing else, they at least displace the critters that were in the Little Spokane Watershed before them. Without the introduced critters, the Little Spokane Watershed would have a much different look and feel about it.

Noxious Introduced Critters

Fourteen introduced critters are considered so harmful that they have been classified as noxious species. There are active programs to remove most of these critters from the watershed. Without these programs at least slowing down the advance of these noxious species, large areas of the watershed could be overrun by these aggressive critters.

Plants make up eleven of these notorious critters. Eight of these belong to the plant class that includes sunflowers: Dalmatian Toadflax, Moth Mullein, Common Mullein, Bull Thistle, Skeletonweed, Spotted Knapweed, White Knapweed and Common Tansy. One plant from the rose class, Purple Loosestrife, is an aggressive water plant found along the Little Spokane and is barely held in check. A grass, Bentgrass, is also considered noxious. The Yellow Flag Iris has invaded the lower section of the Little Spokane, displacing the once abundant cattails and the many birds that thrived on the cattails, not so long ago.

Three animals are considered noxious and can be removed from nature areas whenever they are found. The Bull Frog is extremely destructive of native wildlife and is known to eat small birds. Dogs and Cats are the other two predators that can do considerable damage to the wildlife of the watershed.

Other Introduced Critters

Seventy other critters have been introduced into the watershed. Fifty are plants including: Clovers, Big Bluegrass, Rough Fescue, Timothy, Asparagus, Weeping Willow, Mountain Ash and Norway Maple. The remaining twenty other introduced critters are animals; all fish. These fish include: Brown Trout, Cutthroat Trout, Carp, Goldfish, Bass, Walleye and Shad.

The following are the codes used for the introduced critters: **IN** Introduced Noxious species, **IO** Introduced, Other than noxious species.

Abundance Of Critters In Each Habitat

Each habitat attracts different critters, some only to pass through and some to establish homes in the habitat. How often a particular critter can be seen in a habitat varies. The frequency a critter is expected to be seen in each habitat is listed with the selected critter lists and critter descriptions in each habitat section, and in the critter list in the appendix.

Here are the codes used to show the abundance or frequency of a species for a particular habitat: **A** Abundant, **C** Common, **F** Fairly common, **U** Uncommon, **R** Rare, **V** Vagrant, **K** Known in habitat, **L** Likely in habitat, **M** Missing from habitat.

Migratory critters such as birds, are coded for abundance at the peak of their presence.

Moss and much more

Habitat Overview

Habitats of the Little Spokane Watershed can be categorized into eleven general habitats plus two human related habitats. Each habitat has some different combinations of critters and inter-relationships. Starting with the highest elevation, the habitats are listed below along with some of their more abundant critters.

Subalpine
The highest elevations of the Little Spokane Watershed; including Mt. Spokane and Boyer Mountain. • Subalpine Fir, Beargrass, Yarrow, Glacier Lily, Black Fly, Clark's Nutcracker •

Mountain
The cradle of mountains that forms the edge of the watershed to the east, north and west. • Grand Fir, Western Hemlock, Huckleberry, Miner's Lettuce, Lupine, Mosquito, Bohemian Waxwing, Elk, Moose, Deer Mouse, Snowshoe Rabbit, Black Bear •

Douglas Fir
The north facing slopes which tend to have more shade and moisture. • Douglas Fir, Thimbleberry, Oregon Grape, Yellow Jacket, Bumblebee, Red Crossbill, Pocket Gopher •

Ponderosa Pine
Pine forest habitat that covers much of the watershed. • Ponderosa Pine, Mockorange, Ninebark, Snowberry, Grass Widow, Balsamroot, Yellowbell, Black-capped Chicadee, Red-breasted Nuthatch, Chipmunk, Coyote •

Rockland
Granite and basalt rock outcroppings of the watershed. • Kinnikinnick, Poison Ivy, Licorice-root Fern, Camel Cricket, Blue-tailed Skink, Rock Wren, Marmot •

Bushland
Bushy areas. A favorite area for many birds. • Nootka Rose, Buckbrush, Sumac, Cricket, Magpie, Dark-eyed Junco, Goldfinch, Fox Sparrow, Quail, White-tailed Deer •

Grassland

Meadows and open valleys. • Shooting Star, Larkspur, Bitterroot, Bluebunch Wheatgrass, Idaho Fescue, Buckwheat, Bluebells, Warrior Grasshopper, Canada Goose, Brewer's Blackbird, Crow, Western Bluebird, Killdeer, Meadowlark •

Wetland

Land that is damp, if not wet, much of the year. • Alder, Reed Canary Grass, Smooth Horsetail, Cottonwood, Cattail, Camas, Red-winged Blackbird, Tree Swallow, Great Blue Heron, Mud-dauber Wasp •

Riparian Edge

The edge of land along rivers, creeks, lakes and ponds. • River Birch, Aspen, Paper Birch, Stinging Nettle, Douglas Hawthorn, Red Ossier Dogwood, Dragonfly, Damselfly, Mud Turtle, Water Turtle, Tailed Toad, Cedar Waxwing, Song Sparrow, Raccoon •

Stream

Rivers, streams and creeks. • Steelhead, Sand Roller, Mottled Sculpin, Largescale Sucker, Mallard, Coot, Bank Swallow, Spotted Sandpiper, Osprey, Clam, Spotted Frog, Beaver •

Lake and Pond

Lakes and ponds. • Rainbow Trout, Mountain Whitefish, Mountain Sucker, Bulrush, Duckweed, Water Buttercup, Whirligig Beetle, Pied-billed Grebe, Bufflehead, Painted Turtle •

Disturbed Land

Much of the watershed's land has been disturbed: former agricultural land reverting to nature, timber harvest areas, construction and road building sites. Disturbed land habitat has more introduced species than the other habitats. • Jim Hill Mustard, Bracken, Dalmation Toadflax, Cheatgrass, Mullein, Knapweed, Clover, Bull Thistle, European Starling, Crow •

Human Sites

Urban areas, airports and industrial parks and a quarter mile beyond them, suburban areas and 700 feet beyond them, and rural houses, yards, buildings and roads and 350 feet beyond them. • Honeybee, Apple Maggot, House Fly, Aphid, Earwig, Cockroach, Slug, Robin, Northern Flicker, Rat, Dog, Cat and the many introduced flowers, shrubs and trees that decorate human sites •

Little Spokane Watershed

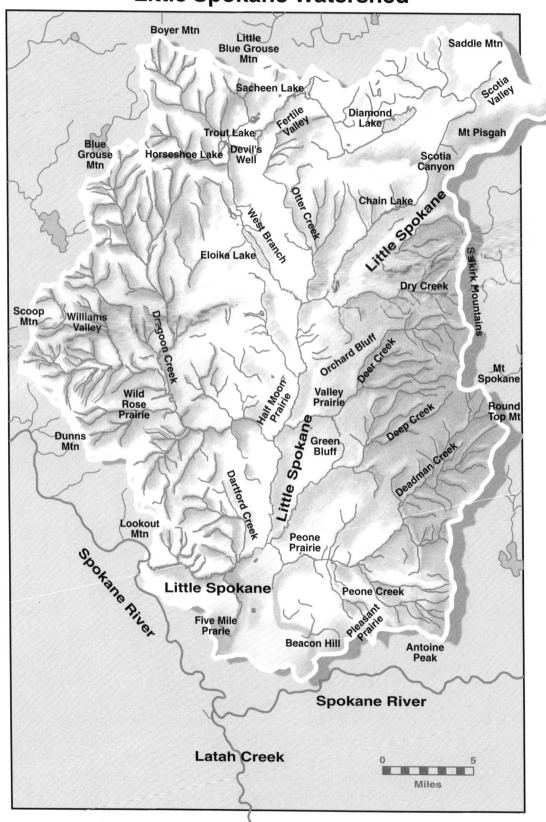

The Little Spokane Watershed

Cradled within forested hills and mountains of eastern Washington is the Little Spokane Watershed, a magnificent treasure of nature. Wildrose Prairie and Williams Valley, along the western edge of the Little Spokane Watershed, send their waters through Dragoon Creek and into the Little Spokane. From the north, Horeseshoe Lake and Eloika Lake's waters flow into the West Branch of the Little Spokane.

From the northeast, just outside of Newport, the Little Spokane begins seeping from the ground, forming a good sized creek within its first couple of miles before making its way through beautiful Scotia Canyon. From the east, Mt. Spokane sends waters cascading along Dry, Deer, Deep and Deadman Creeks. The great Peone Prairie, along the southeast edge of the watershed, sends its waters flowing along its fertile soils. These are the surface waters that make up the Little Spokane Watershed.

Looking across the Little Spokane Watershed from the western edge towards Mt. Spokane

There is also an extraordinary outflowing of water that comes into the Little Spokane Watershed. About ten miles upstream from where the Little Spokane joins with the Spokane River, an underground river flows out of the ground and into the Little Spokane. Starting more than thirty miles away in the Coeur d'Alene Mountain and

An aerial view of the Little Spokane, on the right, joining with the Big Spokane, just beyond Nine Mile Falls. The neck of land lying between the Spokane and Little Spokane Rivers once was the site of a large Indian village and also the early site of fur trading posts.

Rathdrum Prairie in Idaho, these waters flow underground to the Little Spokane and also into the Spokane River.

One place where this underground river comes to the surface is near Waikiki Springs. Walking toward Waikiki springs, along a dry Douglas Fir covered hillside, a person can hear, in the distance, what seems to sound like the roar of a distant ocean. From above the springs a person can see where the roar begins, as water starts to seep out of the hillside. Within 50 feet the water from these many seeps and springs has merged into what could be mistaken for a glacial stream cascading down the hillside. At the bottom of the hillside this cold water forms its own creek that soon flows into the Little Spokane.

What A Watershed Is

A watershed is the region where the surface water comes from that eventually flows into a river or stream. Each river has its own particular watershed region. In this case,

Here, framed by a pine bow, the Little Spokane flows into the Big Spokane. Perhaps the people of the Indian village and fur trading post times had a similar view.

the Little Spokane Watershed is the region for the Little Spokane River and its associated creeks and streams.

The Little Spokane Watershed is part of the larger Spokane - Coeur d'Alene Watershed. The Spokane - Coeur d'Alene Watershed includes five smaller watersheds; Latah Creek, St. Maries, St. Joe, Coeur d'Alene and the Little Spokane. The Spokane - Coeur d'Alene Watershed is part of the much larger Columbia River Watershed, which is about the size of France or Texas.

The Size And Elevation Of The Little Spokane Watershed

The Little Spokane Watershed is a bit larger than the nation of Tahiti. At the farthest points the watershed is a little less than 30 miles long by 25 miles wide. Over 670 square miles of Earth's surface make up the Little Spokane Watershed. It would take about 100 Little Spokane Watersheds to cover the state of Washington, about 5,400 to cover the 50 states, and just over 86,580 Little Spokane Watersheds to cover the land surface of the world; more than 60% of Earth's surface is water.

Mt. Spokane is the highest point in the watershed at 5,878 feet or 1,792 meters above sea level. Where the Little and Big Spokane Rivers meet, the confluence, the elevation is 1,524 feet or 461 meters; a drop of over 4,000 feet in less than 30 miles.

The Little Spokane Watershed's Native Plant and Wildlife History

As yet there has not been adequate comprehensive research of the available documents for references to the native plants and wildlife of the Little Spokane

These three pines have watched this place for over 100 years

Watershed or for that matter the inland Columbia River Watershed. There are several sources that refer directly to the Little Spokane.

One source, *The History of the City of Spokane and Spokane Country Washington,* was written by N. W. Durham in 1912. Based on the records from the Lewis and Clark 1804-1806 expedition, Durham writes: "Captain Lewis wrote: 'The three Indians encountered by Lewis and Clark were evidently from the middle band of the Spokanes, living at a large village at the mouth of the Little Spokane . . .'"

Later in the book, Durham writes, "The site chosen for the Spokane post was the neck of land lying between the Spokane and Little Spokane rivers, a short distance above the joining of the two waters. Cox, circa 1835, describes the site as 'thinly covered with pine and other trees, and close to a trading post of the Northwest company . . .'"

Durham also writes that, "One of the last buffalo in the region was noted in the journal of Dr. George Bucklye, surgeon USA, who descended the Pend d'Oreille in a canoe in the autumn of 1853. From the journal: 'Buffalo were formerly in great numbers in this valley, as attested by the number of skulls seen and by the reports of the inhabitants. For a number of years past none had been seen west of the mountains; but, singular to relate, a buffalo bull was killed at the mouth of the Pend d'Oreille river on the day I passed it. The Indians were in great joy at this, supposing that the buffalo were coming back among them.'"

Salmon, Salmon, Salmon

Salmon were once a primary measure of the Little Spokane Watershed's and the Columbia River Region's quality of life. The following excerpt from Durham gives an idea of what the habitat looked like in the 1870's and most likely what it looked like for thousands of years.

Durham quotes from one of the early settlers, Mrs. Bailey. In her 1870 manuscript, Mrs. Baily describes the area that is today downtown Spokane, "In that day there was a ravine running from Cannon Hill to the river, a little below the falls, known as Little Wolf ditch. For one approaching the settlement from the southwest, the view of the falls and river valley was almost entirely obstructed until the opposite side of the ravine was reached. Then there flashed into view, as if by magic, a scene which, for beauty and grandeur, was surpassed nowhere. Here lay a broad, fertile valley, completely covered with waving bunchgrass, and surrounded by ranges of lofty mountains whose hooded peaks, towering above the fleecy clouds, seemed to fade away into the serene blue of the heavens. Through the valley the river wound its course, now running smoothly, and now rushing with a roar over boulders and cataracts. . . ."

A magnified view of the area where the large Indian village and fur trading posts sites were.

"The country at that time afforded many pastimes for the early settlers. One of the most largely indulged in was the salmon fishing, which began in July, at which time the red salmon, coming up the river from the Columbia, began to make their appearance just below the falls. The white salmon did not come up the river until later in the year, in October."

Possible Further Historic Research

With additional historic research of the Little Spokane Watershed, a better understanding of the habitats, their critters and their inter-relationships can be gained. This research can be invaluable for future habitat restoration projects.

The historian, David H. Chance, outlined a starting point for additional historic research. Research of these sources will no doubt provide additional leads. It would take a professional historian several months to complete this initial research and to write up the findings. References to native plants and wildlife in these sources can be included in the findings within this research time frame. The following list of sources includes the material from the outline.

Archaeological Studies

The nearest archaeological study is the one for Kettle Falls, Washington. This study is of a 9,000 year span that goes from 7000 BC to 1800 AD. There is also a study that has been started at Usk, Washington.

Indian Natural History Research

Dr. Allan H. Smith has extremely detailed and linguistically meaningful field notes on the Kalispel. These notes cover a vast amount of Indian knowledge of natural history subjects and locations, including the upper Little Spokane Watershed.

A view towards a meander of the Little Spokane

Major Written Historic Sources

There is material in Allan Scholz et al. 1985 research of the Spokane River with leads that can be followed. For specific details of the Little Spokane and the confluence there are: the Hudson's Bay Company Archives in Winnipeg, Military sources in the National Archives, Bureau of Indian Affairs sources from the national Archives, and Indian Claims Sources from the National Archives: Spokane, Coeur d'Alene and Kalispel dockets.

Fur Trade And Early Exploration Journals and Records

The fur trade, which was active in the Spokane region from 1800 to 1871 is another source of material. The fur trade in the Spokane region had three distinct periods. First was the Kootenai - Kalispel - Flathead period from

1800 to 1810. The Spokane area was peripheral during this period. From 1810 to 1826 the Spokane House - Fort Spokane period brought significant activity to the Little Spokane Watershed. From 1826 to 1871 the Colville District period had diminishing activity in the Little Spokane Watershed.

One Hudson's Bay Company source lists Spokane and Coeur d'Alene tribal monthly trade statistics for two or three years, from which can be seen the numbers of fur-bearing species that were traded, and some statistics on deer, and elk hides. It may be difficult to tie these counts to particular watersheds, but they certainly would give needed insights about the region.

There is other historical information. An unpublished David Thompson journal refers to a trail up the Little Spokane. After 1826, the northern part of the trail was used by the Hudson's Bay Company between Calispell Lake and Chewelah when the snow was too deep on top.

For direct botanical sources, the David Douglas and Charles Geyer notes can be checked. Both worked on the Spokane. While they may not have gone up the Little Spokane, their botanical notes could be useful reference points.

Military Records

The US Army period began in 1858 with Colonel Wright's campaigns. Military sources from the 1850's have not been combed for native plant and wildlife references. This can be done at the National Archives. There may be material in the Ft. Sherman corpus. Several of the military people may have kept diaries. One of these people, Abercrombie, may have kept a diary of his journey, circa 1877, in the area. Also, there was another expedition just before or after Abercrombie's that probably traversed the length of the Little Spokane.

Dragoon Creek may have been named for the dragoons with Colonel Wright in 1858 - all the more reason to get into the material at the National Archives.

Missionary Records

The Christian Missionary period, both Protestant and Catholic began in 1838. These records may be useful.

Railroad and Timber Records

Railroad and serious timber exploitation of the area both began in 1890. The Great Northern Railway survey of the Little Spokane Valley might be interesting to examine. It would most likely be in Minneapolis.

Newspaper Records

It is important to do a thorough research of newspaper and other journalistic sources prior to 1933, especially for the 19th century. Newspaper and popular journals' research can be done in Spokane, Pullman and Cheney.

County And Other Public Records

Homesteading began around 1885 and continued up into the late 1930's, though at a much reduced frequency after World War I. Land patent files are potentially of interest. Some patent files have quite a bit to say about vegetation on homestead and timber claims.

Spokane County Archives, if anything like Stevens or Pend Oreille county archives, will probably have much more than anyone can imagine. There are state archives at Cheney and in Olympia.

Historic Collections and Diaries

The Walker-Eells corpus has quite a bit of natural history, mainly from Mary Walker, though it is centered, of course, on Tsimikaine Creek. Some of this can be found locally, but some has to be seen at Yale and at Harvard.

Eastern Washington State Historical Society and the Spokane Public Library's Pacific Northwest Collection can also be explored.

Falls on the upper Little Spokane

Habitats, Their Critters and Their Inter-Relationships

Habitats are one of nature's many theaters, where nature's acts of life are played out daily. For the Little Spokane Watershed, eleven natural habitats plus two human-related habitats are the theaters chosen to represent some of the watershed's dynamic inter-relationships. It is not necessary to look far to find drama among the watershed's native plants, wildlife and their habitats. These dramatic inter-relationships, links of life, form particular unending patterns in each of the habitats. These intertwined threads form a unique Little Spokane Watershed tapestry of life.

Lake Habitat, Wetland Habitat, Riparian Habitat and Ponderosa Pine Habitat

Damselfly on alder leaf

Flower and grass

New threads are woven and others are broken. Some inter-relationships can have devastating effects while others allow the watershed to thrive. Human inter-relationships with the Little Spokane Watershed are special. Humans can make conscious choices about how they intend to work with the habitats and critters of the watershed. Human choices shape the inter-relationships humans have with people and nature in the Little Spokane Watershed. Humans also have the ability to anticipate consequences and act in ways that allow the Little Spokane Watershed to become more restorative. Fresh choices can be made by looking more closely at the watershed's web of life to see what can work well and what is less appropriate.

Inter-relationships And Sustainability

Each habitat chapter includes some examples of the habitats' inter-relationships, and what a more sustainable habitat can be like. By allowing each habitat to become more sustainable, the Little Spokane Watershed can become more healthy, thriving and restorative.

These three elements are essential for a more sustainable habitat. Separately they are not enough. A healthy habitat can not remain healthy unless it is both thriving and restorative. A thriving habitat can quickly decline when it is less than healthy or less than restorative. And likewise a restorative habitat may look as if it is doing well. However, without good health and a thriving vibrancy, the habitat can all too quickly slip towards degradation.

In some cases, to allow a habitat to become more sustainable it may be appropriate for restorative activities to take place. These can include planting native plants in former farm fields that are being returned to wildland. Controlled burns can also establish a healthier habitat mosaic. Reduction of large monoculture areas by changing to a healthy biodiversity mix can also be very helpful.

Nature tends towards more stable states, an equilibrium within and between habitats and their critters. This is a general equilibrium with a constant flux of critter populations and their migration patterns in and across various habitats. Nature's relationships tend to regulate population size toward compatible levels of resource renewal and within the maintenance of other conditions required for healthy habitats. By living within these and other carrying capacities, nature tends towards healthy habitats.

Population and disease explosions and the population crashes that follow can happen when inter-relationships are significantly altered over large parts of a watershed. Human activities can alter too much, too fast. What may be of short term benefit to some humans may not be beneficial in the long run to people or nature. Evidence of unfavorable side affects, creeping cumulative affects, unanticipated and unintended consequences, and exceeding the watershed's carrying capacity can be found in the Little Spokane Watershed.

The dumping of toxic and other chemicals into the ground at the Colbert landfill, now an environmental cleanup superfund site, is one example. Not only have wells been contaminated and closed, but hundreds of thousands of gallons of aquifer water are being treated daily to remove many of the toxins, before the water is dumped into the Little Spokane. Human actions like this can have severe affects on the population dynamics of native plants and wildlife and can at least temporarily cause out of control chain reactions of the watershed's inter-relationships.

Quality Of Life Measures

Quality of life measures for each habitat can be one way of examining the health of the watershed. Quality of life measures are touched on for each habitat. Also, the final chapter covers in more detail how some of these measures can be taken.

Ferns and foliage with a fallen tree

Quality of life measures can be used to show how a habitat is becoming more healthy and robust or how the habitat's health is declining. As these measures are more specifically developed, they can more clearly show the progress that each habitat is making toward becoming healthier and more restorative.

A major theme of quality of life measures is to encourage improvements that allow a habitat to become more healthy, thriving and restorative. Much can be done to encourage and nurture this. One essential ingredient, which is too often neglected, are attitudes of working toward a better quality of life. These attitudes can make all the difference in the world.

Progress in quality of life is not by having more than enough, which can eventually become a burden. Progress can be in allowing the Little Spokane Watershed's nature and people to become more healthy, thriving and restorative.

About The Habitat Chapters

The next chapters explore each of the Little Spokane Watershed's habitats. For each habitat the number of critters in each major category of life is listed. Flora, fungus and fauna species that are more abundant are also listed. Some of these critters are then described at the end of each habitat chapter. A complete list of all the critters for each habitat, listed by their abundance, is available as a separate report from the Little Spokane Watershed Council.

The following habitat chapters show more explicitly how some of the inter-relationships of the watershed work, how one inter-relationship is related to another, how one inter-relationship influences another and how these connections, links, and dynamics, are some of what gives life to the Little Spokane Watershed.

A variety of inter-relationships in this mixture of habitats

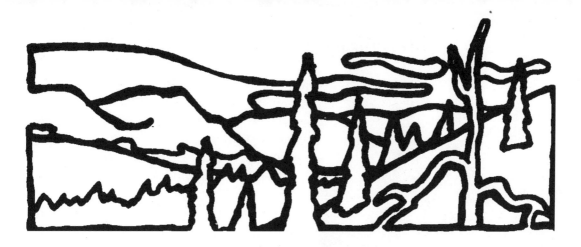

Subalpine Habitat

Subalpine habitat is familiar to anyone who has ever skied or hiked some of the higher elevations in Mount Spokane State Park or Boyer Mountain. Mount Spokane's subalpine elevations afford breathtaking views and offer beauty unsurpassed by any other area in the Spokane region. Subalpine habitat is characterized by a short growing season and low temperatures. This habitat is found at the highest elevation of any of the ecosystems in the Little Spokane Watershed and ranges from approximately 5,000 feet up to the top of Mount Spokane at 5,878 feet. Subalpine habitat can also be found in frost pockets as low as 3,800 feet. In the northern Rocky Mountains and Cascade Range, subalpine habitat is found as high as 8,000 feet, above which erect trees cease to grow and the alpine habitat is found.

Inter-relationships

The most distinguishing features of subalpine communities are the tree species and their distinct distribution. Subalpine fir, Engelmann spruce, and whitebark pine dominate the landscape.

All three species of tree tend to have a clumpy distribution creating an interspersed grove-and-meadow area between dense forest areas and the tree line. This clumpy distribution is a form of timberline succession. Once a tree is established in the open, it is easier for others to get a start next to it, for two reasons. First, most subalpine trees are

Subalpine snag and subalpine fir

A view from subalpine habitat

able to propagate by growing roots from branches that are in contact with the ground. The parent limb feeds the new shoot intravenously for a while. Subalpine soil is characterized by shallow, well-drained silt loams, often with fractured bedrock. This permits water to percolate beyond tree root depth. Intravenous feeding by the parent tree is a huge advantage over growing from a seed.

Second, during spring thaw, dark tree foliage absorbs more of the sun's heat than white snow does, and melts a small well around the larger tree. Also, these wells are more easily formed since the snow accumulation and wind packing is less under the densely growing clumps. This creates a microhabitat with a growing season that may be several weeks longer than the surrounding meadow. Therefore, subalpine trees tend to grow in tight, slowly expanding clumps. This can easily be seen when hiking the back side of Mount Spokane or Mount Kit Carson.

In general, subalpine habitats do not support the diversity of plant or animal species that many lower elevation habitats do. This is generally attributed to the shorter growing season and fewer resources. Few species are adapted to sites with a short growing season and low temperatures. In fact, species diversity is progressively reduced from lower to upper subalpine. Nonetheless, several species thrive in this habitat, in part, because of mutualistic associations that have formed between many of the plant, fungus and animal species.

Whitebark pine and Clark's nutcracker provide a perfect example. Most conifers hide and protect their seeds from seed-eaters as long as possible. The whitebark pine exposes them early and conspicuously, and baits them with rich oils and proteins. Clark's nutcracker, a year-round resident, obliges the tree by collecting the seeds compulsively, selecting the best ones, eating some on the spot and burying the rest for retrieval in the winter. The birds are so industrious that they store two or three times as many seeds as they can consume. The remainder are thus planted. In addition, the strong flying nutcrackers have a typical foraging range of 14 miles and can carry as many as 150 whitebark pine seeds in their throat pouch.

Similarly, migratory hummingbird species, calliope, rufus and black-chinned, may be found in the subalpine community in the late spring and summer. While feeding on the high calorie nectar of plants such as scarlet gilias, the hummingbirds benefit these plants by inadvertently picking up pollen and transferring it to other plants, thereby providing a reproductive advantage.

Not all relationships in a subalpine community are mutually beneficial, mutualistic. Many plant grazers and predators also exist in this habitat. Blue grouse migrate up near timberline in the winter to browse on subalpine fir needles and to escape predation by bobcats, coyotes, and mountain lions in the lower elevations. Pocket gophers spend most of their lives underground where they feed on plant roots and tubers from such plants as beargrass and glacier lily. The presence of pocket gophers is easily determined by gopher cores, small tubular ridges of dirt about 3" wide.

A predator common to nearly anyone who has been hiking on a warm June day is the horse fly. The females, in search of mammal blood, are the pesky ones that buzz around a person's head and bite . They also prey on bear, elk, and smaller mammals. The males feed on pollen and nectar. The occasional red-tailed hawk can be seen floating overhead in search of golden-mantled ground squirrels and other rodents. In addition, the infrequent coyote or bobcat may wander up to the subalpine area, also in search of small mammals to feed on.

One unique critter found on Mt. Spokane is the pika. Pikas are small furry mammals that resemble guinea pigs but belong to the order that includes rabbits. Pikas survived the glaciers and live in the rockpiles around the summit of Mt. Spokane.

One of the most fascinating looking subalpine plants is beargrass. During March through July the flower is unmistakable. It sits atop a 10-25 inch stalk and looks much like a large marshmallow. Around the base are leaves that appear to be grass. However, beargrass is actually in the lily family, Liliaceae, not the grass family, Graminae. It received its name because the leaves make up a small portion of a bear's diet in the spring. However, most browsed plants that are seen are more likely the work of small rodents such as the mountain vole. Beargrass can often be seen growing in large clumps in meadows as well as closed forests in other areas. It can be found from approximately 5,100 feet on up.

Fire is not as common in subalpine habitats as it is in lower areas due to the lack of fuel in these higher elevations. However, evidence in the form of charcoal and tree scars demonstrates that fires have spread through all but the wettest subalpine habitats. These fires may result in stands of lodgepole pine, which thrive in burned-over areas. See the Mountain Habitat section for more on lodgepole pine/fire relationships. However, these stands are quickly replaced or eliminated due to lodgepole pine's shade intolerance and inability to withstand the short growing season and cold temperatures. Grand fir and western hemlock quickly replace lodgepole pine, especially at lower elevations.

Sustainability

Most human activity in subalpine habitats is recreational, although some logging does occur in the lower elevations. Therefore, the subalpine habitat is the least disturbed of any of the habitat types found in the Little Spokane Watershed. However, this is not to say that it is in as pristine condition as it can be. On the contrary, high altitude habitats are especially

A subalpine hillside

Subalpine silhouette

susceptible to degradation due to the short growing season, thin soil, and relatively low species diversity.

Once a subalpine area has been disturbed, it may take hundreds of years for the habitat to repair itself. This is especially true when soil is lost. The already thin soil is an indication that glaciers were late in retreating from subalpine areas after the last ice age ended 10,000 years ago. Consequently, vegetation was delayed in recolonizing high elevation areas. Even today, there is only a very small quantity of living organisms, the biomass, available to add to the soil. The short growing season prevents the rapid accumulation of biomass. Luckily, most people who venture into this high altitude habitat are there only to admire its beauty and are aware of its fragilities.

Quality of Life Measures

The trails through subalpine habitat can be one good measure of subalpine quality of life. Subalpine areas with just a few trails, that people stay on, that are narrow, in good shape and with very little if any erosion are a measure of how careful people are with an area. Rutted trails, double parallel trails, wide trail intersections, trampled vegetation along the trail, litter, human and dog waste show areas where there are too many people for the area. Frequent horseback riding in fragile subalpine areas can increase the rate at which a trail deteriorates.

Forest Habitat Key For Subalpine Habitat

Subalpine forest areas can be found using this part of the forest habitat key. These sub-habitats are in the subalpine habitat or are close to this habitat. The key is a general key for Inland Pacific Northwest conifer forests, so not all the sub-habitats apply to the Little Spokane Watershed. The full key, in the appendix, can be used for the Little Spokane Watershed forests.

Index for Subalpine Habitat

1	6	11	15	A			Subalpine Fir – Oregon Boxwood
1	6	11	15	16	17	A	Mountain Hemlock – Fool's Huckleberry
1	6	11	15	16	17	B	Mountain Hemlock – Beargrass
1	6	11	15	16	18	19	Subalpine Fir – Fool's Huckleberry
1	6	11	15	16	18	20 A	Subalpine Fir – Beargrass
1	6	11	15	16	18	20 B	Subalpine Fir – Grouse Huckleberry
1	6	11	15	16	18	B	White -barked pine – Subalpine Fir

Key for Subalpine Habitat

1.   Coniferous trees other than ponderosa pine present and reproducing

      6.   Red cedar, hemlock or subalpine fir present and reproducing

            11. Red cedar and western hemlock present as non reproducing accidentals if at all; subalpine fir and/or mountain hemlock reproducing well

                  15. Queen's cup and/or fragrant bedstraw usually present; usually with more than 14 undergrowth spp./375 m^2 ; moss–heather, labrador–tea and mountain-heather absent

                  A.   **Subalpine Fir – Oregon Boxwood Habitat**

                  15. Queen's cup and sweet scented bedstraw absent, usually with fewer than 14 undergrowth

                      16. Mountain hemlock reproducing more vigorously than subalpine fir

                          17. Undergrowth with fool's huckleberry well represented

                          A.   **Mountain Hemlock – Fool's Huckleberry Habitat**

                        17. Undergrowth lacking fool's huckleberry, rhododendron and labrador– tea, beargrass or big huckleberry dominant

                        B.   **Mountain hemlock – Beargrass Habitat**

                16. Mountain hemlock absent

                    18. Trees tall, not wind-deformed, forming a closed forest

                      19. Undergrowth with fool's huckleberry, rhododendron or smooth labrador–tea conspicuous

                      A. **Subalpine Fir – Fool's Huckleberry Habitat**

                    19. Fool's huckleberry, rhododendron and labrador–tea absent

                    20. Beargrass or big huckleberry dominant beneath the trees

                      A. **Subalpine Fir – Beargrass Habitat**

                    20. Grouse Huckleberry dominant beneath the trees

                      B. **Subalpine fir – Grouse Huckleberry Habitat**

                18. Trees dwarfed and wind-deformed, occurring as well separated groups or individuals

                  B.   White -barked pine – subalpine fir habitat

Subalpine opening

Summary of Subalpine Habitat Critters

Number of Species by Kingdom

PLANT (PLANTAE)   28

FUNGUS (EUMYCOTA)   5

ANIMAL (ANIMALIA)   24

PROTIST (PROTISTA)   8

BACTERIA & VIRUS (MONERA & VIRUS)   7

TOTAL IDENTIFIED SPECIES   72

Number of Species by Class

Moss (Bryopsida)	1
Horsetail (Equisetopsida)	1
Pine (Pinicae)	5
Magnolia (Magnoliidae)	1
Carnation (Caryophyllidae)	1
Aspen (Dilleniidae)	6
Rose (Rosidae)	3
Sunflower (Asteridae)	5
Grass (Commelinidae)	1
Lily (Liliidae)	4
Mushroom (Basidomycetes)	3
Phragmobasidiomycetes (Phragmobasidiomycetes)	1
Ascomycetes (Ascomycetes)	1
Turbellidia (Turbellidia)	1
Centipede (Chilopoda)	1
Millipede (Diplopoda)	1
Insect (Insecta)	8
Bird (Aves)	7
Mammal (Mammalia)	6
Amoeba (Rhizopoda)	1
Heliozoan (Actimpoda)	1
Foram (Forimaninifera)	1
Sporozoite (Apicomplexa)	1
Slime Mold - Cellular (Acrasiomycetes)	1
Slime Mold - Plasmodial (Myxomycetes)	1
Mildew (Oomycota)	1
Saprobe (Chytridiomycota)	1
Bacteria (Bacteria)	1
Cyanophycota (Cyanophycota)	1
Prochlorophycota (Prochlorophycota)	1
Bacteria Virus (Bacteria Virus)	1
Plant Virus (Plant Virus)	1
Vertebrate Virus (Vertebrate Virus)	1
Invertebrate Virus (Invertebrate Virus)	1

Selected Subalpine Habitat Critters

PLANT (PLANTAE)	28	
Moss (Bryopsida)	1	
Polytrichum juniperinum		A
Horsetail (Equisetopsida)	1	
Scouring Rush		A
Pine (Pinicae)	5	
Engelmann Spruce		C
Lodgepole Pine		F
Pacific Hemlock		A
Subalpine Fir		A
Tamarack		U
Magnolia (Magnoliidae)	1	
False Bugbane		A
Carnation (Caryophyllidae)	1	
Subalpine Sulfur Buckwheat		C
Aspen (Dilleniidae)	6	
Common Pink Wintergreen		C
Fool's Huckleberry (A)		C
Globe Huckleberry		F
Grouse Huckleberry		F
Round-leaved Violet		C
Western Prince's Pine		F
Coolwort Foamflower		F
Swamp Gooseberry		C
Wax Currant		U
Sunflower (Asteridae)	5	
Arrowleaf Groundsel		F
Common Yarrow		F
Red Twinberry		C
Spreading Dogbane		U
Western Hawkweed		F
Grass (Commelinidae)	1	
Elk Sedge		F
Lily (Liliidae)	4	
Beargrass		A
Glacier Lily		A
Starry False Solomon's Seal		F
Western False Solomon's Seal		U

FUNGUS (EUMYCOTA)	5	
Mushroom (Basidomycetes)	3	
Gemmed Amanita		K
Little Brown Cortinarius		L
Witches Butter		L
Phragmobasidiomycetes (Phragmobasidiomycetes)	1	
Gum Drop		K
Ascomycetes (Ascomycetes)	1	
Caloscypha fulgens		L

ANIMAL (ANIMALIA)	24		
Turbellidia (Turbellidia)	1		
Planariidae		L	
Centipede (Chilopoda)	1		
Centipede		L	
Millipede (Diplopoda)	1		
Millipede		L	
Insect (Insecta)	8		
Black Fly		A	
Deer Fly		C	
Horse Fly		C	
Milbert's Tortoiseshell		F	
Mosquito		A	
Mountain Swallowtail		U	
Phoebus Parnassian		F	
Tabanus sp.		C	
Bird (Aves)	7		
Chestnut-backed Chickadee		F	
Clark's Nutcracker		F	
Gray Jay		F	
Mountain Chickadee		U	
Pine Grosbeak		U	
Rock Wren		U	
Rufous Humming Bird		F	
Mammal (Mammalia)	6		
Black Bear		R	
Common Pika		U	
Coyote		F	
Grizzly Bear		M	MS
Human		R	
Yellow-bellied Marmot		U	

* The critters listed here are for all identified species.

Legend - Critters are listed by their common name followed by their abundance in the habitat. Introduced species and species at risk are indicated by type code. • **Abundance Codes: A** Abundant, **C** Common, **F** Fairly common, **U** Uncommon, **R** Rare, **V** Vagrant, **K** Known in habitat, **L** Likely in habitat, **M** Missing from habitat. • **Introduced Species Codes: IN** Introduced Noxious species, **IO** Introduced, Other than noxious species. • **At Risk Codes: MS** Missing, **ED** Endangered, **TH** Threatened, **CD** Candidate, **MN** Monitor, **RGM** Regulated Game, **RNG** Regulated Nongame, **RA** Rare, **PB** Protected Breeding Areas.

Selected Critter Descriptions

Engelmann Spruce *(Picea engelmannii)*

Sub Family:	True Fir (Abies)	**Class:**	Pine (Piniceae)
Family:	Pine (Pinaceae)	**Division:**	Pine (Pinophyta)
Order:	Pine (Pinatea)	**Kingdom:**	Plants (Plantae)

Other Names: Columbian Spruce, Mountain Spruce, Silver Spruce, Spruce, White Spruce
LSW Habitats: SA: C, MT: F

Relationships to Watershed: Engelmann Spruce provide hiding and thermal cover for bear, elk and deer. The trees are used by nuthatches, chickadees, owls and woodpeckers. Spruce Grouse and Blue Grouse feed extensively on buds and needles. Squirrels clip buds and juvenile shoots. Seeds are eaten by squirrels, chipmunks, mice, voles, chickadees, nuthatches, crossbills, and siskins.

Description: Engelmann Spruce are coniferous trees that grow up to 180 feet tall. The crown is pyramidal in shape and the branches are whorled and extend to the ground. The bark is reddish to purplish-brown in color and is thin, loose and scaly. Needles are rigid and 1-2 inches long. They are sharply pointed, bluish green in color, and whorled on the twig. Staminate cones are yellow and from 10-15 mm long while the ovulate cones are oblong, light chestnut brown with thin, papery scales and 1-2 inches long. Both cones hang down from branches. Engelmann Spruce flower from June-July and shed their seeds from September-October.

Look Alikes: Distinct.

Little Spokane Habitat: Engelmann Spruce are found in cold, moist sites in forests that are often dominated by true firs. They are prominent at margins of meadows, streams and lakes. At lower elevations Engelmann Spruce occur along streams with cold air flow. At mid elevations they are found on alluvial terraces, wet benches, bottom land, and seepy slopes on the northerly side, while at timberline Engelmann spruce are found everywhere.

World Habitat: Found from Alaska to California, throughout higher mountains of western Oregon, northern Washington, northern Idaho, western Montana, and northeast Oregon to north central Nevada.

Pacific Hemlock *(Tsuga heterophylla)*

Sub Family:	True Fir (Abies)	**Class:**	Pine (Piniceae)
Family:	Pine (Pinaceae)	**Division:**	Pine (Pinophyta)
Order:	Pine (Pinatea)	**Kingdom:**	Plants (Plantae)

Other Names: Hemlock, Lowland Hemlock, Mountain Hemlock
LSW Habitats: SA: A, MT: C

Relationships to Watershed: Pacific Hemlock provide hiding and thermal cover for wild mammals and are important for watershed protection. Buds are eaten by the Blue Grouse, seeds by siskins and chickadees, and the twigs and leaves by mountain goats.

Description: Pacific Hemlock are coniferous trees that grow to 130 feet tall. They have dark purplish to reddish-brown bark that has deep furrows with narrow rounded ridges. Needles are thickened at the center, 1/2 to 1 inch long and dark green to bluish-green in color. They are 4-sided and have stomatal bloom on all surfaces. The needles are arranged spirally about the twig. Buds are conical and 1/8 inch long. They are red-brown in color and are pointed and sharp. Staminate cones are bluish and 3-4 mm long while the ovulate cones are brownish-purple to deep purple turning brown on maturity. The ovate cones are cylindrical with thin scales that are from 1-3 inches long and broad. They flower from June-July and shed their seeds from August-October.

Look Alikes: May be confused with Western Hemlock (*Tsuga heterophylla*) which has needles of differing lengths arranged in 2-ranks on the twig and cones that are less than 1 inch long. On the Pacific Hemlock the needles appear in a starlike rosette.

Little Spokane Habitat: Pacific Hemlock are found in subalpine to alpine forests and timberlines. They occur on moist, well drained soils. They are seen mostly on the northerly and easterly slopes where moisture is retained late into summer.

World Habitat: Found from Alaska to California, throughout higher mountains of western Oregon, northern Washington, northern Idaho, western Montana, and northeast Oregon to north central Nevada.

Subalpine Fir *(Abies lasiocarpa)*

Subalpine fir

Sub Family:	True Fir (Abies)	**Class:**	Pine (Piniceae)
Family:	Pine (Pinaceae)	**Division:**	Pine (Pinophyta)
Order:	Pine (Pinatea)	**Kingdom:**	Plants (Plantae)

Other Names: Alpine Fir, Balsam Fir, Fir (C), White Balsam Fir
LSW Habitat: SA: A

Relationships To Watershed: Subalpine Fir are the most widely distributed fir in North America. Subalpine Fir stands are important to wildlife as summer range for mule deer, elk and bear. Subalpine Fir forests are used by squirrels, mice, and chipmunks. Birds that use Subalpine Firs are woodpeckers, nuthatches, juncos, chickadees, crossbills, siskins, grouse and owls. Blue Grouse feed heavily on Subalpine Fir and use Subalpine Fir stands year round. Western Spruce Budworm, Tussock Moth, wood rots and fire can damage Subalpine Fir.

Description: Subalpine Fir are coniferous trees up to 100 feet tall with a spirelike crown. Their upper branches are short and stiff and the lower branches are usually drooping. The bark is thin and ash-gray. It is smooth with resin blisters. On older trees the bark is fissured at the base. Needles are 1-1 1/2 inches long, bluish-green with rounded tips. Needles turn upward from a spiral arrangement on the twigs. Buds are rounded, light brown with 3 at the apex of the stem. Staminate cones are bluish and up to 10 mm long. Ovulate cones are deep purple and 2-4 inches long. They are cylindrical and upright on the branch. Cones disintegrate on the tree. Cones appear June to early July and shed their seeds in September.

Look Alikes: Subalpine Fir may be confused with Engelmann Spruce, *Picea engelmannii*, which has sharp pointed needles and the cones fall intact; Grand Fir, *Abies grandis*, whose needles spread out flat; Douglas Fir, *Pseudotsuga menziesii*, which has sharp, pointed reddish buds and the cones fall intact; and White Fir, *Abies concolor*, that are not in this region, whose needles are over 1 1/2 - 2 1/2 inches long.

Little Spokane Habitat: Subalpine Fir are found on subalpine slopes and ridges usually between 5000 and 8000 feet. They can be found at lower elevations along stream courses due to cold air flow. At higher elevations the species occupy northerly and easterly aspects.

World Habitat: Found from Alaska to California, throughout higher mountains of western Oregon, northern Washington, northern Idaho, western Montana, northeast Oregon to north central Nevada.

False Bugbane
(*Trautvetteria caroliniensis*)

		Class:	Magnolia (Magnoliudae)
Family:	Buttercup (Ranunculaceae)	**Division:**	Flower (Magnoliophyta)
Order:	Buttercup (Ranunculales)	**Kingdom:**	Plant (Plantae)

LSW Habitats: SA: A, MT: A, WL: U, RP: C

Relationships To Watershed: False Bugbane is unpalatable and highly toxic.

Description: False Bugbane is a perennial, rhizomatous herb that is 20-32 inches tall. Flowers are inconspicuous white to greenish, blooming May-August and borne in terminal corymbs. Basal leaves have long-petiolate, are 4-10 inches wide and palmately divided into 5 or more lobes. Cauline leaves are alternate and have short petioles.

Corymb Inflorescence - A flat-topped or round-topped flower cluster with the lower flower stalks longer than the upper stalks.

Found On:
False Bugbane
Common Yarrow
Mallow Ninebark

Look Alikes: False Bugbane may be confused with Globeflower (*Trolius laxus*) which has a fruit that is a follicle.

Little Spokane Habitat: False Bugbane may be found in cool, wet sites at upper elevations. Prominent in Subalpine Fir, Grand Fir, Twisted Stalk and Queen's Cup Beadlily communities.

World Habitat: False Bugbane is widely distributed in North America and Japan.

Fool's Huckleberry
(Menziesia ferruginea)

Elliptic Leaf

		Class:	Aspen (Dilleniidae)
Family:	Heath (Ericaceae)	**Division:**	Flower (Magnoliophyta)
Order:	Heath (Ericales)	**Kingdom:**	Plant (Plantae)

Other Names: False Huckleberry, Huckleberry(C), Mock Azalea, Rusty Menziesia, Rusty-leaf
LSW Habitats: SA: C, MT: F, RP: F

Relationships To Watershed: Fool's Huckleberry is poisonous to livestock if eaten in quantity.

Description: Fool's Huckleberry is a straggling deciduous shrub that grows up to 6 feet tall. White to pinkish-white urn-shaped flowers blooming June-July are borne in clusters. New stems are yellow-tan while the older stems are gray-reddish-brown with shredding bark. Leaves are alternate with a whorled appearance, ovate to elliptic, thin and 2 inches long. They are dull light green, glaucous in color, with finely serrated margins. The midvein protrudes from the leaf tip. Fruits are many-seeded ovoid capsules.

Found On:
Fool's Huckleberry
Common Pink Wintergreen
Common Snowberry
Red Twinberry
Spreading Dogbane

Look Alikes: Fool's Huckleberry may be confused with the following: Cascades rhododendron, *Rhododendron albiflorum*, which has white azalea-like flowers; Labrador-tea, *Ledum glandulosum*, which has evergreen leaves with rolled margins; Big Huckleberry, *Vaccinium membranaceum*, which has alternate leaves without a whorled appearance.

Little Spokane Habitat: Fool's Huckleberry is found in moist woods and along stream banks.

World Habitat: Fool's Huckleberry is a native plant widespread in the Pacific Northwest.

Grouse Huckleberry
(*Vaccinium scoparium*)

		Class:	Aspen (Dilleniidae)
Family:	Heath (Ericaceae)	**Division:**	Flower (Magnoliophyta)
Order:	Heath (Ericales)	**Kingdom:**	Plant (Plantae)

Other Names: Grouse Whortleberry, Grouseberry, Huckleberry(B)
LSW Habitats: SA: F, MT: F

Relationships To Watershed: Grouse Huckleberry fruits are readily eaten by birds and animals.

Description: Grouse Huckleberry is a low growing deciduous shrub reaching only 10 inches in height. Small, urn-shaped pinkish flowers bloom in June-August. Grouse Huckleberry plants consist of many slender upright stems, almost broom-like, that are strongly angled. The stems are yellow-green and the buds are tightly sunken in the stem. Leaves are alternate, small, 1/2 inch long, and narrow with shiny light green upper surfaces. They have finely serrate margins. Fruits are small, 1/5 inch, bright red berries.

Look Alikes: Grouse Huckleberry may be confused with dwarf huckleberry (*Vaccinium myrtillus*) which has larger leaves, fewer branches and a bluish to dark red berry.

Little Spokane Habitat: Grouse Huckleberry thrives in high elevation sites with heavy snowpack that are cold and dry.

World Habitat: Grouse Huckleberry is a native plant found from the Cascades east to the Rocky mountains.

Urn-shaped - Pitcher like; hollow or contracted near the mouth like a pitcher or urn.

Found On:
Grouse Huckleberry
Fool'o Huckleberry
Kinnikinnick

Western Prince's Pine
(*Chimaphila umbellata*)

		Class:	Aspen (Dilleniidae)
Family:	Heath (Ericaceae)	**Division:**	Flower (Magnoliophyta)
Order:	Heath (Ericales)	**Kingdom:**	Plant (Plantae)

Other Names: Pipsissewa, Prince's Pine
LSW Habitats: SA: F, MT: F

Relationships To Watershed: Western Prince's Pine is unpalatable.

Serrated Leaf - Toothed along the margin with minute, sharp, forward-pointing teeth.

Found On:
Western Prince's Pine
Blue Elderberry

Description: Western Prince's Pine is a small, rhizomatus evergreen shrub usually 4-12 inches tall. This plant has waxy, whitish-pink to pink flowers blooming in June-August in 3-15 clustered racemes. Leaves are alternate, simple and 2-3 inches long. They are bright green, oblanceolate and whorled with serrated margins. The stem is unbranched, yellowish-green with a woodyish base. Fruits are rounded 5-celled capsules.

Look Alikes: Western Prince's Pine can be confused with Little Pipsissewa, *Chimaphila menziesii*, which usually has less than 3 flowers and dull green to blue-green elliptic leaves.

Capsule - A dry, opening fruit capsule with more than one seed.

Little Spokane Habitat: Western Prince's Pine is found in mid to high elevations with cool, moist sites that may be shady or exposed.

Found On:
Western Prince's Pine
Black Cottonwood
Common Mullein
Common Pink Wintergreen
Fools's Huckleberry
Little Prince's Pine
Pacific Willow
Scouler Willow
Snowbrush Ceanothus

World Habitat: Western Prince's Pine is found in eastern United States and in Eurasia. This plant is widespread throughout the mountains of the Pacific Northwest, from Alaska to southern California and east to the Rocky Mountains of Colorado.

Starry False Solomon's Seal
(*Smilacina stellata*)

		Class:	Lily (Liliidae)
Family:	Lily (Liliaceae)	**Division:**	Flower (Magnoliophyta)
Order:	Lily (Lilales)	**Kingdom:**	Plant (Plantae)

Other Names: False Solomon's Seal, False Spikenard, Star Solomon's Seal, Star-flowered Solomon-plume, Starry Solomon-plume, Western Solomon-plume

LSW Habitat: SA: F

Relationships To Watershed: Starry False Solomon's Seal berries are eaten by grouse.

Description: Starry False Solomon's Seal is a perennial herb that is rhizomatous and low-growing from 8-24 inches tall. Small, white flowers bloom in May-June in few (5-10) 3-inch long terminal racemes. The main stem, rachis, of inflorescence is "zig-zag". Leaves are alternate, simple, sessile, lanceolate and from 2-6 inches long. They are slightly clasping and have parallel venation. The stem is erect, unbranched, green and arched. Fruits are globose berries that are greenish-yellow turning black and are less than 1/2 inch long.

Look Alikes: Starry False Solomon's Seal is readily confused with the following plants: Western False Solomon's Seal, *Smilacina racemosa*, has a many-flowered panicle and leaves that are 3-8 inches long and broader; Twisted Stalk, *Streptopus spp.*, has branched, clasping leaf bases; Fairy Bells, *Disporum spp.*, is branched with rounded leaf bases.

Little Spokane Habitat: Starry False Solomon's Seal is found in cool, moist habitats in closed canopy forests at mid-elevations. Prominent in Subalpine Fir, Grand Fir, Queen's Cup Beadlily, Twinflower and Pacific Yew.

World Habitat: Starry False Solomon's Seal is widespread throughout the United States.

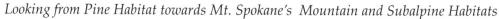

Looking from Pine Habitat towards Mt. Spokane's Mountain and Subalpine Habitats

Mountain Habitat

Mountain habitat inter-relationships are probably the most diverse of any of the land habitats found in the Little Spokane Watershed. This diversity stems from the number of species found in the habitat as well as the number of sub-habitats and forest types. These forest types range from dark, damp stands of mature western red cedar, Engelmann spruce, tamarack, hemlock and grand fir to stands of comparatively young lodgepole pine so thick they are difficult to walk through.

Mountain habitat near one of the headwaters of the Little Spokane

Inter-relationships

In the mountain habitat forests, slow changes continually take place. As some tree species increase in number, size, and vigor, others tend to decrease until they are virtually absent from the area. This series of changes, seral stages, is termed forest succession and the mountain habitat provides a wonderful demonstration of these dynamic inter-actions.

Forest succession common to the mountain habitat starts with lodgepole pine or tamarack (western larch) and terminates with western red cedar, western hemlock, and grand fir. Sometimes the steps of succession can be observed in one area. The process may often look like this: an overstory of tamarack and lodgepole pine, both of which are quick vertical growers; a middle story canopy that consists of Engelmann spruce and Douglas fir; and many grand fir, western red cedar and western hemlock saplings.

Succession occurs because the trees in each story alter their environment enough, by depleting soil nutrients, so the habitat eventually becomes inhospitable to their own species. In this case, lodgepole pine and tamarack are the pioneer species. That is, they are the first coniferous trees to inhabit the area after a disturbance,

Wild Rose

such as a fire or blowdown, creates an opening within a mature forest. Both species out-grow other species because they put most of their growth energy into rapid vertical growth thereby shading-out other potential pioneer species. Both are shade intolerant species, meaning they do best in direct sunlight. Rather than completely blocking sunlight, tamarack and lodgepole pine tend to diffuse it so that only weak sunlight reaches the forest floor. However, this shade alters the habitat enough so that their own offspring and other sun-loving plants are not able to obtain the sunlight they need to survive. Not only do they provide more shade, but they indirectly increase the moisture content of the soil by reducing the amount of water lost to evaporation. The shade

Mountain Bluebells

White Trillium

and additional moisture invite new species to establish themselves.

Tree saplings that are more shade tolerant are better able to survive under these changing conditions. Douglas fir, which is not too shade-tolerant, and Engelmann spruce, which is quite shade-tolerant, do well in environments of moderate shade and moisture. Seeds blown in from adjacent areas or brought in by animals begin to find an ideal environment in which to grow. Like the trees before them, the Douglas fir and Engelmann spruce gradually alter their environment as they grow. Fir and spruce trees spread out their branches to catch the diffuse light. Their relatively flat, densely growing needles catch even more light and further block light from reaching the forest floor giving these species the edge over their predecessors.

Lupine in bloom

As this new habitat creates itself, the habitat becomes ideal for shade-loving species such as grand fir, western hemlock, and western red cedar. Over time these species will grow large enough to dominate the landscape. Cedar and hemlock are especially well-suited to such a habitat. In the Little Spokane Watershed a forest consisting of mature cedar, in the wetter areas, and hemlock is the climax forest. A climax forest signals the end of forest succession. The key point of a climax forest is that the species present do not change their environment as those preceding them did. Instead, they create a stable environment that favors propagation of their own species. If life in a mountain habitat became very stable for a couple hundred years, cedar and hemlock climax forests would become the main forest type.

However, not all forests in the Little Spokane Watershed are climax forests. Rather than being a sequence of successional events, most forests experience disturbance events like fires, floods, winds, landslides, avalanches, and human intervention. These events turn the simple, one, two, three, successional sequence into a tangle of feedback loops and whorls. These forces are considered the rule, not the exception. True climax forests in the mountain habitat are generally found in moist areas such as north facing slopes where the impact of fire is minimal.

Indian Peace Pipe Fungus

Similarly, human suppression of natural wildfires may lead to climax forests in areas that would otherwise be burned over. Naturally occurring intermittent fires disturb the forest and allow other species to establish themselves. These irregular wildfires create a patchwork quilt, a mosaic, of forest types. Fire suppression can lead to even-aged stands and monoculture forests over a large part of the habitat. In these almost sterile forests, when fire strikes, the fire burns hotter and can burn even larger areas. The lack of age and species diversity can have destructive long term consequences for the mountain habitat.

Lodgepole Pine and Fire

Lodgepole pine shows an amazing adaptation to fire. Unlike the fire resistant ponderosa pine, lodgepole pine is not so fire resistant. Rather, its adaptation comes in the form of its ability to reproduce directly following a fire. Lodgepole produces two types of cones. One type is similar to cones of other pines. When mature, it simply opens up and falls to the ground to disperse its seeds. The other type of cone stays on the tree. This cone is sealed shut by resin. When heated by fire, the resin melts, allowing the seeds to drop out. The burned area is extremely fertile ground from the nutrients provided by the ash. Also, other species' seeds need to be imported to the burn area to get started. But lodgepole pine seeds are already present, giving lodgepole a head start.

This advantage is the reason that some stands of trees consist solely of lodgepole pine. Not only do they get started earlier, but they keep their advantage by putting energy into rapid vertical growth so that they are not shaded out by other vegetation. A common practice after logging an area is to burn the slash before replanting with stock trees. This practice may inadvertently sow the area with lodgepole pine seeds. And, although the area is planted with saplings of another species, the lodgepole pine may take over, even when starting from the fire-released seed.

The Mountain Pine Beetle, Fungi, and Lodgepole Pine

When nature's cycles are uninterrupted by humans, lodgepole pine stands occur sporadically within the mountain habitat and consist of young trees. Periodic wildfires remove most large-diameter lodgepole pines and allow smaller ones to replace them. This keeps the mountain pine beetle population relatively stable because they lay their eggs in the larger trees. Fewer large lodgepole pines means fewer beetles. However, repression of wildfires in much of the twentieth century has allowed lodgepole pines to grow larger and has created a heyday for the mountain pine beetle.

The female beetles land on the lower portions of a lodgepole pine trunk and begin to gnaw their way in. As they cut through resin ducts, the tree emits pitch in an effort to drown and push out the beetles. However, each beetle emits pheromones, chemical signals that attract more beetles. If enough beetles attack the tree it may not be able to produce enough pitch to push them all out and the beetles get the upper hand.

The beetles carry a blue stain fungus on special structures in their mouth. When the beetles lay their eggs they also lace the tree with the fungus' spore. The blue stain clogs the water vessels, keeping the nursery area moist, but cutting off the water supply to the rest of the tree. The beetle eggs hatch into hungry larvae that eat their way around the tree, girdling its food supply line. The double whammy from the fungus and the larvae is usually enough to kill the tree. When there are many large lodge pole pines, the beetle can wipe out a large section of forest instead of just a few trees.

The Role of Snags

The natural death of a stand of lodgepole pine or other trees opens up opportunities for birds that rely on dead, standing trees, snags, for food and nest sites. To some people this may not look pretty but snags provide homes for many critters. Birds such as chickadees, nuthatches, wrens, bluebirds, and most woodpeckers have adapted to the natural cycle of trees dying out from lack of sun and the depletion of nutrients. Forest birds, and many others in a variety of habitat types, require snags as a part of their environment. A snag may stand for 20 years or more, providing hunting perches for flycatchers and hawks. If a snag is large enough, it can provide cavities for owls, woodpeckers, chickadees, and squirrels.

At one time forest harvest policies called for the removal of snags to reduce competition for sunlight and to reduce the hazards associated with falling snags during logging operations. Several studies demonstrate that the population of cavity nesting birds is severely reduced under such practices.

Also, a forest is more healthy with an adequate number of snags, since cavity nesting birds feed on insects and often suppress outbreaks of insects such as spruce budworm and the mountain pine beetle. In fact, insects compose roughly 90% of the diet of woodpeckers, with seeds and berries making up the rest.

Big yellow mushroom

How Woodpeckers Make a Living

Woodpeckers resemble perching birds, but differ in a number of specialized traits. Most have two front and two rear toes on each foot, rather than the three-and-one arrangement of perching toes. Strong sharp claws on two-and-two toed feet, plus short stiff tail feathers, give them the grip and bracing they need for hammering the full force of their bodies into the tree.

Sapsucker feeding

Woodpeckers have other adaptations that allow them to live more easily in their habitat. Their brain is encased in air and their neck muscles and skull are fortified. They even have bristle-like feathers covering their nostrils so that sawdust does not enter their lungs. An average day in a woodpecker's life may include 8,000-12,000 blows on a tree or snag. For snatching grubs out of their tunnels, the woodpecker has a barb-tipped tongue much longer than its head. The tongue wraps around the skull in a tiny tubular cavity that allows the tongue to be shot out and reeled back in.

Sustainability

The mountain habitat is the most heavily logged of any of the habitats in the Little Spokane Watershed. Many current logging practices do not encourage regeneration of the natural environment, and may detrimentally affect the habitat. However, the overall benefits of sustainable forestry are beginning to be realized and put into practice.

Sustainable forestry ensures that forest relationships are maintained along with the long-term fertility and health of the land. This means that clear-cuts are generally not an option. Selective cutting of trees can prevent siltation of streams and loss of wildlife habitat. At times small irregular openings can provide areas for early successional plant species which can increase habitat health. Existing roads can be used rather than building new ones. The few remaining old-growth stands can be set aside for the grandeur and diversity they add to the habitat. Nature corridors can be created to link habitats together, thus allowing critter migration and reducing forest fragmentation, resulting in increased biodiversity.

Sustainable forestry also includes restoration of logging sites and replanting logged over areas with a variety of species. These include deciduous hardwoods, as well as conifers from on-site seed sources. This biodiversity can reduce the chances of insect invasions and significantly improve habitat health. Finally, accurate forest carrying capacity studies can be completed before logging operations begin. These

Hummingbird taking advantage of Sapsucker's bark removal

studies can include identifying possible cumulative affects and other repercussions outside the immediate vicinity, including the downstream habitats.

Clearcutting has been an all too common logging practice in which forested slopes are simply cleared of all or almost all trees. The removal of vegetation leaves little to hold the soil in place and can lead to massive sheet erosion. This is particularly true if steps are not taken immediately to replace the vegetation removed during logging. Also poorly located logging roads can cause severe erosion. Siltation of streams from this erosion can kill fish and other aquatic organisms. The loss of what little top soil that develops under conifer trees and the loss of soil nutrients retards regrowth of vegetation.

These practices are ultimately not cost-effective for several reasons: first, they lower the potential for future logging by damaging the soil and water resources needed to regenerate the habitat; second, they lower the potential for enjoying the wealth of nature by damaging the natural beauty of the area; and third, they create hidden, external costs for the community. These external costs include increased road maintenance costs, decreased water quality for residents of the area, and increased potential for further damage from flooding and mud slides.

The affects of clearcutting and other less than sustainable forest practices on wildlife are not small. The magnitude of these affects, greatly depends on factors such as the size of the clearcut, the length of time required for reforestation, and the types of species that are affected. Clearcut areas appear to be similar to wildfire areas except there are far fewer nutrients in clearcut lands.

For large plant eating animals, herbivores, like deer, moose and elk, new open areas provide growth of nutritious forage of the early successional forest plants. Bird species like ruffed grouse, bluebirds and even meadowlarks move into these areas of new forage. This new growth normally begins the year after cutting and lasts up to 20 years.

While providing forage for herbivores, clearcutting destroys their cover, both for concealment and for protection from cold

Northern Pygmy Owl with captured prey

Vole hiding in the grass

Mountain habitat with the haze of forest fire smoke in the background

temperatures and deep snow. Unlike wildfires, logging too often takes the best and leaves the worst. Clearcutting also produces long unbroken rows of slash that impede the travel of large animals.

Quality of Life Measures

The mountain habitat is one of the most popular habitats for hunting. Game species in this habitat include both whitetail and mule deer, elk, blue grouse, spruce grouse, and ruffed grouse. Quality of life can be measured by the health of these and other game animals. Large species range considerable distances. The available, unfragmented nature range areas can be measured.

Another measure can be of the many popular hiking trails in the mountain habitat, particularly in Mt. Spokane State Park. Of course too much of any recreation or activity can damage the mountain habitat. Inadequately maintained trails or just too much foot, horse, or mountain bike traffic can create rutted trails that divert snow-melt in the spring and hasten erosion. Walking off trails can compact soil and damage sensitive plants. These aspects can also be measured.

Forest Habitat Key For Mountain Habitat

Mountain habitat forest areas can be found using this part of the forest habitat key. The full key, in the appendix, can be used for the Little Spokane Watershed forests.

Forest Key Index for Mountain Habitat

1	6	11	12	13	A	Western Red Cedar – Oregon Boxwood
1	6	11	12	13	B	Western Hemlock – Oregon Boxwood
1	6	11	12	14	A	Western Red Cedar – Devil's Club
1	6	11	12	14	B	Western Red Cedar – Ladyfern
1	6	7			B	Grand Fir – Oregon Boxwood

Key for Mountain Habitat

1.   Coniferous trees other than ponderosa pine present and reproducing
     6.   Red cedar, hemlock or subalpine present and reproducing
         11. Red cedar or mountain hemlock reproducing successfully
             12. Uplands; devil's club absent; ladyfern, if present, scarcely half a meter tall
                 13. Hemlock absent; red cedar reproducing successfully
                    A.   **Western Red Cedar – Oregon Boxwood Habitat**
                 13. Hemlock present and reproducing well
                    B.   **Western Hemlock – Oregon Boxwood Habitat**
             12. Moist bottomlands or slopes with seepage; ladyfern usually abundant and well over half a meter tall
                 14. Devil's club abundant; contiguous uplands belonging to the hemlock –boxwood habitat
                    A.   **Western Red Cedar – Devil's Club Habitat**
                 14. Devil's club absent; contiguous uplands usually belonging to the hemlock – boxwood habitat
                    B.   **Western Red Cedar – Ladyfern Habitat**
     7.   Grand fir present and reproducing successfully
              A.   **Grand Fir – Oregon Boxwood Habitat**

Squirrel out on a limb

Summary of Mountain Habitat Critters

Number of Species by Kingdom

PLANT (PLANTAE)   121

FUNGUS (EUMYCOTA)   298

ANIMAL (ANIMALIA)   113

PROTIST (PROTISTA)   8

BACTERIA & VIRUS (MONERA & VIRUS)   7

TOTAL IDENTIFIED SPECIES   547

Number of Species by Class

Moss (Bryopsida)	15
Nornwort (Authocerotae)	2
Fern (Polypodiopsida)	3
Pine (Pinicae)	10
Magnolia (Magnoliidae)	7
Birch (Hamamelidae)	2
Carnation (Caryophyllidae)	7
Aspen (Dilleniidae)	15
Rose (Rosidae)	22
Sunflower (Asteridae)	26
Grass (Commelinidae)	2
Lily (Liliidae)	10
Mushroom (Basidomycetes)	246
Puffball (Gastromycetes)	13
Phragmobasidiomycetes (Phragmobasidiomycetes)	2
Ascomycetes (Ascomycetes)	27
To Be Determined (TBD)	5
Leafy Lichen (Foliose)	3
Fruity Lichen (Fruticose)	2
Turbollidia (Turbellidia)	1
Snail (Gastropoda)	1
Spider (Arachnida)	1
Centipede (Chilopoda)	1
Millipede (Diplopoda)	1
Insect (Insecta)	16
Amphibian (Amphibia)	3
Bird (Aves)	59
Mammal (Mammalia)	30
Amoeba (Rhizopoda)	1
Heliozoan (Actimpoda)	1
Foram (Forimaninifera)	1
Sporozoite (Apicomplexa)	1
Slime Mold - Cellular (Acrasiomycetes)	1
Slime Mold - Plasmodial (Myxomycetes)	1
Mildew (Oomycota)	1
Saprobe (Chytridiomycota)	1
Bacteria (Bacteria)	1
Cyanophycota (Cyanophycota)	1
Prochlorophycota (Prochlorophycota)	1
Bacteria Virus (Bacteria Virus)	1
Plant Virus (Plant Virus)	1
Vertebrate Virus (Vertebrate Virus)	1
Invertebrate Virus (Invertebrate Virus)	1

Selected Mountain Habitat Critters

PLANT (PLANTAE) — 66

Moss (Bryopsida) — 14
- Polytrichum juniperinum — A
- Polytrichum piliferum — A

Fern (Polypodiopsida) — 1
- Oakfern — C

Pine (Pinicae) — 5
- Douglas Fir — A
- Grand Fir — A
- Lodgepole Pine — A
- Pacific Hemlock — C
- Western Red Cedar — C

Magnolia (Magnoliidae) — 3
- False Bugbane — A
- Small Oregon Grape — C
- Western Meadowrue — A

Carnation (Caryophyllidae) — 4
- Broad-leaved Montia — C
- Miner's Lettuce — C
- Sandwort (C) — C
- Subalpine Sulfur Buckwheat — C

Aspen (Dilleniidae) — 6
- Common Pink Wintergreen — C
- Huckleberry (A) — C
- Little Prince's Pine — C
- Pioneer Violet — C
- Quaking Aspen — A
- Round-leaved Violet — C

Rose (Rosidae) — 18
- Big Leaf Lupine — C
- Canby Licoriceroot — C
- Coolwort Foamflower — C
- Douglas Maple — C
- Enchanter's Nightshade — C
- Fireweed — A
- Laceflower — C
- Lovage — C
- Mountain Ash (B) — C
- Mountain Sweet-Cicely — C
- Ocean Spray — A
- Pachistima — A
- Pink Spiraea — C
- Red Osier Dogwood — C
- Snowbrush Ceanothus — C
- Sweet Cicely — C
- Thimbleberry — A
- Woods Strawberry — C

Sunflower (Asteridae) — 10
- Arrowleaf Groundsel — C
- Blue Elderberry — C
- Heartleaf Arnica — C
- Mountain Bluebells — A
- Panicle Bluebells — C
- Pathfinder — C
- Pearly Everlasting — C
- Red Twinberry — A
- Western Coneflower — C
- Western Twinflower — C

Grass (Commelinidae) — 1
- Elk Sedge — C

Lily (Liliidae) — 4
- Beargrass — A
- Glacier Lily — A
- Queencup — C
- White Trillum — C

FUNGUS (EUMYCOTA) — 30

Mushroom (Basidomycetes) — 22
- Brown Almond Smelling Waxy — A
- Cystoderma fallax — C
- Delicious Milk Cap — C
- Delicious Milkcap — C
- Fading Scarlet Waxy Cap — C
- Fetid Armillaria — C
- Golden-spotted Waxy Cap — A
- Honey Mushroom — A
- Laccaria laccata — C
- Larch Waxy Cap — A
- Lilac Mycena — C
- Malodorous Lepiota — C
- Mycena sp. — C
- Pink-fringed Milky — C
- Rosy Larch bolete — C
- Russula olivacea — C
- Short Stemmed Russula — A
- Soapy Trich — C
- Spotted-stalked Milky — C
- Tiger Trich — C
- Western Grisette — C
- Witch's Hat — C

Phragmobasidiomycetes (Phragmobasidiomycetes) — 2
- Gum Drop — A
- Wood Ear — A

Ascomycetes (Ascomycetes) — 1
- Brain Mushroom (A) — C

Leafy Lichen (Foliose) — 3
- Hypogymnia physodes — A
- Parmelia sulcata — A
- Platismatia glauca — C

Fruity Lichen (Fruticose) — 2
- Goatbeard Lichen (A) — A
- Goatbeard Lichen (B) — A

ANIMAL (ANIMALIA) — 20

Insect (Insecta) — 7
- Bark Beetle — C
- Black Fly — A
- Metallic Wood-boring Beetle — C
- Mosquito — A
- Western White — C
- Yellow Jacket — C
- Zephyr Anglewing — C

Bird (Aves) — 12
- Dark-eyed Junco — C
- Evening Grosbeak — C
- Golden-crowned Kinglet — C
- Pine Siskin — A
- Pygmy Nuthatch — C
- Red Crossbill — C
- Swainson's Thrush — C
- Warbling Vireo — C
- Western Tanager — C
- White-crowned Sparrow — C
- Winter Wren — C
- Yellow-rumped Warbler — C

Mammal (Mammalia) — 1
- Western Jumping Mouse — A

* The critters listed here are those listed as abundant and common. Except only the abundant mosses are listed.

Selected Critter Descriptions

Western Red Cedar
(*Thuja plicata*)

Young Western Red Cedar

		Class:	Pine (Pinicae)
Family:	Cedar (Cupressaceae)	**Division:**	Pine (Pinophyta)
Order:	Pine (Pinatae)	**Kingdom:**	Plant (Plantae)

Other Name: Cedar
LSW Habitats: MT: C, DF: U, PP: U

Description: The Western Red Cedar is a large tree that grows up to 60 meters tall. The branches tend to spread or droop slightly and then turn upward. The branchlets are spraylike and strongly flattened horizontally. The bark is gray to reddish-brown and tears off in long fibrous strips. The wood is aromatic. Leaves are scale-like. Pollen cones are minute, numerous and reddish in color. Seed cones have 8-12 scales, are about 1 cm long and occur in loose clusters. They are brown, woody and turned upwards.

Look Alikes: None in the Little Spokane Watershed.

Little Spokane Habitat: Found mostly in moist to wet soils, usually in shaded forests. Cedar grows best on seepages and alluvial sites, but also occurs in drier habitats.

World Habitat: Western Red Cedar occurs throughout the Pacific Northwest.

Lodgepole Pine *(Pinus contorta)*

Sub Family:	Pine (Pinus)	**Class:**	Pine (Pinicae)
Family:	Pine (Pinaceae)	**Division:**	Pine (Pinophyta)
Order:	Pine (Pinatae)	**Kingdom:**	Plant (Plantae)

Other Names: Black Scrub Pine, Coast Pine, Shore Pine, Tamarack Pine
LSW Habitats: SA: F, MT: A, DF: F, PP: F

Relationships To Watershed: Lodgepole Pine provides key summer range for deer and elk. Seeds are eaten by squirrels and chipmunks. The needles are used by blue and spruce grouse. Key agents of mortality are mountain pine beetle, dwarf mistletoe, western gall rust and fire.

Description: Lodgepole Pine is a small coniferous tree that grows up to 80 feet tall. The bark is thin, scaly, gray to dark gray and usually less than 1 inch thick. The leaves are needles in fascicles of 2 that are 1-3 inches long, stiff and often twisted. They are green to yellow-green with ovoid buds that are 1/4 inch long and chestnut-brown in color.

Staminate cones are reddish-green, 8-10 mm long and in clusters. Ovulate cones are subsessile, 1-2 inches long and ovoid in shape. Some cones open after the second year but others remain closed and persist many years on the tree. These cones are purplish-brown and the basal scales are knoblike and armed with long prickles. Cones flower from April-June and shed their seeds from September through October.

Look Alikes: Lodgepole Pine is distinctive with its short needles in 2's and its persistent cones.

Little Spokane Habitat: Lodgepole Pine is found in mountain forests at mid to high elevations. Lodgepole Pine grows across a wide range from low elevations in warm-dry forests to high elevations in cold-moist forests.

World Habitat: Lodgepole Pine is a native plant that is found in Alaska and the Yukon southward to Alberta, Saskatchewan, and through the Rocky Mountains to Colorado. It is also found in the Blue and Wallowa Mountains in Washington, Oregon, Idaho, Utah and Nevada.

Grand Fir *(Abies grandis)*

Sub Family:	True Fir (Abies)	**Class:**	Pine (Pinicae)
Family:	Pine (Pinaceae)	**Division:**	Pine (Pinophyta)
Order:	Pine (Pinatae)	**Kingdom:**	Plant (Plantae)

Other Names: Balsam Fir, Fir (B), Lowland Fir, Lowland White Fir, Silver Fir
LSW Habitats: MT: A, DF: F

Relationships To Watershed: Grand Fir stands are invaluable to wildlife. They provide excellent thermal and hiding cover, snags for cavity nesters, hollow logs for dens, and browse in winter to help sustain deer and elk.

Description: Grand Firs are narrow coniferous trees up to 250 feet tall with open crowns, that are usually rounded. Their bark is smooth, gray to light brown, or ashy brown with 2-3 inch thick furrowed bark in older trees. Inner bark is purplish-red. Needles are 1-1 1/2 inches long, notched at the apex and dark green in color. Needles have stomatal bands on the lower leaf surface with no band on the top and they are arranged two-ranked in flat sprays. Buds are rounded, yellow brown and 3 at the apex of the stem. Staminate cones are yellowish and ovulate cones are yellow-green to green and 2-4 inches long. They are cylindrical, upright on the branch and the brackets are shorter than the scales. Cones disintegrate on the trees and flower from May-June. They shed their seeds in early September.

Look Alikes: Grand Firs may be easily confused with the following: white fir *(Abies concolor)* which has stomatal bands on the top of the leaf and the leaves are longer than 1 1/2 inches; subalpine fir *(Abies lasiocarpa)* which has a stomatal band along the top of the leaf, their leaves are upturned and spirally arranged.

Little Spokane Habitat: Grand Firs are found in a variety of habitats ranging to about the upper elevations of the watershed.

World Habitat: Grand Fir is a native plant that is found from British Columbia to the Bay Area of California and from the Cascades to the Rocky Mountains in Idaho, Montana, Washington and Oregon.

Pacific Yew *(Taxus brevifolia)*

		Class:	Pine (Pinicae)
Family:	Yew (Taxaceae)	**Division:**	Pine (Pinophyta)
Order:	Pine (Pinatae)	**Kingdom:**	Plant (Plantae)

Other Name: Yew
LSW Habitat: MT: U

Relationships To Watershed: Pacific Yew fruit are highly poisonous.

Description: Pacific Yew is an evergreen tree 15-20 feet tall. The bark is very thin, 1/4 inch thick, and scaly with reddish-purple inner bark and a dark purplish or reddish-brown outer bark. The trunk is often contorted. Leaves are linear, 1/2-1 inch long and have a dark green upper surface with a paler underside. They have a pointed apex and appear 2-ranked on the stem. The plant has yellowish staminate cones that appear April-June. Fruits are solitary with fleshy orange to red arils and are poisonous.

Look Alikes: Pacific Yew is the only coniferous species that has a pointed leaf apex and arils instead of cones.

Little Spokane Habitat: Pacific Yew occurs in cool to wet areas in well-drained sites beneath closed tree canopies.

World Habitat: Pacific Yew is a native plant that is found from the Cascades to northern Sierras and east to Montana.

Ternate - In threes. e.g. a leaf with three leaflets.

Found On:
Western Meadowrue

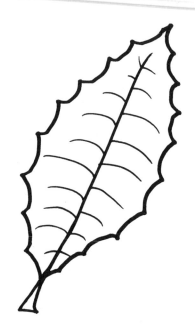

Toothed Leaf

Found On:
Western Meadowrue
Nootka Rose

Western Meadowrue
(Thalictrum occidentale)

		Class:	Magnolia (Magnoliudae)
Family:	Buttercup (Ranunculaceae)	**Division:**	Flower (Magnoliophyta)
Order:	Buttercup (Ranunculales)	**Kingdom:**	Plant (Plantae)

Other Names: Meadowrue
LSW Habitats: MT: A, BU: F, GR: F, DS: U

Relationships To Watershed: Meadowrue is unpalatable.

Description: Western Meadowrue is a dioecious perennial herb that is mid-sized from 1-3 feet tall. It has inconspicuous greenish-white flowers blooming May-July and borne in a panicle. The stigma's are purplish. Leaves are alternate, 3-4 times ternate, green above and pale below. Leaflets are rounded, three lobed and 2-3 times toothed or lobed. Fruits are achenes with three prominent veins on the side.

Look Alikes: Meadowrue may be confused with the following plants: columbines, *Aquilegia spp.*, have leaves that are less dissected and the leaflets are larger; Fendler's meadowrue, *Thalictrum fendleri*, has erect achenes and the stigma's are not purplish.

Little Spokane Habitat: Meadowrue has a wide range of habitats from warm, moist and dry at mid elevations to cool, dry and moist at upper elevations. Prominent in Douglas fir, Rocky Mountain maple and ninebark communities.

World Habitat: Meadowrue is found throughout the Pacific Northwest and Rocky Mountains.

Round-Leaved Violet
(Viola orbiculata)

		Class:	Aspen (Dilleniidae)
Family:	Violet (Violaceae)	**Division:**	Flower (Magnoliophyta)
Order:	Violet (Violales)	**Kingdom:**	Plant (Plantae)

LSW Habitats: SA: C, MT: C, DF: F

Relationships To Watershed: Round-Leaved Violets are unpalatable.

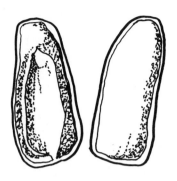

Achene - A small, dry, one-seeded, nut-like fruit.

Found On:
Western Meadowrue
Arrowleaf Groundsel
Bitterbrush
Common Yarrow
Elk Sedge
Ocean Spray
Wapato
Western Coneflower

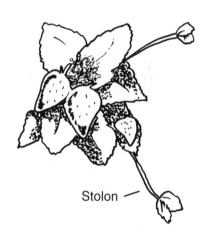

Stolon

Stolon - A horizontal-spreading stem or runner creeping along the ground that roots at the nodes or at the tip, starting a new plant.

Found On:
Round-Leaved Violet

Description: Round-Leaved Violets are low perennial herbs almost 2 inches tall. They have short rootstocks without stolons and the old petiole bases are exposed. Lemon-yellow to golden flowers with the lower three petals purple-veined bloom in May-August. Leaves are round with cordate bases and a round apex. They are thin and small, about 1-2 inches wide.

Look Alikes: Round-Leaved Violets can be easily confused with the following: woodland violet, *Viola glabella*, has cordate-reniform leaves and pointed leaf tips; early blue violet, *Viola adunca* has ovate leaves with acute tips.

Little Spokane Habitat: Round-Leaved Violets are found in cool, moist shaded sites at mid and upper elevations. Prominent in true fir communities.

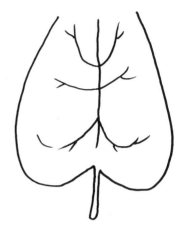

Cordate Leaf - Heart-shaped, with a notch at the base.

Common Pink Wintergreen
(Pyrola asarifolia)

		Class:	Aspen (Dilleniidae)
Family:	Heath (Ericaceae)	**Division:**	Flower (Magnoliophyta)
Order:	Heath (Ericales)	**Kingdom:**	Plant (Plantae)

Other Names: Alpine Pyrola, Liverleaf Wintergreen, Pink Wintergreen, Wintergreen (A)
LSW Habitats: SA: C, MT: C, BU: F, GR: F

Relationships To Watershed: Common Pink Wintergreen is unpalatable.

Description: Common Pink Wintergreen is a low-growing, evergreen perennial herb that is between 6-16 inches tall. Pink, rose or purplish-red flowers bloom in June-September with 10-25 flowers in elongate terminal racemes. The flowers are waxy with a strongly curved style. Leaves are basal, simple and circular to elliptic in shape. They are between 1-3 inches wide, leathery and with an entire margin. They are shiny, dark green above and purplish beneath. Fruit is a capsule.

Look Alikes: Common Pink Wintergreen leaves can often be confused with: Ginger, *Asarum caudatum*, which has cordate to reniform leaves; Round-leaved Violet, *Viola orbiculata*, which has thin, serrated leaves. Common Pink

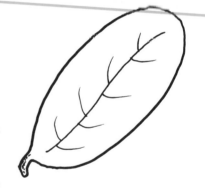

Entire Margin - Leaves without indentation. A leaf with a continuous margin.

Found On:
Common Snowberry
Common Pink Wintergreen
Kinnikinnick
Common Mullein
Scouler Willow
Western Coneflower

Wintergreen has larger, shinier and more leathery leaves than other wintergreens.

Little Spokane Habitat: Common Pink Wintergreen is found in moist, cool mid to upper elevations beneath shady closed canopies. Prominent in true fir and twinflower communities.

World Habitat: Common Pink Wintergreen is found in western United States and across Canada to northeast North America.

Little Prince's Pine
(Chimaphila menziesii)

		Class:	Aspen (Dilleniidae)
Family:	Heath (Ericaceae)	**Division:**	Flower (Magnoliophyta)
Order:	Heath (Ericales)	**Kingdom:**	Plant (Plantae)

Other Name: Little Pipsissewa
LSW Habitat: MT: C

Description: Little Prince's Pine is a small, erect, rhizomatous sub-shrub that is usually less than 6 inches tall. White to pinkish-white waxy flowers bloom in June-August from solitary to 3 in number. Stems are unbranched and may be reddish in color with a woodyish base. Leaves are evergreen, simple, alternate and 1-2 inches long. They are dull green to bluish-green in color with serrated margins. They are widest below the middle. Fruits are rounded 5-celled capsule.

Look Alikes: Little Prince's Pine may be confused with Prince's pine, *Chimaphila umbellata*, which usually contains more than 3 flowers and has shiny green oblanceolate leaves.

Little Spokane Habitat: Found in coniferous woods that are cool and moist.

World Habitat: Little Prince's Pine is a native plant that is widespread in the Pacific Northwest.

Basal Leaves - Leaves from the base of the stem.

Found On:
Common Pink Wintergreen
Common Mullein
False Bugbane
Little Prince's Pine
Idaho Fescue

—Inflorescence

Inflorescence - The flowering part of a plant, the flower cluster.

Woodland Rose
(Rosa gymnocarpa)

Class: Rose (Rosidae)
Family: Rose (Rosaceae)   **Division:** Flower (Magnoliophyta)
Order: Rose (Rosales)   **Kingdom:** Plant (Plantae)

Other Names: Baldhip Rose, Little Wild Rose, Rose (B)
LSW Habitats: MT: F, DF: F

Description: Woodland Rose is a deciduous low shrub that grows up to 3 feet tall. Pink to rose colored flowers bloom June-July. They are small, 1 inch, and borne singly on the stem. Leaves are alternate and odd-pinnately compound with 5 to 7 leaflets that are doubly serrate. The stems are reddish and armed with many fine prickles but no spines.

Look Alikes: Woodland Rose is the only rose with prickles and no spines.

Little Spokane Habitat: Woodland Rose is found in cool, moist areas in grand fir and Douglas fir communities.

World Habitat: Woodland Rose is widespread in the Pacific Northwest.

Cyme Inflorescence - A flat-topped or round-topped flower cluster in which the terminal flower blooms first.

Found On:
Woodland Rose
Woods Rose

Pachistima *(Pachistima myrsinities)*

Class: Rose (Rosidae)
Family: Spindle Tree (Celastraceae)   **Division:** Flower (Magnoliophyta)
Order: Holly (Celastrales)   **Kingdom:** Plant (Plantae)

LSW Habitats: MT: A, DF: C, RK: F

Relationships To Watershed: Pachistima is relished by deer and elk .

Description: Pachistima is an evergreen shrub, low growing up to 2 feet tall. Small maroon flowers bloom April-June in axillary clusters. Leaves are opposite, dark green, glossy, oblanceolate, serrated, thick and leathery. The stems are reddish-brown and ridged to 4 angles. Fruits are small with white arils covering dark brown seeds.

Look Alikes: Pachistima may be confused with bearberries, *Arctostaphylos spp.*, which have alternate, entire leaves.

Little Spokane Habitat: Pachistima is found in open or shaded, well-drained soils. Also occurs on ash soils at higher mountain elevations.

World Habitat: Pachistima is found from British Columbia to California and east to the Rocky Mountains.

Red Twinberry *(Lonicera utahensis)*

		Class:	Sunflower (Asteridae)
Family:	Honeysuckle (Caprifoliaceae)	**Division:**	Flower (Magnoliophyta)
Order:	Teasel (Dispacales)	**Kingdom:**	Plant (Plantae)

Other Names: Honeysuckle (C), Utah Honeysuckle (A)
LSW Habitats: SA: C, MT: A, DF: F

Relationships To Watershed: Red Twinberry is eaten by deer and elk, low in palatability.

Description: Red Twinberry is a deciduous shrub, low to mid-sized with a few erect branches that grows from 3-5 feet tall. Light yellow flowers, with a paired tubular corolla about 1 inch long, bloom May-July. Leaves are opposite, elliptic to ovate and green to dark green in color. They are about 1-2 inches long. The stem is dull gray with a solid white pith. Fruit is a paired, shiny red united berry that is about 1/4 inch long.

Ovate leaf - Egg-shaped and attached at the broad end.

Found On:
Red Twinberry
Western Coneflower

Look Alikes: Red Twinberry is commonly mistaken for Snowberry (*Symphoricarpos spp.*) but the habitats are not overlapping; and Utah Honeysuckle has broader, longer, darker leaves with red fruits.

Little Spokane Habitat: Red Twinberry is found in moist, cool sites in Grand Fir and Subalpine Fir zones. Prominent in Rocky Mountain maple, Douglas Fir and Ninebark communities.

World Habitat: Red Twinberry is found throughout Pacific Northwest, except the Oregon Coast range.

Black Morel *(Morchella angusticeps)*

		Class:	Ascomyocetes (Ascomyccetes)
Family:	True Morel (Morchellaceae)	**Division:**	Ascomycotina(Ascomycotina)
Order:	Discomycetes (Discomycetes)	**Kingdom:**	Fungus (Eumycota)

LSW Habitat: MT: F, DF: F, PP: F, LK: K, HU: F

Relationships To Watershed: Many people hunt and consume Black Morels as a delicacy. Reasonable caution should be used when preparing them as they have low levels of the poison, MMH, which is harmful to one's central nervous system, liver, and kidneys. Cook Black Morels well, in an open pan or parboil for ten minutes to rid this mushroom of the volatile toxin. Morels should not be consumed raw or in large quantities. During the fall, all morel-like mushrooms should be avoided.

Barred Owl

Description: The Black Morel is one of the most distinctive mushrooms and easy to identify. Black Morels vary in size and shape but can be identified by their conic pitted cap that has dark ridges running obscurely vertical. This fungus is hollow and is fastened by the lower edge to the stem.

Look Alikes: May be confused with the following: early morel, Verpa bohemica, which has an unattached cap and the false morels, Cyromitra and Helvella, which have saddle shaped or convoluted caps. Helvella Lacumosa has vertical pits but unlike morels there are no horizontal ridges. All of these fungi should be avoided.

Little Spokane Habitat: Black Morels can be found in conifer forests during the spring and summer depending on elevation and temperature. Recent burn sites are often covered with Black Morels. Sometimes Black Morels can be found in gardens, mulch piles and one year old beauty bark.

Spreading Cup *(Peziza repanda)*

		Class:	Ascomyocetes (Ascomyccetes)
Family:	Cup Fungi (Pezizaceae)	**Division:**	Ascomyocetina(Ascomyccetina
Order:	Discomycetes (Discomycetes)	**Kingdom:**	Fungus (Eumycota)

Other Name: Spreading Peziza, Western Yellow Veil
LSW Habitat: MT: L, HU: L

Relationships To Watershed: Spreading Cup is a brown cup fungi that is widely distributed and common in the Little Spokane Watershed in the winter but fruits all year round.

Description: Spreading Cup is a 3-11 cm. broad or occasionally larger when fully mature, cup-shaped when young but expanding to nearly flat or often wavy, undulating, with the margin often splitting. The fertile upper or inner surface is pale brown to medium brown or tan, or in age somewhat darker, smooth to somewhat wrinkled or convoluted at the center. The exterior, underside is pallid. The flesh is fairly brittle. A stalk is absent or present only as a short, narrowed base.

Look Alikes: Spreading Cup may be confused with *Peziza varia* which has a slightly grayer fertile surface and is widespread on rotting wood or occasionally in basements; *Peziza emileia* which has an ochre-brown fertile surface; *Peziza badioconfusa* which is medium-sized to fairly large with a brown to reddish-brown exterior. Other species that grow on rotting logs are *Pachyella* which has a somewhat gelatinous-rubbery fruiting body that is broadly attached to the substrate and is usually flattened or shallowly cuplike. *Pachyella clypeata* grows 2-8 cm. broad and has a brown to chestnut-brown fertile surface; *Pachyella babingtonii* is minute, 1-5 mm, and cushion-shaped, reddish-brown to purplish-brown, and often somewhat translucent.

Little Spokane Habitat: Spreading Cup is found in solitary, gregarious, or in clusters on logs and branches, especially in hardwoods, lignin-rich humus, etc. Western Yellow Veil is often found in nurseries where wood chip mulch is used.

Townsend's Warbler (*Dendroica townsendi*)

		Class:	Bird (Aves)
Family:	Warbler (Emberizidae)	**Division:**	Vertebrate (Chordata)
Order:	Thrush (Passeriformes)	**Kingdom:**	Animal (Animalia)

LSW Habitats: MT: F, DF: F, PP: U, HU: R

Relationships to Watershed: Townsend's Warbler's diet consists largely or entirely of insects and also a few seeds and plant galls.

Description: The Townsend's Warbler is a small, bright-colored bird, about 4 - 5 inches in length. In the adult male the crown, cheek, throat, and upper breast are black. The black cheek is bordered from above by a yellow eyebrow and below by a broad yellow stripe on the side of the throat. The back is dull olive-green spotted with black. The lower breast is yellow and the belly is white. The adult female is similar, but has an olive-green crown, a dusky cheek, a largely yellow throat, and less black in the back and white in the tail.

Look Alikes: May be confused with the following: Hermit Warbler, *Dendroica occidentalis*, which has entirely golden cheeks, no yellow on the breast, and a primarily gray back; the Black-throated Gray Warbler, *Dendroica nigrescens*, which has paler cheeks and lacks yellow on the breast. Neither of these species have been recorded in the Little Spokane Watershed.

Little Spokane Habitat: Townsend's warblers are found in coniferous forests.

World Habitat: Found in the Pacific Northwest and on the western coast of Canada.

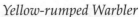
Yellow-rumped Warbler

Snowshoe Rabbit *(Lepus americanus)*

		Class:	Mammal (Mammalia)
Family:	Rabbit (Leporidae)	**Division:**	Vertebrate (Chordata)
Order:	Rabbit (Lagomorpha)	**Kingdom:**	Animal (Animalia)

LSW Habitats: MT: F, DF: F, BU: R, RP: U

Relationships To Watershed: Snowshoe Rabbit forages at night, eating herbaceous vegetation during the growing season and browsing twigs, buds, and bark in winter. Snowshoe Rabbit's predators include lynx, martens, red foxes, and coyotes.

Description: Snowshoe Rabbit is a medium-sized hare, brownish to reddish-brown above and whitish below in summer. The hind feet are relatively quite large. The ears are short and are brownish like the back with dark tips. In winter, the pelage usually changes to white, except for the ear tips which remain dark.

Little Spokane Habitat: Snowshoe Rabbit is a species living in dense coniferous forests or deciduous thickets of alder or willow.

World Habitat: Snowshoe Rabbit is a native species found throughout the Pacific Northwest, except for the arid areas of eastern Washington, eastern Oregon, and southern Idaho. It ranges across subarctic North America from Alaska to Newfoundland and then southward along major mountain ranges to California, New Mexico, and North Carolina.

Flying Squirrel

Northern Flying Squirrel
(Glaucomys sabrinus)

		Class:	Mammal (Mammalia)
Family:	Squirrel (Sciuridae)	**Division:**	Vertebrate (Chordata)
Order:	Rodent (Rodentia)	**Kingdom:**	Animal (Animalia)

Other Names: Flying Squirrel, Squirrel (D)
LSW Habitats: MT: U

Relationships to Watershed: The Northern Flying Squirrel has a varied diet that consists of seeds, nuts, and fungi, and also a wide variety of berries, fruits, blossoms, and even bark. This species is more carniverous than most squirrels and consumes mostly insects, as well as birds and eggs.

Description: The Northern Flying Squirrel is a small nocturnal squirrel with a large head, large black eyes, and soft silky fur. This squirrel has fur-covered membranes on both sides of the body between the fore and hind limbs. The upper parts of the squirrel are brownish to dark grayish while the under parts are ashy gray to light grayish buff.

Look Alikes: This is the only squirrel with side membranes and the only one that is nocturnal.

Little Spokane Habitat: The Northern Flying Squirrel lives in ponderosa pine trees and trees that are higher up in elevation such as lodgepole pine and spruce forests. These squirrels are usually found in the tallest trees and old cabins and abandoned houses. They are rarely found on the ground.

World Habitat: This species is strongly restricted to coniferous forests throughout the Pacific Northwest.

Red Squirrel finishing a pine cone

Western Jumping Mouse
(*Zapus princeps*)

		Class:	Mammal (Mammalia)
Family:	Western Jumping Mouse (Dipodidae)		
		Division:	Vertebrate (Chordata)
Order:	Rodent (Rodentia)	**Kingdom:**	Animal (Animalia)

Other Names: Deer Mouse, Jumping Mouse
LSW Habitats: MT: A, DF: A, PP: A, GR: A

Relationships to Watershed: Western Jumping Mouse usually keeps below the tops of the grass so that only fast movement in the vegetation is apparent. These mice are primarily nocturnal and feed on insects, seeds, and berries.

Description: The Western Jumping Mouse is a medium sized jumping mouse with dark, blackish upper parts, an olive-brown band down the middle of the back, yellowish sides and white under parts. The tail is long and bicolored. The lateral line found between the back and sides is yellowish buff and another band between the sides and belly is clear and pale.

Look Alikes: The only mouse in the Little Spokane Watershed that jumps like a kangaroo when moving.

Little Spokane Habitat: Found in wet meadows, bogs, streamside brush, and moist, grassy, herbaceous places near water. Mostly in forested and subalpine areas.

Pileated Woodpecker

World Habitat: This species occurs throughout British Columbia, excepting the extreme southwest and northeast corners; in the northeast, extreme east, and southeast parts of Washington; in eastern and southcentral Oregon; and in all of Idaho.

Elk *(Cervus canadensis)*

		Class:	Mammal (Mammalia)
Family:	Deer (Cervidae)	**Division:**	Vertebrate (Chordata)
Order:	Deer (Artiodactyla)	**Kingdom:**	Animal (Animalia)

At Risk:	Regulated Game
Other Names:	American Wapiti, Rocky Mountain Elk, Wapiti
LSW Habitats:	MT: F, DF: F, PP: U, GR: R

Description: Elk are large deer-like animals. Their size and height are distinctive; 9 feet tall at the head, 5 1/2 feet tall at the shoulder. Elk have brown or reddish-brown bodies with large yellow or buffy white rump patches. The males have chestnut-brown manes and, in the late summer and fall, heavy, widely spreading antlers; sometimes reaching 5 feet in width.

Look Alikes: Roosevelt Elk, *Cervus roosevelti*, are larger and now usually only seen in Washington's Olympic Peninsula.

Little Spokane Habitat: Elk are found in semi-open forests and the subalpine areas in summer.

World Habitat: Rocky Mountain Elk are found throughout the Pacific Northwest with the exception of western, central and northwestern British Columbia. Rocky Mountain Elk are also found on Vancouver Island.

A tiny waterfall

Douglas Fir Habitat

Douglas fir habitat has the most patchy distribution of any of the forest habitats in the Little Spokane Watershed. It generally occurs at elevations below that of the mountain habitat, although it can still occupy elevations as high as 5,000 feet. The most common area in which Douglas fir habitat is found in the Little Spokane Watershed is on the north side of lower elevation slopes. The warmer, drier south slopes are usually occupied by drought-tolerant ponderosa pine. The Douglas fir do much better in the cooler, more moist north facing slopes.

Inter-relationships

Douglas Fir

The Douglas fir was named after David Douglas, a Scottish naturalist who is often credited with being the first European to describe the Douglas fir in 1825. Actually, Archibold Menzies, another Scot, described the Douglas fir in 1791 while visiting the northwest on one of Captain Vancouver's ships. Douglas called it a pine. Later taxonomists tried out "yellow-leafed-fir", "spruce", and finally "false-hemlock", while sticking with fir for the common name. Actually, it is none of them.

Like hemlocks and cedars, also misapplied European names, Douglas fir is a Pacific Rim genus. There are three species within this genus in Japan and China and one in a tiny mountainous area of Southern California. In 1826 David

Pathway through older Douglas Fir

Moss covered log enfolded with new life

Douglas introduced the seeds to Europe and it has been grown abroad with great success, especially in New Zealand and Scotland.

In the Little Spokane Watershed and other areas of the foothills of the Rocky Mountains, a 100 foot Douglas fir is considered large. However, in the much wetter forests of the Cascades and northern Coast Range, Douglas firs may reach heights of 165-295 feet and diameters of 3-6 feet. The trees do not begin to develop these old-growth characteristics until they are 175-250 years old.

In the relatively dry foothills of the Inland Pacific Northwest, Douglas fir can displace pines whose shade tolerance is very low. This allows Douglas fir to become the climax species in these sites, growing in the shade and moisture provided by the pine trees. In the more moist higher elevations, the more shade tolerant species such as true firs, the grand fir in the Little Spokane Watershed, hemlock, and cedar will generally displace Douglas fir when forest succession is undisturbed for several hundred years.

Fire suppression has played a major role in allowing Douglas fir to replace ponderosa pine as the climax species in some lower elevation areas. Prior to the suppression of forest fires, any Douglas fir saplings that may have been able to get a start within the ponderosa pine stand would have been eliminated by fires which historically burn through ponderosa pine stands every 5-20 years.

Tamarack

Another conifer common to the Douglas fir habitat is the tamarack, also called western larch. This is definitely one of the more interesting coniferous trees in the watershed. Many people use the terms evergreen and conifer interchangeably and the tamarack demonstrates why this is not accurate. A conifer is simply a woody plant that has needle-like or scale-like leaves and produces seeds in a cone. An evergreen is a plant that does not lose all of its leaves at one time during the year and is always green (thus the term evergreen). It just so happens that most conifers in this area are also evergreens. The tamarack however, produces cones; it is a true conifer, but loses its needles in the late fall and is therefore deciduous. In the spring, intense chartreuse needles are seen sprouting in whorls from short peg like spurs. In the winter a tamarack can be distinguished from an aspen or cottonwood by its coniferous form – single, straight trunk and symmetrical branching – and can be distinguished from a dead evergreen by the pegs on its twigs and its distinctive pattern of bark development.

Apparently the tamarack has found a system that works well. It is a tree that is successful in a variety of habitats, but does best in areas with full sunlight and ample groundwater. This helps the tamarack make up for photosynthetic time lost due to the shedding of its needles. Deciduous needles also make the tamarack more resilient in the wake of defoliating insect attacks. Because tamaracks produce a whole new crop of needles every year anyway, producing another crop is not as difficult to do as it is for other insect defoliated conifers. Production of the new crop of needles in the spring does require significant energy. It takes about three weeks to replace the root energy stores used to grow the new needles.

Birds

One of the more common birds in this habitat is the red crossbill, a small perching bird that is aptly named. The crossbill does in fact have a bill that is crossed - the lower mandible hooks upward almost as much as the upper one hooks downward. The design allows the birds to pry cone scales apart to extract the seeds. The jaws also open wide for the bird's tongue to glean aphids and terrestrial insects. Crossbills will migrate to wherever some kind of conifer is bearing a good cone crop. A shower of conifer seed coats and seed wings often means a crossbill flock is above.

Golden Waxy Cap Mushrooms

An old Douglas Fir stump provides a home for moss and lichen

Northern Saw-whet owl

A more familiar but just as interesting bird is the common raven. Ravens can be distinguished from their smaller cousin the crow by the raven's larger size, heavier "Roman nose" effect of the bill, ruffed throat and breast, a wedge-shaped tail and by a guttural croak rather than the crow's "caw".

The raven is the largest of all perching birds, order Passeriformes. It is considered to be among the most intelligent and most recently evolved bird, avian, order. Passeriformes have, by far, the greatest number of species, an indicator of current success and rapidity of evolution. The success of ravens may also be attributed to the flexibility of their diet. They are able to eat almost anything edible, including nestlings, eggs, seeds, insects, fruit, rodents and even hares.

Quality of Life Measures

Human activities in the Douglas fir habitat include hunting for both whitetail and mule deer, elk, and both ruffed and blue grouse. Hiking and bird watching are also popular in this habitat. Quality of life measures for hunting, hiking and bird watching can come from observations of the people on these activities. As the watershed's quality of life improves there will be more and diverse species seen.

Because of the proximity to human habitation, Douglas fir habitat often provides home for humans as well as wildlife. This habitat has yet to see the numbers and spread of human populations that the ponderosa pine habitat has seen in the last 130 years. In part this is due to the steeper, shadier north facing slopes of Douglas fir habitat. As quality of life improves in the watershed, the sprawl of human habitation can be reduced, the density of where people live can increase along with nature buffers around the human habitation areas, and more native plants can remain on building sites.

Large ant mound

Forest Habitat Key For Douglas Fir Habitat

Douglas Fir forest areas can be found using this part of the forest habitat key.

The full key, in the appendix, can be used for the Little Spokane Watershed forests.

Index for Douglas Fir Habitat

1	6	7	9		A	Douglas Fir - Pinegrass Habitat
1	6	7	9		B	Douglas Fir - Pinegrass, Kinnikinnick Phase Habitat
1	6	7	8	10	A	Douglas Fir - Ninebark Habitat
1	6	7	8	10	B	Douglas Fir - Snowberry Habitat

Key for Douglas Fir Habitat

1. Coniferous trees other than ponderosa pine present and reproducing
   6. Red cedar, hemlock and subalpine fir absent, or at least not reproducing
      7. Grand fir absent; undergrowth lacking, queen's cup, twinflower, wintergreen, Big huckleberry, and round–leaved violet
         8. Pinegrass, often with much elk sedge or low northern sedge, very conspicuous in the undergrowth; shrubs other than kinnikinnick or huckleberry
            9. Kinnikinnick and huckleberry unrepresented
               A. **Douglas Fir – Pinegrass Habitat**
            9. Kinnikinnick present; huckleberry usually present
               B. **Douglas Fir – Pinegrass, Kinnikinnick Phase Habitat**
         8. Pinegrass, elk sedge and low northern sedge poorly represented, if at all present; shrubs other than kinnikinnick or huckleberry dominant
            10. Ninebark and/or ocean–spray well represented
               A. **Douglas Fir – Ninebark Habitat**
            10. Ninebark and ocean-spray absent; snowberry and/or shiny–leaf spiraea abundantly represented
               B. **Douglas Fir – Snowberry Habitat**

Wild Strawberry

Summary of Douglas Fir Habitat Critters

Number of Species by Kingdom

PLANT (PLANTAE)   90

FUNGUS (EUMYCOTA)   119

ANIMAL (ANIMALIA)   117

PROTIST (PROTISTA)   8

BACTERIA & VIRUS (MONERA & VIRUS)   7

TOTAL IDENTIFIED SPECIES   341

Number of Species by Class

Moss (Bryopsida)	16
Nornwort (Authocerotae)	1
Fern (Polypodiopsida)	1
Pine (Pinicae)	6
Magnolia (Magnoliidae)	5
Carnation (Caryophyllidae)	3
Aspen (Dilleniidae)	5
Rose (Rosidae)	20
Sunflower (Asteridae)	25
Grass (Commelinidae)	2
Lily (Liliidae)	6
Mushroom (Basidomycetes)	94
Puffball (Gastromycetes)	5
Phragmobasidiomycetes (Phragmobasidiomycetes)	2
Ascomycetes (Ascomycetes)	10
To Be Determined (TBD)	1
Crusty Lichen (Crustose)	1
Leafy Lichen (Foliose)	6
Turbellidia (Turbellidia)	1
Snail (Gastropoda)	2
Spider (Arachnida)	1
Centipede (Chilopoda)	1
Millipede (Diplopoda)	1
Insect (Insecta)	28
Amphibian (Amphibia)	2
Reptile (Reptilia)	4
Bird (Aves)	56
Mammal (Mammalia)	21
Amoeba (Rhizopoda)	1
Heliozoan (Actimpoda)	1
Foram (Forimaninifera)	1
Sporozoite (Apicomplexa)	1
Slime Mold - Cellular (Acrasiomycetes)	1
Slime Mold - Plasmodial (Myxomycetes)	1
Mildew (Oomycota)	1
Saprobe (Chytridiomycota)	1
Bacteria (Bacteria)	1
Cyanophycota (Cyanophycota)	1
Prochlorophycota (Prochlorophycota)	1
Bacteria Virus (Bacteria Virus)	1
Plant Virus (Plant Virus)	1
Vertebrate Virus (Vertebrate Virus)	1
Invertebrate Virus (Invertebrate Virus)	1

Selected Douglas Fir Habitat Critters

PLANT (PLANTAE)	41	
Moss (Bryopsida)	14	
Aluacomnium androgynum		C
Aluacomnium androgynum		C
Brachythecium albicans		C
Brachythecium campestre		C
Brachythecium salebposum		C
Ceratodon purpureus		C
Dicranum fuscescens		C
Funaria hygrometrica		C
Homalothecium nevadense		C
Polytrichum juniperinum		A
Polytrichum piliferum		A
Racomitrium hetrostichum		C
Rhacomitrium canescens		C
Torula ruralis		C
Pine (Pinicae)	1	
Douglas Fir		A
Magnolia (Magnoliidae)	1	
Small Oregon Grape		A
Rose (Rosidae)	9	
Mallow Ninebark		C
Nootka Rose		C
Ocean Spray		A
Pachistima		C
Redstem Ceanothus		C
Snowbrush Ceanothus		C
Thimbleberry		A
Wild Strawberry		C
Woods Rose		C
Sunflower (Asteridae)	13	
Arrowleaf Groundsel		C
Common Snowberry		C
Common Yarrow		C
Honeysuckle (B)		C IO
Low Fleabane		C
Orange Honeysuckle		C
Oregon Boxwood		C
Pathfinder		C
Pearly Everlasting		C
Ragwort		C
Western Hawkweed		C
Western Twinflower		C
Wild Aster		C
Grass (Commelinidae)	2	
Elk Sedge		A
Pinegrass		C
Lily (Liliidae)	1	
Glacier Lily		C
FUNGUS (EUMYCOTA)	26	
Mushroom (Basidomycetes)	20	
Brown Almond Smelling Waxy		A
Clavaria cristata		C
Cystoderma fallax		C
Fading Scarlet Waxy Cap		C
Fetid Armillaria		A
Golden Chanterelle		C
Golden-spotted Waxy Cap		A
Honey Mushroom		A
Laccaria laccata		C
Malodorous Lepiota		C
Olive Brown Waxy		C
Pink-fringed Milky		C
Rosy Larch bolete		C
Scaly Pholiota		C
Short Stemmed Russula		A
Soapy Trich		C
Spotted-stalked Milky		C
Tiger Trich		C
Western Grisette		C
Witch's Hat		C
Phragmobasidiomycetes		
(Phragmobasidiomycetes)	1	
Gum Drop		A
Ascomycetes (Ascomycetes)	1	
Brain Mushroom (A)		C
Crusty Lichen (Crustose)	1	
Usnea spp		C
Leafy Lichen (Foliose)	3	
Hypogymnia physodes		A
Parmelia sulcata		A
Platismatia glauca		C
ANIMAL (ANIMALIA)	27	
Insect (Insecta)	11	
Ant		C
Bark Beetle		C
Bumblebee		C
Bumblebee spp		C
Lorquin's Admiral		C
Pearly Crescentspot		C
Satyr Anglewing		C
Tussock Moth		A
Western Tiger Swallowtail		C
Yellow Jacket		C
Zerene Fritillary		C
Bird (Aves)	14	
Chipping Sparrow		C
Common Raven		C
Dark-eyed Junco		C
Evening Grosbeak		C
Golden-crowned Kinglet		C
Great Horned Owl		C
Hermit Thrush		C
Pine Siskin		A
Pygmy Nuthatch		C
Red Crossbill		C
Swainson's Thrush		C
Warbling Vireo		C
Western Tanager		C
Winter Wren		C
Mammal (Mammalia)	2	
Western Jumping Mouse		A
White-tailed Deer		C RGM

* The critters listed here are those identified as abundant and common.

Legend - Critters are listed by their common name followed by their abundance in the habitat. Introduced species and species at risk are indicated by type code. • **Abundance Codes: A** Abundant, **C** Common, **F** Fairly common, **U** Uncommon, **R** Rare, **V** Vagrant, **K** Known in habitat, **L** Likely in habitat, **M** Missing from habitat. • **Introduced Species Codes: IN** Introduced Noxious species, **IO** Introduced, Other than noxious species. • **At Risk Codes: MS** Missing, **ED** Endangered, **TH** Threatened, **CD** Candidate, **MN** Monitor, **RGM** Regulated Game, **RNG** Regulated Nongame, **RA** Rare, **PB** Protected Breeding Areas.

Selected Critter Descriptions

Douglas-Fir (*Pseudotsuga menziesii*)

Sub Family:	True Fir (Abies)	**Class:**	Pine (Pinicae)
Family:	Pine (Pinaceae)	**Division:**	Pine (Pinophyta)
Order:	Pine (Pinatae)	**Kingdom:**	Plant (Plantae)

Other Name: Fir (A)
LSW Habitats: MT: A, DF: A, PP: U

Relationships To Watershed: Douglas Fir provide valuable cover and foraging habitat for deer and elk. Squirrels eat the seeds and store them in caches. Songbirds eating the seeds are Clark's Nutcracker, nuthatches, crossbills, juncos and siskins. Blue Grouse eat the needles.

Description: Douglas Fir is a large coniferous tree that grows to between 130-150 feet tall. The crown is compact and the tree has a pyramidal shape with branches ascending and drooping. The leader is stiffly erect. Bark on young trees is thin and smooth with resin blisters that are gray. On older trees the bark is rough, thick, reddish-brown and has irregular deep furrows with corky grayish to reddish brown layered plates. Needles are 3/4-1 inch long and blue green to yellow green to purplish-green in color. They have a blunt apex, whitish stomata on the upper surface and 2 stomatal bands below. The needles are in a spiral arrangement on the twig. Buds are shiny, sharp pointed, conical and reddish-brown to brown in color. Staminate cones are orange-red while the ovulate cones are yellowish-green to purplish-green becoming reddish-brown and 2-4 inches long at maturity. A 3-lobed bract extends beyond the scale with the center lobe being the longest. The cones flower April-May and shed their seeds August-September.

Look Alikes: Douglas Fir may be confused with the following: Grand Fir, *Abies grandis*, whose needles are in 2-ranked flat sprays, thicker, broader and do not contain stomatal bloom on the top of the leaf; Subalpine Fir, *Abies lasiocarpa*, which has needles that are spirally arranged like the Douglas-Fir but the leaves are upturned to spiral rather than oriented spirally.

Doug Fir cones with their mouse tail bracts

Little Spokane Habitat: Douglas Fir are found in moist to dry areas near the timberline.

Tamarack (*Larix occidentalis*)

Sub Family:	True Fir (Abies)	**Class:**	Pine (Pinicae)
Family:	Pine (Pinaceae)	**Division:**	Pine (Pinophyta)
Order:	Pine (Pinatae)	**Kingdom:**	Plant (Plantae)

Other Names: Larch, Western Larch
LSW Habitats: SA: U, MT: F, DF: F, RK: U

Relationships To Watershed: Tamarack forests provide habitat for elk, deer and bear. Blue Grouse and Spruce Grouse eat the needles. Crossbills eat the seeds. Trees quickly establish after fire and grow rapidly and dominate as fire pioneers.

Description: Tamarack is a coniferous tree that grows to 140-180 feet tall. It consists of a long, clear bole with a short crown of horizontal, radiating branches. Young

Russula Mushroom emerging

trees have thin, scaly grayish-brown bark while the older trees have thick, flattened plates between deep furrows. Needles are deciduous and are bunched in 15-30 needles in a spur. They are pale green, 1-2 inches long and turn brilliant yellow in autumn. Buds are 1/8 inch, rounded and chestnut brown in color. Staminate cones are 1/2 inch long and yellow while the ovulate cones are 1 inch long and oblong. They have reddish-brown scales that are reflexed and bracts with a prominent central spine that is longer than the scales. They flower from May-June and shed their seeds from September to October.

Look Alikes: Tamarack is very distinctive but may be confused with ponderosa pine, *Pinus ponderosa*, if one only looks at the bark, however the rest of the tree is very different.

White Shooting Star

Little Spokane Habitat: Tamarack grows on moist, deep soils as well as dryer gravels. Tamarack is found in north and east exposures at lower elevations, and on all exposures in the moist mid and upper elevational range. It is especially prominent on ash influenced soils.

World Habitat: Tamarack is a native plant found in southern British Columbia, south on the east side of the Cascades to central Oregon, across northern Washington to northeast Montana, northern Idaho and in southeast Washington and northwest Oregon.

Small Oregon Grape
(Berberis repens)

		Class:	Magnolia (Magnoliudae)
Family:	Barberry (Berberidaceae)	Division:	Flower (Magnoliophyta)
Order:	Buttercup (Ranunculales)	Kingdom:	Plant (Plantae)

Other Names: Creeping Oregon Grape, Oregon Grape (B)
LSW Habitats: MT: C, DF: A, PP: C, RK: F

Relationships To Watershed: Small Oregon Grape leaves will attract deer.

Description: Small Oregon Grape is a low growing, creeping shrub usually less than 12 inches tall. Buttery yellow flowers in racemes bloom in March-June. The plant is rhizomatous and often forms dense patches. Leaves are evergreen, alternate and pinnately compound with 5 to 7 leaflets. The margins have spinose teeth, like holly, and the leaflets are less than twice as long as broad, dull green and non-glossy above. Fruits are dark blue berries with a glaucous dusting.

Look Alikes: Small Oregon Grape may be confused with tall Oregon grape, *Berberis aquifolium*, which has longer leaflets that are 7 to 9 in number and are lighter in color and glossy.

Little Spokane Habitat: Small Oregon Grape thrives in dry well-drained sites often on steep mountain or canyon slopes.

World Habitat: Small Oregon Grape is a native plant that is found in eastern Washington and eastern Oregon.

Compound Leaf - A leaf separated into two or more distinct leaflets.

Leaflet - A division of a compound leaf

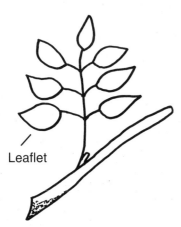

Leaflet

Pinnate Leaf - A compound leaf with leaflets arranged on opposite sides of a common axis.

Found On:
Blue Elderberry
Common Yarrow
Small Oregon Grape
Woods Rose
Woodland Rose

Spinose - Bearing spines.

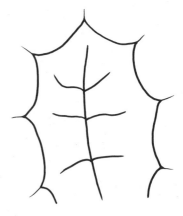

Found On:
Small Oregon Grape

Doubly Serrate Leaf or Biserrate Leaf - Doubly saw-tooth, the teeth of a serrate leaf are also serrate.

Found On:
Thimbleberry
Mallow ninebark
Mountain Maple
Thimbleberry

Thimbleberry (*Rubus parviflorus*)

		Class:	Rose (Rosidae)
Family:	Rose (Rosaceae)	**Division:**	Flower (Magnoliophyta)
Order:	Rose (Rosales)	**Kingdom:**	Plant (Plantae)

LSW Habitats: MT: A, DF: A, RK: U, BU: F

Relationships To Watershed: Thimbleberry fruit is eaten by bears, raccoons, ground squirrels, skunks, grouse and grosbeaks.

Description: Thimbleberry is a deciduous, low to mid-size shrub from 3-5 feet in height. White to pinkish white flowers bloom May-July with 3-7 large flowers in flat-topped panicles. Alternate leaves are simple, up to 6 inches long and 8 inches broad, and palmately 5-lobed with long petioles. The leaves have doubly serrated margins, are dark green above and are soft with small hairs. Stems are light brown, cane like and unarmed. The bark is papery and thin. Fruits are thimble-like red aggregates of drupelets.

Aggregate Fruit - A cluster or group of small fleshy fruits, drupelets, that originate from a number of separate pistils in a single flower.

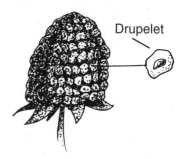

Drupelet

Found On:
Thimbleberry

Thimbleberry in flower

Look Alikes: Thimbleberry, with maple-like leaves, can be mistaken for Rocky Mountain maple (*Acer glabrum*). Thimbleberry leaves are alternate while maples have opposite leaves.

Little Spokane Habitat: Thimbleberry is found in moist sites along stream banks in canyon bottoms to forested communities. At higher elevations, to 9,000 feet, Thimbleberry can be found on exposed sites, avalanche chutes.

World Habitat: Thimbleberry is widespread from Alaska to Mexico and from the Great Lakes westward to the Pacific Coast.

White Spiraea *(Spiraea betulifolia)*

		Class:	Rose (Rosidae)
Family:	Rose (Rosaceae)	**Division:**	Flower(Magnoliophyta)
Order:	Rose (Rosales)	**Kingdom:**	Plant (Plantae)

Other Names: Flattop Spiraea, Shiny-leaf Spiraea
LSW Habitats: PP: C, GR: C

Relationships To Watershed: White Spiraea is low in palatability and increases with disturbance such as skidding and overgrazing.

Description: White Spiraea is a deciduous, rhizomatous shrub; low growing from 8-24 inches tall. Small white flowers bloom June-July in a dense flat-topped corymb of up to 4 inches across. White Spirea has alternate, ovate leaves that are 1-3 inches long. They are green above and paler below with coarsely double serrated margins from the mid margin to the apex. The stem is erect with a light yellow-brown color. Fruit is a glabrous follicle with 5 in a cluster.

Spiraea in bloom

Look Alikes: White Spiraea may be confused with the following: Hawthornes, *Crataegus spp.*, are armed and have leaves that are serrated from midpoint to apex; Serviceberry, *Amelanchier spp.*, leaves are darker green, with coarse serrations above the midpoint of the leaf and with a distinctive paralleling venation.

Little Spokane Habitat: White Spiraea is found in warm, dry sites beneath ponderosa pine and Douglas-fir and in warm, moist sites beneath successional grand fir. White Spirae forms patches with other rhizomatous plants such as snowberry, ninebark, pinegrass and elk sedge.

World Habitat: White Spiraea is found south in the Cascades to north central Oregon and eastward to the Rocky Mountains.

Woods Rose (*Rosa woodsii*)

Rose with beetle exploring the flower

		Class:	Rose (Rosidae)
Family:	Rose (Rosaceae)	**Division:**	Flower (Magnoliophyta)
Order:	Rose (Rosaloo)	**Kingdom:**	Plant (Plantae)

Other Name: Rose (C)
LSW Habitats: DF: C, PP: C, GH: C, RP: C

Relationships To Watershed: Woods Rose hips are eaten by bear, grouse and quail.

Description: Woods Rose is a deciduous shrub, low to mid-sized from 3-7 feet tall. Small 1-2 inch flowers bloom May-July, clustered in 3-5 inch terminal cymes. Alternate leaves are odd-pinnately compound with 5-9 leaflets that are singly serrate. The stems are armed with stout, straight to slightly curved spines. Fruits are red hips with the calyx persisting on the hip at fruiting time.

Look Alikes: Woods Rose is very similar to Nootka Rose, *Rosa nutkana*, which has a solitary larger flower.

Little Spokane Habitat: Woods Rose is found in warm, dry sites.

World Habitat: Woods Rose is found only in North America from eastern Washington to southern California and east to Wisconsin, Montana and Texas.

Mountain Maple (*Acer glabrum*)

		Class:	Rose (Rosidae)
Family:	Maple (Aceraceae)	**Division:**	Flower (Magnoliophyta)
Order:	Maple (Sapindales)	**Kingdom:**	Plant (Plantae)

Other Name: Rocky Mountain Maple
LSW Habitats: MT: F, DF: F, RP: C

Relationships To Watershed: Mountain Maple persists in open savanna as an early to mid seral species in true fir communities. Browsed readily by deer and elk.

Description: Mountain Maple is a deciduous shrub or small tree from 3 to 33 feet tall. Flowers are small and greenish-yellow, blooming in April-June in axillary clusters. Leaves are opposite, simple and palmately lobed with 3-5 main veins. The leaves are 2-5 inches in diameter, dark green above with reddish tints and paler below. The petiole can be either green or red and is the same length as the leaf blade. The stem is smooth with reddish-brown bark that turns gray with age. The buds are opposite, red, ovate and often paired. Fruit is a double samara that is 1 inch long and joined at acute or right angles.

Lobed Leaf - Lobes that are less than half way to the base or midvein

Found on:
Mountain Maple
Mallow Ninebark
Ocean Spray
Thimble Berry
Wax Currant
Western Meadowrue

Orange Honeysuckle vine twists up the branches

Look Alikes: Mountain Maple is the only maple in the inland Pacific Northwest; however, it may be confused with: ninebark, *Physocarpus spp.*, and currant and gooseberry species, *Ribes spp.* Mountain Maple leaves are opposite while the look-alikes have alternate leaves.

Little Spokane Habitat: Mountain Maples are found in moist seepage sites under grand fir and Douglas-fir communities. They also occur in riparian communities from low elevation canyon bottoms to mid-mountain streamsides. They are prominent in grand fir, Douglas fir and ninebark communities.

World Habitat: Mountain Maples are found east of the Cascades in Washington and Oregon and extending east to Idaho and western Montana. Also found in the Blue and Wallowa mountains.

White-flowered Hawkweed
(*Heiracium umbeliatum*)

*Black Blister Bettle
on flower stalk*

		Class:	Sunflower (Asteridae)
Family:	Sunflower (Compositae)	**Division:**	Flower (Magnoliophyta)
Order:	Sunflower (Asterales)	**Kingdom:**	Plant (Plantae)

Other Names: Hawkweed (B), White Hawkweed
LSW Habitats: MT: F, DF: F

Relationships To Watershed: White-flowered Hawkweed is palatable to deer and elk.

Description: White-flowered Hawkweed is a perennial herb that grows to about 12-30 inches tall. White flowers bloom June-August with few to many heads. The involucre is glabrous to hairy and blackish-green in color with stellate hairs. Lower leaves are elliptic with a petiole, the middle and upper cauline leaves are reduced and sessile. Leaves are alternate and the margins are entire to wavy.

Look Alikes: White-flowered Hawkweed may be confused with Western Hawkweed (*Hieracium albertinum*) when the flowers are absent. Western hawkweed has yellow flowers and the stems and leaves are long and hairy. The lower leaves are sessile to shortly petiolate.

Little Spokane Habitat: White-flowered Hawkweed is found in Douglas-fir to subalpine fir communities at cool, moist, mid-elevations in the mountains.

World Habitat: White-flowered Hawkweed is a native plant that is widespread throughout the Pacific Northwest.

Elk Sedge (*Carex geyeri*)

		Class:	Grass (Commelinidae)
Family:	Sedge (Cyperaceae)	**Division:**	Flower (Magnoliophyta)
Order:	Reed (Cyperales)	**Kingdom:**	Plant (Plantae)

LSW Habitats: SA: F, MT: C, DF: A

Relationships To Watershed: Elk Sedge is a heavy sod former that is a fierce competitor with associated rhizomatous grasses and shrubs on forested sites. Elk Sedge is highly drought tolerant. In early spring elk feed heavily on Elk Sedge.

Description: Elk Sedge consists of loosely clustered culms from rhizomes. Elk Sedge appears grass-like. It is an evergreen perennial and the culms are 8-20 inches tall and triangular in shape. Leaves are flat, tough, 3-ranked with brownish dried tips. The basal sheaths are shiny tan to brown. The inflorescence consists of a solitary bractless terminal spike. The flowers are 1-3 pistillate with brownish scales below and bloom April-July. Fruits are a large 3-angled achene.

Look Alikes: Elk Sedge may be confused with pinegrass (*Calamagrosis rubescens*) whose leaves are lighter green and not basally arranged. Elk Sedge also has a tuft of hair at the leaf collar, awned florets, reddish culm bases.

Little Spokane Habitat: Elk Sedge is found in warm, dry lower to mid elevations in forested sites to cool, dry upper elevations.

World Habitat: Elk Sedge is a native plant found mainly east of the Cascades from British Columbia to northern California, Utah, and Colorado.

Golden Chanterelle (*Cantharellus cibarius*)

Family:	Chanterelle (Cantharellaceae)	**Class:**	Mushroom (Basidomycetes)
Order:	Aphyllophorales (Aphyllophorales)	**Division:**	Mushroom (Basidiomycotina)
		Kingdom:	Fungus (Eumycota)

Other Names: Yellow Chanterelle
LSW Habitats: MT: L, DF: C, RP: U

Relationships To Watershed· Golden Chanterelle is one of the best-known and best-liked mushrooms of the west and elsewhere. They often grow in great abundance year after year in the same woods. Deer, squirrels, elk, and other rodents eat Golden Chanterelles. Squirrels store this mushroom in trees for their winter food.

Description: Golden Chanterelle is a mushroom with a cap that is golden to dark egg yellow and sometimes shaded with tan. It is smooth and at first rounded and then upturned. The center is more or less sunken and the margin is ruffled. They are 2-12 inches wide and the flesh is white with yellow tones, sometimes with yellow. The fertile surface is the same as the cap color to pale yellow with shallow, blunt-edged ridges and interlacing veins running down the stalk. The stalk is yellow to whitish, sometimes bruising orange. It is usually smooth and occasionally tapers from a larger base. The stalk is from 1-4 inches long.

Look Alikes: Golden Chanterelle may be confused with the following mushrooms. White Chanterelle, *Cantharellus subalbidus*, which is white and stains rusty yellow when handled. False Chanterelle, *Hygrophoropsis aurantiaca*, with a cap that is most often orange and sometimes brown, it is dry and suede-like with the flesh being the same color or lighter than the cap. Hypomyces Lactifluorum has a more mutated look without distinctive ridges. Sealy Chanterelle, Gomphus Floccosus, with a cap that is deeply depresed to fluted and a darker orange. Sealy Chanterelle has large wooly scales that run up the center to the edges

A white colored mushroom

More Fungi and Lichen

Fairy Ring Mushrooms

Lichen and moss well established on a stump

Lignicolous mushroom

Chicken Of The Woods

Lentinus Lepideus, possibly

Brain Mushroom

of the surface. Sealy Chanterelle also has accumulative liver damaging effects.

Little Spokane Habitat: Golden Chanterelle may be found in late summer to late fall, often under Douglas fir, hemlock, or spruce, in old or second-growth forests and in the surrounding hills and lower mountains.

Rubber Boa (*Charina bottae*)

Class: Reptiles (Reptilia)
Family: Boa (Boidae)   **Division:** Vertebrate (Chordata)
Order: Snake (Squamata)   **Kingdom:** Animal (Animalia)

LSW Habitats: DF: R, PP; R, RK: R, RP: R

Relationships To Watershed: Rubber boa snakes kill their food by constriction. Their primary diet consists of small mammals, although birds and lizards are sometimes taken.

Description: Rubber boa snakes have short, stout bodies with short, blunt, prehensile tails. They range from 355-725 mm long. Their heads are rounded, blunt, and not distinct from the neck. Eyes are small with a vertical pupil. The plates on top of the head are large and irregular. Body scutes are small and smooth and the anal plate is single with a small spur on either side. The dorsal surface is uniformly brown, grayish or yellowish or greenish brown. The ventral surface is yellow.

Look Alikes: Distinct from other snakes by its tubelike appearance and docility.

Little Spokane Habitat: Rubber boas are found primarily in humid, mountainous regions, although they also occur in drier, lowland localities. This species is highly nocturnal.

World Habitat: Rubber boas are a prominent native species ranging throughout the Pacific Northwest. Their habitat ranges from British Columbia south to the San Bernadino Mountains in California and east to western Montana, western Wyoming, and Utah.

Little Brown Myotis (*Myotis lucifugus*)

Class: Mammal (Mammalia)
Family: Plainnose Bat (Vespertilionidae) **Division:** Vertebrate (Chordata)
Order: Bat (Chiroptera)   **Kingdom:** Animal (Animalia)

Other Names: LBM, Little Brown Bat
LSW Habitats: DF: R, WL: U, ST: U, LK: U

Relationships To Watershed: Little Brown Myotis bats emerge at dusk to feed. They are opportunistic hunters, eating a great variety of insect prey. They hunt in the valleys and nearby hills in Ponderosa Pine forests, openings of trees, and over bluffs, lakes, rivers and irrigation flumes.

Description: The Little Brown Myotis bat is a medium-size species of *Myotis*. The fur color is extremely variable, it ranges from yellow or olive to blackish. The fur on its underside is lighter, varying from light brown to tan. Its dorsal fur is long and glossy. The wing membranes and ears are dark brown.

Look Alikes: Little Brown Myotis can be differentiated from the Fringed Myotis, *Myotis thysanodes*, Northern Long-eared Myotis, *Myotis septentrionalis*, Western Long-eared Myotis, *Myotis evotis*, and Keen's Long-eared Myotis, *Myotis keenii*, because they all have larger ears and a larger prominence in front of the ear, a tragus, than the Little Brown Myotis. The absence of a keel on the slender spur of the ankle joing, a calcar, distinguishes it from the Long-Legged Myotis, *Myotis volans*, California Myotis, *Myotis californicus*, and Western Small-footed Myotis, *Myotis ciliolabrum*.

Little Spokane Habitat: Little Brown Myotis exploits a wide range of habitats, from arid grassland and Ponderosa Pine forest to humid coastal forest and northern boreal forest. They range from sea level on the coast to over 2000 meters above sea level. Summer roosts are in buildings and other human-made structures, tree cavities, rock crevices, caves and under the bark of trees.

World Habitat: Little Brown Myotis is a widespread species that inhabits most of North America as far north as the tree-line.

Black Bear (*Ursus americanus*)

		Class:	Mammal (Mammalia)
Family:	Bear (Ursidae)	**Division:**	Vertebrate (Chordata)
Order:	Carnivore (Carnivora)	**Kingdom:**	Animal (Animalia)

Other Name: Bear
LSW Habitats: SA: R, MT: U, DF: U, PP: U

Relationships To Watershed: Black Bears are the most omnivorous of all North American mammals. Most of their animal food is small, however. They feed on vegetables, flesh or insect material as well as other mammals.

Description: Black Bears are the smallest of North American bears. Color phases range from blue-black through black, brown, cinnamon, blond, gray, to white. The black and brown phases are the most common, the former being more numerous in the wetter, coastal areas and the latter better represented in the drier, interior regions. The average adult individual may weigh 200-300 pounds. The fur is relatively long and shaggy. The nails are short and black.

Look Alikes: Black Bears may be confused with grizzly bears (*Ursis arctos*) which have distinctive shoulder humps and a dished profile.

Little Spokane Habitat: Black Bears prefer forested or wooded habitats, as well as swamps. Black bears commonly visit open berry patches in burns or subalpine areas when the fruit is ripe.

World Habitat: Black Bears are a native species occurring throughout the Pacific Northwest, though usually not found in open, non-forested areas.

A dusting of snow on a critter hide-away next to the tree trunk

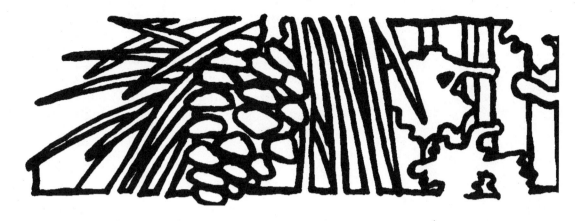

Ponderosa Pine Habitat

Ponderosa pine habitat is probably the most familiar habitat to the people who live in the greater Spokane area. Ponderosa pine habitat covers more of the Little Spokane Watershed than any other single habitat type. With the exception of introduced domesticated trees, ponderosa pine is the only conifer that thrives in the comparatively low elevations, generally below 4,000 feet, of the Little Spokane Watershed, Spokane Valley, and the surrounding areas of the region. Anyone who has spent a summer in this area also knows how hot and dry it can be. These two characteristics, in combination with well drained soils, are the most defining of this habitat type. Summer temperatures can easily climb to over 100 degrees with little or no precipitation throughout the hottest part of the year.

Inter-relationships

The ponderosa pine has found its niche in the world by adapting to an environment that is inhospitable to other conifers and is very successful in doing so. In fact ponderosa pine is the most widely distributed tree in the American West.

Lone Pine framed by a Douglas Fir branch. Cottonwoods mark the bank's edge, the riparian edge, of the Little Spokane. The south facing slope in the background is a Ponderosa Pine forest. The field is being nurtured back to a more restorative habitat. Some of the noxious weeds have been removed and thousands of native plants have been added. A recently planted Ponderosa Pine is in the foreground.

Scarlet Gilia's bright red flowers

Walking along a pine forest path

Ponderosa pine habitat shows the extent of the hot, dry climate of much of the mountainous West, from central Mexico into Canada. It can generally be found between the lower elevation steppe, the scablands, high desert, and Palouse in this region, and the higher elevation mountain habitat.

One reason for the ponderosa's versatility is its extraordinary resistance to drought. Its main adaptation is its root system that snakes down as far as 36 feet and sprawls out as far as 100 feet on either side of the trunk in search if water. Instead of tapering into fine, hairy rootlets the way most trees do, ponderosa roots are boldly and simply branched. This gives the tree enough root surface-area to absorb moisture when it is abundant, but prevents the tree from pumping the soil dry when moisture is scarce.

Above ground, the long evergreen pine needles have thick skin and breathing pores that are sunken out of the wind, preventing loss of moisture from evaporation. However, when soil water is abundant, the tree is able to exhale water vapor at an amazing rate, which helps keep it cool on hot summer afternoons. Amazingly, the ponderosa can drink in traces of water through its leaves and transport it to its roots. By reversing the normal process of water intake, the ponderosa pine is able to take advantage of night dew and foggy weather.

The open, park-like look of an old ponderosa pine forest is a direct result of decades of drought, fire and root competition between trees. The trees are widely spaced, each one having its own helping of moisture and nutrients. Plants in the understory are pruned back by regular lightning fires. Mature ponderosas are the most fire-resistant trees in their range, thanks to thick bark, branches high off the ground and high crowns, but young pines are vulnerable. The sapling stands a good chance of surviving fires to reach immune size if it grows away from other trees because other saplings and the needle litter under large trees are the two main fuels for fire. Bunchgrass and balsam root also provide fuel for fire. Saplings growing under a mature ponderosa stand little chance of surviving a fire, hence the park-like spacing.

Canopy densities vary greatly in ponderosa pine stands, particularly since the suppression of wildfires. Two broad classifications within ponderosa pine habitat are the bunchgrass habitat and the shrub habitat. Generally speaking, tree density is greater in the shrub habitat because these areas are more moist than the bunchgrass site, although both are considered dry.

Growth amidst the pine neetles

The ponderosa-bunchgrass habitat can be divided further into three sub-habitats; Idaho fescue habitat; bluebunch wheatgrass habitat with stony soil; and needle-and-thread grass habitat with conspicuously sandy soil.

Similarly, the ponderosa-shrub habitat reveals three sub-habitats, each based on the presence of a particular species of shrub; bitterbrush habitat with well drained sandy or stony soil; ninebark habitat with ninebark and ocean spray and soil consisting of loam or stony loam; and snowberry habitat with Wood's rose, nootka rose, shiny-leaf spirea, or chokecherry.

Snowberries wet from recent rain

Forest Key For Ponderosa Pine Habitat

Ponderosa Pine forest areas can be found using this part of the forest key. The full key, in the appendix, can be used for Little Spokane Watershed forest lands.

Forest Key Index for Ponderosa Pine Habitat

Ponderosa Pine – Grass

1	2	3	A		Ponderosa Pine – Idaho Fescue
1	2	3	B		Ponderosa Pine – Bluebunch Wheatgrass

Ponderosa Pine – Shrub

1	2	3	C		Ponderosa Pine – Needle -and-Thread
1	2	4	A		Ponderosa Pine – Bitterbrush
1	2	4	5	A	Ponderosa Pine – Ninebark
1	2	4	5	B	Ponderosa Pine – Snowberry

Forest Key Decision Table for Ponderosa Pine Habitat

1. Ponderosa pine present; other conifers absent
   - 2. Undergrowth dominated by grasses; shrubs inconspicuous; dwarf mistletoe usually abundant
     - 3. Idaho fescue is principal grass
       - A. **Ponderosa Pine – Idaho Fescue Habitat**
     - 3. Bluebunch wheat grass the principal grass; soil usually with high stone content
       - B. **Ponderosa Pine – Bluebunch Wheatgrass Habitat**
     - 3. Needle–and–thread the principal grass; soil conspicuously sandy
       - C. **Ponderosa Pine – Needle–and–Thread Habitat**
   - 2. Shrubs conspicuous in undergrowth
     - 4. Bitterbrush well represented; soil sandy or stony; dwarf mistletoe usually present
       - A. **Ponderosa Pine – Bitterbrush Habitat**
     - 4. Bitterbrush and dwarf mistletoe absent; soil a loam or stony loam
       - 5. Ninebark and/or ocean–spray well represented
         - A. **Ponderosa Pine – Ninebark Habitat**
       - 5. Ninebark and ocean–spray absent; undergrowth dominated by snowberry, wood's rose, nootka rose, shiny–leaf spiraea or chokecherry
         - B. **Ponderosa Pine – Snowberry Habitat**

Red-breasted Nuthatch

A bird common to ponderosa pine habitats and the mountain habitats is the red-breasted nuthatch, a small bird that seems equally comfortable walking head-first down a tree as it does walking up one. Nuthatches have feet that are similar to those of woodpeckers, which enable them to cling to tree bark in the upright position, but nuthatches also have long strong toes and sharp, curved claws that work like grappling hooks on the blocks of bark. They glean insects from the bark and eat seeds, often

Young Pine replacing a stump

from the underside of cones, which may be missed by their rightside-up-counterparts. Red-breasted nuthatches are also a cavity nesting species that require dead or dying tree tops to build their nest cavities.

Coyote

Coyotes are probably one of the most loved and most hated animals in the West. They are loved because they are so cunning and adaptable. There are many stories and legends of the coyotes' many talents and travails. Coyotes are also regarded by some, especially ranchers and farmers, as a pest that should be eliminated. In fact coyotes today are America's most bountied, poisoned, and targeted predator.

Ironically, predator control has done coyotes more good than harm. Historically, wolves ruled the forests, leaving coyotes to range over the steppes, brushy mountains, and prairies. But during the nineteenth century, guns and traps wiped out most wolves from most of the western states, allowing coyotes to replace the wolf in most of the wolf's original range. This includes most of the Little Spokane Watershed, although coyotes remain more abundant in brushy than in forested terrain as can be demonstrated by their success in the open ponderosa pine habitats.

Also coyote numbers have increased because of their adaptability to human modified habitats. Coyotes feed on domestic cats and small dogs. They can be found along much of the Little Spokane Watershed.

Coyotes are too small to significantly limit deer or sheep numbers, although some people in the west choose to believe otherwise. Though preferring small mammals and birds, coyotes are prepared to subsist through hard times on grasshoppers, or on fruit, on winter-killed deer and elk, or occasionally on fawns. Coyotes have the fastest running- speed of any American predator, which enables them to capture hares. To run down weakened deer, they work as a pack, like wolves, but this is rare. Usually they hunt alone or pair up cleverly, one partner either decoying or flushing prey while the other lurks.

If you see hair-filled scat along a trail you can bet it is a coyote's. Scat and urine play a critical role in coyote interaction, acting as a graffiti signature full of scents that can later be "read" by other canine passers-by. The

*Lycaenid butterfly
on pine needles*

Grass Widow flower

Lichen on Pine bow

Fly on Woods Rose leaflet

long nose in the dog family really does aid in scent detection. Coyotes are able to detect the passage of other animals a mile of two away or several days previous. No less important is their ability to read scent posts for data about the condition and activities of fellow coyotes. While wolves scent mark their territory, it is no longer believed that coyotes do the same, and it is increasingly doubted that coyotes are territorial at all, with the possible exception during the reproductive season when pups are around.

Sustainability

Ponderosa pine ranks second nationally, after Douglas fir, in lumber production. Most knotty pine paneling comes from young ponderosas. A bigger threat to ponderosas, however, is the seemingly evergrowing expanse of human habitats. This is especially true of the interior Pacific Northwest and of the Little Spokane Watershed in particular. Mixed in with many of the domesticated tree species around Spokane are many large ponderosas. In addition, historic photos show what is now Spokane was dominated by ponderosas.

As successful as they appear to be now, ponderosas in less dry areas may gradually be displaced by the Douglas fir if fire is not allowed to act out its natural role. Many land managers are now caught in a catch-22; ponderosas need fire to control succession, but fires have been suppressed for so long that fuel in the form of needles, dead branches, and even dead trees, have accumulated to the point that an uncontrolled fire would more than likely kill any size ponderosa and burn larger areas than if smaller periodic fires had been allowed. Even worse is the increasing chance of wildfires or fires started by humans that can burn much larger areas than if natural fire or controlled burns had been done on a periodic basis. With an established pattern of prescribed burning, protective fire patterns can be established. This can allow a healthier ponderosa pine habitat to establish itself.

Quality of Life Measures

Ponderosa pine habitat covers a large part of the Little Spokane Watershed and has considerable effects on the other habitats. The fragmentation of the habitat from roads, development and other human activities is one aspect that can be measured. Quality of life for the habitat can improve as the habitat becomes unfragmented through the use of nature corridors that link isolated ponderosa pine habitat together. Some farm land is being returned to wildland and can be linked to other more native habitats. The number of acres being returned to ponderosa pine habitat is another measure of progress towards better habitat quality of life; as is the number of acres that have been re-planted with native plants. Critter counts, including bird counts, are another way to measure the habitat's quality of life.

A field returning to ponderosa pine habitat

Summary of Ponderosa Habitat Critters

Number of Species by Kingdom

PLANT (PLANTAE)   110

FUNGUS (EUMYCOTA)   127

ANIMAL (ANIMALIA)   146

PROTIST (PROTISTA)   8

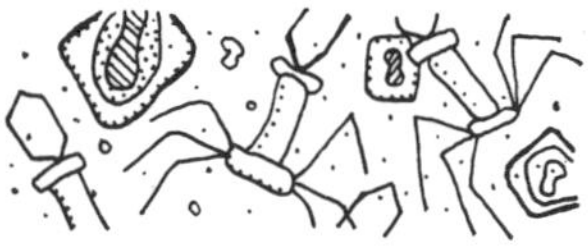

**BACTERIA & VIRUS
(MONERA & VIRUS)**   7

Number of Species by Class

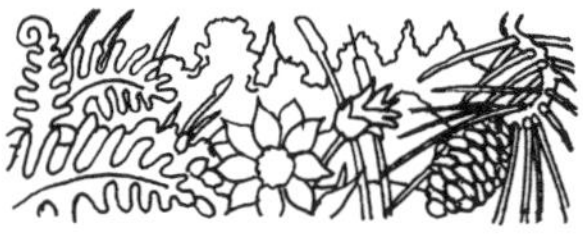

Moss (Bryopsida)	15
Nornwort (Authocerotae)	1
Pine (Pinicae)	5
Magnolia (Magnoliidae)	2
Carnation (Caryophyllidae)	9
Aspen (Dilleniidae)	9
Rose (Rosidae)	27
Sunflower (Asteridae)	29
Grass (Commelinidae)	6
Lily (Liliidae)	7
Mushroom (Basidomycetes)	82
Puffball (Gastromycetes)	6
Phragmobasidiomycetes (Phragmobasidiomycetes)	2
Ascomycetes (Ascomycetes)	12
To Be Determined (TBD)	3
Crusty Lichen (Crustose)	7
Leafy Lichen (Foliose)	8
Fruity Lichen (Fruticose)	7
Turbellidia (Turbellidia)	1
Spider (Arachnida)	2
Centipede (Chilopoda)	1
Millipede (Diplopoda)	1
Insect (Insecta)	39
Amphibian (Amphibia)	4
Reptile (Reptilia)	5
Bird (Aves)	63
Mammal (Mammalia)	30
Amoeba (Rhizopoda)	1
Heliozoan (Actimpoda)	1
Foram (Forimaninifera)	1
Sporozoite (Apicomplexa)	1
Slime Mold - Cellular (Acrasiomycetes)	1
Slime Mold - Plasmodial (Myxomycetes)	1
Mildew (Oomycota)	1
Saprobe (Chytridiomycota)	1
Bacteria (Bacteria)	1
Cyanophycota (Cyanophycota)	1
Prochlorophycota (Prochlorophycota)	1
Bacteria Virus (Bacteria Virus)	1
Plant Virus (Plant Virus)	1
Vertebrate Virus (Vertebrate Virus)	1
Invertebrate Virus (Invertebrate Virus)	1

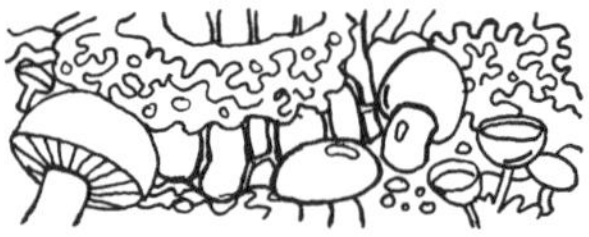

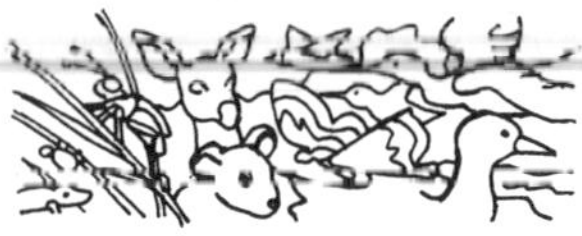

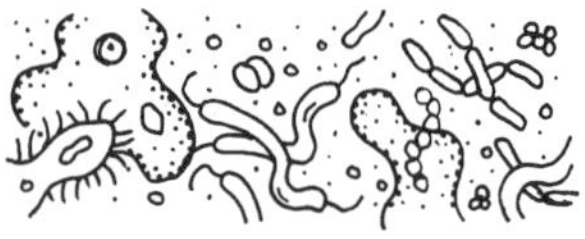

TOTAL IDENTIFIED SPECIES   398

Selected Ponderosa Habitat Critters

PLANT (PLANTAE)	67		
Moss (Bryopsida)	14		
Aluacomnium androgynum		C	
Aluacomnium androgynum		C	
Brachythecium albicans		C	
Brachythecium campestre		C	
Brachythecium salebposum		C	
Ceratodon purpureus		C	
Dicranum fuscescens		C	
Polytrichum juniperinum		A	
Polytrichum piliferum		A	
Pine (Pinicae)	1		
Ponderosa Pine		A	
Magnolia (Magnoliidae)	2		
Sagebrush Buttercup		A	
Small Oregon Grape		C	
Carnation (Caryophyllidae)	3		
Jagged Chickweed		C	IO
Knotweed		C	
Sheep Sorrel		C	IO
Aspen (Dilleniidae)	3		
Kinnikinnick		C	
Shooting Star (B)		A	
Rose (Rosidae)	20		
Whitlow Grass		A	
Bitterbrush		A	
Blue Lupine		C	
Ceanothus		C	
Chokecherry		A	
Cinquefoil		C	
Dwarf Mistletoe		C	
Mallow Ninebark		A	
Mock Orange		A	
Nootka Rose		C	
Pale Cinquefoil		C	
Redstem Ceanothus		C	
Small-flowered Fringecup		C	
Smooth Fringecup		C	
Snowbrush Ceanothus		C	
Sticky Geranium		C	
Wax Currant		C	
Western Serviceberry		A	
White Spiraea		C	
Wild Strawberry		C	
Woods Rose		C	
Sunflower (Asteridae)	14		
Arrowleaf Balsamroot		C	
Arrowleaf Groundsel		C	
Blue Lips		C	
Common Snowberry		A	
Common Yarrow		C	
Cut-leaf Daisy		A	
Indian Blanket		C	
Montana Goldenrod		C	
Narrow-leaved Collomia		C	
Ragwort		C	
Salmon Collomia		C	
Spreading Dogbane		A	
Wild Aster		A	
Yellow Beardtongue		C	
Grass (Commelinidae)	3		
Bluebunch Wheatgrass		C	
Pinegrass		C	
Small Fescue		C	

Lily (Liliidae)	7		
Glacier Lily		C	
Grass Widow		A	
Mariposa Lily		C	
Western False Solomon's Seal		C	
Wild Onion (A)		C	
Wild Onion (C)		C	
Yellowbell		C	
FUNGUS (EUMYCOTA)	19		
Mushroom (Basidomycetes)	9		
Delicious Milk Cap		C	
Delicious Milkcap		C	
Fly Agaric (B)		C	
Glutinous Waxy Cap		A	
Lyophyllum atratum		C	
Man On horseback		C	
Matsutake		C	
Olive Brown Waxy		A	
Short Stemmed Russula		A	
Puffball (Gastromycetes)	2		
Puffball (B)		C	
Puffball (C)		C	
Crusty Lichen (Crustose)	1		
Evernia mesomorpha		A	
Leafy Lichen (Foliose)	6		
Cetraria candensis		C	
Hypogymnia enteromorpha		A	
Hypogymnia imsaugii		C	
Hypogymnia phyoodoo		A	
Parmelia sulcata		A	
Platismatia glauca		C	
Fruity Lichen (Fruticose)	1		
Letharea vulpina		A	
ANIMAL (ANIMALIA)	26		
Insect (Insecta)	10		
Ant		C	
Bark Beetle		C	
Bumblebee		C	
Bumblebee spp		C	
Least Wood Nymph		C	
Ochre Ringlet		C	
Pearly Crescentspot		C	
Robber fly		C	
Sawfly		C	
Yellow Jacket		C	
Amphibian (Amphibia)	1		
Western Toad		C	
Bird (Aves)	12		
Black-capped Chickadee		C	
Chipping Sparrow		C	
Common Raven		C	
Dark-eyed Junco		C	
Downy Woodpecker		C	
Evening Grosbeak		C	
Great Horned Owl		C	
House Finch		C	
Pygmy Nuthatch		C	
Red Crossbill		C	
Red-breasted Nuthatch		C	
Warbling Vireo		C	
Mammal (Mammalia)	3		
Human		C	
Western Jumping Mouse		A	
White-tailed Deer		C	RGM

* The critters listed here are identified as abundant and common. Except a few common mosses have been omited.

Legend - Critters are listed by their common name followed by their abundance in the habitat. Introduced species and species at risk are indicated by type code. • **Abundance Codes: A** Abundant, **C** Common, **F** Fairly common, **U** Uncommon, **R** Rare, **V** Vagrant, **K** Known in habitat, **L** Likely in habitat, **M** Missing from habitat. • **Introduced Species Codes: IN** Introduced Noxious species, **IO** Introduced, Other than noxious species. • **At Risk Codes: MS** Missing, **ED** Endangered, **TH** Threatened, **CD** Candidate, **MN** Monitor, **RGM** Regulated Game, **RNG** Regulated Nongame, **RA** Rare, **PB** Protected Breeding Areas.

Selected Critter Descriptions

Pine cone, pine needles and lichen

Ponderosa Pine *(Pinus ponderosa)*

Sub Family:	Pine (Pinus)	**Class:**	Pine (Pinicae)
Family:	Pine (Pinaceae)	**Division:**	Pine (Pinophyta)
Order:	Pine (Pinatae)	**Kingdom:**	Plant (Plantae)

Other Names: Blackjack Pine, Bull Pine, P. Pine, Pondosa Pine, Western Yellow Pine, Yellow Pine, Yellow Pondosa Pine

LSW Habitats: MT: U, DF: U, PP: A, RK: A, BU: F, GR: U, RP: C, DS: C, HU: A

Relationships To Watershed: Elk, deer, porcupines and rabbits browse on the pine needles. Mice, chipmunks and ground squirrels eat the roots and stems. Juncos, finches, siskins, grosbeaks, sparrows and chickadees eat pine seeds. Thickets help to hide deer and elk. Cavity nesters make their homes in standing pine snags. Eagles, turkeys and hawks use trees for roosts and nests. Fire is needed to promote pine dominance and to discourage fir. Ponderosa Pine is highly resistant to fire with its thick bark, open stands, smooth trunks, boles, that are free of lower limbs and deep root systems. Ponderosa Pine's seeds readily germinate in mineral soils after a fire.

Pine bow with cone

Description: Ponderosa Pine is a large coniferous tree growing up to 180 feet tall. Ponderosa Pine's bark is dark brown to black on young trees, becoming yellow-brown to cinnamon-red as the trees mature. There are large flat plates between deep furrows on the older trees, the scales of plates look like "jigsaw puzzle" pieces. Needles are in groups of 3 and are 5-8 inches long. They are green to yellow-green in color, flexible and have a basal sheath that is 1/4-3/4 inch long. Male cones, staminate cones, are yellow to purplish and are strongly clustered. Female cones, ovulate cones, are deep reddish-purple maturing to reddish-brown to brown and are 3-6 inches long and ovate. The cones are stalkless, sessile, with chocolate brown scales containing a thickened prickly tip. Cones flower from May-June and shed their seeds in September.

Look Alikes: Ponderosa Pines are the only 3-needled pine in the western United States.

Little Spokane Habitat: Ponderosa Pines are found on warm, dry sites over a broad spectrum of soils with their best development on deep sandy gravels and loam.

World Habitat: Ponderosa Pine is a native tree found from British Columbia to Baja California, mostly east of the Cascades but occasionally west of the Cascades in southwestern Washington and western Oregon. Ponderosa Pine is found east to southeastern British Columbia, Montana and the Dakotas, south in the Rocky Mountains to western Texas and northern Mexico.

Chokecherry (*Prunus virginiana*)

		Class:	Rose (Rosidae)
Family:	Rose (Rosaceae)	**Division:**	Flower (Magnoliophyta)
Order:	Rose (Rosales)	**Kingdom:**	Plants (Plantae)

L&W Habitats: ⅅℾ: U, ℾℾ: A, ⅃Ⅼ: ℾ, ℾℾ: ℂ

Relationships To Watershed: Chokecherry provides mule deer browse. The fruits are eaten by grouse, magpies, rabbits and bears.

Description: Chokecherry is a tall shrub that reaches heights of 3-15 feet. The stems have purplish-gray bark with reddish-brown twigs. Leaves are alternate and oblong-ovate to obovate. They are 2-4 inches long and finely serrate. They are dark green and lustrous above and pale green below. The leaf apex is acute and the base is rounded with a petiole that is about 1 inch long. White flowers bloom May-July with elongated racemes up to 6 inches long and drooping. The fruit is a drupe about 3/8 inch in diameter and red to purple to black in color.

Look Alikes: Chokecherry may be easily confused with the following: bittercherry (*Prunus emarginata*) which has glands on the leaf base whereas chokecherry has glands on the petiole at the base of the leaf; serviceberry, *Amelanchier alnifolia*, has leaves that have no glands and leaf veins which are strongly paralleling.

Little Spokane Habitat: Chokecherry is found from seepy outcrops in the cold desert sagebrush-grasslands to the lower elevation forests. It occupies cool, moist foothills, mountains and canyon habitats.

World Habitat: Chokecherry is a native plant found across Canada and the northern United States. It is very widespread in the Pacific Northwest.

Mallow Ninebark
(Physocarpus malvaceus)

Class: Rose (Rosidae)
Family: Rose (Rosaceae)
Order: Rose (Rosales)
Division: Flower (Magnoliophyta)
Kingdom: Plant (Plantae)

Other Name: Ninebark
LSW Habitats: DF: C, PP: A, RK: U, BU: A

Relationships To Watershed: Mallow Ninebark is low in palatability and is browsed sporadically. Ninebark has severe regeneration difficulty but is vigorous and aggressive following fires.

Description: Mallow Ninebark is a deciduous shrub mid to tall in height and up to 6 feet tall. Small white flowers bloom from May to July in terminal corymbs. Mallow Ninebark has alternate, deciduous, maple-like leaves with 3 palmate lobes. The leaf margins are doubly serrate. The stems and bark are reddish to grayish-brown with loose, shredding bark. Fruits are paired, many seeded hairy follicles.

Palmate - Lobed, veined, or divided from a common point.

Found On:
Mallow Ninebark
False Bugbane
Mountain Maple
Thimbleberry

Robin feasting on Serviceberries

Look Alikes: Mallow Ninebark may be confused with the following plants: Ocean spray, *Holodiscus discolor*, which has leaves that are not palmately lobed like a maple; Sticky Currant, *Ribes viscosissimum*, has leaves which are glandular and sticky to the touch.

Little Spokane Habitat: Mallow Ninebark may be found in canyon slopes and bottoms beneath Ponderosa Pine and Douglas-Fir as well as on nonforested shrubland sites.

Follicle - A dry, opening fruit with a single seed and an opening along a single side.

Found On:
Mallow Ninebark

World Habitat: Mallow Ninebark is found in North America from southern Alberta and British Columbia, Washington, Oregon, Montana, Wyoming and Utah.

Western Serviceberry
(Amelanchier alnifolia)

		Class:	Rose (Rosidae)
Family:	Rose (Rosaceae)	**Division:**	Flower (Magnoliophyta)
Order:	Rose (Rosales)	**Kingdom:**	Plant (Plantae)

Other Names: Saskatoon Serviceberry, Serviceberry (A), Western Shadbush

LSW Habitats: PP: A, RK: R, GR: C

Relationships To Watershed: Western Serviceberry is browsed by deer, elk, sheep, and goats. Grouse eat the berries in summer and the buds in winter. This is one of the first shrubs to flower in the canyons in early spring.

Description: Western Serviceberry is a shrub or small tree that is from 5-20 feet tall. The stem is reddish brown and ages to gray. It has alternate branching with alternate leaves that are flattened or truncated at the base with coarse dentations on margins above the mid-point of the leaf. Veins are strongly paralleling and the blades are 1/2-1 inch long. White flowers bloom March-July with racemes of 3 to 20 flowers. Fruits are are dark purplish, globose pomes.

Look Alikes: Western Serviceberry may be confused with the following: Hawthornes, *Crataegus* spp., which have thorns; Cherries, *Prunus* spp., which have glands on the petiole or at leaf base; Spiraea, *Spiraea* spp., which has a distinctive venation and serration to the leaf.

Little Spokane Habitat: Western Serviceberry is typically found on canyon slopes and in open forest savannas. It is an early seral species in ponderosa pine-dominated woodlands.

World Habitat: Western Serviceberry is a native plant widespread throughout the Pacific Northwestern states.

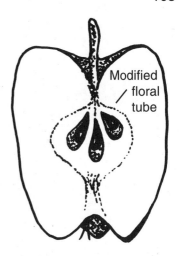

Modified floral tube

Pome - A fruit with a core. A modified floral tube surrounds the core.

Found On:
Western Serviceberry

Tubular Flower - With the form of a tube or cylinder.

Found On:
Wax Current
Red Twinberry

Wax Currant (Ribes cereum)

		Class:	Rose (Rosidae)
Family:	Gooseberry (Grossulariaceae)	**Division:**	Flower (Magnoliophyta)
Order:	Rose (Rosales)	**Kingdom:**	Plant (Plantae)

Other Name: Squaw Currant
LSW Habitats: SA: U, PP: C, BU: F

Description: Wax Currant is a stiff, multi-branched, mid-sized shrub that grows up to 5 feet tall. The stem is unarmed and gray to reddish-brown in color. Leaves are alternate and very small, less than 1 1/4 inches in diameter. The upper surface is waxy and the margins are double serrated. Leaves are indistinctly 3-5 lobed. Greenish-white tubular flowers bloom in April-June and are borne in drooping clusters of 3-5. Fruits are bright red or orange berries.

Look Alikes: Wax Currant is very distinct.

Little Spokane Habitat: Wax Currant is found in the forest fringe on warm, dry sites.

World Habitat: Wax Currant is native plant found on the east slopes of the Cascades and eastward to the Rocky Mountains.

Common Snowberry *(Symphoricarpos albus)*

		Class:	Sunflower (Asteridae)
Family:	Honeysuckle (Caprifoliaceae)	**Division:**	Flower (Magnoliophyta)
Order:	Teasel (Dispacales)	**Kingdom:**	Plant (Plantae)

Other Name: Snowberry
LSW Habitats: DF: C, PP: A, RK: A, BU: F

Relationships To Watershed: Common Snowberry is poisonous. Palatability is low for livestock, but moderate on winter range for deer.

Description: Common Snowberry is a deciduous, rhizomatous, low growing shrub about 2-4 feet tall. White or pinkish bell-shaped flowers bloom May-June in 3-5 flowered racemes. Leaves are opposite, elliptic and 1-2 inches long. The margins are entire. Stem branching is opposite. Mature stems shred and have a hollow dark pith while the juvenile branches may not be hollow. The bark is grayish in color. Fruits are white, round and berrylike, 3/8 inch, and they persist long after the leaves fall in winter.

Snowberry blossoms turning to berries

Look Alikes: Common Snowberry may be confused with the following: Mountain

Snowberry, *Symphoricarpos oreophilus*, has tubular flowers and a solid, dark pith; Utah Honeysuckle, *Lonicera utahensis*, has larger leaves and a solid white pith.

Little Spokane Habitat: Common Snowberry can tolerate warm, dry sites where seepages or rock crevasses provide moisture in nonforested communities. Optimum conditions are on warm, moist, well-drained soils under Ponderosa Pine and Douglas Fir communities.

World Habitat: Common Snowberry is widespread throughout northern North America.

Pinegrass *(Calamagrostis rubescens)*

		Class:	Grass (Commelinidae)	
Family:	Grass (Gramineae)	**Division:**	Flower (Magnoliophyta)	
Order:	Grass (Poales)	**Kingdom:**	Plant (Plantae)	

LSW Habitats: MT. F, DF: C, PP: C, DS: F

Awn - A narrow, bristle-like appendage of grass

Found On:
Pinegrass
Cheatgrass
Idaho Fescue

Relationships To Watershed: Pinegrass resists fires and its palatability increases after a fire. This grass forms dense mats that will resist tree establishment. Lightly eaten for forage except in spring when succulent and in fall when rains and frosts soften the leaves.

Description: Pinegrass is a strongly rhizomatous perennial. Culms grow up to 3 feet tall and their bases are reddish. The leafage is usually about 12-16 inches tall. Leaves are flat, drooping blades about 1/8 inch wide and are mostly basally arranged. Auricles are lacking and a collar of conspicuous hairs is diagnostic. This grass seldom flowers but when it does they are in spikelike panicles from 3-6 inches long. There is one flower per spikelet and the awns are twisted, bent and attached near the base of the lemma and extend a little longer than the spikelet. They flower from June-August.

Fritillary, orange colored butterfly

Look Alikes: Pinegrass may be confused with Elk Sedge, *Carex geyeri*, which has only basal leaves that are dark green, coarse and 3-ranked. The stem is triangular and the inflorescence is a brown cigar-like spike.

Little Spokane Habitat: Pinegrass is found in warm-dry to cool-dry sites at mid-elevations.

World Habitat: Pinegrass is a native plant found in British Columbia south into the Cascades to southern California throughout the Pacific Northwest and south in the Rockies to Colorado.

Western False Solomon's Seal
(*Smilacina racemosa*)

		Class:	Lily (Liliidae)
Family:	Lily (Liliaceae)	**Division:**	Flower (Magnoliophyta)
Order:	Lily (Liliales)	**Kingdom:**	Plant (Plantae)

Other Name: False Solomon's Seal
LSW Habitats: SA: U, MT: F, DF: F, PP: C, RK: F, GR; F, RP: C

Relationships To Watershed: Western False Solomon's Seal's berries are eaten by grouse.

Description: False Solomon's Seal is a perennial herb that is strongly rhizomatous, mid sized from 1-3 feet tall, with many small, white flowers blooming April-July in a terminal panicle up to 5 inches long. Leaves are alternate, simple, sessile and lanceolate. They are 3-8 inches long with parallel venation and are slightly clasping. The stem is erect, unbranched, green and is arched or curved downward. Fruit is a globose berry that is green-brown to red and 1/2 inch or less.

Look Alikes: False Solomon's Seal is readily confused with the following plants: starry false Solomon's seal, *Smilacina stellata,* has a few-flowered raceme and leaves that are 2-6 inches long and narrower; twisted stalk, *Streptopus amplexifolius,* is branched with a clasping leaf base; wartberry fairybells, *Disporum trachycarpum,* is branched with rounded leaf bases.

Little Spokane Habitat: False Solomon's Seal is found in warm moist to warm dry habitats in relatively open forested stands, often on outcroppings. Prominent in Douglas fir, grand fir, Rocky Mountain maple, big huckleberry and ninebark communities.

World Habitat: False Solomon's Seal is widespread throughout the United States.

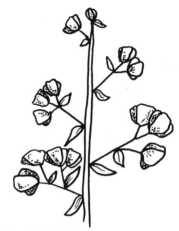

Panicle Inflorescence - Branched flower cluster with flowers maturing from the bottom upward

Found On:
Western False Solomon's Seal
Cheatgrass
Coolwort Foamflower
Idaho Fescuc
Ocean Spray
Redstem Ceanothus

Lanceolate Leaf - Lance-shaped; much longer than wide, with the widest part below the middle.

Found On:
Western False Solomon's Seal
Wapato

Sculptured Puffball
(*Calvatia sculpta*)

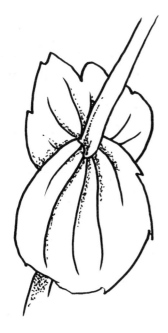

Class:	Puffball (Gastromycetes)
Division:	Mushroom (Basidimycotina)
Order: True Puffball (Lycoperdales)	**Kingdom:** Fungus (Eumycota)

Other Name: Sierran Puffball
LSW Habitats: PP: K

Relationships To Watershed: Sculptured Puffball is a spectacular mushroom to find when it is in good condition. The abrupt pyramidal peaks covering the surface make it the most striking puffball. It is also one of the tastiest, assuming one likes this strong flavored family in the first place. Like all puffballs this sculptured beauty should be eaten only when young and the flesh is all white. This family is one of the few fungi known as a food source for Native Americans as well as being used for medicinal purposes. Natives and pioneers applied the flesh or dried spores to burns and cuts to stop bleeding and to heal wounds.

Clasping Leaves - Wholly or partly surrounding the stem.

Found On:
Western False Solomon's Seal

Description: Sculptured Puffball is round to pear shaped and definitely not smooth. They are 2 to 6 inches in diameter with a white surface that is covered with a landscape of little pyramids. When mature the spore mass is a dark olive-brown.

Little Spokane Habitat: Sculptured Puffball grows under ponderosa pine and other conifers, in open areas, and periodically on the side of dirt roads. It likes moisture and warmth and therefore shows up from late spring to early fall depending on the weather.

Look Alikes: There is one other puffball with similar ornamentation, Calbovista subscupta, but it has flatter warts. Aminita magniverrucata has a cap that is constructed in the same way but it is a gilled mushroom atop a stalk.

Long-toed Salamander (*Ambystoma macrodactylum*)

		Class:	Amphibians (Amphibia)
Family:	Salamander (Ambystomatidae)	**Division:**	Vertebrate (Chordata)
Order:	Salamander (Caudata)	**Kingdom:**	Animal (Animalia)

LSW Habitats: MT: U, DF: U, PP: U, LK: F

Relationships To Watershed: Long-toed Salamanders live below ground during hot, dry or freezing weather. During these times you can find them above ground only during mating season. Salamanders migrate to the breeding ponds from October-April depending on the local climate. Long-toed salamanders are the first amphibians to breed in the spring in the Pacific Northwest. Their food consists of spiders, lepidopteran larvae, crickets, earthworms, flies, snails, slugs, aphids, collembolans, flies, beetle larvae, amphipods and other terrestrial and aquatic invertebrates. They are preyed upon by garter snakes and bullfrogs.

Description: Long-toed Salamanders are small lizard-like animals, dark gray to black in color, with a yellow, tan or olive green dorsal stripe that runs from the head, down the back and to the end of the tail. The stripe has uneven borders. Unlike a lizard's scaly skin, the skin of this salamander is smooth and has prominent costal grooves. The sides, abdomen and chest of the salamander are white, silver or blue and have green-brown to green-black speckles. Adults reach about 6 1/4 inches in total length.

Look Alikes: Long-toed Salamanders may be confused with the following: Dunn's Salamander, *Plethodon dunni*, and Western Red-backed Salamande, *Plethodon vehiculum*, both of which have yellow to green-yellow dorsal stripes but they also have nasolabial grooves and short toes. Neither of these salamanders occur in the Little Spokane Watershed.

Little Spokane Habitat: Long-toed salamanders may exist in a wide variety of habitats, from semiarid sagebrush deserts, dry woodlands, humid forests, alpine meadows to all kinds of intermediate habitats.

World Habitat: Long-toed Salamanders are found from southeast Alaska, British Columbia, western Alberta through western Montana, Idaho, Washington, Oregon and into California. Long-toed Salamanders used to be more prominent. However, the introduction of some fish into the North Cascades ecosystem has led to a decrease in Long-toed Salamanders. The reason for the decrease may be because they are unable to coexist with this fish, probably because the fish eat the salamander larvae.

Western Toad *(Bufo boreas)*

		Class:	Amphibians (Amphibia)
Family:	True toad (Bufonidae)	**Division:**	Vertebrate (Chordata)
Order:	Frog (Anura)	**Kingdom:**	Animal (Animalia)

Other Name: Natterjack Toad
LSW Habitats: MT: R, DF: U, PP: C, BU: U, WL: U, HU: F

Relationships To Watershed: Western Toads feed on flying insects, spiders, crayfish, sowbugs and earthworms. They are preyed on by garter snakes, coyotes, raccoons, crows and ravens. However, they deter many predators because they secrete a mild, white poison from the parotoid glands and larger warts as a deterrent to predators.

Description: Western Toad color varies and is usually green to brown. The underside of the toad is green with dark spots. It has a light stripe that is yellow or pale green that runs down the center of the back. The stripe begins at the nostrils and runs to the posterior of the body. The skin of the back, sides and upper legs are covered with small warts and the skin is dry. The parotoid glands located behind the eyes are oblong swellings that are a little larger than the eyes. The pupils are horizontal ovals.

Look Alikes: Western Toad is the only toad in the watershed. They may be confused with the woodhouse toad, *Bufo woodhousii*, which has distinct cranial crests that are L-shaped bony ridges between and behind each eye and barely enters South Eastern Washington.

Western Toad on a stump

Little Spokane Habitat: Western Toads are found from sea level to high mountainous areas. They live in a variety of habitats such as sand dunes and ponderosa pine forests. They are nocturnal during the dry weather. Toads forage during daylight on rainy or overcast days. The mature toads go to water to breed.

World Habitat: Western Toads are found in north eastern Mexico throughout the western United States and Canada into southeastern Alaska.

Gopher Snake *(Pituophis melanoleucus deserticola)*

		Class:	Reptiles (Reptilia)
Family:	Colubrid Snake (Colubridae)	**Division:**	Vertebrate (Chordata)
Order:	Snake (Squamata)	**Kingdom:**	Animal (Animalia)

Other Name: Bull Snake, Pine Gopher Snake
LSW Habitats: DF: U, PP: U, GR: U, RP: R

Relationships To Watershed: Gopher Snakes are generally day-active but they are also active during warm nights. They are largely terrestrial, but they are good climbers and sometimes search for prey in bushes and trees. Their primary prey is rodents, but they occasionally eat rabbits and birds. Gopher snakes are eaten frequently by birds of prey such as the red-tailed hawk. Gopher snakes can give an impressive aggressive display when encountered. When approached they may puff up, hiss loudly, strike vigorously. The tip of the tail may be rapidly vibrated, and if this is done in dry leaves the resulting sound is not unlike the whir of a rattlesnake. It has also been suggested that the color pattern of gopher snakes is mimetic of that of the western rattlesnake.

Description: Gopher Snakes are large heavy bodied snakes, up to four feet in length. They have dark brown or black blotches on a tan or light brown background. Gopher snakes have a row of dorsal blotches flanked on each side by a row of lateral blotches. There is a characteristic dark crescent passing between the eyes and down to the angle of the jaw on each side. The rostral scale is large, and the dorsal scales are keeled except for several lower rows on each side. The anal plate is entire, there are usually 8 upper labials, and 12-13 lower labials. Males have relatively longer tails than females.

Look Alikes: Gopher snakes are often called bullsnakes, which are also a gopher snake subspecies of the Eastern United States.

Little Spokane Habitat: Gopher Snakes occur in a great variety of habitats including prairies, coniferous forests, and deserts. They are generally absent from dense forests and high mountains in the Pacific Northwest and seem to be most common in semi-arid brush areas adjacent to farms.

World Habitat: Gopher Snakes are widely distributed over most of western United States and parts of adjacent Canada. They are also found in southeastern United States. There are 10 recognized subspecies.

Black-capped Chickadee (*Parus atricapillus*)

		Class:	Bird (Aves)
Family:	Chickadee (Paridae)	**Division:**	Vertebrate (Chordata)
Order:	Thrush (Passeriformes)	**Kingdom:**	Animal (Animalia)

LSW Habitats: DF: U, PP: C, RP: C

Relationships to Watershed: This chickadee feeds primarily on spiders and their eggs.

Description: The black-capped chickadee is a small songbird that has a black cap and bib. The cheeks are large and white. They are gray above and on the long tail and whitish below with light rust or buff sides and flanks.

Look Alikes: May be confused with the mountain chickadee, *Parus gambeli*, which has a black head and bib as well as a black mask over the eyes.

Little Spokane Habitat: The black-capped chickadee inhabits mixed and deciduous woodlands, thickets, and orchards.

World Habitat: They inhabit most of northern United States and southern Canada.

Porcupine *(Erethizon dorsatum)*

		Class:	Mammal (Mammalia)
Family:	Porcupine (Erethizontidae)	**Division:**	Vertebrate (Chordata)
Order:	Rodent (Rodentia)	**Kingdom:**	Animal (Animalia)

LSW Habitats: MT: F, DF: U, PP: F, BU: U

Relationships To Watershed: Porcupines are excellent climbers and spend much of their time among the branches of large trees, where they are comparatively safe and where much of their winter food is obtained. They are entirely vegetarian, and eat a wide range of plants. In summer most of their food is of low vegetation, clover, lupines, geranium, aster, parsnip, grass, many marsh plants, and a great variety of upland plants. They also consume leaves and tips of numerous shrubs and small bushes, berries, fruits, and occasionally garden vegetables. They are very fond of apples and sweet potatoes. In autumn and winter their food is largely twigs and bark of bushes and trees, and where the snow is deep almost entirely of tree bark. The outer rough bark is scraped off and thrown down and only the green inner bark and cambium layer next to the wood are eaten. Porcupines fall prey mostly to mountain lions, bobcats, lynx, fishers, and wolverines.

Description: Porcupines are large, blackish or yellowish rodents covered with long hairs interspersed with short sharp spines, quills, which are found especially on the back and tail. Quills are modified hairs which are loosely attached. When provoked, the porcupine erects them and, with a slap of the tail, drives them home. Back-slanting barbs at the tips then cause the quills to work in deeper. The body is stocky and the animal's movements are slow and deliberate. The length of porcupines is between 28-30 inches long and they weigh between 20-25 pounds.

Porcupine took the bark off this pine

Look Alikes: None.

Little Spokane Habitat: Porcupines are most abundant in coniferous forests but also inhabit deciduous woodlands. They occur on the plains most frequently in riparian habitats and are also found in open sagebrush areas.

World Habitat: Porcupines are a native species found throughout the entire Pacific Northwest, excluding Vancouver and Queen Charlotte Islands.

Coyote *(Canis latrans)*

		Class:	Mammal (Mammalia)
Family:	Dog (Canidae)	**Division:**	Vertebrate (Chordata)
Order:	Carnivore (Carnivora)	**Kingdom:**	Animal (Animalia)

LSW Habitats: SA: F, MT: F, DF: F, PP: F, RK: F, BU: F, GR: F, WL: F, RP: F, DS: F, HU: R

Relationships To Watershed: Coyotes prey mostly on small animals, but larger prey is occasionally taken.

Description: Coyotes resemble a slender, medium-sized, domestic dog, grayish-brown in color with shades of red on the legs, feet, and ears. Their large, pointed ears usually face forward, but can be moved in other directions. Coyotes have a graceful, springing gait. The general light coloration of the coyote, causing it to blend in with most vegetation and rocks is distinctive.

Look Alikes: Coyotes may be confused with wolves, however coyotes have a more pointed muzzle and are smaller in size. They may also be confused with many domestic dogs, however coyote tails are bushier and are held down when they run.

Little Spokane Habitat: Coyotes are most numerous in open prairies or desert type habitats. They are less common, but present, in the denser forest and subalpine and alpine areas. They have become adapted to living on ranches and to visiting farmsteads and rural settlements where they may prey on the house cats at the edges of town. They are well adjusted to living near humans. Their numbers are said to be increasing.

World Habitat: Coyotes are native animals that occur throughout the Pacific Northwest with the exception of coastal British Columbia and Vancouver and Queen Charlotte Islands.

Rockland Habitat

Rockland Habitat is more difficult to categorize than the forest habitats due to its intermixing nature. Rockland occurs wherever a rock outcropping becomes exposed. This is usually due to erosion, major earth movements or as a result of the last basalt flows that formed the scablands and then were carved out by the great Missoula floods. Generally, in the Little Spokane Watershed, most of the rockland is hot and dry. There is little diversity and poor growing conditions. These outcroppings occur within other habitat types, primarily the lower elevation habitats of ponderosa pine, bush land, grassland, and even disturbed and human habitats.

Granite rockland facing the Little Spokane

Because rockland habitats are islands within other habitats, critter migration in and out plays a major role in the inter-relationships that develop. Similarly, the relatively small size of rockland habitat limits the animal population to relatively small animals. An excellent place to observe an example of rockland habitat in a natural setting is along the stretch of the Little Spokane River that flows through the Little Spokane Natural Area. The Indian Painted Rock Trail runs along the river and several rock outcroppings are observable from the trail. When observing rockland it is best to stay on trails to reduce damage to this fragile habitat.

Rock outcroppings in the Little Spokane Watershed are composed of two major types of rock - basalt and granite. Basalt is the most abundant surface rock in Washington and in the Earth's crust as a whole. It is also the darkest of our major lava mixes.

Gutsy pine in the rocks

Basalt lava erupts in several styles. One of them, the basalt flood, is technically a volcano, but not a mountain. Between 12 and 18 million years ago giant fissures, or large cracks in the earth's surface, opened up all along southeast Washington and northeast Oregon. Out from these fissures, some of which were up to 100 miles long, flowed millions of tons of liquid rock. There were as many as 150 of these massive hot liquid rock flows, each one bringing another layer of rock up to two miles thick. In total, hot lava flooded more that 62,000 square miles, almost two-thirds the size of Washington State.

Over the eons, erosion carved out channels in the basalt while windblown soil accumulated on top. The last ice age, which ended about 10,000 years ago, contributed substantially to the current terrain that we see in the Little Spokane Watershed. Ice and flood waters scoured out valleys, exposing the basalt. The scablands southwest of Spokane had up to 150 feet of top soil torn away by the last ice age's great floods, exposing the basalt rock layer, the scabland. The Little Spokane Watershed however, was more protected as the flood waters surged through the Spokane Valley. Erosion by wind and water will similarly erode soil and soft rock, but will leave the harder basalt in place. The results are seemingly gravity-defying structures such as Bowl and Pitcher near the Little Spokane Watershed.

Granite is also a major component of the rockland habitat in the Little Spokane Watershed. Granite's salt and pepper appearance is easily distinguished from basalt's dark hue. Like basalt, granite's origins are also from molten rock – ignacious, fire, rock. However liquid granite rock slowly cooled below Earth's surface while basalt quickly cooled on Earth's surface.

The difference in appearance is a result of how long the lava was able to cool and its mineral makeup. The liquid rock that formed the basalt, we see today, flowed out onto the surface of the Earth and cooled relatively quickly and formed small, tight crystals. Granite, although from the same origin as basalt, never made it to the surface of the Earth. Instead granite was forced into the subterranean fingers and chambers where it cooled very slowly, over hundreds of thousands of years, allowing its atoms plenty of time to precipitate out in an organized manner, forming larger mineral crystals. If the underground chamber is large enough, such as those found below volcanoes, the molten rock will cool to form what is called a batholith. Over time, the softer surrounding material may erode away, leaving the granite exposed in the shape in which it cooled, which may appear very irregular when viewing the surrounding landscape. Probably the most famous granite structure of this sort in North America is Half Dome in Yosemite National Park.

Inter-relationships

The rock outcroppings that are exposed in the Little Spokane Watershed are far from the most biologically diverse habitat in the area. However, several critters have adapted to life in this seemingly barren landscape. Many of the plants are either grasses or non-woody-stemmed plants, forbs, that die back in the summer. Reptiles such as the western skink, small mammals like the yellow-bellied marmot and chipmunk, and birds like rock wrens and canyon wrens are among those that find excellent denning sites in these areas. Because food is relatively scarce, they often leave the rockland and search in adjacent habitats. In general few large mammals are found in rockland habitat.

Yellow-bellied Marmot

The yellow-bellied marmot is a relatively large member of the squirrel family which locates its burrow in rock outcroppings to escape the phenomenal digging prowess of their worst enemy, the badger. Marmots may often be heard before they are seen and can easily be distinguished by their high-pitched shriek. Marmots are slow when compared to other prey and rely on their shrieks as an early warning system when predators approach.

Like many squirrels, marmots take their hibernation seriously. They put on enough fat to constitute as much as half their body weight, and then they head underground for as long as eight months.

An interesting adaptation that low-elevation yellow-bellied marmots have developed is that of aestivation, as opposed to hibernation. When the summer heat dries up spring's herbs and grasses, marmots respond by going underground and going into a sort of summer hibernation, aestivation, as early as late June. In doing so, they allow their body temperatures to vary and require little food or water. Instead, they use energy in the form of fat that has accumulated on their bodies.

The main difference between aestivation and hibernation is the extent of body temperature change. Both are aimed at conserving energy during lean times and do so by reducing the animal's

Marmot checking it all out

metabolic rate. However, aestivation is generally a response to high temperatures and scarcity of water while hibernation is a response to extreme cold. In hibernation, the animal actually goes into a state of hypothermia, allowing its core body temperature to drop, thereby saving considerable energy. In aestivation, the body temperature remains constant. Marmots are able to go directly from aestivation into hibernation as the temperature cools in the early fall. They emerge from their burrow in late February or March, waking only occasionally to eat stored food, stretch, or excrete.

Western Skink

Rockland habitat brings to mind images of reptiles basking on a sunny rock on a cool summer morning. Indeed, the rockland habitat is home to the infamous western skink, perhaps more commonly known as the blue-tailed skink. True to its name, this lizard, when it is young, has a bright blue tail that is thought to be used to bait predators and to divert the strike away from the lizards head. When touched, the tail breaks off and thrashes wildly, keeping the predator busy while the skink shimmies out of reach. Skinks are often found under stones.

These fragile tails are built to break off. A wall of cartilage passes through each vertebrae, creating a weak point where muscles and blood sinuses are also modified to allow for an easy break. If in danger, a skink may even break off its own tail by pressing against something, thus leaving its pursuer with nothing but a wriggling blue tail.

Losing a tail is a trick that works only once, and there is a definite energy cost associated with growing a new tail. The new tail grows in slowly and is never as

Skink

long or colorful as the first one. Nor does it have the fracture planes that allow it to break off again. Losing a tail may also mean losing some stored fat that might have gotten the lizard through a lean time. And, of course, growing a new tail requires significant energy that must be borrowed from breeding or feeding activities.

Sustainability

Like the ponderosa pine habitat, the rockland habitat is most adversely affected by the mere presence of humans. Even walking off trails in rocklands can be very destructive to this habitat. Fragile plants are crushed, rocks are easily disturbed and erosion can be accelerated, especially on steep slopes. It may seem that there are plenty of these rock outcroppings around. Even within the city of Spokane some yards include rock formations. However, looking more closely at the rocklands one can see

Sun on the rocks above the Little Spokane

the creeping loss of rockland and the fragmentation of nature around the rocklands. The loss of links of nature between rocklands and the surrounding habitats adversely affects the critters of the rocklands. With the restoration of nature corridors between habitats, the rocklands can become more healthy. Then the western skinks and other rockland critters can better flourish.

Quality of Life Measures

The quality of life in rocklands can be measured with critter counts in specific areas, for plants, animals, fungi and lichens. As rocklands become more healthy, certain critter populations will increase. For example, skinks will be noticed more often.

Summary of Rockland Habitat Critters

Number of Species by Kingdom

PLANT (PLANTAE)   67

FUNGUS (EUMYCOTA)   18

ANIMAL (ANIMALIA)   47

PROTIST (PROTISTA)   8

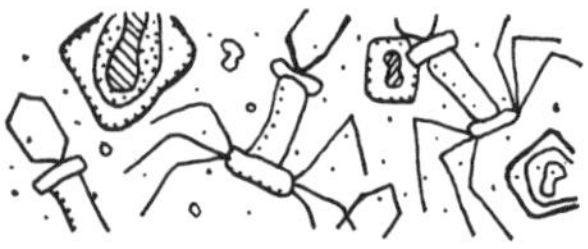

**BACTERIA & VIRUS
(MONERA & VIRUS)**   7

TOTAL IDENTIFIED SPECIES   147

Number of Species by Class

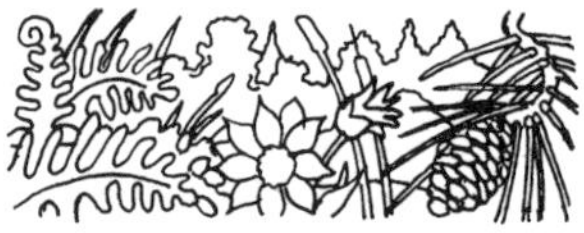

Moss (Bryopsida)	14
Club Moss (Isoetopsida)	1
Fern (Polypodiopsida)	4
Pine (Pinicae)	2
Magnolia (Magnoliidae)	1
Carnation (Caryophyllidae)	4
Aspen (Dilleniidae)	6
Rose (Rosidae)	15
Sunflower (Asteridae)	17
Grass (Commelinidae)	1
Lily (Liliidae)	2
Crusty Lichen (Crustose)	9
Leafy Lichen (Foliose)	8
Fruity Lichen (Fruticose)	1
Turbellidia (Turbellidia)	1
Spider (Arachnida)	1
Centipede (Chilopoda)	1
Millipede (Diplopoda)	1
Insect (Insecta)	3
Reptile (Reptilia)	7
Bird (Aves)	18
Mammal (Mammalia)	15
Amoeba (Rhizopoda)	1
Heliozoan (Actimpoda)	1
Foram (Forimaninifera)	1
Sporozoite (Apicomplexa)	1
Slime Mold - Cellular (Acrasiomycetes)	1
Slime Mold - Plasmodial (Myxomycetes)	1
Mildew (Oomycota)	1
Saprobe (Chytridiomycota)	1
Bacteria (Bacteria)	1
Cyanophycota (Cyanophycota)	1
Prochlorophycota (Prochlorophycota)	1
Bacteria Virus (Bacteria Virus)	1
Plant Virus (Plant Virus)	1
Vertebrate Virus (Vertebrate Virus)	1
Invertebrate Virus (Invertebrate Virus)	1

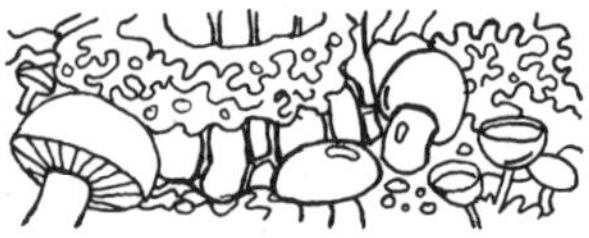

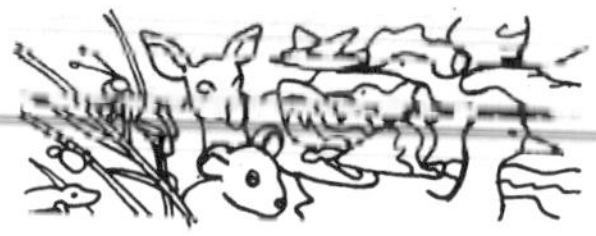

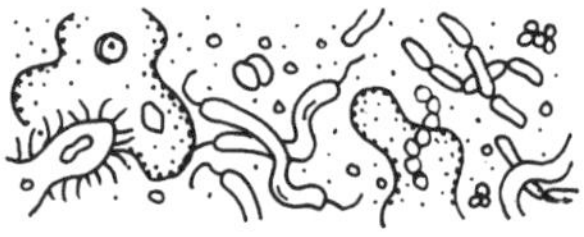

Selected Rockland Habitat Critters

PLANT (PLANTAE)	47	
Moss (Bryopsida)	14	
Brachythecium albicans		C
Brachythecium campestre		C
Brachythecium salebposum		C
Ceratodon purpureus		C
Funaria hygrometrica		C
Grimmia apocarpa		F
Grimmia montana		C
Homalothecium nevadense		C
Pholia nutans		F
Polytrichum juniperinum		A
Polytrichum piliferum		A
Racomitrium hetrostichum		C
Rhacomitrium canescens		C
Torula ruralis		C
Club Moss (Isoetopsida)	1	
Selaginella		C
Fern (Polypodiopsida)	2	
Licorice-Root Fern		F
Rocky Mountain Woodsia		C
Pine (Pinicae)	1	
Ponderosa Pine		A
Magnolia (Magnoliidae)	1	
Small Oregon Grape		F
Carnation (Caryophyllidae)	2	
Canyon Heather		F
Field Chickweed		F
Aspen (Dilleniidae)	3	
Holboellis Rockcress		C
Kinnikinnick		C
Pacific Willow		F
Rose (Rosidae)	11	
Alumroot		C
Bitterbrush		A
Chokecherry		F
Mock Orange		C
Ocean Spray		A
Pachistima		F
Poison Ivy		F
Roundleaf Alumroot (B)		F
Stonecrop		A
Swale Desert Parsley		F
Western Saxifrage		F
Sunflower (Asteridae)	10	
Bellflower		C
Common Mullein		F IN
Common Snowberry		A
Common Yarrow		C
Cut-leaf Daisy		C
Microsteris		A
Wild Aster		A
Wooly Groundsel		F
Yellow Beardtongue		C
Yellow Indian Paintbrush		C
Grass (Commelinidae)	1	
Bluebunch Wheatgrass		C
Lily (Liliidae)	1	
Western False Solomon's Seal		F

FUNGUS (EUMYCOTA)	9	
Crusty Lichen (Crustose)	6	
Acarospora chlorophana		F
Candelariella vitellina		F
Diploschistes scruposus		F
Hypocenomyce (Lecidea) scalaris		C
Lecanora rupicola		C
Xanthoria elegans		C
Leafy Lichen (Foliose)	3	
Parmelia saxatilis		C
Parmelia sulcata		C
Umbilicaria spp.		C
ANIMAL (ANIMALIA)	12	
Insect (Insecta)	2	
Cave Cricket		F
Sand Cricket		F
Reptile (Reptilia)	2	
Western Rattlesnake		F
Western Skink		F
Bird (Aves)	5	
Bank Swallow		A
Cliff Swallow		A
Common Raven		F
Eastern Kingbird		F
Great Horned Owl		C
Mammal (Mammalia)	3	
Coyote		F
Yellow Pine Chipmunk		F
Yellow-bellied Marmot		F

* The critters listed here are identified as abundant, common and fairly common.

Legend - Critters are listed by their common name followed by their abundance in the habitat. Introduced species and species at risk are indicated by type code. • **Abundance Codes: A** Abundant, **C** Common, **F** Fairly common, **U** Uncommon, **R** Rare, **V** Vagrant, **K** Known in habitat, **L** Likely in habitat, **M** Missing from habitat. • **Introduced Species Codes: IN** Introduced Noxious species, **IO** Introduced, Other than noxious species. • **At Risk Codes: MS** Missing, **ED** Endangered, **TH** Threatened, **CD** Candidate, **MN** Monitor, **RGM** Regulated Game, **RNG** Regulated Nongame, **RA** Rare, **PB** Protected Breeding Areas.

Selected Critter Descriptions

Kinnikinnick
(Arctostaphylos uva-ursi)

		Class:	Aspen (Dilleniidae)
Family:	Heath (Ericaceae)	**Division:**	Flower (Magnoliophyta)
Order:	Heath (Ericales)	**Kingdom:**	Plant (Plantae)

Other Names: Bearberry, Sandberry
LSW Habitats: MT: F, DF: F, PP: C, RK: C, HU: F

Relationships To Watershed: Kinnikinnick berries are edible by wildlife. Its mat-forming characteristics make it good for erosion control protection on highly disturbed sites.

Description: Kinnikinnick is a trailing evergreen shrub that is up to 6 inches tall. White to pinkish urn-shaped flowers bloom in June-July in few-flowered racemes. Stems are brownish to reddish with shredding bark. Leaves are alternate, thick and leathery. They are 1/2-1 inch long, spatulate in shape with entire margins, have a rounded tip and are dark green above. Fruits are round, bright red, berry-like drupe.

Look Alikes: Kinnikinnick may be confused with Pinemat Manzanita, *Arctostaphylos nevadensis*, which has a pointed leaf tip, is more erect and has a brown-red berry; Twinflower, *Linnaea borealis*, and Oregon Boxwood, *Pachistima mysinites*, which both have opposite leaves with serrated margins.

Little Spokane Habitat: Kinnikinnick is found under sunny stands of Ponderosa Pine, Lodgepole Pine and in Grand Fir-dominated communities. Kinnikinnick is common on sandy soils and glacial soil in cool moist canyon bottoms.

World Habitat: Kinnikinnick is found in the Cascades throughout Oregon and Washington to the Rocky Mountains.

Drupe - A fleshy or pulpy fruit in which the seed has a stony covering.

Found On:
Kinnikinnick
Chokecherry

Spur - A stiffly projecting part of a branch.

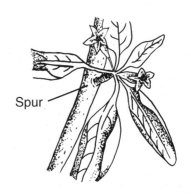

Spur

Found On:
Bitterbrush

Bitterbrush *(Purshia tridentata)*

		Class:	Rosidae (Rosidae)
Family:	Rose (Rosaceae)	**Division:**	Flower (Magnoliophyta)
Order:	Rose (Rosales)	**Kingdom:**	Plant (Plantae)

Other Name: Antelope Brush
LSW Habitats: PP: A, RK: A, BU: C, GR: U

Relationships To Watershed: Bitterbrush is an extremely important winter range browse species for deer, antelope and elk. Rodents cache or eat bitterbrush seeds in great quantities. The species name "tridentata" refers to the three-lobed (tri) leaf (dentata).

Description: Bitterbrush is an erect, stiff and abundantly branched mid-sized shrub that grows up to 8 feet tall. Stems are reddish-brown that become gray-reddish brown as the shrub matures. Spur shoots are common. Pale yellow flowers bloom April-July and are borne singly at each leaf cluster. Leaves are alternate and wedge-shaped. They are about 3/4 inch long, clustered on spur shoots, gray-green above and white to gray below. The margins are rolled under and the leaves are 3-lobed at the apex. Fruits are tear-shaped achenes with a tapered beak.

Look Alikes: Bitterbrush may be confused with Sagebrush, *Artemisia* spp., which has leaves that are silvery, hairy and odoriferous.

Little Spokane Habitat: Bitterbrush grows in sandy, gravelly and rocky soils in cold desert shrub lands and beneath Ponderosa Pine at the forested fringe on warm dry sites.

Ocean Spray in bloom

World Habitat: Bitterbrush is a native plant that is found east of the cascades in Washington, and Oregon and northern California, and eastward to western Montana, Wyoming and Colorado.

Ocean Spray *(Holodiscus discolor)*

		Class:	Rose (Rosidae)
Family:	Rose (Rosaceae)	**Division:**	Flower (Magnoliophyta)
Order:	Rose (Rosales)	**Kingdom:**	Plant (Plantae)

Other Names: Creambrush, Indian Arrowwood, Mountain Spray
LSW Habitats: MT: A, DF: A, RK: A

Relationships To Watershed: Ocean Spray resprouts basally following fire and increases with disturbance. This plant may be heavily browsed on winter ranges.

Description: Ocean Spray is a deciduous shrub that is mid-sized from 3-9 feet tall. Ocean Spray is erect, multi-branched, with a vase-like form. Small, creamy to white flowers bloom July-August in dense, large pyramidal panicles that often droop in a "spray". The old dried inflorescences usually overwinter. The leaves are alternate, 1-3 inches long with a triangular shape and a truncated base. The margins are shallowly lobed with coarse teeth. Leaves are pale green above and white and hairy below. The stems are grayish-red in color with the young stems ridged and the older bark shredding. Fruit is a small 1-seeded achene.

Look Alikes: Ocean Spray may possibly be confused with currants, gooseberries, *Ribes spp.*, or ninebark, *Physocarpus malbacus*, when not in flower. Leaf margins are distinctive. Look for old dried inflorescences from previous years.

Little Spokane Habitat: Ocean Spray is found on open rocky or gravelly colluvial slopes and beneath warm, dry tree species, including ponderosa pine, Douglas-fir, in open forested stands.

World Habitat: Ocean Spray is widespread from British Columbia to southern California, Montana, Idaho and Oregon.

Truncate Leaf Base - The leaf base squared at the end as if cut off.

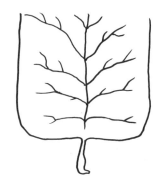

Found On:
Ocean Spray
Western Serviceberry

Poison Ivy *(Rhus radicans)*

		Class:	Rose (Rosidae)	
Family:	Maple (Aceraceae)	**Division:**	Flower (Magnoliophyta)	
Order:	Maple (Sapindales)	**Kingdom:**	Plant (Plantae)	

Poison ivy - leaves of three let them be

Other Name: Poison Oak
LSW Habitat: RK: F

Relationships To Watershed: Poison Ivy has little survival value to the plant, unlike nettle stingers which are an effective defense against browsing. Poison Ivy could be considered an accident of biochemistry, or one of the commonest allergies in humans. Other species don't seem to be susceptible to the plant's poison. They gather the nectar, or browse the leaves with pronounced indifference.

Description: Poison Ivy is an erect, perennial woody shrub. Leaves are narrowly pointed with few lobes. The leaves are compound with leaflets almost always in 3's. Leaflets are around 2-5 inches long. New foliage is reddish and glossy in the spring. Foliage loses its gloss as the plant matures, and by midsummer some leaflets may turn crimson while others go from green to yellow just before dropping in the fall. Greenish-white flowers occur in dense erect clusters and are about 1/4 inch in diameter. They produce translucent white berries in bunches that are single-seeded and striped longitudinally. These berries are present by late summer and into winter long after the leaves have fallen. Many plants may fail to fruit.

Poison ivy along a rock

Look Alikes: Poison Ivy tends to grow on or near white oak because its leaflets seem to mimic the oak leaves in shape, sheen and shade.

Little Spokane Habitat: Poison Ivy is found in dry, hot, sunny, rocky locations.

World Habitat: Poison Ivy is a native plant found in the east of the Cascades into central Washington and Oregon, east to the Atlantic coast and south to Mexico.

Western Skink *(Eumeces skiltonianus)*

		Class:	Reptiles (Reptilia)
Family:	Skink (Scincidae)	**Division:**	Vertebrate (Chordata)
Order:	Snake (Squamata)	**Kingdom:**	Animal (Animalia)

Other Name: Blue-Tailed Skink, Skink
LSW Habitats: PP: F, RK: F, GR: U

Relationships To Watershed: Western Skinks prey on arthropods, crickets, beetles, moths, grasshoppers and flies. The bright blue tail is a distraction tool from predators. Predators grab for the tail and it is damaged or lost but allows the skink to escape without having its vital organs damaged.

Description: Western Skinks are small shiny lizards patterned with longitudinal stripes and often with bright blue tails when they are young. They have a middorsal dark stripe and a dorsolateral chocolate to olive-brown stripe on each side. Between the side stripes and middorsal dark stripe, there are two white to cream-colored stripes on

Skull on mossy rock

Millipede among the rocks

each side. The chin and belly are light gray and mottled with bluish or greenish spots. The bright blue tail fades to blue-gray or brown-gray in larger individuals. The males are red in color on the chin and the side of the head during breeding season.

Look Alikes: The only skink in the Little Spokane Watershed.

Little Spokane Habitat: Western Skinks are found in canyons, open woodlands and forests up to 2100 meters in elevation. They prefer rocky habitats with some moisture. Blue-tailed Skinks can be found in rotting logs, under surface litter and under large flat stones covering the cool, moist earth.

World Habitat: Blue-tailed Skinks are a native species found in the Pacific Northwest.

Western Rattlesnake
(Crotalus viridis oreganus)

		Class:	Reptiles (Reptilia)
Family:	Rattlesnake (Viperidae)	**Division:**	Vertebrate (Chordata)
Order:	Snake (Squamata)	**Kingdom:**	Animal (Animalia)

Other Name: Rattlesnake
LSW Habitats: RK: F, GR: U, DS: U, HU: U

Relationships To Watershed: Western Rattlesnakes feed mainly on small mammals and are important economically as controllers of rodent pests. Birds are occasionally eaten.

Description: Western Rattlesnakes have long, stout bodies with short tails that end in horny rattles or buttons. Adult length ranges between 600-1575 mm. The head is broad, especially at the back, and holds a triangular shape that is distinct from the neck. The eye has a vertical pupil. This snake has a deep pit between the eyes and the snout. This "pit" functions as a heat-sensing organ and is used to detect the usual warm-blooded prey of the snake. The scutes on the top of the head are small and the body scutes are strongly keeled.

The ground color is brown, tan, olive, or gray, with a series of large dark brown blotches along the back. A series of smaller blotches appears on each side of the body below the large blotches. Ground color between bands may be somewhat lighter towards the tail than on the rest of the body. The top of the head usually shows ground color with a dark band running from below the eye to the corner of the jaw. Underparts are yellowish-white, sometimes brownish. The rattle at the end of the tail consists of a series of loosely interlocked horny segments which produce a characteristic buzzing sound when the tail is vibrated rapidly.

Rattlesnakes typically use the rattle when they are disturbed. Western rattlesnakes are the only venomous snakes in the Little Spokane Watershed. The venom is produced in a gland above the angle of the jaw. The fangs are two specialized teeth at the front of the upper jaw. They are like small hypodermic needles that are used to inject the venom into the prey. This can be used for feeding and for defense.

Look Alikes: The only rattlesnake in Washington.

Little Spokane Habitat: Western rattlesnakes are generally restricted to dry habitats where there is some shelter available in the summer. They also live in talus slopes in sagebrush and lightly forested areas. In winter they use rock outcrops and talus slopes that function as "dens" in which the snakes hibernate.

World Habitat: Western rattlesnakes are a native species that range over most of the western half of North America with a few gaps.

Ferns among the rocks

Yellow-bellied Marmot
(*Marmota flaviventris*)

		Class:	Mammal (Mammalia)
Family:	Squirrel (Sciuridae)	**Division:**	Vertebrate (Chordata)
Order:	Rodent (Rodentia)	**Kingdom:**	Animal (Animalia)

Other Name: Marmot
LSW Habitats: SA: U, RK: F, GR: U, HU: F

Relationships To Watershed: Yellow-bellied Marmots consume a diet that includes both grasses and forbs. They avoid toxic plants selecting species that are succulent and actively growing. Predators include coyotes, badgers, hawks, eagles, and bobcats. Marmots are important prey species for larger predators.

Cliff swallow makes a home under a bridge

Description: Yellow-bellied Marmots are short-legged, short-tailed creatures about the size of a house cat. They are the largest members of the versatile squirrel family. The general coloration of the Yellow-bellied Marmot is a grizzled yellowish-brown sprinkled with white above. Their underparts are orange-yellow, as also are their feet and cheeks. Their total length is about 24 inches.

Look Alikes: The hoary marmot, *Marmota caligata*, is larger, whitish and not known to occur in the watershed subalpine area.

Little Spokane Habitat: Yellow-bellied Marmots are found in a typical habitat that includes boulders, balsatic outcrops, abandoned buildings, piles of logs or lumber, and the roadside banks. Marmots can be found at all elevations in the Little Spokane Watershed.

World Habitat: Yellow-bellied Marmots are a native species that range from southern British Columbia and Alberta southward to California and New Mexico. They are entirely absent from the Pacific Coast Range.

Big Brown Bat *(Eptesicus fuscus)*

		Class:	Mammal (Mammalia)
Family:	Plainnose Bat (Vespertilionidae)	**Division:**	Vertebrate (Chordata)
Order:	Bat (Chiroptera)	**Kingdom:**	Animal (Animalia)

LSW Habitats: PP: U, RK: U

Relationships to Watershed: Big Brown Bats are nocturnal, meaning they are active only at night. The bat consumes insects which it catches in midair. The Big Brown Bat has poor eyesight and thus uses sonar and great hearing to locate its prey. During the day the bat will hide away in a dark place, such as buildings, usually some distance from the ground.

Description: The Big Brown Bat is a medium to large sized bat, reddish-brown to brown in color. This bat has blackish wing and tail membranes and ears. The Big Brown Bat's short ears barely reach the tip of its nose when laid forward. The under parts are slightly lighter than the above parts. The Big Brown Bat has long oily fur.

Look Alikes: Although this bat resembles many of the *Myotis* species, it can be readily identified by its large size, large head and long fur.

Little Spokane Habitat: The Big Brown Bat inhabits forested areas near water, farmsteads, and metropolitan and urban areas in cities and towns.

World Habitat: The Big Brown Bat has a large range that extends from northern South America to southern Canada.

Bat asleep during the day

Bobcat *(Lynx rufus)*

		Class:	Mammal (Mammalia)
Family:	Cat (Felidae)	**Division:**	Vertebrate (Chordata)
Order:	Carnivore (Carnivora)	**Kingdom:**	Animal (Animalia)

LSW Habitats: MT: R, RK: U, RP: U

Relationships To Watershed: Bobcats feed on rabbits, ground squirrels, mice, and birds. While the bobcat is the most common wild cat south of the United States - Canadian border, it is rarely seen except by accident because it is a very shy animal.

Description: Bobcats are short-tailed, long-legged cat-like animals with sharp-pointed ears. Their fur is gray and spotted with brown or black. The pelage on the sides and back is reddish to grayish. The ear tassels and sideburns are only moderately developed. They weigh fifteen to twenty pounds with a body length of about 30 inches.

Look Alikes: Bobcats may be confused with the lynx, *Lynx canadensis*, which has longer legs and much larger feet than the bobcat. The lynx does not have spots on the body and legs, is not as reddish in color and has a plain, black-tipped tail.

Little Spokane Habitat: Bobcats are fairly common in broken, rocky areas and logged-over and forested land, also second growth timber.

World Habitat: Bobcats are a native species found in Washington, Oregon, California and Idaho. They are also found in southern and eastern-central British Columbia.

Rockland habitat above the riparian and bushland habitats

Bushland Habitat

Bushland habitat is found mostly at low elevations of the watershed, often near human habitat. Bushland habitat is distinguished by the presence of woody shrubs and some relatively small deciduous trees and a marked absence of coniferous trees, except for the occasional ponderosa pine. These areas receive very little moisture and what moisture they do receive comes mostly in the form of snow.

Inter-relationships

Bushland habitat is often interspersed with ponderosa pine habitat to form a mosaic of forest and open areas. Bushland habitat may also be found between the ponderosa pine habitat and the even drier grassland habitat. An area that is currently bushland habitat may be abandoned farmland that is making the transition back to wildland. Many bushland habitats are but one step in the transition of a grassland habitat into a forest habitat. This may be a natural process or one caused by the suppression of wildfires.

Because bushland habitat presents such a harsh environment, relatively few species are adapted to it. Thus, species

Blending into the grass edge a deer looks up. Here the bushland habitat blends with riparian, rockland and ponderosa pine habitats.

*Mud Dauber Wasp nest
in the foliage*

Puffball, Calvatia Booniana

diversity is somewhat less than habitats such as the mountain or riparian habitats with their more numerous and diverse critters. The exception to this is in the summer when the number of bird species, many of them summer breeders, visit the bushland habitat to feast on an abundant crop of seeds.

The Ever-present Role of Fire

Like all of the undisturbed low elevation habitats in the Little Spokane Watershed, bushland is adapted to frequent fires caused by lightning strikes. Before the suppression of fires, fire would clear an area every few years. After a fire, healthy bushland quickly regenerates. In doing so, nutrients for the next generation of growth are released and the soil becomes richer.

Snowbrush ceanothus, also known as evergreen ceanothus and buckbrush, demonstrates this type of adaptation. Snowbrush invades burns, including clearcuts in higher elevations. Its seeds are activated by the heat of a fire and the increased soil warmth of the new clearing. The young shoots grow slowly, but easily crowd out annuals in three or four seasons. The roots host nitrogen-fixing bacteria, a nutrient that is necessary for further vegetation growth.

Tick on fabric looking for warm moist skin to attach to. Ticks attach to humans, deer and other animals to feed on their blood. Check for and remove ticks after walking through tick habitats.

Deer

By far the largest mammal found with any regularity in bushland habitat are deer, both mule deer and white tail deer. Mule deer prefer bushland habitat. Whitetail occasionally wander into an open brushy area, but are more of a forest dweller. They can most easily be distinguished by their tails. The mule deer has a conspicuous black tip on its tail, and the white tail blatantly waves its white tail as it runs away. The waving white tail is believed to be an adaptive response to predators. In effect, the deer is saying to the predator, "I see you so don't even bother trying to catch me." This is especially beneficial to a doe who may have vulnerable fawns nearby.

Browsing deer provide a critical component to the bushland habitat by stimulating plant growth on woody shrubs and grasses that are being eaten. At first it may sound odd that killing part of a plant will enhance its growth, but this works like domesticated house plants. To get them to become shrubbier, parts are pruned off of the plant. Many wild, woody plants respond the same way.

Birds

Many bird species spend time foraging for seeds in the bushland habitat. The combination of food availability and cover from predators attracts these birds. Some of these species are migratory birds that stop over in the Little Spokane Watershed while on their way north for the summer or south for the winter. They move down from higher elevations during inclement weather. Examples include the house wren and black-headed grosbeak. Other species are year-round residents, such as the white-breasted nuthatch and black-billed magpie.

Sustainability

Bushland habitats provide valuable links of life just as every habitat type does and can be allowed to become more restorative. This means allowing natural cycles to proceed uninterrupted. Bushland habitats constitute a very small proportion of the undeveloped lands in the Little Spokane Watershed and do not provide a great deal of material that can be harvested or extracted. More biodiversity can result when there is less human interference within the bushland's natural cycles. This simply means, that when possible, they should be left alone.

Cedar Waxwing blending in with the foliage

Quality of Life Measures

Bushland habitat quality of life can be measured by how quickly the habitat is transitioning toward its more mature stages. The biodiversity of bushland habitat is also a measure of quality of life.

Summary of Bushland Habitat Critters

Number of Species by Kingdom

PLANT (PLANTAE) 27

FUNGUS (EUMYCOTA) 26

ANIMAL (ANIMALIA) 79

PROTIST (PROTISTA) 8

**BACTERIA & VIRUS
(MONERA & VIRUS)** 7

Number of Species by Class

Moss (Bryopsida)	3
Pine (Pinicae)	1
Magnolia (Magnoliidae)	4
Carnation (Caryophyllidae)	1
Aspen (Dilleniidae)	2
Rose (Rosidae)	12
Sunflower (Asteridae)	3
Lily (Liliidae)	1
Mushroom (Basidomycetes)	20
Puffball (Gastromycetes)	1
Phragmobasidiomycetes (Phragmobasidiomycetes)	1
To Be Determined (TBD)	1
Crusty Lichen (Crustose)	2
Leafy Lichen (Foliose)	1
Turbellidia (Turbellidia)	1
Spider (Arachnida)	1
Centipede (Chilopoda)	1
Millipede (Diplopoda)	1
Insect (Insecta)	8
Amphibian (Amphibia)	3
Reptile (Reptilia)	1
Bird (Aves)	52
Mammal (Mammalia)	11
Amoeba (Rhizopoda)	1
Heliozoan (Actimpoda)	1
Foram (Forimaninifera)	1
Sporozoite (Apicomplexa)	1
Slime Mold - Cellular (Acrasiomycetes)	1
Slime Mold - Plasmodial (Myxomycetes)	1
Mildew (Oomycota)	1
Saprobe (Chytridiomycota)	1
Bacteria (Bacteria)	1
Cyanophycota (Cyanophycota)	1
Prochlorophycota (Prochlorophycota)	1
Bacteria Virus (Bacteria Virus)	1
Plant Virus (Plant Virus)	1
Vertebrate Virus (Vertebrate Virus)	1
Invertebrate Virus (Invertebrate Virus)	1

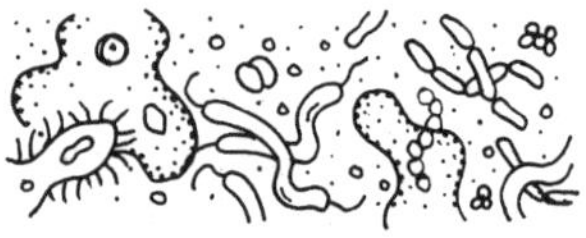

TOTAL IDENTIFIED SPECIES 147

Selected Bushland Habitat Critters

PLANT (PLANTAE)	24		
Moss (Bryopsida)	3		
Ceratodon purpureus		C	
Funaria hygrometrica		C	
Polytrichum juniperinum		A	
Pine (Pinicae)	1		
Ponderosa Pine		F	
Magnolia (Magnoliidae)	4		
Blue Clematis		F	
Oregon Grape		F	
Western Meadowrue		F	
Western Virgin's Bower		F	
Aspen (Dilleniidae)	1		
Common Pink Wintergreen		F	
Rose (Rosidae)	11		
Bitter Cherry		F	
Bitterbrush		C	
Ceanothus		C	
Golden Currant		F	
Mallow Ninebark		A	
Mountain Ash (B)		C	
Nootka Rose		A	
Snowbrush Ceanothus		A	
Swamp Gooseberry		F	
Wax Currant		F	
Western Sumac		F	
Sunflower (Asteridae)	3		
Arrowleaf Groundsel		F	
Common Snowberry		F	
Prickly Phlox		C	
Lily (Liliidae)	1		
Death Camas		C	
FUNGUS (EUMYCOTA)	4		
Mushroom (Basidomycetes)	1		
Malodorous Lepiota		F	
Crusty Lichen (Crustose)	2		
Rhizocarpon geographicum		C	
Xanthoria polycarpa		C	
Leafy Lichen (Foliose)	1		
Parmelia sulcata		C	

ANIMAL (ANIMALIA)	37		
Spider (Arachnida)	1		
Tick		F	
Insect (Insecta)	5		
California Tortoiseshell		F	
Field Cricket		F	
Russet Hairstreak		F	
Snowy Tree Cricket		F	
Western Tiger Swallowtail		C	
Bird (Aves)	23		
American Goldfinch		F	
American Robin		C	
Black-billed Magpie		C	
Black-headed Grosbeak		F	
Blue-winged Teal		F	
Brewer's Blackbird		A	
California Quail		C	IO
Calliope Hummingbird		F	
Cedar Waxwing		C	
Chipping Sparrow		C	
Dark-eyed Junco		C	
Eastern Kingbird		F	
Great Horned Owl		C	
House Finch		C	
House Wren		C	
Mountain Bluebird		C	
Mountain Chickadee		F	
Orange-crowned Warbler		F	
Ruby-crowned Kinglet		C	
Spotted Towhee		F	
Warbling Vireo		C	
Western Meadowlark		F	
White-crowned Sparrow		C	
Mammal (Mammalia)	8		
Coyote		F	
Human		C	
Masked Shrew		C	
Mule Deer		F	RGM
Raccoon		F	
Striped Skunk		F	
White-tailed Deer		C	RGM
Yellow Pine Chipmunk		F	

* The critters listed here are those identified as abundant, common and fairly common.

Legend - Critters are listed by their common name followed by their abundance in the habitat. Introduced species and species at risk are indicated by type code. • **Abundance Codes: A** Abundant, **C** Common, **F** Fairly common, **U** Uncommon, **R** Rare, **V** Vagrant, **K** Known in habitat, **L** Likely in habitat, **M** Missing from habitat. • **Introduced Species Codes: IN** Introduced Noxious species, **IO** Introduced, Other than noxious species. • **At Risk Codes: MS** Missing, **ED** Endangered, **TH** Threatened, **CD** Candidate, **MN** Monitor, **RGM** Regulated Game, **RNG** Regulated Nongame, **RA** Rare, **PB** Protected Breeding Areas.

Selected Critter Descriptions

Nootka Rose (*Rosa nutkana*)

		Class:	Rose (Rosidae)
Family:	Rose (Rosaceae)	**Division:**	Flower (Magnoliophyta)
Order:	Rose (Rosales)	**Kingdom:**	Plant (Plantae)

Other Name: Rose (A)
LSW Habitats: DF: C, PP: C, BU: A

Relationships To Watershed: Nootka Rose is low in palatability but the hips are important winter food for grouse and quail.

Description: Nootka Rose is a deciduous shrub low to mid-sized, from 2-6 feet tall. Large, 2-3 inch pink flowers bloom May to July, solitarily at the end of the branch. Alternate leaves are odd-pinnately compound with 5-7 leaflets that are serrate to doubly serrate. The stems are armed with pairs of straight to slightly curved spines. The fruits are large purplish-red hips with sepals remaining on the hip at fruiting time.

Hip - A fleshy berry-like structure surrounding numerous small, dry one-seeded nut-like frut.

Found on:
Nootka Rose
Woods Rose

Look Alikes: Nootka Rose is very similar to the woods rose (*Rosa woodsii*) which has smaller flowers in terminal clusters.

Little Spokane Habitat: Nootka Rose lives in wooded or moist areas.

World Habitat: Nootka Rose is found only in North America from the Cascades to the Rockies in the Pacific Northwest.

Bracket fungi and moss on decomposing limb

Snowbrush Ceanothus
(*Ceanothus velutinus*)

		Class:	Rose (Rosidae)
Family:	Buckthorn (Rhamnaceae)	**Division:**	Flower (Magnoliophyta)
Order:	Buckthorn (Rhamnales)	**Kingdom:**	Plant (Plantae)

Other Names: Buckbrush, Evergreen Ceanothus, Snowbrush
LSW Habitats: MT: C, DF: C, PP: C, BU: A, DS: C

Relationships To Watershed: Snowbrush Ceanothus is a nitrogen-fixing plant. The seeds require scarification in order to germinate.

Description: Snowbrush Ceanothus is a very aromatic erect shrub that grows from 2-10 feet tall. Stems are green with very smooth bark and are alternately branched. Leaves are evergreen, alternate, thick and very glossy or shiny dark green above and paler below. There are three main veins that branch from the leaf base and the edges often curl downward. Small white flowers bloom June-August in dense pyramidal shaped racemes. Fruits are small capsules containing 3 seeds that explode following intense heat.

Look Alikes: Snowbrush Ceanothus may be confused with redstem ceanothus, *Ceanothus sanguineus*, which has deciduous leaves and reddish stems.

Little Spokane Habitat: Snowbrush Ceanothus is found in open, sunny slopes.

World Habitat: Snowbrush Ceanothus is a native plant widespread in the mountainous Pacific Northwest.

Ruffed grouse hen waiting for chicks to hatch

Ruffed Grouse *(Bonasa umbellus)*

		Class:	Bird (Aves)
Family:	Grouse (Phasianidae)	**Division:**	Vertebrate (Chordata)
Order:	Grouse (Galliformes)	**Kingdom:**	Animal (Animalia)

At Risk: Regulated Game
LSW Habitats: DF: U, BU: U, RP: U

Relationships To Watershed: Ruffed Grouse feeds on tree buds which makes it conspicuous in tree tops, usually at dawn or dusk, during winter when snow covers the ground. Ruffed Grouse are preyed upon by mammals, owls and raptors. Almost completely herbivorous browsers, Ruffed Grouse eat foliage of woody plants, twigs, catkins, buds, and fleshy fruits. Quaking Aspen buds are their primary winter food, along with buds, catkins and

Ruffed grouse chicks hatching

Blue Clematis flower head

*Blue Clematis over taking
a bush*

leaves from Hazelnuts, Willow, Birch, Cherry and Apple family species. In the summer and fall Serviceberry, Elderberry, Cherry, Blackberry, Strawberry, Hawthorn, Rose and Dogwood fruits are eaten. Clover foliage is also a major food. Young grouse eat insect larvae, beetles, flies, snails, spiders, ants and sedge seeds.

Description: Ruffed Grouse are ground-dwelling gamebirds about 17 inches in length. Overall color is brown-red or brown-gray with a small crest and black ruffs on the sides of the neck. The tail has a wide dark band at the tip. Males display themselves by raising their crest and ruff and fanning their tail while beating their wings to make a low, drumming noise. Wings are short and rounded; birds tend to "explode" from underbrush into flight and fly short distances to safety.

Look Alikes: Ruffed Grouse may be confused with: Sharp-tailed grouse, *Tympanuchus phasianellus*, which is chunkier and generally lighter brown in color. It has a pointed tail and lives in more open cove.

Spruce grouse, *Dendragapus canadensis*, which is generally darker with a prominent rust-colored or yellowish band on the tip of the tail. Spruce grouse are crestless and the males have a dark throat and breast. Spruce Grouse are found in open coniferous forests with dense undergrowth. The adult blue grouse, *Dendragapus obscurus*, is larger and darker.

Blue Grouse, *D. obscurus*, which are larger and darker, are found in open coniferous forests and mixed woodlands, brushy lowlands and mountain slopes, and higher altitudes in winter. Blue Grouse also lack crests and males are an overall sooty-gray color.

Little Spokane Habitat: Ruffed Grouse is found in forests with deciduous trees with dense undergrowth, especially where aspens are present.

World Habitat: Ruffed Grouse is found from Alaska south to northern California across to northeastern Canada and the Appalachians.

Black-chinned Hummingbird
(*Archilochus alexandri*)

		Class:	Bird (Aves)
Family:	Hummingbird (Trochilidae)	**Division:**	Vertebrate (Chordata)
Order:	Swift (Apodiformes)	**Kingdom:**	Animal (Animalia)

LSW Habitats: BU: U, HU: U

Relationships to Watershed: In addition to necter the Black-chinned Hummingbird's diet consists of spiders.

Description: The smallest of all birds are included in the Hummingbird family. Hummingbirds are usually iridescent, with needle-like bills for sipping nector from flowers and with wing motion so rapid as to appear blurred. The Black-chinned Hummingbird is 3 1/3 - 3 3/4 inches in length. The males have dark green upperparts and a black chin bordered below by an iridescent purple-violet band with a distinct white collar. The dark tail is shallowly notched. Females are green above and whitish below, with an immaculate throat and a slight tinge of buff on the flanks. The bill is long and very slightly decurved. Both sexes show a small white spot behind their eyes.

Boxelder bug on clematis

Look Alikes: The female Anna's hummingbird, *Calypte anna*, may be confused with the female black-chinned hummingbird, but it is slightly larger and has grayer

Oregon Grape flowering

underparts and some red spotting on the throat. The female Costa's hummingbird, *Calypte costae*, is also very similar to the female, but is seldom seen in the region.

Little Spokane Habitat: Commonly found in riparian woodlands of canyons and lowlands.

World Habitat: Found in the western United States.

Western Screech Owl (*Otus kennicottii*)

		Class:	Bird (Aves)
Family:	Owl (Strigidae)	**Division:**	Vertebrate (Chordata)
Order:	Owl (Strigiformes)	**Kingdom:**	Animal (Animalia)

LSW Habitats: PP: U, BU: R, HU: U

Relationships to Watershed: Western Screech Owl's diet varies to include arthropods, amphibians, reptiles and fish. The owls are nocturnal and hunt only at night.

Description: In the Pacific Northwest there are screech owls that are rufus, red, in color. But most are a deep brown-grey above with narrow black streaks. The underparts are white with dark streaks and wide crossbar markings. The tail is strongly dark and faintly barred with brown and the wings show 2 rows of white spots and some white barring on primaries.

Fawn Angle Butterfly resting

Look Alikes: Easily confused with the eastern screech owl, however this owl does not occur in western United States.

Little Spokane Habitat: The western screech owl favors riparian woodlands.

World Habitat: Found on the western side of the United States.

Gray Catbird feeding a grasshopper to the young

Yellow Pine Chipmunk *(Eutamias amoenus)*

		Class:	Mammal (Mammalia)
Family:	Squirrel (Sciuridae)	**Division:**	Vertebrate (Chordata)
Order:	Rodent (Rodentia)	**Kingdom:**	Animal (Animalia)

Other Name: Chipmunk (A)
LSW Habitats: MT: F, DF: F, PP: F, RK: F, BU: F, DS: U

Relationships To Watershed: Yellow Pine Chipmunks eat insects and any available plant food during the spring, turning more and more to seeds and grains as these ripen. These animals disappear underground with the coming of the first snows of winter and reappear in the spring.

Description: Yellow Pine Chipmunks are squirrels of medium size, about eight inches long. They have sharply contrasting black and white stripes set against a brown or gray-brown background. Their ears are dark, sooty gray or black with conspicuous white post-auricular patches. The sides are bright yellow or orange. The rump is grayish and the belly white or buffy.

Look Alikes: Yellow Pine Chipmunks may be confused with the Golden-mantled Ground Squirrels, *Spermophilus lateralis*, which are much larger and do not have stripes on their face and along their sides. The red tailed chipmunk is distinguished from the Yellow Pine Chipmunk by its redish tail underside. Several other species of chipmunks look very similar but are not present in the Little Spokane Watershed.

Little Spokane Habitat: Yellow Pine Chipmunks are found abundantly in yellow pine forests as well as mountain meadows and clearings, logged or burned-over lands, and in other open places that are bushy or rocky. Yellow Pine Chipmunks are also found in high mountains, rock debris, talus, slopes and road cuts.

World Habitat: Yellow Pine Chipmunks are a native species found in southern and central British Columbia, the mountains of Washington, central and eastern Oregon, and most of Idaho.

Yellow Pine Chipmunk

White-tailed Deer *(Odocoileus virginianus)*

		Class:	Mammal (Mammalia)
Family:	Deer (Cervidae)	**Division:**	Vertebrate (Chordata)
Order:	Deer (Artiodactyla)	**Kingdom:**	Animal (Animalia)

At Risk: Regulated Game
Other Name: Virginian Deer
LSW Habitats: MT: F, DF: C, PP: C, BU: C, RP: C, DS; C, HU: U

Relationships To Watershed: White-tailed Deer browse on a wide variety of shrubs and trees and also softer plants. Deer are preyed upon by Coyotes, Wolves, and Humans. They are often stunned and hit by automobiles.

Description: White-tailed deer are probably the most abundant deer in the U.S. They are a medium-sized deer reaching 3 1/2 feet at the shoulder and weighing up to 300 pounds. They are reddish to tan in summer and bluish-gray in winter. Their bushy tail is white underneath and is carried as a distinctive flag when the animal runs. The buck's antlers are in the form of single right and left beams with the tines branching therefrom. They gallop by means of a "rocking-horse" gait in which the hind feet are placed ahead of the forefeet and they can reach speeds of 40 miles per hour. They can jump 8 feet high and 30 feet horizontally.

Look Alikes: White-tailed Deer may be confused with the mule deer which does not have a white tail.

White-tailed Deer on a morning walk

Little Spokane Habitat: White-tailed Deer are found in dense forests, deciduous woods, and extensive brushy places of low to intermediate elevations, as well as marshy areas near water. They seek thickly vegetated habitats.

World Habitat: White-tailed Deer occur irregularly east of the Cascades in southern British Columbia and in Washington. They are also found in proper habitat in Oregon, except for the southeastern desert area and in Idaho, except for southern desert region.

Grassland Habitat

Grassland habitat is characterized by extremely dry and usually treeless areas at low elevations. Mostly grasses and some flowering plants make their home in the grasslands. Ponderosa pine and bushland habitats are interspersed with grassland habitat. Unlike the massive grass plains east of the Rocky Mountains, the grasslands of the Little Spokane Watershed are not large open expanses. However, they do have many of the same characteristics and critters as their larger counterparts.

Wildflowers and grasses. Looking across Wildrose Prairie to the north and east.

Inter-relationships

Grasses and other Small Native Plants

To survive the driest parts of the year, grasses grow gigantic root systems covered with fibrous root hairs to take advantage of even the slightest trace of water. Most of the biomass of this habitat is underground. A single plant may have as much as 2 to 3 miles of end-to-end roots. Most grasses grow rapidly in the early spring when moisture is available, and then go semidormant for the hottest summer months. When cool, moist weather returns in the fall, the grasses come out of dormancy for some last-minute growing. When temperatures begin to dip below freezing, the plants again go dormant until the spring thaw comes.

Besides climate, grasses have had to adapt to the constant pruning by grass-eating animals such as deer and historically bison which have been recorded in the area. Most plants grow from their tips and lose their ability to grow vertically when this tip is lost. Grasses, however, grow from their base, so that when an animal bites off the tops, they simply grow out again. This is also the reason lawns are cut so often.

Grasses, yarrow and teasel

Grassland habitat also has excellent adaptation to wildfires. Grasses can quickly put up new shoots after a fire. The reservoir of nutrients stored underground not only allows grasses to remain alive during the hot dry weather, but these same nutrients allow grasses to quickly come back after a fire.

A number of broad-leafed native plants with non-woody stems, called forbs, also inhabit the grasslands. These include shooting star in wetter areas, and balsamroot and blue lupine in the drier areas. Forbs grow deep, branched taproots in search of moisture and therefore do not compete with the more shallow roots of grasses. Many of these forbs produce brilliantly colored flowers in the spring.

Like so many of the habitats in the Little Spokane Watershed, grassland habitat health depends on periodic wildfires. In the past, every 5 to 15 years, fire would cleanse the area of vegetation, leaving the roots unharmed. Within weeks of a fire, a vigorous rebirth of grass sprouts appears.

Wildlife and Grassland Inter-relationships

Wildlife in the grassland habitat of the Little Spokane Watershed often come to this habitat in search of food but do not set up permanent residence there. In the vast grasslands of the Great Plains, birds have adapted to nesting on the ground since they have no alternative. In the Little Spokane Watershed, the small size of the grasslands allows animals such as birds and deer to leave in order to seek better shelter, generally in the form of wooded areas and brushy areas. In the spring grasslands are often wet areas that receive early migrating birds.

Beetle on teasel

Pocket Gopher

Small burrowing mammals such as the northern pocket gopher are year round residents to the grassland habitat. These rodents have adapted themselves for digging. Their legs are stubby and muscular, tipped with long, sharp claws that scoop dirt like the blade of a shovel.

The gopher's large yellow side teeth and incisors protrude outside their lips enabling them to cut roots and remove dirt without swallowing a mouthful. The 'pocket' in the pocket gopher's name comes from their special cheek pouches that are used to hold food. These pockets turn inside out like pants' pockets for easy cleaning. To further keep dirt out of their system, their ears have valves that close and their eyelids fit so tightly that not even fine-grained sand can make its way in.

Part of a gopher's diet consists of roots and tubers from plants such as camas and balsamroot, which may dangle down into its chamber. The favorite foods of the gopher, however, are succulent green leaves and stems, such as shooting star and lupine, that can only be found up on the surface.

Gopher burrows are centers for feeding, resting, traveling, hiding, and giving birth. The horizontal, main tunnel is 4 to 12 inches beneath the ground and has many short branches that the gopher uses for

Grassland below the hills and along the river edge

exits, entrances, or as storage areas for food. The nest chamber is built 18 to 24 inches underground.

All this burrowing is good for the soil. It lifts sublevel soil up to the surface so that air, water, and solvents can break down minerals and make them available to plants. The loosened soil also allows nutrients from dead plant material to percolate down to the lower levels along with oxygen and water. The improved drainage slows spring runoff and allows deep-rooted plants like balsamroot to flourish.

Animals also benefit from gopher excavation. Many species occupy abandoned gopher holes, including ground squirrels, gopher snakes that hide their entrance under a mound of soil, and meadow voles. Hawks fly over these gopher areas looking for a day's feast. Gophers also benefit from their own actions because the continual disturbance tends to favor the growth of soft-stemmed plants, which happen to be their preferred foods.

Sustainability

Grassland habitats in the Little Spokane Watershed can be utilized and allowed to become more restorative at the same time. Probably the single largest threat to grasslands is overgrazing by domestic cattle. Unlike bison that graze as a herd from one area to the next, cattle graze for long periods of time in the same area. Cattle often then graze the plants down to stubble from which it is very difficult for the plants to recover. Rotation of

Downy woodpecker eating mullein seeds

cattle to other plots of land allows grasslands to regenerate naturally. Also, periodic controlled fires can replicate the cleansing action of lightning fires.

In addition to allowing areas to regrow, bison also disperse when drinking at water holes. Domestic cattle tend to congregate in one area, thereby destroying the stream banks and turning the stream into a muddy wallow when left in an area too long. Bison also have hooves that are shaped so that they turn up the soil rather than compacting it, as domestic cattle do.

While there are some historic reports of some bison in the area, the bunch grasses and easily compacted soils of the Little Spokane would not be very supportive of large buffalo herds. Yet, some landowners are discovering the benefits of raising bison in place of cattle. Aside from benefiting the land, bison are less prone to disease and cold. Similarly, bison meat currently brings a higher price on the market and is naturally lower in fat than beef.

Quality of Life Measures

Grasslands quality of life can be measured with transects that count the critters in the grassland habitat. These transect measures can be used to examine the biodiversity of various areas. Over time these measures can be compared to see what kinds of increases and decreases there are.

Balsamroot in bloom

Summary of Grassland Habitat Critters

Number of Species by Kingdom

PLANT (PLANTAE)   149

FUNGUS (EUMYCOTA)   23

ANIMAL (ANIMALIA)   112

PROTIST (PROTISTA)   8

BACTERIA & VIRUS (MONERA & VIRUS)   7

TOTAL IDENTIFIED SPECIES   299

Number of Species by Class

Moss (Bryopsida)	3
Pine (Pinicae)	2
Magnolia (Magnoliidae)	3
Carnation (Caryophyllidae)	10
Aspen (Dilleniidae)	9
Rose (Rosidae)	26
Sunflower (Asteridae)	68
Grass (Commelinidae)	20
Lily (Liliidae)	8

Mushroom (Basidomycetes)	19
Puffball (Gastromycetes)	3
Leafy Lichen (Foliose)	1

Turbellidia (Turbellidia)	1
Earthworm (Oligocheata)	1
Spider (Arachnida)	1
Centipede (Chilopoda)	1
Millipede (Diplopoda)	1
Insect (Insecta)	40
Amphibian (Amphibia)	2
Reptile (Reptilia)	5
Bird (Aves)	50
Mammal (Mammalia)	10

Amoeba (Rhizopoda)	1
Heliozoan (Actimpoda)	1
Foram (Forimaninifera)	1
Sporozoite (Apicomplexa)	1
Slime Mold - Cellular (Acrasiomycetes)	1
Slime Mold - Plasmodial (Myxomycetes)	1
Mildew (Oomycota)	1
Saprobe (Chytridiomycota)	1

Bacteria (Bacteria)	1
Cyanophycota (Cyanophycota)	1
Prochlorophycota (Prochlorophycota)	1
Bacteria Virus (Bacteria Virus)	1
Plant Virus (Plant Virus)	1
Vertebrate Virus (Vertebrate Virus)	1
Invertebrate Virus (Invertebrate Virus)	1

Selected Grassland Habitat Critters

PLANT (PLANTAE)	76	
Moss (Bryopsida)	3	
Ceratodon purpureus	C	
Funaria hygrometrica	C	
Polytrichum juniperinum	A	
Magnolia (Magnoliidae)	2	
Meadow Larkspur	A	
Sagebrush Buttercup	A	
Carnation (Caryophyllidae)	5	
Jagged Chickweed	C	IO
Knotweed	C	
Narrow-leaved Spring Beauty	C	
Western Spring Beauty	C	
Wyeth Buckwheat	C	
Aspen (Dilleniidae)	3	
Shooting Star (A)	A	
Shooting Star (B)	A	
Whitlow Grass	A	
Rose (Rosidae)	20	
Blue Lupine	A	
Cinquefoil	C	
Crane's Bill	C	IO
Gray's Lomatium	C	
Hairy Vetch	C	IO
Large-fruit Lomation	C	
Nevada Deervetch	C	
Nine-leaved Lomatium	C	
Old Man's Whiskers (A)	C	
Pale Cinquefoil	C	
Pepper and Salt	C	
Redstem Ceanothus	C	
Saxifrage (A)	C	
Small-flowered Fringecup	C	
Smooth Fringecup	C	
Spanish Clover	C	
Sticky Geranium	C	
Western Serviceberry	C	
White Spiraea	C	
Woods Rose	C	
Sunflower (Asteridae)	27	
Arrowleaf Balsamroot	A	
Bellflower	C	
Big Sagebrush	A	
Blanket Flower	C	
Blue Lips	C	
Brown-eyed Susan	C	
Common Yarrow	C	
Cut-leaf Daisy	A	
Fleabane	C	
Goldenweed	C	
Hairy Albert	C	
Indian Blanket	C	
Lemonweed	C	
Low Fleabane	C	
Low Pussytoes	C	
Microsteris	A	
Montana Goldenrod	C	
Narrow-leaved Collomia	C	
Prickly Phlox	C	
Salmon Collomia	C	
Spreading Dogbane	A	
Twin Arnica	C	

Western Hawkweed	C	
Whiteleaf Phacelia	C	
Wooly Plantain	C	
Yellow Beardtongue	C	
Yellow Indian Paintbrush	C	
Grass (Commelinidae)	10	
Bluebunch Wheatgrass	A	
Bulbous Bluegrass	A	IO
California Oatgrass	C	
Cheatgrass	A	IO
Idaho Fescue	A	
Japanese Brome	C	IO
Junegrass	C	
One-spike Oatgrass	A	IO
Rye Grass	C	
Small Fescue	C	
Lily (Liliidae)	6	
Death Camas	C	
Grass Widow	A	
Mariposa Lily	C	
Wild Onion (A)	C	
Wild Onion (C)	C	
Yellowbell	C	
FUNGUS (EUMYCOTA)	2	
Puffball (Gastromycetes)	2	
Puffball (B)	C	
Puffball (O)	C	
ANIMAL (ANIMALIA)	25	
Earthworm (Oligocheata)	1	
Lumbriculida	C	
Insect (Insecta)	10	
Bee fly	C	
Blister Beetle	C	
Least Wood Nymph	C	
Lesser Migratory Grasshopper	A	
Ochre Ringlet	C	
Robber fly	C	
Tiger Beetle	C	
Tumbling Flower Beetle	C	
Warrior Grasshopper	A	
Western White	C	
Reptile (Reptilia)	1	
Common Garter Snake	C	
Bird (Aves)	11	
American Crow	C	
American Robin	C	
Brewer's Blackbird	A	
Canada Goose	C	
Cedar Waxwing	C	
Horned Lark	C	
Mourning Dove	C	
Ring-necked Pheasant	C	
Savannah Sparrow	C	
Vesper Sparrow	C	
Western Meadowlark	C	
Mammal (Mammalia)	2	
Human	C	
Western Jumping Mouse	A	

* The critters listed here are those identified as abundant and common.

Legend - Critters are listed by their common name followed by their abundance in the habitat. Introduced species and species at risk are indicated by type code. • **Abundance Codes: A** Abundant, **C** Common, **F** Fairly common, **U** Uncommon, **R** Rare, **V** Vagrant, **K** Known in habitat, **L** Likely in habitat, **M** Missing from habitat. • **Introduced Species Codes: IN** Introduced Noxious species, **IO** Introduced, Other than noxious species. • **At Risk Codes: MS** Missing, **ED** Endangered, **TH** Threatened, **CD** Candidate, **MN** Monitor, **RGM** Regulated Game, **RNG** Regulated Nongame, **RA** Rare, **PB** Protected Breeding Areas.

Selected Critter Descriptions

Nine-leaved Lomatium *(Lomatium triternatum)*

		Class:	Rose (Rosidae)
Family:	Parsley (Umbelliferae)	**Division:**	Flower (Magnoliophyta)
Order:	Parsley (Umbellales)	**Kingdom:**	Plant (Plantae)

Other Names: Biscuitroot (A), Wild Dill
LSW Habitat: GR: C

Relationships To Watershed: Nine-leaved Lomatium may serve as a larval food plant for butterflies and other insects preferring the Umbelliferae families. Fruits may be eaten by seed-eating birds. Nine-leavedLomatium is a possible forage plant for mammalian herbivores and has a history of human use as a vegetable and tea plant.

Description: Nine-leavedLomatium is a perennial forb, 8-32 inches tall. Yellow flowers bloom May - July in compound umbels with unequal rays. Thin, linear leaves generally divided into three leaflets, cleft 2-3 times into long narrow segments 1 to 10, at most 20, cm long, giving the appearance of three "tridents" fused at the ends of the leaves. The root is elongated and thickened but not tuberous. Fruit is a dry schizocarp, oblong to elliptic with wings.

Look Alikes: Nine-leavedLomatium may be confused with other linear-leaved lomatiums including Leiburg's Lomatium, *L. orogenioides*, found in meadows and moist bottomlands, which has white flowers; Slender-Fruit Lomatium, *L. leptocarpum*, found on open slopes to meadows and swales especially in heavy clay soils, which has very linear to narrow fruits; and Swale Lomatium, *L. ambiguum*, which is widespread on open slopes and flats, but has a globe-shaped root and does not have an involucel, a secondary whorl of bracts immediately below the flower cluster.

Little Spokane Habitat: Nine-leavedLomatium is found on open slopes and meadows, dry to fairly moist soil, lowland to mid-mountain habitats. Prominent in deeper soil bunchgrass and shrub-grass communities.

World Habitat: Found from southern Alberta and British Columbia to Colorado, Utah, and California.

Spreading dogbane

Spreading Dogbane
(Apocynum androsaemifolium)

		Class:	Sunflower (Asteridae)
Family:	Dogbane (Apocynaceae)	**Division:**	Flower (Magnoliophyta)
Order:	Gentian (Gentianales)	**Kingdom:**	Plant (Plantae)

Other Name: Low Dogbane
LSW Habitats: SA: U, MT: U, DF: U, PP: A, GR: A

Relationships To Watershed: Spreading Dogbane can be toxic to livestock.

Description: Spreading Dogbane is a perennial shrub formed by rhizomes. The stems are erect, branched, leafy and often reddish. The plant grows from 20-70 cm. tall and has a milky sap. Leaves are opposite, narrowly oval to elliptic or oblong. They are short-stalked, 3-8 cm long, spreading and drooping in appearance. Leaf tops are hairless and green while underneath they are paler and usually hairy. Spreading Dogbane has sweet scented, pink or whitish flowers with pink veins. The flowers are bell-shaped with flaring lobes. They are 6-8 mm long and found in terminal and lateral clusters. Fruits are very long, 5-12 cm, paired, skinny, cylindrical pods that contain numerous seeds, each with a long tuft of cottony hairs.

Look Alikes: Spreading Dogbane may be confused with hemp dogbane, *Apocynum cannabinum*, which has yellow-green leaves that are held upright and has greenish-white flowers that are only 2-5 mm long.

Little Spokane Habitat: Spreading Dogbane is found on open hillsides and ridges, on dry, warm, well-drained sites, fields, meadows, roadsides, and also in dry forest.

World Habitat: Spreading Dogbane is a native plant found in much of Canada and all but the southeastern United States.

Opposite Leaves - Leaves across from one another at the same node. Not alternate or whorled.

Found On:
Spreading Dogbane
Common Snowberry
Mountain Maple
Red Twinberry

Oblong Leaf

Found On:
Spreading Dogbane

Common Yarrow
(Achillea millefolium)

		Class:	Sunflower (Asteridae)
Family:	Sunflower (Compositae)	**Division:**	Flower (Magnoliophyta)
Order:	Sunflower (Asterales)	**Kingdom:**	Plant (Plantae)

Other Names: Milfoil, Yarrow
LSW Habitats: SA: F, MT: F, DF: C, PP: C, RK: C, GR: C, DS: A

Relationships To Watershed: Common Yarrow is the most common plant in the Pacific Northwest. Common Yarrow is eaten primarily by deer, pronghorn antelope and sheep when it is succulent in early season. Sage grouse also eat Common Yarrow.

Description: Common Yarrow is an aromatic perennial herb that is rhizomatous. White flowers bloom April-October in numerous heads of 3-5 white rays in a flat-topped corymb. Leaves are alternate, pinnately dissected with the cauline leaves being sessile and the lower leaves having petioles. They grow up to 6 inches long and have a fern-like appearance. The stem is erect and from 4-40 inches tall. It is a single stem with some side branches. Fruit is an achene.

Look Alikes: Common Yarrow has fern-like leaves that are very distinctive. Scarlet Gilia, *Gilia aggregata*, leaves are also pinnated but do not have any fine leaflets. At subalpine and alpine elevations over 8000 feet, the variety *alpicola* is differentiated by dark brown to black involucral bract margins.

Little Spokane Habitat: Common Yarrow grows in a wide range of sites. From plains to subalpine in dry, open areas. Common Yarrow can exist with a wide variety of plants from bunchgrass to forests.

World Habitat: Common Yarrow is wide ranging from Manitoba to British Columbia, south to Kansas, New Mexico, Arizona, California and northern Mexico.

Ray Flower - A ray or strap-like, ligulate, flower of the sunflower family. Not a disk flower.

Found On:
Common Yarrow
Western Coneflower

Bluebunch Wheatgrass *(Agropyron spicatum)*

		Class:	Grass (Commelinidae)
Family:	Grass (Graminae)	**Division:**	Flower (Magnoliophyta)
Order:	Grass (Poales)	**Kingdom:**	Plant (Plantae)

LSW Habitats: PP: C, RK: C, GR: A

Relationships To Watershed: Highly palatable and nutritious. Used extensively by elk.

Description: Bluebunch Wheatgrass is a caespitose, tufted, perennial that may exhibit rhizomatous tendencies at higher elevations on warm, moist sites. Leafage is usually 12-16 inches tall and the culms are up to 3 feet tall. Blades are flat to slightly inrolled and are prominently veined on the upper surface with a bluish appearance. The auricle at the leaf base on the culm is reddish to purplish. The inflorescence consists of an erect spike that is 3-6 inches long and the spikelets are one per node that is 1/2-3/4 inch long, and 6-8 florets. Glumes are acute to acuminate and the lemma is awned and up to 3/4 inch long. Flowers bloom June-August.

Look Alikes: Bluebunch Wheatgrass may be confused with the following: bearded wheatgrass, *Agropyron caninum*, has crowded spikelets; intermediate wheatgrass, *Agropyron intermedium*, is unawned; pubescent wheatgrass, *Agropyron trichophonem*, is short and pubescent.

Little Spokane Habitat: Bluebunch Wheatgrass lives on hot, dry slopes in grasslands to warm dry forest fringe. Bluebunch Wheatgrass is found on shallow soil scablands.

World Habitat: Bluebunch Wheatgrass is found from Alaska to California and east to the Dakotas and New Mexico. Bluebunch Wheatgrass is widespread east of the Cascades.

Idaho Fescue *(Festuca idahoensis)*

Family:	Grass (Graminae)	Class:	Grass (Commelinidae)
Order:	Grass (Poales)	Division:	Flower (Magnoliophyta)
		Kingdom:	Plant (Plantae)

Other Names: Blue Bunchgrass, Fescue (D)
LSW Habitats: PP: F, GR: A

Relationships To Watershed: Idaho Fescue is relished by elk in canyons in the spring.

Description: Idaho Fescue is a strongly caespitose perennial that is nonrhizomatous. The foliage is between 3-10 inches tall with the culms growing up to 2 1/2 feet tall. Basal leaves are fine, 2-5 inches long with a green to bluish cast. They have tightly inrolled blades without auricles. The inflorescence consists of a narrow panicle that is 3-6 inches long with erect and ascending spikelets.

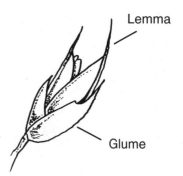

Spikelet - The grasses and sedges flower unit, ultimate flower cluster.

Lemma

Glume

Found On:
Idaho Fescue
cheatgrass
Pinegrass

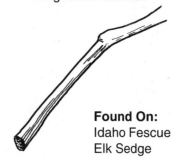

Clum - A hollow or pithy stalk or stem, of grasses, sedges and rushes.

Found On:
Idaho Fescue
Elk Sedge

Cespitose - growing in tufts or clumps

Found On:
Idaho Fescue

Brome

Death Camas

There are 5-7 florets per spikelet. Lemma is stout, straight and has a short awn about 1/8 of an inch. They flower from May-July.

Look Alikes: Idaho Fescue may be confused with the following: Western Fescue (*Festuca occidentalis*) whose leaves are light green, shorter and the panicle is open and drooping; Rough Fescue (*Festuca scabrella*) is unawned; Sheep Fescue (*Festuca ovina*) has a congested panicle and the foliage is yellow-green; Green Fescue (*Festuca viridula*) which has flat blades.

Little Spokane Habitat: Idaho Fescue is found from grasslands to dry and rocky mountain slopes and meadows. It is often associated with bluebunch wheatgrass and extends with Prairie Junegrass into the Ponderosa Pine forest fringe.

World Habitat: Idaho Fescue is a native grass found from British Columbia southward in the Olympics and Cascades to Sierras and eastward to the Rockies.

Death Camas
(*Zigadenus venenosus*)

		Class:	Lily (Liliidae)
Family:	Lily (Liliaceae)	**Division:**	Flower (Magnoliophyta)
Order:	Lily (Liliales)	**Kingdom:**	Plant (Plantae)

Other Names: Deadly Zigadenus, Grassy Death Camas, Meadow Death Camas
LSW Habitats: RK: U, BU: C, GR: C

Relationships To Watershed: Death Camas has the greatest rangeland use in the spring when it's succulent. Sheep are primary class of livestock lost to poisoning from the high concentrations of alkaloids. Fatal losses are greatest on early use of spring rangeland where death camas occurs. The bulbs are poisonous to humans.

Description: Death Camas is a perennial which has an ovoid bulb up to 1 inch long. The bulb has a dark coat. Stems are slender, from 8-20 inches long and have few cauline leaves. Death Camas has white to cream-colored flowers with unequal tepals, the outer being ovate and pointed at the tip and the inner being longer up to 8 mm.

Flowers bloom March-July in a 4-8 inch long raceme that has some branching at the raceme base. Death Camas can be extremely poisonous if eaten.

Look Alikes: Death Camas may be confused with the following: Glaucous Zigadenus, *Zigadenus elegans*, which has larger flowers with the tepals being greater than 8 mm; Panicled Death Camas, *Zigadenus paniculatus*, which has its inflorescence being a panicle and only staminate flowers occur at the inflorescence base; Common Camas, *Camossia quamash*, which has purple to blue flowers.

Little Spokane Habitat: Death Camas is found in openings of the lower mountain forests, sagebrush slopes, and grassy slopes and ridges. It is also found in moist meadows, vernal depressions and seepages with common camas, *Camassia quamash*.

World Habitat: Death Camas is a native plant that is found in British Columbia, south along the east base of the Cascades to north central Oregon; east to Alberta and Saskatchewan; south in the Rockies to Colorado. Death Camas is common in eastern Washington, eastern Oregon, northern Idaho and Montana.

Raceme Inflorescence - An unbranched elongated flower cluster with stalked flowers blooming from bottom upward

Found On:
Death Camas
Pink Wintergreen
Kinnikinnick
Small Oregon Grape
Snowbrush
  Ceanothus
Swamp
  Gooseberry
Wapato
Western Prince's
  Pine
Western Serviceberry

Cauline Leaves - Leaves coming from the stem above ground level

Common Garter Snake
(*Thamnophis sirtalis fitchi*)

		Class:	Reptiles (Reptilia)
Family:	Colubrid Snake (Colubridae)	**Division:**	Vertebrate (Chordata)
Order:	Snake (Squamata)	**Kingdom:**	Animal (Animalia)

Other Name: Garter Snake
LSW Habitats: DF: U, PP: U, GR: C, RP: U, ST: U, HU: C

Relationships To Watershed: Common garter snakes feed primarily on frogs, toads, and salamanders. Small mammals, birds, fish, and even other reptiles are occasionally taken. Like most snakes, this species usually attempts to escape when approached, but some large individuals flatten the head and body and strike viciously. In addition to biting, garter snakes have especially repulsive secretions from the anal musk glands. When captured the snake writhes its body, smearing fecal material and musk over itself and its captor.

Found On:
Death Camas
Common Mullein
Common Yarrow
False Bugbane
Western False Solomon's
  Seal
White-flowered Hawkweed

Scarlet Gilia 's red flowers

Description: Common garter snakes are large, up to 132 cm, heavy-bodied snakes that, throughout most of the Little Spokane Watershed, have some red coloration along the sides of the body and seven upper labials. They are characterized by 19 rows of keeled dorsal scales, 7 upper labials, 10 lower labials, and an average of 163-165 ventrals in males and 158-159 in females, and an average of 81-86 caudals in males and 72-79 in females. In the Pacific Northwest, a dorsal stripe is present but variably expressed, and the lateral stripes are similarly variable.

Look Alikes: The western terrestrial garter snake may also be found in the watershed.

Little Spokane Habitat: Common garter snakes are most common in wet meadows and along water courses, but can be found far from water in open valleys and in deep coniferous forests. They range in elevation from sea level to 2400 meters.

World Habitat: Common garter snakes are the most widespread native snake in North America, ranging from the Atlantic to the Pacific oceans and from the Gulf of Mexico to Fort Smith in the Northwest Territories. The common garter snake is absent from southwestern United States.

Western Racer
(Coluber constrictor mormon)

		Class:	Reptiles (Reptilia)
Family:	Colubrid Snake (Colubridae)	**Division:**	Vertebrate (Chordata)
Order:	Snake (Squamata)	**Kingdom:**	Animal (Animalia)

Other Names: Blue Racer, Racer
LSW Habitats: DF: R, PP: U, BU: R, GR: U

Labials - The upper and lower lip segments of a snake.

Upper Labials

Lower Labials

Yellow salsify

Relationships To Watershed: Western racers consume frogs, lizards other snakes, small mammals, birds, and insects.

Description: Western Racers are snakes with long and slender bodies and long, whip-like tails. Their lengths are from 560-1980 mm. Their heads are large and distinct from the neck. Eyes are large with a round pupil. Body scutes are smooth and the anal plate is divided. The adult dorsal color uniform is grayish or olive becoming greenish or bluish on the lower sides. The ventral color is yellow. They are very agile and very speedy snakes. They are often aggressive and strike readily, sometimes vibrating the tail as well.

Look Alikes: Eleven racer subspecies are somewhat defined. All others occur outside the Pacific Northwest.

Little Spokane Habitat: Western Racers are generally active during daylight. The Racer is also an able climber and is sometimes found in the bushes. Its usual habitat is open, sparsely treed country, but Racers may pass the winter in more forested areas.

World Habitat: Western Racers are a native species occurring over most of the United States and adjacent parts of southern Canada. They are absent from the southwestern United States and the northern Mississippi River area.

Grasshopper on blade of grass

Turkey Vulture *(Cathartes aura)*

		Class:	Bird (Aves)
Family:	Vulture (Cathartidae)	**Division:**	Vertebrate (Chordata)
Order:	Hawk (Falconiformes)	**Kingdom:**	Animal (Animalia)

LSW Habitats: RK: U, GR: U

Relationships To Watershed: Turkey vultures feed on virtually any dead animals down to the size of tadpoles. Nests are found in caves or in hollow stumps with narrow entrances. They are usually made of raked stones, dry leaves and wood chips.

Description: Turkey vultures are large, blackish, soaring raptors with a 6-foot wingspread. They have a small-looking, naked red head with a rather long tail. The light gray secondaries and primaries contrast strongly with the bird's otherwise blackish-brown plumage. The wings are held in a shallow V, called a dihedral, while the bird is in flight. The outer primaries are separated while in flight.

Look Alikes: Turkey vultures may be confused with the following species: bald and golden eagles, *Haliaeetus leucocephalus* and *Aquila chrysaetos*, which hold wings

Teasel

horizontally and not in a V; osprey, *Pandion haliaetus*, which have a kink in the wings when soaring and are white underneath.

Little Spokane Habitat: Turkey vultures are usually seen soaring and perching with wings spread on utility poles and dead trees. They may also be observed roosting in tall woods, or at road kills along highways. They are much harder to find on windless or rainy days.

World Habitat: Turkey vultures are found in southern Canada south to Mexico, Gulf of Mexico, and southern Florida. Found throughout the United States.

Northern Harrier (*Circus cyaneus*)

		Class:	Birds (Aves)
Family:	Hawk (Accipitridae)	**Division:**	Vertebrate (Chordata)
Order:	Hawk (Falconiformes)	**Kingdom:**	Animal (Animalia)

LSW Habitats: GR: F, WL: F

Relationships to Watershed: Northern Harrier's diet consists mainly of voles, but it also includes birds, snakes, frogs, insects and carrion. The Harrier hunts its prey primarily on the wing, quartering fields and marshes. Usually the Northern Harrier hunts within about a ten mile radius, flying up to 100 miles a day.

Description: The Northern Harrier is a slender-bodied hawk with long tail and wings, long slender yellow legs and a conspicuous white rump patch. Adult males are pale gray on the head, back, wings and tail. The tail is also crossed with 6-8 gray-brown bands. The neck, throat, and upper breast are gray becoming paler gray to whitish on the lower breast and belly. The eyes are yellow. Adult females are brownish on the head, back, and wings and the tail is crossed with 6-8 dark brown bands. The neck, throat, and breast are light brown to cream-colored and streaked with darker brown. The eyes are brown.

Look Alikes: May be confused with the Red-tailed Hawk (*Buteo jamaicensis*) and the Rough-legged Hawk (*Buteo lagopus*) which are both larger, have broader wings and proportionately shorter tails.

Butterfly on grass

Butterfly on daisy

Little Spokane Habitat: The Northern Harrier is a bird that inhabits marshlands, grasslands, and prairies. It nests on the ground in dense cover, or occasionally in deeper, more bulky nests built in shallow water.

World Habitat: Common throughout the U.S. and into Canada.

Red-tailed Hawk
(*Buteo jamaicensis*)

		Class:	Birds (Aves)
Family:	Hawk (Accipitridae)	**Division:**	Vertebrate (Chordata)
Order:	Hawk (Falconiformes)	**Kingdom:**	Animal (Animalia)

At Risk: Regulated Non-game
LSW Habitats: MT: U, PP: F, GR: F

Relationships To Watershed: Red-tailed Hawks consume a primary diet of small rodents and rabbits, but also feed on a variety of other mammals including birds, snakes, lizards, and large amphibians.

Red-tailed Hawk

Description: Red-tailed Hawks are large, stocky and broad-winged birds. They are brown to dark brown on the upperparts, often lighter brown on the head and nape, and mottled with white or rufous on the mantle. The upper tail coverts may be whitish suffused with rufous or, more commonly, rufous with brownish or darker rufous barring. The tail is reddish, usually brick-red, with a narrow black subterminal band and a narrow white tip. On the underparts these birds are cream-colored, with variable cinnamon to black streaking on the sides of the breast, a broad band of dark barring and streaking across the belly, and barring on the legs. The wing linings are whitish, with a brown or chestnut-brown patagial stripe and a dark, crescent-shaped wrist patch. The primaries and secondaries are crossed with 6 to 8 narrow dark bars. Dark morphs occur. Immature Red-tailed Hawks have a brown banded tail instead of a red tail.

Red-tailed hawk soaring

Look Alikes: Red-tailed Hawks may be confused with Swainson's Hawks, *Buteo swainsoni,* which only rarely visit the Little Spokane Watershed during migration. Swainson's hawks lack belly bands, have dark bibs in adults and some immatures, and have pale wing linings and dark flight feathers. Ferruginous Hawks, *Buteo regalis,* are larger and immaculate below, with

Cinquefoil flowers

rusty brown legs, whitish tail; Rough-legged Hawk, *Buteo lagopus*, which has large, dark wrist patches and the tail is white at the base and is usually seen in the winter; Red-shouldered Hawk, *Buteo lineatus*, is smaller, has a white crescent-shaped wing patch on outer primaries, adults have 4-7 white bands in tail; Broad-winged Hawk, *Buteo platypterus*, which is notably smaller, with no distinguishing marks on underwings, with no belly bands and 2 white bands in the tail. The last two hawks, Red-Shouldered and Broad-Winged, are not present in Eastern Washington.

Little Spokane Habitat: Red-tailed Hawks are found in a wide variety of habitats, ranging from open woodlands to fields.

World Habitat: Red-tailed Hawks are found in most areas of the United States, Canada, West Indies and Central America.

Brewer's Blackbird *(Euphagus cyanocephalus)*

		Class:	Birds (Aves)
Family:	Warbler(Emberizidae)	**Division:**	Vertebrate (Chordata)
Order:	Thrush(Passeriformes)	**Kingdom:**	Animal (Animalia)

LSW Habitats: BU: A, GR: A, WL: A, LK: A, DS: A, HU: A

Relationships to Watershed: Brewer's Blackbirds feed on spiders, small crustaceans, snails, grass and some forb seeds.

Description: Brewer's Blackbirds are short, chunky birds, 8-10 inches in length. They have conical, sharp-pointed bills and rather flat profiles. The adult male is completely

Cinquefoil

black, and in good light there is a purple iridescence on the head and a green iridescence on the body. Their eyes are creamy white or very pale yellow. The female is mostly smooth, dusty-gray on the lower back, wings, and tail. The eyebrow and throat are paler gray, but do not contrast sharply with the darker crown and face. The eyes are dark brown.

Look Alikes: Brewer's Blackbird male may be confused with the Rusty blackbird, *Euphagus carolinus*. The Rusty blackbird has a bulkier head with a longer bill. They are bulkier overall and have a shorter tail. The female Rusty's eyes are usually dull medium-yellow.

Little Spokane Habitat: The Brewer's Blackbird is common in open country.

World Habitat: Found throughout western U.S.

Northern Pocket Gopher
(*Thomomys talpoides*)

		Class:	Mammal (Mammalia)
Family:	Pocket Gopher (Geomyidae)	**Division:**	Vertebrate (Chordata)
Order:	Rodent (Rodentia)	**Kingdom:**	Animal (Animalia)

Other Name: Pocket Gopher
LSW Habitats: MT: Г, DГ: Г, GΠ: U, DO: Г

Lupine

Kestrel with grasshopper

Relationships To Watershed: Northern Pocket Gophers are nonselective vegetarians, feeding on a variety of roots, bulbs, tubers, and leaves.

Description: Northern Pocket Gophers are small rodents with small eyes and ears, short fur, a relatively short and sparsely haired tail, long foreclaws, heavy shoulders, and small hips for turning in a tunnel. They spend most of their lives underground in tunnels, much as moles do. They are about 8 inches in length and yellowish to grayish-brown in color.

Look Alikes: Often called a mole, which it does not resemble, but closely resembles other species of Pocket Gophers , none of which occur in Eastern Washington.

Little Spokane Habitat: Northern Pocket Gophers seek semiopen areas with fairly deep, soft soil for burrowing. They are most commonly found in mountain meadows, grassy prairies, dry slopes, and pine forest floors.

World Habitat: Northern Pocket Gophers are native gophers found in the intermountain west and adjacent northern plains, ranging from the Prairie Provinces of Canada southward to New Mexico, and from the Sierra and Cascade mountains eastward to Minnesota.

A few remains of a disintigrated tree

Wetland Habitat

Wetland habitat in the Little Spokane Watershed does not fit a stereotype. Wetlands can range from a small seep on a hillside or a damp area in a meadow to springs and even marshes. One definition of wetlands is: "areas that are inundated or saturated by surface or ground water at a frequency and duration sufficient to support . . . a prevalence of vegetation typically adapted for life in saturated soil conditions [and include] marshes, shallow swamps, lakeshores, bogs, muskegs, wet meadows, and estuaries. . . ."

Fallen tree becoming part of the wetland

Snipe among heron tracks

The wetlands of the Little Spokane Watershed are found mostly in flatlands where water accumulates, although these areas may be close to hills or mountains. In many wetland areas a stream may be found nearby which may in part feed the wetland area. Some streams may also run directly into a flatland thereby creating a wetland. It may or may not have an outlet.

A wetland may also be found along a natural wetness gradient between permanently flooded and better drained soils. In other words, a wetland may occur at the periphery of a pond or lake. Rather than having a well defined shore, there may be a region that is marsh-like for at least part of the year.

Because much of the Little Spokane Watershed is in a semi-arid environment, many areas that display wetland characteristics during wetter portions of the year may not appear to be a wetland during the late summer and fall. These areas must be dominated by wetland types of plant communities characterized by species like scouring rush, sedges and cattails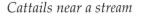

The most successful species are those that can exploit the best of the marsh yet can escape to another habitat when the wetland is flooded or dries up. During seasons of high precipitation or snow melt, the wetlands act like a giant sponge, absorbing much of the water. Wetlands also slow floodwaters. Where functional wetlands have been reduced or eliminated, more severe flooding may result.

A heron colony makes its home in the cottonwoods across the stream

Cattails near a stream

Inter-relationships

Cattails

A plant often found in year-round wetland habitats is the cattail. The fuzzy brown head of the cattail can hold as many as 250,000 seeds, each equipped with a fluffy parachute that catches in the wind or floats atop the water. Cattails also reproduce by sending out a horizontal stem called a rhizome. This stem puts down roots and sends up shoots, creating an entirely new plant.

Each autumn the cattail sends its remaining nutrients into the rhizome before the upper stalk dies. The nutrient rich rhizomes remain alive beneath the winter ice, relying on dead, hollow stalks to snorkel air down to them. The starch of the rhizome fuels early growth in the spring.

The rhizome is also a favorite food of the muskrat who will dive deep to dig them up from the bottom. The rafts of floating plants sometimes seen in a marsh are often the result of feeding by a muskrat. However, the cattail sometimes uses this uprooting to its advantage by floating to new areas and taking root again.

Under balanced conditions, the small-scale harvest of cattails by muskrats can benefit the marsh by providing habitat to migratory waterfowl such as mallards, ring-necked ducks, pintails, goldeneyes and many others. The patches of water opened up by muskrats are used as resting and feeding areas.

Marsh Life

Most vegetation in open marshes grows near the edge due to the shallow water. Plants can utilize unrestricted sunlight while receiving ample moisture much of the year. These thick clusters of plants dampen wave action and create a stable harbor in which frogs, toads, and salamanders lay their eggs. Insects also lay their eggs between, under, and on the plants, providing an

Purple Loosestrife is an invasive noxious weed that can overtake wetlands and stream banks

A former meander, now a wetland filled in with iris

Heron atop cottonwood

abundant source of food to amphibians. In turn, these amphibians give wading birds such as the great blue heron, snakes such as the western terrestrial garter snake, and land mammals such as the coyote and raccoon something to hunt.

The still-standing stalks of last year's plants provide valuable habitat for a variety of breeding birds. Red-winged blackbirds, yellow-headed blackbirds, and marsh wrens stake out their breeding grounds among the cattails. American coots and waterfowl such as northern pintails, redheads, and mallards raise their young in the relative safety of the dense vegetation. As a bonus, each plant harbors the larvae of various insects, providing the high protein diet that ducklings need.

Wetland habitat also provides resources for marsh wrens and shore birds such as common snipes, Virginia rails, and soras. Shore birds are especially well suited at extracting insects from mud or sand. The long, needle-like beaks of shorebirds are very sensitive to touch. The bird probes the soil with its beak and when an insect is detected, the beak automatically snaps shut on the prey.

Sustainability

The wealth of life in wetlands is remarkable. An abundance of decaying organisms quickly recycles nutrients of fallen plants and dead animals. These recycled nutrients are then used by other critters for further growth. When the system is in balance, the wetland habitat continues to be productive. Unfortunately, wetland areas are extremely sensitive to outside interference.

The natural successional pattern for wetlands is for open ponds to become marshes that will become meadows. This pattern can be observed in beaver ponds in the area. Fire in the past has slowed the process down, as have floods which redistribute the sediment and nutrients. Without these, ponds become marshes and marshes become meadows at a faster rate.

Horsetail and watercress

A wetland that is drained and turned into agricultural land loses most of its wetland values and functions. But other actions can be almost as detrimental. Like much of the wildlife, grazing cattle prefer the succulent vegetation of the wetland habitat to that of the upland areas. A herd of cattle that is pastured too long in a wetland area can quickly mow down the green plants, leaving a trampled mudhole. Fertilizer runoff adds excess nutrients to the wetland. Algae thrive on this, creating algae blooms that can choke out other life.

There is more. Because of their sensitivity, the only truly sustainable human relationship with these habitats is to do as little to them as possible. Theoretically, this should not be too difficult since most damage done to wetlands is the indirect result of other actions rather than a deliberate assault on the habitat itself.

Sustainable wetlands depend on more proactive stewardship than some of the other habitats. This responsibility is being taken on by more people as they realize how important wetland habitats are.

Quality of Life Measures

One quick measure of wetland habitat quality of life as a whole is to compare the area that was wetland before 1900 with the area of today's wetlands. Washington state has lost more than 50 percent of its wetlands in the past 150 years. Recognizing that further degradation will create even more serious issues, Washington state has made a commitment to future generations that there should be no further net loss of wetlands. Much can be done in the Little Spokane Watershed to restore wetland values and function where possible and to allow wetlands to become more healthy, thriving, and restorative.

An abundance of vegetation in this wetland

Summary of Wetland Habitat Critters

Number of Species by Kingdom

PLANT (PLANTAE)   71

FUNGUS (EUMYCOTA)   4

ANIMAL (ANIMALIA)   53

PROTIST (PROTISTA)   16

**BACTERIA & VIRUS
(MONERA & VIRUS)**   7

TOTAL IDENTIFIED SPECIES   151

Number of Species by Class

Moss (Bryopsida)	5
Horsetail (Equisetopsida)	3
Magnolia (Magnoliidae)	6
Birch (Hamamelidae)	2
Carnation (Caryophyllidae)	7
Aspen (Dilleniidae)	6
Rose (Rosidae)	5
Sunflower (Asteridae)	16
Water Plantain (Alismatidae)	1
Grass (Commelinidae)	9
Duckweed (Arecidae)	1
Lily (Liliidae)	10
Mushroom (Basidomycetes)	4
Turbellidia (Turbellidia)	1
Spider (Arachnida)	1
Centipede (Chilopoda)	1
Millipede (Diplopoda)	1
Insect (Insecta)	3
Amphibian (Amphibia)	2
Bird (Aves)	35
Mammal (Mammalia)	9
Amoeba (Rhizopoda)	1
Heliozoan (Actimpoda)	1
Foram (Forimaninifera)	1
Sporozoite (Apicomplexa)	1
Zooflagellate (Zoomastigophera)	1
Ciliate (Ciliophora)	1
Dinoflagellates (Dinoflagellata)	1
Golden Algae (Chrysophyta)	1
Diatom (Bacillumiophyta)	1
Euglena (Euglenopphyta)	1
Green Algae (Chlorophyta)	1
Brown Algae (Phaeophyta)	1
Slime Mold - Cellular (Acrasiomycetes)	1
Slime Mold - Plasmodial (Myxomycetes)	1
Mildew (Oomycota)	1
Saprobe (Chytridiomycota)	1
Bacteria (Bacteria)	1
Cyanophycota (Cyanophycota)	1
Prochlorophycota (Prochlorophycota)	1
Bacteria Virus (Bacteria Virus)	1
Plant Virus (Plant Virus)	1
Vertebrate Virus (Vertebrate Virus)	1
Invertebrate Virus (Invertebrate Virus)	1

Selected Wetland Habitat Critters

PLANT (PLANTAE)	50		
Moss (Bryopsida)	5		
Ceratodon purpureus		C	
Drepanocladus aduncus		C	
Mniaceae spp.		C	
Plagiomnium insigne		C	
Polytrichum juniperinum		A	
Horsetail (Equisetopsida)	3		
Field Horsetail		F	
Scouring Rush		C	
Smooth Horsetail		C	
Magnolia (Magnoliidae)	1		
Buttercup (B)		F	
Birch (Hamamelidae)	2		
Mountain Alder		A	
Paper Birch		F	
Carnation (Caryophyllidae)	4		
Bluntleaf Sandwort		C	
Longstem Chickweed		C	
Menzies' Silene		C	
Sticky Chickweed		C	IO
Aspen (Dilleniidae)	5		
Black Cottonwood		C	
Pacific Willow		A	
Scouler Willow		C	
Shooting Star (A)		F	
Stinging Nettle		C	
Rose (Rosidae)	4		
Cup Clover		F	
Small-bead Clover		F	
Touch-me-not		F	
Yampah		F	
Sunflower (Asteridae)	12		
Annual Paintbrush		F	
Bedstraw		C	
Blue Elderberry		F	
Cudweed		F	
Heterocodon		C	
Indian Paintbrush		C	
Longhorn Plectritis		F	
Marsh Speedwell		F	
Mule's Ears		F	
Needle-leaf Navarretia		C	
Owl's Clover		F	
Self-heal		C	
Water Plantain (Alismatidae)	1		
Wapato		F	
Grass (Commelinidae)	8		
Bulrush (C)		C	
Common Cattail		C	
Mannagrass		F	
Panic Grass		F	

Redtop		C	IO
Reed Canary Grass		A	IO
Short-awn Foxtail		F	
Timothy		C	IO
Duckweed (Arecidae)	1		
Skunk Cabbage		C	
Lily (Liliidae)	4		
Camas		C	
Claspleaf Twisted Stalk		F	
Western Blue Flag		C	
Wild Onion (B)		C	
FUNGUS (EUMYCOTA)	2		
Mushroom (Basidomycetes)	2		
Leccinum insigne		F	
Shaggy Mane		F	
ANIMAL (ANIMALIA)	25		
Insect (Insecta)	2		
Gray Hairstreak		F	
Redlegged Grasshopper		C	
Bird (Aves)	17		
Barn Swallow		C	
Black Tern		F	
Brewer's Blackbird		A	
Cliff Swallow		C	
Common Yellowthroat		C	
Great Blue Heron		F	MN
Great Horned Owl		F	
Mallard		C	
Marsh Wren		F	
Northern Harrier		F	
Northern Rough-winged Swallow		C	
Osprey		C	MN
Red-winged Blackbird		A	
Tree Swallow		C	
Tundra Swan		C	
Yellow-headed Blackbird		C	
Yellow-throat		F	
Mammal (Mammalia)	6		
Coyote		F	
Dusky Shrew		C	
Masked Shrew		C	
Muskrat		F	
Striped Skunk		F	
Vagrant Shrew		C	
PROTIST (PROTISTA)	1		
Green Algae (Chlorophyta)	1		
Green Algae		C	

* The critters listed here are identified as abundant, common and fairly common.

Legend - Critters are listed by their common name followed by their abundance in the habitat. Introduced species and species at risk are indicated by type code. • **Abundance Codes: A** Abundant, **C** Common, **F** Fairly common, **U** Uncommon, **R** Rare, **V** Vagrant, **K** Known in habitat, **L** Likely in habitat, **M** Missing from habitat. • **Introduced Species Codes: IN** Introduced Noxious species, **IO** Introduced, Other than noxious species. • **At Risk Codes: MS** Missing, **ED** Endangered, **TH** Threatened, **CD** Candidate, **MN** Monitor, **RGM** Regulated Game, **RNG** Regulated Nongame, **RA** Rare, **PB** Protected Breeding Areas.

Selected Critter Descriptions

Mountain Alder *(Alnus incana)*

		Class:	Birch (Hamamelidae)
Family:	Birch (Betulacae)	**Division:**	Flower (Magnoliophyta)
Order:	Oak (Fagales)	**Kingdom:**	Plant (Plantae)

Other Names: Alder, Thinleaf Alder
LSW Habitats: MT: F, WL: A, RP: A

Lenticel - A slightly raised, somewhat corky, often lens-shaped area on the surface of a young stem

Relationships To Watershed: Mountain Alders are nitrogen-fixing plants which benefit the soil and other plants. They are low to moderately palatable for wildlife.

Found On:
Mountain Alder

Description: Mountain Alders are large, deciduous shrubs usually 15 to 20 feet tall. Their flowers are catkins that develop before their leaves. Male catkins are clustered and drooping while the female catkins are small, cone-like clusters on short stalks. They bloom from April to May. Leaves are alternate with doubly serrated margins with an acute or rounded tip. They are of dull green color and they average 2-4 inches with 1/2-1 inch long petioles. The stems are hairy at first and when mature they are grayish-brown with orangish lenticels on the bark. Branching of the plant is alternate. Fruits are small, wingless nutlets enclosed in the female catkins.

Look Alikes: Mountain Alder is readily confused with Sitka alder, *Alnus sinuata*, which has sharply pointed winter buds. The Thinleaf Alder has rounded, blunt buds.

Alder leaves

Little Spokane Habitat: Mountain Alders prefer seepages and areas of high water table. They are often prevalent along streams and meadow margins at lower mountain elevations.

World Habitat: Mountain Alders are found east of the Cascade crest to the Rocky Mountains of Idaho and Montana.

Pith - The spongy central tissue in some stems and roots

Found On:
Blue Elderberry
Common Snowberry
Elk Sedge
Red Twinberry
Small Oregon Grape

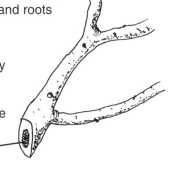

Pith

Blue Elderberry *(Sambucus cerulea)*

		Class:	Sunflower (Asteridae)
Family:	Honeysuckle (Caprifoliaceae)	**Division:**	Flower (Magnoliophyta)
Order:	Teasel (Dispacales)	**Kingdom:**	Plant (Plantae)

Other Name: Elderberry (A)
LSW Habitats: MT: C, PP: R, WL: F, RP: F

Umbel Inflorescence - A flat topped or convex flower cluster arising from a common point, like the struts on a umbrella

Description: Blue Elderberry is a deciduous shrub or small tree with pithy stems. Elderberry flowers are white and borne in a compound, flat-topped umbel. Leaves are pinnately to bipinnately compound and the leaflets are serrated. Fruits are berrylike, juicy and have 3-5 small, seedlike stones within. The fruits are coated with a waxy powder, glaucous, and appear pale powdery blue.

Found On:
Blue Elderberry

Look Alikes: Blue Elderberry may be confused with black elderberry (*Sambucus racemosa*) which has a pyramidal umbel and the fruits are black or purplish-black.

Little Spokane Habitat: Blue Elderberry is very widespread and diverse. It is found in many habitats throughout the Little Spokane Watershed

World Habitat: Blue Elderberry is a widespread native species.

Skunk Cabbage *(Lysichitum americanum)*

		Class:	Duckweed (Arecidae)
Family:	Duckweed (Lemnaceae)	**Division:**	Flower (Magnoliophyta)
Order:	Duckweed (Arales)	**Kingdom:**	Plant (Plantae)

LSW Habitats: WL: C, RP: C, ST: U

Skunk Cabbage

Relationships To Watershed: Skunk Cabbage smells like dead animals, dog dung and stale urine. It is the odor that attracts carrion beetles, blowflies, or other insects that normally lay their eggs on small things that can be eaten by their larvae. While the insects are hanging out on the spike they pick up pollen that they then carry to other flowers for pollination.

Description: Skunk Cabbage is a robust perennial that grows from 30-150 cm tall. This plant grows from fleshy upright underground stems. The leaves are clustered in a large basal rosette and are lanceolate to broadly elliptic in shape. They are very large (to 1.5m long by 0.5m wide), thin and tapering to short, stout winged stalks. There are numerous flowers of greenish-yellow color arranged on a spike on a thick fleshy axis. This is hooded by a bright yellow large bract that appears before or with the leaves in early spring. The fruits are berry-like and pulpy, green to reddish in color and embedded in the fleshy flower spike. This plant has a skunky odor, especially when flowering.

Look Alikes: Skunk Cabbage is distinct.

Little Spokane Habitat: Skunk Cabbage is found near swamps, fens, muskeg, wet forests, mucky seepage areas and wet meadows at low to mid elevations.

World Habitat: Skunk Cabbage is found from Alaska to California, east to Montana and Idaho.

Western Blue Flag
(*Iris missouriensis*)

		Class:	Lily (Liliidae)
Family:	Iris (Iridaceae)	**Division:**	Flower (Magnoliophyta)
Order:	Lily (Liliales)	**Kingdom:**	Plant (Plantae)

Other Names: Blue Flag Iris, Iris (A)
LSW Habitats: WL: C

Stinging nettles

Blue flag flower

Relationships To Watershed: Western Blue Flag is poisonous, especially the rhizomes.

Description: Western Blue Flag has large, delicate pale blue or blue-violet flowers that often have purple veins. They bloom at the top of a stout leafless stalk that grows from dense clumps of tough sword-shaped leaves.

Look Alikes: Western Blue Flag is distinct.

Little Spokane Habitat: Western Blue Flag is found

Iris seed head

in meadows and stream banks, always where moisture is abundant until flowering time.

World Habitat: Found from British Columbia to southern California, east of the Cascade Mountains and Sierra Navada, east to southern New Mexico, Colorado, and North and South Dakota.

Pacific Tree Frog *(Pseudacris regilla)*

		Class:	Amphibians (Amphibia)
Family:	True Frog (Ranidae)	**Division:**	Vertebrate (Chordata)
Order:	Frog (Anura)	**Kingdom:**	Animal (Animalia)

At Risk: Candidate Species
Other Names: Tree Frog
LSW Habitats: PP: U, BU: R, GR: R, WL: U, RP: U, ST: U, LK: U, HU: R

Relationships To Watershed: Pacific Tree Frogs have sticky pads on the front and hind toes that enable them to climb freely about vegetation in search of food such as spiders and insects.

Pacific tree frog

Canary reed grass

Description: Pacific tree frogs have conspicuous dark masks extending from the nostrils to the shoulders, and relatively long, slender legs. The toes are tipped by round toe pads and webbing is extremely limited. Above, the smooth, moist skin may appear green, brown, reddish, bronze, or pale gray. Most individuals are marked above with a Y-shaped figure between the eyes and irregular, dark stripes or blotches on the back. The belly and chest are creamy white and rough textured.

Look Alikes: Pacific tree frogs have distinctive toe pads present on the tips of their toes. Other frogs have distinct spots.

Little Spokane Habitat: Pacific tree frogs live in a variety of habitats, at times quite far from the nearest body of water. Suitable habitats may include woodlands, meadows, pastures, and even many urban sites.

World Habitat: Pacific Tree Frogs are the most widely distributed frog in Washington and Oregon.

Great Blue Heron *(Ardea herodias)*

		Class:	Bird(Aves)
Family:	Heron (Ardeidae)	**Division:**	Vertebrate (Chordata)
Order:	Heron (Ciconiformes)	**Kingdom:**	Animal (Animalia)

At Risk: Monitor Species
Other Name: Heron, Great Blue
LSW Habitats: WL: F, RP: F, ST: F, LK: C

Relationships To Watershed: Great Blue Heron usually hunt by standing motionless in shallow water and waiting for prey to come within striking distance. The Great Blue Heron nests in colonies, heronries, of many nests. Several heronries occur along the Little Spokane. With reduced human interference the heronries have greater chances of remaining in the Little Spokane Watershed.

Great blue heron

Description: Great Blue Heron is a large lean bird, standing about 4 feet tall with a wingspan of 7 feet. Great Blue is one of the largest long-legged birds widely found in the West. They fly with slow, labored wingbeats. The adult has a white head with the sides of the crown and nape black, and short plumes projecting to the rear. The neck is light gray, with a whitish ventral stripe. The bill is large and yellowish, the body is blue-gray and the legs are dark.

Look Alikes: Great Blue Heron may be confused with the following species: great egret, *Casmerodius albus*, is pure white, smaller with a less massive bill and black legs and feet; sandhill crane (*Grus canadensis*) which has entire plumage rather uniform gray or gray-brown, a red crown and a black bill, it flies with its neck fully extended.

A rush seed head

Little Spokane Habitat: Great Blue Heron are found in all wetland environments.

World Habitat: Great Blue Heron are found in south-central Canada, most of the United States, Mexico and South America.

Sora *(Porzana carolina)*

		Class:	Bird(Aves)
Family:	Rail(Rallidae)	**Division:**	Vertebrate (Chordata)
Order:	Rail(Gruiformes)	**Kingdom:**	Animal (Animalia)

LSW Habitats:　WL: U

Relationships to Watershed: Soras often feed at the edge of openings in the marsh or along watercourses. They feed on seeds, snails and other inverts.

Description: Sora is a small bird with a plump body and a yellow bill. It is mostly brown on the upperparts and wings, with heavily barred flanks. The sides of the head and foreneck are gray and the face is black.

Look Alikes: Sora may be confused with the Virginia Rail, *Rallus limicola*, which has brighter plumage and a long, thin bill. Also the Yellow Rail, *Coturnicops noveboracensis*, which does not occur in the watershed and is smaller, has a buff back that is streaked and checkered with very dark markings.

Little Spokane Habitat: Sora inhabits densely vegetated freshwater and salt marshes as well as damp meadows.

World Habitat: Found throughout northern U.S. and southern British Columbia.

Rushes

Common Yellowthroat *(Geothlypis trichas)*

		Class:	Bird(Aves)
Family:	Warbler (Emberizidae)	**Division:**	Vertebrate (Chordata)
Order:	Thrush (Passeriformes)	**Kingdom:**	Animal (Animalia)

Other Name:　Yellowthroat
LSW Habitats:　WL: C, ST: F, LK: F

Relationships to Watershed: Common Yellowthroats feed on spiders and seeds.

Description: Common Yellowthroat is a small, 4 1/2 - 5 3/4 inches, brightly colored bird. The adult male has plain brown-olive upperparts. A broad black mask extends fron the bill and forehead over the eyes across the cheeks to the side of the neck. The mask is bordered posteriorly with a pale blue-gray band. The bird has a bright, warm yellow chin, throat, and breast and a white belly. The adult female lacks the mask. The female's coloring is more brown than olive-brown and the yellow chin and white belly are the same as the male.

Look Alikes: Fairly distinct, especially the males.

Little Spokane Habitat: Common Yellowthroats are found wherever bushes, vines, tangles, or cattails provide sufficient cover. They can be found nesting along streams, ponds, marshes, roadsides, wood margins, brushy pastures, rejuvenated clear-cut forests, and even brushy openings well within the forest.

World Habitat: Found throughout the U.S. and up into Canada.

Yellow-headed Blackbird
(Xanthocephalus xanthocephalus)

		Class:	Bird (Aves)
Family:	Warbler (Emberizidae)	**Division:**	Vertebrate (Chordata)
Order:	Thrush (Passeriformes)	**Kingdom:**	Animal (Animalia)

LSW Habitats: WL: C, LK: C

Relationships to Watershed: The diet consists of spiders, grasses and forb seeds.

Description: Yellow-headed Blackbird is a robin-sized marsh blackbird. The adult male is mostly black with a bright golden-yellow head and breast, a small black mask connects the eyes and the bill. There is a white patch on the wings. The female is noticeably smaller than the male and much duller. It is dusky-brown with a breast and face that are golden-yellow.

Yellow-headed blackbird

Look Alikes: None.

Little Spokane Habitat: The Yellow-headed Blackbird is a marsh-nesting bird that is found mixed with other blackbirds in pastures and agricultural fields and around feedlots.

World Habitat: This bird is common over the western two-thirds of North America.

Riparian Habitat

Riparian habitats are a transition zone found between water bodies and upland areas. Lands along perennially and intermittently flowing rivers and streams, shores of lakes, and reservoirs with stable water levels are typical riparian areas. The word 'riparian' comes from a Latin word for riverbank or river edge.

Rivers, streams, and lakes provide vast amounts of this edge habitat; the vegetative transition between land and water. Riparian habitats offer wildlife the bounties of both water and land.

Healthy riparian habitat can be heavily shaded moist areas. Plants thrive in the moist nutrient-rich soil. Riparian habitats in the Little Spokane Watershed are dominated by broadleaf-deciduous trees like cottonwood, aspen, alder, willow and shrubs like mockorange and ninebark.

A meander along the lower Little Spokane

A garden of life along this riparian edge

River and stream edges are especially important habitats. Unlike other freshwater habitats, lakes and ponds, that have limited, circular shorelines, the river and stream edge becomes a continuous nature corridor that can stretch unbroken for miles. Too often the riparian habitat is the only remaining bit of natural vegetation found in highly developed areas or the only area where large animals can find shade. Elk, moose, and other migrating wildlife use these corridors to safely travel from their high-altitude summer ranges to their lowland winter ranges.

In addition to visual cover and protection from predators, wildlife also find that the temperature in riparian areas fluctuates less than the surrounding areas. The vegetation that overhangs the banks insulates the air, keeping temperatures cool in the summer and somewhat warmer in the winter. Riparian areas also provide easy access to drinking water, protected sites for burrows and nests, and a sunny spot for fruit-producing shrubs to grow, such as elderberry and thimbleberry. Muddy banks are a great place to look for tracks of upland animals that visit the water throughout the day.

Beetle overpowered by ants

Spring view of riparian habitat

Inter-relationships

All Kinds of Critters

Riparian areas serve as havens for all kinds of critters. In fact, riparian habitats have a higher proportion of use by wildlife than any other habitat. However, it is impossible to completely separate the inter-relationships between riparian habitats and the stream and lake habitats; or for that matter, to separate any habitat inter-relationships, they are all inter-related, they 'inter-are'.

Many animals may migrate between these habitats. Amphibians are not necessarily restricted to being submerged in water for their entire lives. Many venture from the water into the riparian habitat when sufficient shade and ground moisture are available.

Massive numbers of insects thrive along riparian habitats. The moist surroundings and plentiful water provide ideal habitat for insects. This habitat includes many plant types; shrubs, the woody stemmed plants; herbs or herbaceous plants, the non woody stemmed plants; forbs, the broad leaf non woody stemmed plants like wildflowers; grasses; rushes, with their hollow pithy stems; and sedges, with a solid stem. In turn, the plentiful insects provide vast quantities of food for birds, amphibians, and reptiles, as well as the fish in the adjacent stream or lake.

Transforming into a dragonfly

Insects a Plenty

Fly on barbed wire

Insects are by far and away the most diverse and successful class of animals on earth. Over half a million species have been named and described and many times more remain to be discovered.

Dragonfly hovering above the water

The majority of an insect's life cycle entails changing, metamorphosis, from a wingless larva, which does most or all of the eating and growing, to a pupa, a transforming, resting stage and finally to an adult who propagates the species.

Sustainability

The riparian habitat is probably the most crucial of all the habitats, as it provides much needed habitat for wildlife. It is difficult to determine what habitat types should be given priority in terms of allowing them to become more restorative. All habitats are crucial to particular species as well as contributing to other factors such as water quality and reduction of erosion.

Sustainable riparian habitats should be relatively simple to keep healthy since they are generally narrow bands along waterways, often in flood zones, and provide little in the way of land useful to agriculture, industry, or homes. Similarly, they do not provide much in the way of "harvestable" resources with the possible minor exception of wild berries, which are essential for birds.

Riparian habitats provide people with excellent opportunities for viewing wildlife in their natural surroundings with usually minor disturbances to the critters daily lives. This can be considered when determining the value and function of the land and what is gained as riparian lands become more restorative.

Quality of Life Measures

Logging and grazing practices can severely affect riparian habitat. Logging even in adjacent upland areas can increase the amount of light in a riparian habitat, decrease the moisture and increase erosion. Over grazing can increase the sediment in the water and reduce vegetation near water which can increase water temperature.

Cottonwoods catching the sunlight

Beaver hut along the riparian edge

Summary of Riparian Habitat Critters

Number of Species by Kingdom

PLANT (PLANTAE) 80

FUNGUS (EUMYCOTA) 18

ANIMAL (ANIMALIA) 175

PROTIST (PROTISTA) 16

**BACTERIA & VIRUS
(MONERA & VIRUS)** 7

TOTAL IDENTIFIED SPECIES 296

Number of Species by Class

Moss (Bryopsida)	24
Nornwort (Authocerotae)	2
Horsetail (Equisetopsida)	1
Fern (Polypodiopsida)	1
Pine (Pinicae)	2
Magnolia (Magnoliidae)	3
Birch (Hamamelidae)	3
Carnation (Caryophyllidae)	6
Aspen (Dilleniidae)	7
Rose (Rosidae)	17
Sunflower (Asteridae)	9
Grass (Commelinidae)	1
Duckweed (Arecidae)	1
Lily (Liliidae)	3
Mushroom (Basidomycetes)	18
Turbellidia (Turbellidia)	1
Earthworm (Oligocheata)	1
Spider (Arachnida)	1
Centipede (Chilopoda)	1
Millipede (Diplopoda)	1
Insect (Insecta)	86
Eel, Lamprey (Cyclostomata)	2
Amphibian (Amphibia)	4
Reptile (Reptilia)	5
Bird (Aves)	62
Mammal (Mammalia)	11
Amoeba (Rhizopoda)	1
Heliozoan (Actimpoda)	1
Foram (Forimaninifera)	1
Sporozoite (Apicomplexa)	1
Zooflagellate (Zoomastigophera)	1
Ciliate (Ciliophora)	1
Dinoflagellates (Dinoflagellata)	1
Golden Algae (Chrysophyta)	1
Diatom (Bacillumiophyta)	1
Euglena (Euglenopphyta)	1
Green Algae (Chlorophyta)	1
Brown Algae (Phaeophyta)	1
Slime Mold - Cellular (Acrasiomycetes)	1
Slime Mold - Plasmodial (Myxomycetes)	1
Mildew (Oomycota)	1
Saprobe (Chytridiomycota)	1
Bacteria (Bacteria)	1
Cyanophycota (Cyanophycota)	1
Prochlorophycota (Prochlorophycota)	1
Bacteria Virus (Bacteria Virus)	1
Plant Virus (Plant Virus)	1
Vertebrate Virus (Vertebrate Virus)	1
Invertebrate Virus (Invertebrate Virus)	1

Selected Riparian Habitat Critters

Category / Critter	Count / Abundance	Extra Code
PLANT (PLANTAE)	46	
Moss (Bryopsida)	13	
Aluacomnium androgynum	C	
Aluacomnium androgynum	C	
Brachythecium albicans	C	
Brachythecium campestre	C	
Brachythecium salebposum	C	
Ceratodon purpureus	C	
Dicranum fuscescens	C	
Funaria hygrometrica	C	
Homalothecium nevadense	C	
Mniaceae spp.	C	
Polytrichum juniperinum	A	
Polytrichum piliferum	A	
Torula ruralis	C	
Horsetail (Equisetopsida)	1	
Scouring Rush	C	
Pine (Pinicae)	1	
Ponderosa Pine	C	
Magnolia (Magnoliidae)	1	
False Bugbane	C	
Birch (Hamamelidae)	3	
Mountain Alder	A	
Paper Birch	C	
River Birch	A	
Carnation (Caryophyllidae)	3	
Broad-leaved Montia	C	
Longstem Chickweed	C	
Sticky Chickweed	C	IO
Aspen (Dilleniidae)	6	
Black Cottonwood	A	
Pacific Willow	A	
Pioneer Violet	C	
Quaking Aspen	A	
Scouler Willow	C	
Stinging Nettle	C	
Rose (Rosidae)	10	
Chokecherry	C	
Coolwort Foamflower	C	
Douglas Hawthorn	C	
Douglas Maple	C	
Mountain Maple	C	
Red Osier Dogwood	C	
Small-bead Clover	C	
Swamp Gooseberry	C	
Thimbleberry	C	
Woods Rose	C	
Sunflower (Asteridae)	5	
Arrowleaf Groundsel	C	
Heterocodon	C	
Indian Paintbrush	C	
Needle-leaf Navarretia	C	
Western Coneflower	C	
Grass (Commelinidae)	1	
Common Cattail	C	
Duckweed (Arecidae)	1	
Skunk Cabbage	C	
Lily (Liliidae)	1	
Western False Solomon's Seal	C	
FUNGUS (EUMYCOTA)	6	
Mushroom (Basidomycetes)	6	
Brown Almond Smelling Waxy	C	
Delicious Milk Cap	C	
Golden-spotted Waxy Cap	C	
Honey Mushroom	A	
Russula olivacea	C	
Velvet Foot	C	
ANIMAL (ANIMALIA)	52	
Insect (Insecta)	35	
Aquatic Dance Fly	A	
Aquatic Longlegged Fly	A	
Biting Midge	A	
Checkered Beetle	A	
Convergent Lady Beetle	A	
Damsel Bug	A	
Damselfly	A	
Dragon Fly	A	
Gall Wasp	A	
Geometrid Moth	A	
Glow-worm	A	
Ground Beetle	A	
Leaf Bug	A	
Leafhopper	A	
Lorquin's Admiral	C	
March Fly	A	
Meadow Grasshopper	A	
Metallic Wood-boring Beetle	A	
Moth Fly	A	
Mourning Cloak	C	IO
Pale Checkerspot	C	
Pelecorhynchidae	A	
Primitive Crane Fly	A	
Satyr Anglewing	C	
Sawfly	C	
Seed Bug	A	
Shore Fly	A	
Skimmer	A	
Spring Blue	A	
Syrphid Fly	A	
Tent Caterpillar	A	
Tiger Beetle	C	
Tiger Moth	A	
Yellow Jacket	C	
Zerene Fritillary	C	
Bird (Aves)	15	
American Robin	C	
Bank Swallow	A	
Black-capped Chickadee	C	
Common Raven	C	
Eastern Kingbird	C	
Great Horned Owl	C	
Hermit Thrush	C	
Killdeer	C	
Lazuli Bunting	C	
Mountain Chickadee	C	
Red-breasted Nuthatch	C	
Song Sparrow	C	
Warbling Vireo	C	
Winter Wren	C	
Yellow Warbler	C	
Mammal (Mammalia)	2	
Striped Skunk	C	
White-tailed Deer	C	RGM
PROTIST (PROTISTA)	1	
Green Algae (Chlorophyta)	1	
Green Algae	C	

* The critters listed here are identified as abundant and common.

Legend - Critters are listed by their common name followed by their abundance in the habitat. Introduced species and species at risk are indicated by type code. • **Abundance Codes: A** Abundant, **C** Common, **F** Fairly common, **U** Uncommon, **R** Rare, **V** Vagrant, **K** Known in habitat, **L** Likely in habitat, **M** Missing from habitat. • **Introduced Species Codes: IN** Introduced Noxious species, **IO** Introduced, Other than noxious species. • **At Risk Codes: MS** Missing, **ED** Endangered, **TH** Threatened, **CD** Candidate, **MN** Monitor, **RGM** Regulated Game, **RNG** Regulated Nongame, **RA** Rare, **PB** Protected Breeding Areas.

Selected Critter Descriptions

Scouring Rush *(Equisetum hyemale)*

		Class:	Horsetail (Equisetopsida)
Family:	Horsetail (Equisetaceae)	**Division:**	Horsetail (Arthrophyta)
Order:	Horsetail (Equisetales)	**Kingdom:**	Plant (Plantae)

Other Name:　Dutch Rush
LSW Habitats:　SA: A, WL: C, RP: C, DS: C

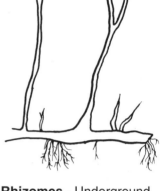

Relationships To Watershed: Scouring Rush is a very hearty plant. It was the first plant to shoot up through the debris of Mount St. Helens in May 1980. Scouring Rush are also known to grow up through cracks in the asphalt on highway shoulders. This plant received its name from its scouring abilities due to the silica-hardened gritty bumps on its skin.

Rhizomes - Underground, often elongated stems, distinguished from a root by the presence of nodes, buds, or scale-like leaves

Description: Scouring Rush is a stout, rhizomatous plant. Its stems are unbranched, hollow and evergreen. They are 1.5 m tall, 3-10 mm thick and have between 14-50 ridges. The stems are bluish-green in color while the sheaths are green to ashy-gray with black bands at the tip and in the middle. The teeth are dark brown to blackish in color. The cones are short-stalked and up to 2.5 cm long. They are hard-pointed and persistent.

Found on
Coolwort Foamflower
Common Snowborry
Common Yarrow
Pinegrass
Spreading Dogbane
Western False Solomon's Seal
Western Prince's Pine
Scouring Rush

Scouring rush and mullein

Look Alikes: Scouring Rush may be confused with northern scouring-rush, *Equisetum variegatum*, which is smaller, thinner and has fewer ridges.

Little Spokane Habitat: Scouring Rush is common on moist to wet sites. It is often found on the banks of major streams and rivers as well as in shaded alluvial forests. This plant also does well in disturbed sites such as roadsides and old fields. It is found at low to mid elevations.

World Habitat: Scouring Rush is found in the Pacific Northwest and south to California and Florida.

Paper Birch *(Betula papyrifera)*

		Class:	Birch (Hamamelidae)
Family:	Birch (Betulaceae)	**Division:**	Flower (Magnoliophyta)
Order:	Oak (Fagales)	**Kingdom:**	Plant (Plantae)

Other Name: Birch (A)
LSW Habitats: MT: F, WL: F, RP: C

Description: Paper Birch is a small to medium-sized deciduous tree that grows to 30 meters tall. The bark is white to copper-brown in color, smooth and marked with brown horizontal lines of raised pores. The bark peels off in papery strips. Leaves are alternate and oval to round in shape. They are sharp-pointed, up to 10 cm long, dull green above, and pale and hairy below. The leaf margins are doubly toothed. Male and female catkins occur on separate trees and are between 2-4 cm long. They flower at the same time or even before the leaves emerge in spring. The catkins break up at maturity. Fruits are nutlets with wings that are broader than the body.

Birch branch decomposing

Look Alikes: Paper Birch may be confused with bitter cherry whose leaves are oblong to oval and less pointy tipped.

Little Spokane Habitat: Paper Birch grows in open to dense woods, and usually prefers a moist environment. It is typically found on well-drained sites but it is also on or around bogs and other wetlands.

Red Osier Dogwood in bloom

World Habitat: Paper Birch is found from Alaska south, mostly east of the Cascades, to northeastern Oregon, east to the Atlantic coast and south to northern Idaho and to Montana, Colorado, Iowa, Illinois and North Carolina.

Petiole - The leaf stalk

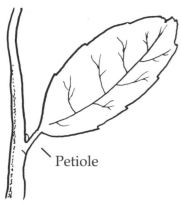

Petiole

Found On:
Arrowleaf Groundsel
Chokecherry
Common Yarrow
False Bugbane
Mountain Alder
Mountain Maple
Quaking Aspen
Redstem Ceanothus
Round-leaved Violet
Thimble Berry
Western Coneflower
White-flowered Hawkweed

Black Cottonwood
(Populus trichocarpa)

		Class:	Aspen (Dilleniidae)
Family:	Aspen (Salicaceae)	**Division:**	Flower (Magnoliophyta)
Order:	Aspen (Salicales)	**Kingdom:**	Plant (Plantae)

Other Name: Cottonwood
LSW Habitats: MT: U, WL: C, RP: A, ST: A, LK: A

Relationships To Watershed: Black Cottonwood resin is an anti-infectant which is used by bees to protect their hives from intruders. Bees seal the intruders, such as mice, in the resin which helps prevent decay and damage to the hive.

Description: Black Cottonwood is a large deciduous tree that grows up to 50 meters tall. The old bark is deeply furrowed and dark gray in color. The buds of this tree are very sticky and fragrant.

Leaves are alternate, thick, and oval in shape. They are from 5-15 cm long with a rounded to heart-shaped base and a sharp-pointed tip. The leaf margin has fine round-teeth. The upper leaf surface is shiny bright green and the under-surface is pale and often stained with patches of brown resin. The leaf stalks are round.

Male and female catkins are found on separate trees. They flower before the leaves appear in spring. Fruits are round, green, hairy capsules that split into 3 parts and expel seeds covered with white fluffy hairs.

Heron flying from nest in a Cottonwood

Gazing up into Cottonwood Branches

Look Alikes: Black Cottonwood bark is fairly distinctive.

Little Spokane Habitat: Black Cottonwood is found on moist to wet sites. They are typically found in bottomlands bordering rivers, streams, lakes and marshes.

World Habitat: Black Cottonwood is common in the Pacific Northwest, also from Alaska to Baja California, on both sides of the Cascades, to southwestern Alberta, western Montana, Wyoming, and Utah. It is, however, a regressing tree species.

Pacific Willow *(Salix lasiandra)*

Family: Aspen (Salicaceae)
Order: Aspen (Salicales)

Class: Aspen (Dilleniidae)
Division: Flower (Magnoliophyta)
Kingdom: Plant (Plantae)

Other Names: Red Willow, Willow (D)
LSW Habitats: PP: F, RK: F, WL: A, RP: A, LK: F

Relationships To Watershed: Pacific Willow is a food-plant for the caterpillars of a number of butterflies and moths. The Western Tiger Swallowtail, Mourning-cloak and Lorquin's Admiral are all found on the leaves of willows.

Description: Pacific Willow is a tall, slender tree or shrub that grows to 12 meters. The bark is fissured and yellowish-brown colored on older trees with brown, glabrous branches. The twigs are glossy with yellow, duckbill shaped buds. Stipules are prominent on the Pacific Willow and have a kidney shape to them.

Leaves are alternate and lance-shaped tapering to a long tip. They range from 5-15 cm long with finely toothed margins. The leaves are regularly about five times as long as wide and taper to a slender point. Young leaves are reddish and densely hairy while older leaves are not hairy but have a whitish bloom beneath.

Flowers are catkins with the male and female occurring on separate trees. The male catkins grow up to 7 cm long while the females grow up to 12 cm long. They have pale yellow bracts that are hairy and present after flowering. Catkins appear with the leaves in spring. Fruits are smooth capsules that are from 4-8 mm long.

Look Alikes: Pacific Willow is unmistakable when its catkins are out, for the male catkins have from 4-9 stamens while other

Alternate Leaves -
Leaves arranged singly, not opposite.

Found on:
Arrowleaf Groundsel
Black Cottonwood
False Bugbane
Kinnikinnick
Mountain Alder
Nootka Rose
Pacific Willow
Paper Birch
Scouler Willow
Swamp Gooseberry
Wax Currant
Western Meadowrue

Catkins Inflorescence -
A flower cluster consisting of a dense spike of unisexual flowers.

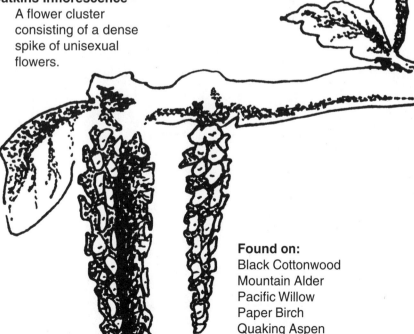

Found on:
Black Cottonwood
Mountain Alder
Pacific Willow
Paper Birch
Quaking Aspen
Scouler Willow

Pacific Willow with galls. A gall is an abnormal swelling of plant tissue caused by insects, microorganisms, or external injury.

Quaking Aspen leaves

willows have only one or two. May be confused with the following: Soft-leaved Willow, *Salix sessilifolia*, which has leaves that are hairy when mature; Sitka Willow, *S. sitchensis*, which has leaves that are hairy when mature; Piper Willow, *S. piperi*, whose leaves are 2-3 times as long as wide and are generally broadest near the middle with bluntly toothed margins; and Scouler Willow, *S. scouleriana*, which is almost independent of water and whose leaf blades are widest above the middle with smooth margins.

Little Spokane Habitat: Pacific Willow is found on river banks, floodplains, lakeshores, and wet meadows. It is often seen standing in quiet, shallow river backwaters.

World Habitat: Pacific Willow is found in the Pacific Northwest. Also from Alaska, Yukon, and back to California, New Mexico and South Dakota.

Quaking Aspen
(*Populus tremuloides*)

		Class:	Aspen(Dillendiidae)
Family:	Aspen (Salicaceae)	Division:	Flower (Magnoliophyta)
Order:	Aspen (Salicales)	Kingdom:	Plant (Plantae)

Other Names: Aspen, Trembling Aspen
LSW Habitats: MT: A, RP: A, ST: A, LK: A, DS: A

Relationships To Watershed: Quaking Aspen leaves are a choice browse for wildlife from elk and beaver to grouse and pika.

Description: Quaking Aspen is generally less than 10 meters tall, growing in easily recognized thickets. The thickets are formed from growth by root suckers, which means that one thicket is usually from the same plant and genetically identical, a clone. This becomes apparent in the fall when the leaves begin to change color. Members of a clone will all turn colors at the same time, while the color changes will vary from one clone to the other.

The bark is powdery white, and the powder can be rubbed away with a finger. The bark is smooth on young trees, becoming darker and rough on older trees. Leaves are up to about 5-6 cm long and are mostly heart-shaped with fine serrations around the margins. The petioles are flexible and strongly flattened at right angles to the blades which enable the leaves to quiver in even the gentlest breeze. Female and male catkins occur on separate trees. The fruits are 1/4 inch conical seedpods that split in 2 to release minute seeds.

Western Baneberry leaf with berries. The berries are bright red.

Look Alikes: Quaking Aspen is easily identified by its bark and leaf shape.

Little Spokane Habitat: Quaking Aspen invades after conifers are logged. They also fill in avalanche tracks and are found along streambeds.

World Habitat: Quaking Aspen is the widest-ranging American tree that covers much of Alaska, Canada, the Northeast and North Central states, the Rocky Mountains, the Pacific Northwest, and the Sierra Madre south to Guanajuato.

Swamp Gooseberry
(*Ribes lacustre*)

		Class:	Rose (Rosidae)
Family:	Rose (Rosaceae)	**Division:**	Flower (Magnoliophyta)
Order:	Rose (Rosales)	**Kingdom:**	Plant (Plantae)

Other Names: Prickly Gooseberry, Swamp Black
LSW Habitats: SA: C, MT: F, BU: F, RP: C

Relationships To Watershed: Swamp Gooseberry are unpalatable. They are the principal species being eradicated as host for white pine blister rust.

Lady Bugs

Description: Swamp Gooseberry are deciduous shrubs, mid-sized up to 6 feet tall. Yellowish-green to pinkish-white flowers bloom in April-July in drooping racemes of 7-15. Alternate leaves are maple-like and 5-lobed. They are up to 2 inches wide with a deeply incised and serrated margin. The upper surface is glossy and the underside is velvety. The stems are armed with spines at nodes and prickles in between with a smooth reddish-brown color. Fruits are purple-black berries with glandular hairs.

Sessile - without a stock
Found on:
Arrowleaf Groundsel
Common Yarrow

Western False
   Solomo's Seal
White-flowered
   Hawkweed

Look Alikes: Swamp Gooseberry may be confused with other gooseberries, *Ribes spp.*, that are armed but the glossy, deeply-incised maple-like leaves are fairly diagnostic.

Little Spokane Habitat: Swamp Gooseberry are found in cool, moist to wet forests and openings in the forest.

Butterflies resting

World Habitat: Swamp Gooseberry is common throughout the west. From Alaska to California in both Olympic mountains and the Cascades and as far east as the Dakotas, Michigan, Pennsylvania and Colorado.

Coolwort Foamflower
(Tiarella trifolata unifoldata)

		Class:	Rose (Rosidae)
Family:	Saxifrage (Saxifragaceae)	**Division:**	Flower (Magnoliophyta)
Order:	Rose (Rosales)	**Kingdom:**	Plant (Plantae)

LSW Habitats: SA: F, MT: C, DF: U, RP: C

Relationships To Watershed: Coolwort Foamflower is unpalatable.

Description: Coolwort Foamflower is a perennial, rhizomatous herb that is low to mid sized from 8-20 inches tall. White flowers bloom in June-August in 5-merous bell-shaped elongated panicles.

Look Alikes: Coolwort Foamflower may be confused with mitreworts, *Mitella spp.*, which has capsules that are saucer-shaped or goldthread, *Coptic occidentalis*, which has shiny leaves.

Little Spokane Habitat: Coolwort Foamflower may be found near cool, moist streamsides and bottom locations. It is prominent in subalpine fir and queen's cup beadlily communities.

World Habitat: Coolwort Foamflower is widespread in the Pacific Northwest.

Arrowleaf Groundsel
(Senecio triangularis)

		Class:	Sunflower (Asteridae)
Family:	Sunflower (Compositae)	**Division:**	Flower (Magnoliophyta)
Order:	Sunflower (Asterales)	**Kingdom:**	Plant (Plantae)

I SW Habitats: SA: F, MT: C, DF: C, PP: C, BU: F, GR: F, RP: C, DS: F

Relationships To Watershed: Arrowleaf Groundsel is palatable to deer and elk.

Cow Parsnip

Description: Arrowleaf Groundsel is a perennial herb that is 1-5 feet tall. Yellow flowers bloom in June-September in numerous heads of flat-topped inflorescence. The leaves are numerous, alternate and triangular-shaped. They are 2-8 inches long with the lower leaves large and having long petioles and the upper leaves becoming smaller and sessile. Fruits are achenes.

Immature American Redstart

Look Alikes: Arrowleaf Groundsel is easily recognized.

Little Spokane Habitat: Arrowleaf Groundsel is found in cool, wet, moist soils at upper elevations under spruce, subalpine fir, and in riparian habitats. It is prominent in twisted stalk, meadowrue and tall bluebell communities.

Song Sparrow feeding open mouths

World Habitat: Widespread in the mountains of the western United States.

Lorquin's Admiral
(*Limenitis lorquini*)

Sub Family: Milkweed Butterflies (Danainae)
        Class: Insect (Insecta)
Family: Brush-footed Butterfly (Nymphalidae)
        Division: Joint-legd. Invrt. (Arthropda)
Order: Butterfly (Lepidoptera)
        Kingdom: Animal (Animalia)

LSW Habitats: DF: C, RP: C, HU: R

Relationships to Watershed: Lorquin's Admiral butterflies are more interested in animal droppings, carrion and decaying fruit than they are in flowers.

Description: The Lorquin's Admiral is a black butterfly with orange wing tips. There are small white dashes surrounding the exterior of the wing and a line of white patches following the curve of the wing about a third of the way into the wing.

Look Alikes: Other admirals are similar but do not occur in the watershed.

Little Spokane Habitat: The larvae are found on willow, cottonwood, and poplar trees, while the butterflies can be found in open clearings.

World Habitat: This butterfly occurs over the entire Pacific Northwest.

Lorquin's Admiral

Mourning Cloak *(Nymphalis antiopa)*

Sub Family:	Milkweed Butterflies (Danainae)	**Class:**	Insect (Insecta)
Family:	Brush-footed Butterfly (Nymphalidae)	**Division:**	Joint-legged Invertebrate (Arthropda)
Order:	Butterfly (Lepidoptera)	**Kingdom:**	Animal (Animalia)

Introduced: Introduced Species
LSW Habitats: RP: C, HU: U

Relationships To Watershed: Mourning Cloak may be found on the following host plants: willows, cottonwood, aspen, maples, siberian elm, paper birch, cow sorrel, rose, thimbleberry and alder.

Description: Mourning Cloak is a butterfly with wings that are bordered by yellow. Along the yellow border are blue spots. The majority of the wing is dark in color.

Little Spokane Habitat: Mourning Cloak frequents tree-lined streams in the sagebrush steppes and woodlands, and occasionally visits yards in residential areas.

World Habitat: Mourning Cloak is an introduced species that occurs throughout the Pacific Northwest. This butterfly ranges throughout the United States.

Raccoon *(Procyon lotor)*

		Class:	Mammal (Mammalia)
Family:	Raccoon (Procyonidae)	**Division:**	Vertebrate (Chordata)
Order:	Carnivore (Carnivora)	**Kingdom:**	Animal (Animalia)

LSW Habitats: MT: R, DF: U, PP: U, BU: F, RP: F, ST: F, LK: F

Relationships To Watershed: Raccoon are opportunistic omnivores that feed on carrion, small mammals, birds, crayfish, insects, fruits, grains, nuts, and whatever else is available. The sense of touch is highly developed in raccoons, and this may account for their well-known habit of washing or feeling foods.

Young Raccoon on the way

Coprinus Mushroom on Cottonwood Bark.

Close-up view of Coprinus

A young skunk on a visit

Description: Raccoon are medium-sized, stocky carnivore with grizzled blackish-gray upper parts. They have a black mask over their eyes and cheeks, and a conspicuously ringed bushy rail. Their toes are long and fingerlike. They usually have a conspicuous hump in the back. Their snouts and ears are pointed.

Look Alikes: None in the Little Spokane Watershed.

Little Spokane Habitat: Raccoon prefer woods and brushy areas near fresh or salt water. They occupy dens in hollow trees and old squirrel nests. They also inhabit caves and mines, abandoned buildings, haystacks, muskrat lodges, and occasionally ground dens.

World Habitat: Raccoon are a native species that range throughout most of North America, from central Canada south to Panama.

Striped Skunk *(Mephitis mephitis)*

	Class:	Mammal (Mammalia)	
Family:	Weasel (Mustelidae)	**Division:**	Vertebrate (Chordata)
Order:	Carnivore (Carnivora)	**Kingdom:**	Animal (Animalia)

Other Name: Skunk
LSW Habitats: DF: U, PP: U, BU: F, WL: F, RP: C, DS: U, HU: U

Relationships To Watershed: Striped Skunks are opportunistic omnivores. Their diet includes mostly beetles and grasshoppers, mainly because of their abundance. Other foods include carrion, small mammals, frogs, lizards, birds, eggs, fruit, worms, spiders, grubs, and garbage.

Description: Striped Skunks are cat-sized mammals about 30 inches long including 7 1/2 inches of bushy tail. Their shiny black fur is long and harsh with soft underfur. They are marked with a broad white stripe down each side of their body, from the top of the head to the base of the tail. They also have a narrow white stripe down the center of their head between their eyes. Their legs are short with strong curved claws.

Their most well-known method of defense is ejecting a nauseous fluid from their anal glands. This amber-colored fluid may travel up to 12 feet and has a most disagreeable and lasting odor that may spread over a radius of 1/2 mile. It can cause blindness if ejected directly into the eyes and it burns the skin and hair. It is not used against another skunk.

Skunks face heavy mortality on roads from vehicles because they stand their ground and rely on their nauseous fluid to resist attack instead of running from danger.

Look Alikes: None.

Little Spokane Habitat: Striped Skunks exhibit no obvious habitat preference but apparently avoid dense forests and marshy areas where dry den sites are unavailable.

World Habitat: Striped skunks are a native species that are found throughout all of the United States and adjacent areas of Canada and Mexico, except coastal marshes and the most arid southwestern deserts.

A view from riparian habitat

Moose *(Alces alces)*

		Class:	Mammal (Mammalia)
Family:	Deer (Cervidae)	**Division:**	Vertebrate (Chordata)
Order:	Deer (Artiodactyla)	**Kingdom:**	Animal (Animalia)

At Risk: Regulated Game
LSW Habitats: MT: U, RP: U, ST: U, LK: U

Relationships To Watershed: Moose are the largest animal in the Little Spokane Watershed.

Description: Moose are large deer that stand 7 or more feet tall at the shoulders. Adults weigh 900-1000 pounds and are

Young Moose

similar in size to horses. Cows are about 3/4 the size of bulls. Moose are blackish-brown in color with a protuberant, rounded snout; short tail, and a "bell" or flap of skin hanging underneath the throat. The males have massive palmate antlers with tines projecting from the edges. Moose are the largest deer in the world.

Look Alikes: There is no other critter like a moose.

Little Spokane Habitat: Moose prefer shrubby, mixed coniferous and deciduous forests, particularly near water. They are commonly found in immediate vicinity of lakes, both mountain and alpine, where they feed on submerged aquatic vegetation. Moose are also found in marshy or swampy areas along streams and rivers.

World Habitat: Moose are a native mammal found in British Columbia, northeastern Washington, northern and eastern Idaho and in the Okanogan Highlands of Washington. Their numbers increase significantly with adequate protection, especially from poaching.

Moose ambling along Horseshoe Lake of the Little Spokane West Branch

Stream Habitat

Stream habitats in the Little Spokane Watershed are made up of a series of small mountain streams that eventually flow together to form the main river of the Little Spokane. Stream habitats also include the aquifer outflows into the lower sections of the Little Spokane.

The major differences among streams are volume of water and speed of flow. Although there is no ideal way of classifying streams into distinct groups, geologists distinguish them by their relative age. By age, geologists mean the erosion or deposition stage, not fixed periods of time. The stages are similar to humans; youth, maturity, and old age. Each is directly related to the steepness of the stream, channel gradient, and hence to the stream's speed. In general, young streams have greater gradients and flow quickly while old streams have low gradients and flow more slowly.

Little Spokane starting from mountain habitat

Stream habitat changes considerably between the higher and lower elevations. The narrow faster flowing higher elevation streams provide habitat for winter wren, varied thrush, northern water thrush and various species of shrew. At the lower elevations of the Little Spokane, streams are wider and slower, providing habitat more to the liking of raccoon, mink, common and hooded merganser and several species of bat.

In the Waikiki Springs area, about ten miles upstream from where the Little Spokane goes into the Spokane River, there is an unusual amount of aquifer water

Aquifer spring flowing out of the hillside

Aquifer water cascading down the hillside

added to the Little Spokane. Here aquifer water significantly adds to the volume of the Little Spokane through a series of seeps and springs. This water coming out of the hillsides creates unique microhabitats which bring additional dynamics to the watershed.

One large outpouring of aquifer water starts about halfway up a dry hillside. There many seeps and springs come together releasing their waters down the hillside. From a distance a loud rush of water, almost like ocean waves, can be heard as these waters run together, cascading down the hillside. At the bottom of the hill, the water is like a glacial stream high in the mountains rushing down the last rocks to its stream bed. All this happens in less than a couple hundred feet. This steam is called Wai Nui which is Hawaiian for big fresh water.

Inter-relationships

How Streams Develop Themselves

The relatively small size of many of the Little Spokane's streams indicate that they are young streams. These youthful streams are characteristic of mountainous areas where water flows rapidly and erodes quickly. They transport solids by carrying smaller particles in suspension and rolling or pushing larger rocks and debris along the bottom. The faster the water moves, the larger the rocks it moves. The harder rocks in the stream path tend to erode more slowly and result in the formation of rapids and riffles.

Youthful streams tend to flow straighter than older streams and the water in youthful streams is generally shallow except for small pools such as those found below waterfalls and fallen logs. Spring high water helps undercut the banks, providing additional habitat for fish and other critters.

The lower section has characteristics of an old stream with a large series of meanders and old oxbows. The winding meanders weave their way through broad floodplains. They slow the flow of the stream and allow more and wetter habitats to thrive. The floodplains act as giant sponges. During spring floods new channels can be formed by cutting off a part of a meander curve. This abandoned meander curve, an oxbow, becomes a pond and eventually fills in becoming part of the floodplain.

Where streams have been channelized, the value and function of the floodplains can be significantly degraded. The flow of the stream is much faster in channelized streams and the ability of the floodplain to act as a sponge is significantly reduced. During floods the channelized water runs even faster which can cause additional damage further downstream.

Riffles and Pools

Turbulent flows add oxygen to water, making these younger streams much

Sunlight reflected off riffles along a Little Spokane meander

higher in dissolved oxygen than ponds or lakes. Because of this, biological communities in these streams differ substantially from ponds or lakes. In streams food webs are mostly predatory because of the decrease in biomass from plants. Lakes and ponds have a large stationary food source, plankton, which is quickly washed away in streams. Streams replenish food supplies from organic materials washed into the stream by runoff.

As water in the rapids encounters the friction of the rocky bottom, the ensuing turbulence raises particles of sand and silt and keeps them suspended in the water. When this silt-laden water slams against a boulder or log, the rebounding wave is forceful enough to pick up and carry even larger particles. The result is that riffles are usually swept clean of all movable sand and other particles, leaving only heavier cobbles and gravel. This tidy rocky bed supports more kinds of life than a shifting bed of scouring sands. Riffles allow the rocky surfaces to become homes for insect larvae, planaria, algae, and other critters that attach themselves to these welcoming rocks. Stonefly nymphs, black fly larvae, caddisfly larvae, tadpoles and the tailed frog can all be found here.

Salmon Beds

These cleaned gravel stream beds are perfect places for salmon to spawn. Less than 100 years ago these streams were the initial homes of tens of thousands of salmon before they made their journey to the Pacific Ocean. After their life in the ocean, they returned home to the Little Spokane to spawn the next generation of salmon before they died.

Some of the dams built on the Spokane and Columbia rivers were built without fish passages which prevented the annual salmon migrations, locking the salmon out of the watershed. With the re-establishment of adequate passages to and from the Pacific Ocean, salmon can once again bring an abundance of life to the Little Spokane Watershed.

Moss covered log in clear water

A Turbulent Life

For some organisms the current in these riffles is a blessing. The current acts as a continuous conveyer belt delivering bits of food from upstream such as leaves and twigs that have fallen into the stream or insects that have been dislodged from the rocks. The constant churning of the water mixes oxygen into the water while continuously flushing away wastes.

This same current creates a challenge along the banks by constantly prying loose anything that is not well anchored in place. Stream critters are outfitted in a variety of ways to battle the force of moving water. Some simply avoid the current by living in the eddies behind rocks or burrowing into the stream bed. Snails, stonefly nymphs, and flatworms find refuge on the quiet underside of rocks.

Other organisms actually use the current to keep them plastered against the rock or to help them snag a passing meal. The caddisfly larva, hydropsyche, builds a funnel-shaped net attached to a rock. Periodically, it creeps out from its crevice to harvest the tiny plants and animals caught in the net. Black fly larvae have feathery brushes on their heads that comb bits of food from the passing water. The adults line up on the rocks in dense colonies, their legs clamped tightly to the slippery rocks.

Also growing on the tops of rocks are colonies of algae, bacteria and other tiny creatures. The slimy stream algae are familiar to anyone who has tried to pick their way across a stream, stepping only on rocks. Luckily, stream algae reproduce new generations of algae faster than any other kind of algae, quickly replacing the colony scraped off when boots slip and slide across these rocks.

For many animals, places where the water is still and deep are more appealing than turbulent water. Such pools may contain crayfish and various fish such as cutthroat trout. These fish feed on nearly any aquatic

Garter snake eating a sculpin that was caught in the stream

insect they can find, as well as the large number of other insects that fall from trees and bushes overhead.

Amphibians do not necessarily spend all of their time in the water. They are, after all, amphibious. All amphibians hatch in water as gilled, water-breathing, legless, swimming larvae, later metamorphosing into adults that spend time on land, returning to the water to breed. Amphibians lack an effective moisture barrier in either their skin or their eggs, so to avoid deadly drying they must return to the water frequently, venturing from it mainly at night or in the shade.

Nymphs of mayflies, damsel flies, and dragonflies are also common in stream pools. During the summer months, the air above a stream comes alive as the stream larvae crawl out among the rocks and begin to transform into flying adults. Hatching insects float up from the bottom and struggle to break free from the surface or they crawl onto rocks or logs. Those that hesitate are whisked down stream to hungry trout. Those that make it to the air are often scooped up by bats, flycatchers, swallows, and swifts. Those that stop to rest on the leaves of streamside shrubs may wind up in the beaks of warblers, sparrows, and thrushes. Life is full of unexpected surprises for aquatic insects. It quickly becomes understandable why many of these insects make so many offspring just to keep their species alive, which in turn allows other species to make a living.

Another beginning of the Little Spokane

Heron colony nests high in the cottonwoods

Sustainability

Streams are very important not only to the critters that live there, but also to the thousands of other species that rely on the streams for their food, shelter, and drinking water. Too often streams become less than healthful due to human practices that pollute the water. Sometimes only the symptoms of the unhealthful streams are treated instead of the actual issues. Powerful chemicals or even biocides are used on stream water in an attempt to make the water safer for humans to drink.

One of the most insidious threats to clear, clean-running streams is the removal of streamside vegetation. Once there are no roots to hold the soil, vast plumes of silt may bleed into the water, irritating the gills of fish and amphibians while blocking the light that algae need to grow. Unsustainable logging practices too near streams can also send large silt plumes down stream.

When this silt settles to the bottom, it chokes the gravel community. As the smothered community decays, it uses more and more oxygen. At the same time, the unfiltered sun heats the stream, thus reducing the stream's ability to hold dissolved oxygen. This forces out sensitive species such as trout, amphibians, and many aquatic insects. Once a critter population cycle has been disrupted, these negative effects may compound their impact on the remaining populations, sending them into a long term decline. It can take many years to once again establish thriving, healthy populations.

Equally alarming results occur when acids, toxic chemicals, fertilizers and biocides such as insecticides, fungicides, herbicides, and pesticides, get into the stream from less than sustainable human practices. Rather than the normal cleaning action of a stream current, the current merely spreads the contaminants over a larger area down stream.

A more sustainable relationship between humans and the stream habitat can benefit everyone. Many people involved in agriculture depend on stream water for irrigation, cattle, and even for their own use. Steps are being taken to minimize these and other impacts on streams and to allow streams to become more healthy and more restorative.

Wood duck on its box nest

Cattle are being fenced off from streams and watered through use of gravity fed watering troughs that reduce damage to streams. This allows stream vegetation to thrive, stream temperature to stay cooler, less raw organic matter to go into the stream, and the fish and invertebrate habitats to become more restorative. Irrigation-intensive crops are being replaced with crops requiring less water. Activities that may cause loss of vegetation along the stream banks are being avoided by many of the people who live and work in the Little Spokane Watershed.

Quality of Life Measures

Many invertebrates have adapted to streams by attaching to rocks. Studies can be made of the macro-invertebrates in the streams. Because invertebrates vary in their tolerance to pollution, they can be divided into three groups: Class I, pollution intolerant; Class II, somewhat pollution tolerant; and Class III, pollution tolerant.

By studying the invertebrate diversity in a stream, you can get a feel for the health of the stream and nearby habitats. The macro-invertebrates can be counted and compared to other steam counts, and baselines can be established. As stream health becomes more restorative, the macro-invertebrate counts will improve, showing the increase in biodiversity. As biodiversity increases some critters can become more abundant and critters seldom seen in recent years can re-establish themselves.

Another sign of restorative stream health is that water quality measures can show marked improvement and stream flows can increase. Unfortunately over the past 30 years, the annual stream flow of the Little Spokane has declined by about 25 percent. An example of reversing this destructive trend is to reduce irrigation during dry summers and to see the almost immediate increase in stream flows.

Instead of dry stream beds and the associated loss of life, healthier stream beds can be encouraged. As these flow rates increase, the Little Spokane Watershed can become more healthy. With more shade over the streams, insect counts will increase along with the numbers and kinds of birds. Measures of biodiversity will significantly increase as the streams become more restorative.

A lower Little Spokane meander and oxbow

Summary of Stream Habitat Critters

Number of Species by Kingdom

PLANT (PLANTAE)   18

FUNGUS (EUMYCOTA)   0

ANIMAL (ANIMALIA)   276

PROTIST (PROTISTA)   15

**BACTERIA & VIRUS
(MONERA & VIRUS)**   7

TOTAL IDENTIFIED SPECIES   316

Number of Species by Class

Magnolia (Magnoliidae)	1
Aspen (Dilleniidae)	5
Rose (Rosidae)	3
Sunflower (Asteridae)	4
Grass (Commelinidae)	2
Duckweed (Arecidae)	1
Lily (Liliidae)	2
Hydrozoa (Hydrozoa)	1
Turbellidia (Turbellidia)	2
Clam (Pelecypoda)	1
Snail (Gastropoda)	3
Earthworm (Oligocheata)	2
Leech (Hirudinea)	1
Crustacean (Crustacea)	11
Centipede (Chilopoda)	1
Millipede (Diplopoda)	1
Insect (Insecta)	140
Bony Fish (Osteichthyes)	45
Amphibian (Amphibia)	2
Reptile (Reptilia)	3
Bird (Aves)	54
Mammal (Mammalia)	9
Amoeba (Rhizopoda)	1
Heliozoan (Actimpoda)	1
Foram (Forimaninifera)	1
Sporozoite (Apicomplexa)	1
Zooflagellate (Zoomastigophera)	1
Ciliate (Ciliophora)	1
Dinoflagellates (Dinoflagellata)	1
Golden Algae (Chrysophyta)	1
Diatom (Bacillumiophyta)	1
Euglena (Euglenopphyta)	1
Green Algae (Chlorophyta)	1
Brown Algae (Phaeophyta)	1
Red Algae (Rhodophyta)	1
Mildew (Oomycota)	1
Saprobe (Chytridiomycota)	1
Bacteria (Bacteria)	1
Cyanophycota (Cyanophycota)	1
Prochlorophycota (Prochlorophycota)	1
Bacteria Virus (Bacteria Virus)	1
Plant Virus (Plant Virus)	1
Vertebrate Virus (Vertebrate Virus)	1
Invertebrate Virus (Invertebrate Virus)	1

Selected Stream Habitat Critters

PLANT (PLANTAE)	15		
Magnolia (Magnoliidae)	1		
Indian Pond Lily		F	
Aspen (Dilleniidae)	5		
Black Cottonwood		A	
Geyer's Twinpod		F	
Quaking Aspen		A	
Slender Willow		F	
Watercress		C	
Rose (Rosidae)	3		
Purple Loosestrife		A	IN
Red Osier Dogwood		C	
Touch-me-not		F	
Sunflower (Asteridae)	2		
American Brooklime		C	
Wild Mint		C	
Grass (Commelinidae)	2		
Common Cattail		A	
Panic Grass		F	
Lily (Liliidae)	2		
Tiger Lily		F	
Yellow Flag Iris		A	IN
ANIMAL (ANIMALIA)	150		
Hydrozoa (Hydrozoa)	1		
Hydra sp.		F	
Turbellidia (Turbellidia)	1		
Tricladidae		F	
Clam (Pelecypoda)	1		
Clam		F	
Snail (Gastropoda)	3		
Lymnea auriculais		F	
Lymnea stagnalis		F	
Pisidium sp.		F	
Earthworm (Oligocheata)	2		
Lumbriculidae		F	
Naididae		F	
Leech (Hirudinea)	1		
Piscicola sp.		F	
Crustacean (Crustacea)	7		
Calanoid		F	
Cyclopoid		F	
Gammarces lacustris		F	
Gammaridae		F	
Harpacticoid		F	
Pacifastacus sp.		F	
Talitridae		F	
Insect (Insecta)	92		
Aeshna sp.		F	
Allocosmoecus sp.		F	
Alloperla sp.		F	
Amphicosmoecus canax		F	
Amphineura sp.		F	
Anabolia bimaculata		F	
Antocha sp.		F	
Apatania sp.		F	
Asynarchus aldinus		F	
Atherix sp.		F	
Attenella margarita		F	
Bezzia sp.		F	
Brychius sp.		F	
Calineura californica nymphs		F	
Chelifera sp.		F	
Chloroperla sp.		F	

Cinygmula sp.		F	
Clinocera sp.		F	
Cnephia sp.		F	
Coptomus sp.		F	
Despaxia augusta		F	
Dicosmoecus gilvipes		F	
Dicranata sp.		F	
Diura knowltoni		F	
Drunella flavilinea		F	
Drunella grandis		F	
Ecclisomyia sp.		F	
Rove Beetle		C	
Stonefly		A	
Bony Fish (Osteichthyes)	6		
Bridgelip Sucker		F	
Carp		C	IO
Rainbow Trout		F	RGM
Smallmouth Bass		F	IO
Walleye		C	IO
White Crappie		F	IO
Amphibian (Amphibia)	1		
Bull Frog		F	IN
Reptile (Reptilia)	1		
Western Painted Turtle		F	RNG
Bird (Aves)	31		
American Coot		F	
American Dipper		F	
American Robin		C	
Bank Swallow		A	
Blue-winged Teal		F	
Canada Goose		F	
Cedar Waxwing		C	
Cinnamon Teal		F	
Cliff Swallow		F	
Common Goldeneye		F	
Common Merganser		C	
Common Yellowthroat		F	
Gray Catbird		F	
Great Blue Heron		F	MN
Great Horned Owl		C	
Greater Yellowlegs		F	
Green-winged Teal		F	
Lesser Scaup		C	
Mallard		C	
Mountain Chickadee		C	
Northern Oriole		F	
Northern Pintail		F	
Northern Waterthrush		F	
Song Sparrow		C	
Spotted Sandpiper		F	
Spotted Towhee		F	
Varied Thrush		F	
Violet-green Swallow		A	
Willow Flycatcher		C	
Winter Wren		C	
Yellow Warbler		F	
Mammal (Mammalia)	3		
Mink		F	
Muskrat		F	
Raccoon		F	
PROTIST (PROTISTA)	1		
Green Algae (Chlorophyta)	1		
Green Algae		C	

* The critters listed are identified as abundant, common and fairly common. Except not all the fairly common insects.

Selected Critter Descriptions

Bridgelip Sucker
(Catostomus columbianus)

		Class:	Bony Fish (Osteichthyes)
Family:	Sucker (Catostomidae)	**Division:**	Vertebrate (Chordata)
Order:	Carp, Sucker (Cypriniformes)	**Kingdom:**	Animal (Animalia)

LSW Habitat: ST: F

Relationships To Watershed: Bridgelip Suckers eat food of unknown origin. However, the flattened mouth and sharp-edged lower jaw suggest they probably feed by scraping algae from rocks. Like almost all other suckers, they probably also feed to some extent on aquatic insect larvae and crustaceans.

Description: Bridgelip Suckers are fish having from 11-14, usually 12, dorsal rays. Bridgelip Suckers have incompletely cleft lower lips and very slight notches in the corners of their mouths.

Look Alikes: Bridgelip Suckers may be confused with the Mountain Sucker, *Catomus platyrhynchus*, which has more distinct notches between the upper and lower lips and has 10 or 11 dorsal rays.

Stream, riparian and pine habitats

Little Spokane Habitat: Bridgelip Suckers inhabit the quiet areas in the backwaters or the edges of the main current of rivers with sand or mud bottoms.

World Habitat: Bridgelip Suckers are only found in the Columbia and Fraser river watersheds.

Minnows

Smallmouth Bass
(Micropterus dolomieni)

		Class:	Bony Fish (Osteichthyes)
Family:	Sunfish (Centrarchidae)	**Division:**	Vertebrate (Chordata)
Order:	Perch (Perciformes)	**Kingdom:**	Animal (Animalia)

Introduced: Introduced Species
LSW Habitats: ST: F, LK: F

Relationships To Watershed: Smallmouth Bass usually feed on minnows, sunfish, darters, madtom catfish, and lampreys.

Description: Smallmouth Bass have small mouths and the maxillaries usually do not extend beyond the centers of the eyes. The spinous and soft-rayed components of the dorsal fin are rather broadly joined. This bass has about 67-81 scales in the lateral line.

Look Alikes: Smallmouth Bass may be confused with the largemouth bass, *Micropterus salmoides*, in which the maxillary extends beyond the posterior of the eye. The spinous and soft-rayed components of the dorsal fin are separated to the base and the largemouth bass has 58-69 scales in the lateral line.

Little Spokane Habitat: Smallmouth Bass usually inhabit cool, clear streams or lakes with some current. They are usually found in areas with a substrate of rock, boulders, gravel or sand. In lakes they are found around rocky reefs and gravel bars.

Belted Kingfisher

World Habitat: Smallmouth Bass are an introduced species that had an original range from the middle of Minnesota east to southern Quebec, southeast to northern Georgia, west to Oklahoma, and north to Minnesota.

Fallen limbs

White Crappie *(Pomoxis annularis)*

		Class:	Bony Fish (Osteichthyes)
Family:	Sunfish (Centrarchidae)	**Division:**	Vertebrate (Chordata)
Order:	Perch (Perciformes)	**Kingdom:**	Animal (Animalia)

Introduced:	Introduced Species
LSW Habitat:	ST: F

Relationships To Watershed: White Crappies feed on zooplankton, insects and other fishes.

Description: White Crappies have a compressed body with anal and dorsal fins of about equal size. They usually have 5 or 6 dorsal spines.

Look Alikes: White Crappies may be confused with the black crappie, *Pomoxis nigromaculatus*, whose base of the

Spotted sandpiper

dorsal fin is longer than the white crappie. The black crappie has 7 or 8 dorsal spines.

Little Spokane Habitat: White Crappies do not depend on rooted vegetation and are found in turbid waters that are more alkaline.

World Habitat: White Crappies are an introduced fish whose original range was from central Minnesota east to eastern New York, south to Alabama, west to central Texas and northeastern Mexico and north to eastern South Dakota.

Wood Duck *(Aix sponsa)*

		Class:	Bird (Aves)
Family:	Waterfowl (Anatidae)	**Division:**	Vertebrate (Chordata)
Order:	Waterfowl (Anseriformes)	**Kingdom:**	Animal (Animalia)

At Risk: Regulated Game
LSW Habitat: RP: U, ST: U, LK: U

Relationships to Watershed: The Wood Duck is the most highly colored duck. Wood Ducks feed on seeds, acorns, berries, grains, aquatic and terrestrial insects and other invertebrates.

Description: Both sexes of Wood Duck have crested heads, white bellies, and long tails. The male's crest is iridescent green with 2 white streaks, one extending back from the bill, the other from the eye. The white throat has 2 prongs extending upward. The

Wood duck pair

burgundy chest is stippled with white and separated from the bronze side feathers by a "finger" of black and white. A red eye and a partially red bill complete this colorful array. The female has a gray head and crest, an elliptical white eye patch, and a grayish-brown chest and sides with whitish spots.

Look Alikes: The Wood Duck may be confused with the following: American Wigeon, *Anas americana*, has a large white speculum and lacks a crest. Hooded Merganser, *Lophodytes cucullatus*, which has a slender bill and white patches on the wings. The male has a white fan on its head.

Little Spokane Habitat: The Wood Duck inhabits areas of placid waters of streams, ponds, swamps, wooded sloughs, and lakes. They nest in tree cavities and nest boxes, sometimes in cities and towns adjacent to rivers and lakes.

World Habitat: Found in the Pacific Northwest down to California and on the eastern side of the United States.

Cedar waxwing

Beaver dam across stream

Beaver *(Castor canadensis)*

		Class:	Mammal (Mammalia)
Family:	Beaver (Castoridae)	**Division:**	Vertebrate (Chordata)
Order:	Rodent (Rodentia)	**Kingdom:**	Animal (Animalia)

LSW Habitats: ST: U, LK: U

Relationships To Watershed: Beavers consume many kinds of aquatic and herbaceous plants, among them the bark and cambium from aspen, willow, cottonwood, birch, or alder trees, and cattails. Beaver impoundments are important in irrigation and reforestation, and in forming habitats for trout, aquatic

Sandpiper along water edge

birds, and other fur-bearing animals such as mink and river otter. Trapping and the gradual encroachment of humans and their alterations of the environment, however, are making the future difficult for the beaver in many parts of the Pacific Northwest.

Description: Beavers are large dark brown rodents with large blunt heads and distinctive, flattened, scale-covered tails. Some individuals may weigh as much as 30 to 60 pounds. The beaver has large, webbed hind feet. The beaver measures about forty inches in length.

Look Alikes: While swimming, beavers resemble Muskrats or Otters, but out of the water they cannot be confused with other animals because of their distinct tails. This beaver species is the only beaver species in the Pacific Northwest.

Little Spokane Habitat: Beavers sometimes live in burrows dug into the banks of larger rivers. More commonly, however, they build their familiar lodges and dams in streams and lakes. Many times the dams built in streams will produce beaver ponds behind them. Entrances to the lodges are below the level of winter ice formation, allowing access during the year-round activity of the animals.

World Habitat: Beavers are a native species common throughout the Pacific Northwest.

Muskrat on the move

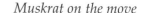

Muskrat
(Ondatra zibethica)

		Class:	Mammal (Mammalia)
Family:	Vole (Microtidae)	**Division:**	Vertebrate (Chordata)
Order:	Rodent (Rodentia)	**Kingdom:**	Animal (Animalia)

LSW Habitats: WL: F, RP: U, ST: F, HU: F

Muskrat on the bank

Relationships To Watershed: Muskrats feed mostly on aquatic vegetation, including roots, stems, bulbs, and leaves of cattails, bulrushes, sedges, lilies, and pondweeds. They also consume crayfish, clams, snails, fish, and frogs.

Description: Muskrats are the largest of the voles, about the size of a small house cat, with dense dark-brown fur, short ears, and a naked, laterally compressed tail. The under parts are dark gray to silvery gray. Their aquatic specializations include large, partly webbed feet, laterally rotated ankles, laterally compressed tail, dense, waterproof underfur, and lips that close behind front teeth.

Look Alikes: Beaver when tail is not visible.

Little Spokane Habitat: Muskrats are found in marshes and swamps, and along streams, rivers, and lakes, mostly in the lowlands.

World Habitat: Muskrats are a native species occurring extensively and commonly in suitable habitats throughout the Pacific Northwest with the exception of the mountains of southcentral Oregon, and southwestern British Columbia.

Mink *(Mustela vison)*

		Class:	Mammal (Mammalia)
Family:	Weasel (Mustelidae)	**Division:**	Vertebrate (Chordata)
Order:	Carnivore (Carnivora)	**Kingdom:**	Animal (Animalia)

LSW Habitats: ST: F

Relationships to Watershed: Mink prey heavily on muskrats but also consume crayfish, fish, rodents, and waterfowl.

Description: The mink is a large, semiaquatic weasel-like animal that is rich brownish in color with white patches on the chin. Their coat, pelage, is dense, soft, glossy, and water-repellent. The tail is only moderately bushy.

Look Alikes: Distinct.

Little Spokane Habitat: Minks are only found around water. Dens are near water in hollow logs, bank cavities, or old muskrat lodges or burrows.

World Habitat: The range of the mink in North America extends from Alaska and Canada southward to the Gulf of Mexico.

Beaver hut along stream

Lake and Pond Habitat

Lakes are large inland bodies of water that have at least some wave action at the surface. Also, the water is usually deep, at some point in the lake. The main difference between a lake and a pond is the depth, although there are no clear-cut differences. A lake is deep enough to have a layer that does not receive any energy in the form of sunlight whereas sunlight is able to penetrate to the bottom of a pond anywhere within its waters.

Lakes may be either natural or human-made. In either case, water is entrapped in a basin. Lakes abound in glacial regions such as northeast Washington. The lake habitat within the Little Spokane Watershed is represented primarily by Diamond Lake, Sacheen Lake, Trout Lake, Horseshoe Lake, and Eloika Lake, all of which are in the northern half of the watershed.

Headwaters of Little Spokane near Newport, WA

Inter-relationships

No matter how they were created, lakes are all headed for the same future. Water entering them brings silt and organic matter from the surrounding slopes. Aquatic plants and animals find their way in and begin to take root, multiply, and die. Their remains add nutrients and encourage the growth of even more organisms. As the bottom builds up with silt and organic matter, plants can take root farther and farther into the center, helping to pump the lake dry by giving their moisture to the surrounding air. Slowly, a lake becomes a pond, then a marsh, a wet

Turtles enjoying the sun

meadow, a shrub swamp, and perhaps eventually a forest. For deep lakes, this future may be millions of years away.

Lake Layers

The deep layer of a lake that receives no sunlight is generally colder than the upper layer that is warmed directly by the sun. Life thins out in this cold layer where it is too dark for green plants to grow.

In the warmer, sunnier layer nearer the surface, billions of microscopic plants and animals float on or near the top, utilizing the sun's energy and heat. These microscopic creatures form the basis of the food chain that supports insects, fish, amphibians, birds and mammals. When this cloud of microscopic life dies, the remains filter down through the cold, dark layer and settle on the lake bottom. Here life abounds again. Organisms such as bacteria, bloodworms, midges, flatworms, and other organisms consume the debris and convert it to nutrients such as nitrogen and phosphorous compounds.

These nutrients, however, do not just rise to the surface waters where they are needed by plants. Nor does oxygen produced by these plants automatically sink to

Lily pads in flower

the lower layer where it is needed by decomposers. Since cold water is denser and heavier than warm water, the two layers separate. Winds that ripple across the surface circulate the warm layer with itself, but leave the cold layer unruffled.

Due to the large temperature fluctuations throughout the year in the Little Spokane Watershed, a twice yearly phenomenon called overturn breaks down the barrier between them and causes the waters to mix and share their resources. In the fall, the sun-warmed upper layer begins to cool down until it reaches the same or lower temperature as the lower layer. When this occurs, the layering breaks down, and brisk winds are able to stir the water all the way to the bottom. This is termed fall turnover. The same thing happens in reverse in the spring. The icy upper layer thaws, and the whole lake reaches the equilibrium temperature. Winds stir it from top to bottom, mixing plant nutrients from the depths with fresh oxygen from the surface.

Ducklings along the water edge

Wildlife

For wildlife, the greatest advantage of a lake over a pond is the size and depth. In large lakes, loons have enough room to set up territories. The waters are deep enough to allow the loons, along with mergansers and grebes to dive after young fish, such as trout and perch. Other diving birds such as ruddy ducks, ring-necked ducks, and redheads reach for more remote submerged vegetation. Their special diving adaptations include streamlined bodies, legs that are placed back for propulsion, and the ability to tolerate buildup of carbon monoxide while diving.

Osprey also frequent lakes during the spring and summer. Oftentimes, the loud splash of an osprey diving into the water to catch a fish can be heard from far away. Osprey are the only bird of prey that will plunge into the water feet first to capture fish from a depth of one to three feet. Bald eagles merely pick up fish from the surface.

Along the shallow edges of a lake, the profusion of plants provides shade and protection to a number of animals. Rails, bitterns, marsh wrens, coots, and both

Lily pads soon to bloom

Mallard and ducklings

yellow-headed and red-winged blackbirds build their nests above the water in the thick tufts of emergent plants. Teals, pintails, and widgeons teach their young to tip-up for food in the shallows, and long-legged herons and egrets stand statue-still, waiting for the hapless minnows to swim within striking distance.

The shallow, sunlit, warm waters close to shore, the littoral zone, make a diverse microhabitat. This habitat includes algae, snails, clams, insects that eat plants (herbivores), insects that eat animals (carnivores), crawfish, small fish, and amphibians.

The sunlit open-surface water, the limnetic zone, is less diverse but can include larger populations of phytoplankton that are grazed on by zooplankton. These are eaten by small fish which are eaten by larger fish.

Sustainability

Like all aquatic habitats, the balance in the lake habitat is easily upset by outside disturbances. The two most destructive factors contributing to the demise of lake habitats are human created; the introduction of outside species, especially fish, and eutrophication, the term applied when a lake receives too many nutrients.

The introduction by humans of non-native species, whether intentionally or accidentally, can throw off the balance in a lake. Introduced fish may feed preferentially on one type of plant or animal, thereby reducing their numbers and possibly eliminating a food source for native species. For example, the introduction of carp to lakes can indirectly change the level of algae in the lake. Carp will selectively feed on large plankton. The large plankton are more efficient at reducing algae growth than are the smaller plankton. By eliminating the large plankton, algae growth may increase. This can contribute to eutrophication of a lake.

Eutrophication is the term applied to the result of an increase in nutrients in either lakes or streams. Some pollutants may increase productivity by stimulating the growth of large populations of algae blooms and water weeds that upset more healthier balances. This results in an upset in the carbon dioxide-oxygen balance in the water. The increased algae may kill off other plants by using an excessive amount of carbon dioxide and producing too much oxygen for some fish to survive.

As algae populations grow larger, they begin to die off. Bacteria that decompose the algae use up the oxygen supply. Fish kills are the result of this decreasing oxygen supply.

Allowing Lakes To Be More Restorative

Lakes provide habitat for many critters including large numbers of migratory waterfowl; ducks, geese, and swans. Allowing a lake to become polluted or introducing non-native critters can be bad news for everyone and everything. It is easy to control the introduction of non-native species but it requires everyone to think about the consequences and act in more restorative ways. Keeping outside nutrients and waste out of a lake is more difficult, particularly in agricultural areas where fertilizers are common. With the application of chemical biocides and fertilizers done more carefully, lake habitats can become more restorative.

Quality of Life Measures

Periodic monitoring of nutrients in the water is one measure of lake and pond quality of life. The variety of aquatic plants and other aquatic species is another measure of lake and pond health. The reduction in the amount of sewage and other pollutants going in to lakes and ponds is yet a third quality of life measure.

Great blue heron fishing

Summary of Lake and Pond Habitat Critters

Number of Species by Kingdom

PLANT (PLANTAE)   39

FUNGUS (EUMYCOTA)   0

ANIMAL (ANIMALIA)   171

PROTIST (PROTISTA)   14

**BACTERIA & VIRUS
(MONERA & VIRUS)**   7

TOTAL IDENTIFIED SPECIES   232

Number of Species by Class

Magnolia (Magnoliidae)	3
Carnation (Caryophyllidae)	2
Aspen (Dilleniidae)	9
Rose (Rosidae)	4
Sunflower (Asteridae)	8
Water Plantain (Alismatidae)	3
Grass (Commelinidae)	8
Duckweed (Arecidae)	1
Lily (Liliidae)	1
Hydrozoa (Hydrozoa)	2
Turbellidia (Turbellidia)	1
Roundworm (Acari)	1
Clam (Pelecypoda)	1
Snail (Gastropoda)	1
Leech (Hirudinea)	1
Crustacean (Crustacea)	6
Centipede (Chilopoda)	1
Millipede (Diplopoda)	1
Insect (Insecta)	10
Bony Fish (Osteichthyes)	44
Amphibian (Amphibia)	7
Reptile (Reptilia)	2
Bird (Aves)	78
Mammal (Mammalia)	7
Amoeba (Rhizopoda)	1
Heliozoan (Actimpoda)	1
Foram (Forimaninifera)	1
Sporozoite (Apicomplexa)	1
Zooflagellate (Zoomastigophera)	1
Ciliate (Ciliophora)	1
Dinoflagellates (Dinoflagellata)	1
Golden Algae (Chrysophyta)	1
Diatom (Bacillumiophyta)	1
Euglena (Euglenopphyta)	1
Green Algae (Chlorophyta)	1
Brown Algae (Phaeophyta)	1
Mildew (Oomycota)	1
Saprobe (Chytridiomycota)	1
Bacteria (Bacteria)	1
Cyanophycota (Cyanophycota)	1
Prochlorophycota (Prochlorophycota)	1
Bacteria Virus (Bacteria Virus)	1
Plant Virus (Plant Virus)	1
Vertebrate Virus (Vertebrate Virus)	1
Invertebrate Virus (Invertebrate Virus)	1

Selected Lake and Pond Habitat Critters

Critter	Count	Abundance	Risk
PLANT (PLANTAE)	26		
Magnolia (Magnoliidae)	3		
Indian Pond Lily		F	
Spearwort		C	
Water Buttercup		C	
Carnation (Caryophyllidae)	1		
Colored Smartweed		C	
Aspen (Dilleniidae)	6		
Black Cottonwood		A	
Pacific Willow		F	
Peach Willow		F	
Quaking Aspen		A	
Shooting Star (B)		F	
Willow (B)		F	
Rose (Rosidae)	2		
Red Osier Dogwood		C	
Water Parsnip		C	
Sunflower (Asteridae)	3		
Beggartick		F	
Marsh Scullcap		C	
Wild Mint		C	
Water Plantain (Alismatidae)	3		
Pondweed		F	
Wapato		F	
Water Plantain		F	
Grass (Commelinidae)	6		
Bulrush (A)		F	
Common Cattail		A	
Panic Grass		F	
Short-awn Foxtail		C	
Spike Rush		C	
Tule		A	
Duckweed (Arecidae)	1		
Duckweed		A	
Lily (Liliidae)	1		
Tiger Lily		F	
ANIMAL (ANIMALIA)	82		
Roundworm (Acari)	1		
Round Worm		C	
Snail (Gastropoda)	1		
Gastropoda		C	
Leech (Hirudinea)	1		
Hirudinea		F	
Crustacean (Crustacea)	6		
Copepoda		A	
Crayfish		C	
Cyclops		A	
Daphnia		A	
Decapoda		C	
Seed Shrimp		A	
Insect (Insecta)	11		
Aeshnidae		A	
Amphipoda		F	
Backswimmer		C	
Diving Beetle		F	
Dixid Midge		C	
Hydrophilus sp.		F	
Midge		A	
Mosquitoe		C	
Tropisternus sp.		F	
Water Boatman		A	
Whirligig Beetle (B)		A	
Bony Fish (Osteichthyes)	5		
Carp		C	IO
Channel Catfish		C	IO
Rainbow Trout		C	RGM
Smallmouth Bass		F	IO
Walleye		C	IO
Amphibian (Amphibia)	4		
Bull Frog		F	IN
Long-toed Salamander		F	
Pacific Treefrog		C	
Tiger Salamander		F	
Reptile (Reptilia)	1		
Western Painted Turtle		C	RNG
Bird (Aves)	48		
American Coot		A	
American Goldfinch		C	
American Robin		C	
American Wigeon		F	
Bank Swallow		A	
Barn Swallow		C	
Barrow's Goldeneye		F	
Black Tern		F	
Blue-winged Teal		F	
Bonaparte Gull		F	
Brewer's Blackbird		A	
Bufflehead		F	RGM
Canada Goose		C	
Cedar Waxwing		C	
Cinnamon Teal		C	
Cliff Swallow		C	
Common Goldeneye		F	
Common Merganser		F	
Common Yellowthroat		F	
Eared Grebe		C	PB
Great Blue Heron		C	MN
Greater Yellowlegs		F	
Green-winged Teal		F	
House Finch		C	
Killdeer		C	
Least Sandpiper		F	
Lesser Scaup		F	
Lesser Yellowlegs		F	
Long-billed Dowitcher		F	
Mallard		C	
Marsh Wren		F	
Northern Oriole		F	
Northern Pintail		F	
Northern Rough-winged Swallow		C	
Northern Shoveler		F	
Osprey		C	MN
Pectoral Sandpiper		F	
Pied-billed Grebe		F	PB
Red-winged Blackbird		A	
Ring-billed Gull		F	
Semipalmated Sandpiper		F	
Song Sparrow		C	
Spotted Sandpiper		F	
Tree Swallow		C	
Tundra Swan		C	
Violet-green Swallow		A	
Western Sandpiper		F	
Yellow-headed Blackbird		C	
Mammal (Mammalia)	1		
Raccoon		F	

* The critters listed here are identified as abundant, common and fairly common. Except a few fairly common animals.

Legend - Critters are listed by their common name followed by their abundance in the habitat. Introduced species and species at risk are indicated by type code. • **Abundance Codes: A** Abundant, **C** Common, **F** Fairly common, **U** Uncommon, **R** Rare, **V** Vagrant, **K** Known in habitat, **L** Likely in habitat, **M** Missing from habitat. • **Introduced Species Codes: IN** Introduced Noxious species, **IO** Introduced, Other than noxious species. • **At Risk Codes: MS** Missing, **ED** Endangered, **TH** Threatened, **CD** Candidate, **MN** Monitor, **RGM** Regulated Game, **RNG** Regulated Nongame, **RA** Rare, **PB** Protected Breeding Areas.

Selected Critter Descriptions

Wapato *(Sagittaria cuneata)*

Class: Water Plantain (Alismatidae)
Family: Water Plantain (Alismataceae)   **Division:**   Flower (Magnoliophyta)
Order: Water Plantain (Alismatales)   **Kingdom:**   Plant (Plantae)

Other Name: Arrowhead, Arumleaf Arrowhead, Tule Potato
LSW Habitats: WL: F, LK: F

Relationships To Watershed: Wapato tubers are eaten by ducks.

Description: Wapato is an aquatic, perennial, non-woody plant that is tuber-bearing. Plants are dioecious, with the female flowered plants having a shorter peduncle than the male flowered plants. Flowers are white, and borne in whorls of 3 in a simple, bracteate raceme. Inflorescences have bracts from 10-30 mm that are lanceolate in shape. Leaf blades are sagittate in shape and borne on a long stem pointing forward.

Look Alikes: Wapato may be confused with awl-leaf arrowhead, *Sagittaria subulata*, which has leaves without blades and is rhizomatous instead of tuber-bearing.

Little Spokane Habitat: Wapato is found in moist ponds and ditches.

World Habitat: Wapato is a native plant that is found from northern British Columbia south to the eastern

Wapato in grass

Sagittate Leaf - Arrow shaped leaf with the basal lobes directed downward.

Found On:
Wapato

Pedicel - Stalk of single flowers on a flower cluster.

Peduncle - Stalk of a solitary flower or a flower cluster.

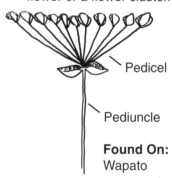

Pedicel

Pediuncle

Found On:
Wapato

Tuber - A swollen, fleshy, usually underground stem, such as the potato, bearing buds from which new plant shoots arise.

Found On:
Wapato

Cascades in Washington and Oregon and to southern California. Eastward it extends to New York, Illinois, Utah, New Mexico and northern Texas.

Bulrush *(Scirpus microcarpus)*

		Class:	Grass (Commelinidae)
Family:	Sedge (Cyperaceae)	**Division:**	Flower (Magnoliophyta)
Order:	Reed (Cyperales)	**Kingdom:**	Plant (Plantae)

Other Names: Small-fruit Bulrush, Small-flowered Bulrush
LSW Habitats: LK: F

Description: Bulrush is a tall plant of the sedge family. Stems are usually clustered from a sturdy rhizome. They are stout, triangular and leafy. Bulrush grows to 1.5 meters tall. The leaves are several and occur from both the base and the stem. They are flat and from 10-15 mm wide. The inflorescence has numerous short spikelets in small clusters at the ends of spreading stalks. The fruits are pale with lens-shaped, pointy-tipped achenes.

Beak - A narrow or prolonged tip, as on some fruits and seeds.

Found On:
Wapato
Bitterbrush
Blue Elderberry

Look Alikes: None.

Little Spokane Habitat: Found in swamps, sloughs, streambanks, wet ditches and clearings. They are common at low to mid elevations.

World Habitat: Found in the Pacific Northwest.

Tule *(Scirpus lacustris)*

		Class:	Grass (Commelinidae)
Family:	Sedge (Cyperaceae)	**Division:**	Flower (Magnoliophyta)
Order:	Reed (Cyperales)	**Kingdom:**	Plant (Plantae)

Other Names: American Great Bulrush, Bulrush, Softstem Bulrush
LSW Habitats: LK: A

Description: Tules are stout perennials that stems from a thick, scaly reddish-brown rhizome. The stems are cylindrical, erect and form in rows along the rhizomes. They are from 1-3 m tall. The leaves are few and form mostly at or near the base of the stem. The inflorescence occur several to many in an open to compact, branched terminal cluster. The spikelets are brown. Fruits are egg-shaped achenes that are each surrounded by several fragile whitish bristles.

Lily flower

Look Alikes: None.

Little Spokane Habitat: Found in marshes, muddy shores and shallow water at low elevations.

World Habitat: Found throughout the Pacific Northwest.

Common Cattail *(Typha latifolia)*

		Class:	Grass (Commelinidae)
Family:	Cattail (Typhaceae)	**Division:**	Flower (Magnoliophyta)
Order:	Cattail (Typhales)	**Kingdom:**	Plant (Plantae)

Other Name: Cattail
LSW Habitats: WL: C, RP: C, ST: A, LK: A

Relationships To Watershed: Common Cattail provides important habitat and food for many marsh animals, including wrens, blackbirds, waterfowl and muskrats.

Description: Common Cattail is a perennial that stems out from coarse rhizomes. The stems are pithy, unbranched, cylindrical and 1-3m tall. Leaves are alternate, flat, narrow (1-2 cm) and long (1.5-5 feet) and they give the appearance of a grass. The stalks in which the flower is borne are 3-10 feet tall. The flowers are minute, chaffy and found in a dense, round, smooth spike of two distinct portions. The upper part is the male part which is thicker when flowering but withers when fruiting begins. The lower part is the female part which thickens and turns dark brown in fruit. The fruits are tiny nutlets (1 mm) with numerous long slender hairs at the base that are designed to float in wind or water.

Look Alikes: Common Cattail may be confused with the big bulrushes or tules, *Scirpus spp.* which grow in similar habitats but these plants have few short basal leaves and an open flower cluster.

Little Spokane Habitat: Common Cattail need moist soils and are found near marshes, ponds, lakeshores, wet ditches and slow-flowing or quiet waters. They range from low to mid elevations.

Sunlight on lily pads

World Habitat: Common Cattails are found from Alaska to Mexico, east to most of southern Canada and throughout the United States, Eurasia and north Africa.

Tiger Lily *(Lilium columbianum)*

		Class:	Lily (Liliidae)
Family:	Lily (Liliaceae)	**Division:**	Flower (Magnoliophyta)
Order:	Lily (Liliales)	**Kingdom:**	Plant (Plantae)

Other Names: Columbia Lily, Oregon Lily
LSW Habitats: ST: F, LK: F

Description: Tiger Lily is a perennial plant that stems from a deep-seated, oval white bulb with thick scales. The plant grows up to 1.2 meters tall. The leaves are narrowly lance-shaped and usually arranged in several whorls of 6-9 on the stem. Flowers are bright orange with deep-red or purple spots near the center. They are large and showy, nodding down with their petals curved backwards. There are few to many flowers at the top of the stem. Fruits are barrel-shaped capsules with low ridges.

Look Alikes: Unique.

Tiger lily flower

Little Spokane Habitat: Found in meadows, thickets, open forest and clearings from low to subalpine elevations.

World Habitat: Ranges from southern British Columbia to northwestern California, east to northern Nevada and northern Idaho.

Rainbow Trout *(Salmo gairdneri)*

		Class:	Bony Fish (Osteichthyes)
Family:	Salmon, Trout (Salmonidae)	**Division:**	Vertebrate (Chordata)
Order:	Salmon, Trout (Salmoniformes)	**Kingdom:**	Animal (Animalia)

Other Name: Steelhead
At Risk: Regulated Game
LSW Habitats: ST: F, LK: C

Relationships To Watershed: Rainbow Trout feed primarily on foods that are associated with the bottom, such as aquatic insects, amphipods, aquatic worms, and fish eggs. Occasionally they eat small fish.

Description: Rainbow Trout are game fish of the salmon family. They usually have 11 or 12 rays in the dorsal fins, and typically 10 rays in the pelvic fin. They have a reddish stripe which is often, but not always, present along the side. They are uniformly silver until they darken toward spawning time.

Look Alikes: Rainbow Trout may be confused with cutthroat trout, *Salmo clarki*, which has red-orange "slash marks" on the underside of the lower jaw and has basibranchial (hyoid) teeth behind the tongue.

Little Spokane Habitat: Rainbow Trout prefer cool water, less than 70 degrees with plenty of oxygen, although they can survive from 32 degrees up to 80 degrees. In lakes where surface waters warm above 70 degrees in the summer, trout will move to deeper, cooler water if the oxygen content is sufficient there. Rainbow Trout are tolerant of a wide range of salinities.

World Habitat: Originally, Rainbow Trout ranged from northern Mexico to southeastern Alaska, and inland to the tributaries of the upper Columbia River, to Hell's Canyon Dam on the Snake River and to the Clearwater and Salmon Rivers in Idaho. Human activities have eliminated the anadromous form south of San Francisco.

Channel Catfish *(Ictalurus punctatus)*

		Class:	Bony Fish (Osteichthyes)
Family:	Catfish (Ictaluridae)	**Division:**	Vertebrate (Chordata)
Order:	Catfish (Siluriformes)	**Kingdom:**	Animal (Animalia)

Introduced:	Introduced Species
Other Name:	Catfish
LOW Habitat:	LR: C

Relationships To Watershed: Channel Catfish feed by sight and by taste, using their whiskers, barbels, and consume a variety of food items. They usually feed at night, and their primary food consists of small fish, insects, seeds, crayfish, aquatic insect nymphs, spiders, and vegetation.

Description: Channel Catfish have small and slender heads. The upper jaw protrudes over the lower jaw. Generally, the sides have scattered dark irregular spots, but these are absent in very small and very large channel catfish. This species has a deeply forked tail.

Look Alikes: Channel Catfish may be confused with the brown bullhead, *Ictalurus nebulosus*, which does not have a deeply forked tail. The head is larger than the channel catfish. Also, the bullhead has nearly equal jaws.

Little Spokane Habitat: Channel Catfish are found most often in clear lakes, reservoirs, and streams, but they can survive in muddy waters. In streams they are usually found in moderate to swift current over sand, gravel and rubble bottoms, and sometimes over mud bottoms. They are seldom found in dense aquatic vegetation.

World Habitat: Channel Catfish are an introduced species that originally occurred from central Montana and southern Saskatchewan east to southern Ontario and New York, southeast along the western Appalachian Mountains to Georgia and eastward through most of Florida, west to eastern New Mexico and northeast Mexico and north to Montana.

Walleye *(Stizotedion vitreum vitreum)*

		Class:	Bony Fish (Osteichthyes)
Family:	Perch (Percidae)	**Division:**	Vertebrate (Chordata)
Order:	Perch (Perciformes)	**Kingdom:**	Animal (Animalia)

Introduced: Introduced Species
LSW Habitats: ST: C, LK: C

Relationships To Watershed: Walleye feed on insects and fish such as yellow perch, whitefish, ciscoes, goldeneyes, sticklebacks, sculpins, suckers, and minnows.

Description: Walleye can be identified by the 2 spines in the anal fin, 2 separate dorsal fins with a dark spot at the base of the spiny first dorsal, and canine teeth in a large, terminal mouth. The lower edge of the caudal fin has a white margin.

Little Spokane Habitat: Walleye are found mainly in large lakes and streams. They travel in loose schools in open water near or on the bottom.

World Habitat: Walleye are an introduced species whose original range was from the central and northern Mississippi river system east to North Carolina, northward to the Hudson Bay region and Labrador, and northwest to the MacKenzie River and Saskatchewan River systems.

Tiger Salamander *(Ambystoma tigrinum melanostictum)*

		Class:	Amphibian (Amphibia)
Family:	Salamander (Ambystomatidae)	**Division:**	Vertebrate (Chordata)
Order:	Salamander (Caudata)	**Kingdom:**	Animal (Animalia)

Other Name: Blotched Tiger Salamander
LSW Habitats: LK: F

Relationships to Watershed: The Tiger Salamander's diet consists of a variety of invertebrates including earthworms, insects, snails and slugs. They may also prey on small vertebrates including other amphibians.

Description: The Tiger Salamander is a large, heavy-bodied animal of the amphibian class with a broad head and small, protruding eyes. Tiger Salamander has olive or pale-yellow spots, bars or blotches with indistinct borders set between a network of black markings. The pattern fades as it extends onto the gray chest and belly.

Look Alikes: The Tiger Salamander's appearance varies greatly from yellow spots to black lines. The Long-toed Salamander has a black stripe.

Little Spokane Habitat: The terrestrial adults are seldom seen but may be abundant near lakes and ponds. They are active at night and during spring rains as they migrate to and from the breeding ponds.

World Habitat: The Tiger Salamander ranges from Mexico through the central midwest and eastern U.S. and into southern Canada. In Washington this subspecies occurs in the Columbia Basin and northeastern Washington.

Bull Frog *(Rana catesbeiana)*

		Class:	Amphibians (Amphibia)
Family:	True frog (Ranidae)	**Division:**	Vertebrate (Chordata)
Order:	Frog (Anura)	**Kingdom:**	Animal (Animalia)

Introduced: Introduced Noxious Species
LSW Habitats: ST: F, LK: F

Bullfrog in duckweed

Relationships To Watershed: Bull Frogs feed on insects, earthworms, crayfish, fish, tadpoles, frogs, salamanders, snakes, small turtles, birds and small mammals. They also feed on juniper berries, small fruits, wood, bark, seeds and coniferous needles. Bull frogs are extremely destructive to native species and should be removed whenever they are found.

Description: Bull Frogs are the largest frogs in the watershed. They have conspicuous ridges that run posteriorly from the eyes down to the shoulders behind the conspicuous tympanum. Dorsally they are green to greenish-brown in color while ventrally they are white to cream with various dark mottling. The male bull frog has a tympanum that is two times as large as their eyes while on the females it is the same size as the eye. These frogs give a loud chirp or squeak when they are startled and jump into the water. Male bull frogs give a deep resonating call in late spring and summer to warn off other males or attracting females for breeding.

Look Alikes: Bull frogs may be confused with the green frog, *Rana clamitans*, which does not occur west of the Mississippi. The Green Frog has prominent dorsolateral folds which extend midway down both sides of the back.

Bull frog, an introduced menace

Little Spokane Habitat: Bull frogs are highly aquatic and they inhabit almost any permanent water including ponds, lakes, mill ponds, reservoirs, sluggish irrigation ditches, slow moving streams and rivers.

World Habitat: Bull frogs are native to eastern and midwestern United States and southeastern Canada. However, they have been introduced in the Pacific Northwest. They were introduced to western Oregon in the 1920-1930's. The introduction of the bullfrog into the area has led to the slow disappearance of the spotted frog. West of the Cascades the bull frog is also destroying western pond turtles.

Western Painted Turtle (*Chrysemys picta*)

		Class:	Reptiles (Reptilia)
Family:	Water and Box Turtle (Emydidae)	**Division:**	Vertebrate (Chordata)
Order:	Turtle (Testudines)	**Kingdom:**	Animal (Animalia)

At Risk: Regulated Non-game
Other Name: Painted Turtle
LSW Habitats: ST: F, LK: C

Relationships To Watershed: Western Painted Turtles are omnivorous feeders, and feed on most kinds of plants and small animals in their waters. The younger turtles tend to be carnivorous, becoming more herbivorous as they grow older. The eggs of these turtles are preyed upon by terrestrial predators such as skunks and raccoons and the hatchlings may be preyed upon by bullfrogs and raccoons.

Description: Western Painted Turtles are distinguished by red color on the ventral shell, or plastron, and on the undersides of the marginal scutes of the carapace. There is an irregular dark pattern that is displayed on the central part of the plastron that has outward extensions along the seams between the plates. The sides of the head, throat, legs and tail are marked by contrasting longitudinal lines, which are usually light yellow but may range from yellow to red. The carapace is smooth and olive to almost black in color.

Look Alikes: None in the Little Spokane Watershed.

Little Spokane Habitat: Western Painted Turtles are highly aquatic. They usually occupy marshy ponds or small lakes, but are also found in slow-moving streams and quieter backwaters of rivers. They prefer muddy bottoms with considerable aquatic vegetation.

World Habitat: The Western Painted Turtle is found from the Atlantic to Pacific Oceans in southern Canada and the northern United States. They are widespread in the southeast, along the Mississippi River and on the northern plains of the United States, but absent from the Great Basin, southwest, and Pacific Coast.

Turtle on log

Western Grebe (*Aechmophorus occidentalis*)

		Class:	Bird (Aves)
Family:	Grebe (Podicipedidae)	**Division:**	Vertebrate (Chordata)
Order:	Grebe (Podicipediformes)	**Kingdom:**	Animal (Animalia)

At Risk: Monitor Species
LSW Habitat: LK: U

Relationships to Watershed: Western Grebe's diet consists of mostly fish, aquatic inverts, few amphibians and feathers.

Description: Western Grebe is a small to medium-size diving bird with a long swanlike neck. Western Grebe has bright red eyes and a long sharp bill that is dull greenish-yellow. They have a white throat that continues to their belly. The top of the head, back of the neck, and the back are dark grayish-black. Like all grebes, they lose their coloration in the winter, when most of the population leaves the area.

Look Alikes: May be confused with Clark's Grebe, *Podiceps clarkii*. They can be differentiated by a few characteristics. The Western Grebe's eyes are completely surrounded by black feathers while the Clark's Grebe's eyes are surrounded by white feathers. The Clark's Grebe's bill is bright orange-yellow compared to the dull greenish-yellow bill of the Western Grebe.

Little Spokane Habitat: Western Grebe are found in marshes and lakes.

World Habitat: Western Grebe range from British Columbia to central Mexico on the West Coast, and from California and Washington inland to the Dakotas. They are rarely found on the East Coast.

Mallard female

Mallard (*Anas platyhynchos*)

		Class:	Bird (Aves)
Family:	Waterfowl (Anatidae)	**Division:**	Vertebrate (Chordata)
Order:	Waterfowl (Anseriformes)	**Kingdom:**	Animal (Animalia)

LSW Habitats: WL: C ST: C, LK: C

Relationships To Watershed: Mallards feed on seeds and shoots of sedge, grass, and aquatic vegetation, grain, acorns, insects, and aquatic invertebrates.

Description: Mallards are a common wild duck from which the domestic duck is descended. Mallard males have green heads and necks separated from the dark brown chest by a narrow white ring. At rest, the folded wings form a dark line separating the gray sides and back. The black rump and tail coverts contrast with the white outer tail feathers. Mallard females are rather uniformly mottled brown, lighter and less mottled on the head and belly. In flight, an iridescent patch of dark blue, the speculum, bordered in front and back by white can be seen. The broad wings and short tail make the wings look as though they are placed farther back on the body than in other species.

Look Alikes: Northern Shoveler has a green head also, but the bill is very large and the chestnut is in the flanks. Female ducks and eclipse ducks have a superficial resemblance.

Osprey taking off from nest

Little Spokane Habitat: Mallards hang out in lakes, marshes, and swamps. They are often seen congregating in flocks and forming huge "rafts".

World Habitat: Mallards are found throughout the United States into Canada.

Osprey with fresh catch

Osprey *(Pandion haliaetus)*

		Class:	Birds (Aves)
Family:	Hawk (Acolpltridae)	**Division:**	Vertebrate (Chordata)
Order:	Hawk (Falconiformes)	**Kingdom:**	Animal (Animalia)

At Risk: Monitor Species
LSW Habitats: WL: C, ST: U, LK: C

Relationships To Watershed: Osprey feed almost exclusively on live fish. They usually hover at 30-100 feet and dive for fish. They also take rodents, birds, small vertebrates and crustaceans. Their large stick nests, which can be made of sod, cow dung, seaweed, rubbish, etc., are typically built in dead trees, but may also be found on telephone poles, windmills, old duck blinds, and channel markers.

Description: The Osprey is a large bird of prey of the hawk family. Osprey are brown to brownish-black above and white below, having brownish-black marks on the wrist and buff to brown speckling on the breast. The head is white with a dark crown and a wide, dark brown eye stripe. While in flight, one can tell an osprey by the white underparts and the crook in the long, narrow wings, as well as by the blackish marks at the wrist.

Look Alikes: Osprey may be confused with other raptors but the white plumage, their fishing habit and the definite crook in the wings while in flight, are distinctive.

Little Spokane Habitat: Osprey are typically associated with water. However, when suitable nest sites are unavailable near water, they may nest considerable distances inland.

World Habitat: Osprey are found from northwestern Alaska and north-central Canada south to Baja California, Sonoran coast, and the Gulf states.

Red-winged Blackbird
(*Agelaius phoeniceus*)

		Class:	Birds (Aves)
Family:	Warbler (Emberizidae)	**Division:**	Vertebrate (Chordata)
Order:	Thrush (Passeriformes)	**Kingdom:**	Animal (Animalia)

LSW Habitats: PP: U, WL: A, LK: A, HU: R

Relationships to Watershed: Red-winged Blackbirds feed on spiders, grass and forb seeds.

Description: The adult male is entirely black except for a bright reddish or reddish-orange shoulder patch. The patch has a buff-whitish border. The female is dark brown above, tinged with black and gray, and has a light or buff eyebrow. Their pale underparts are heavily streaked with blackish-brown

Look Alikes: May be confused with the Tricolored Blackbird, *Agelaius tricolor*. The male tricolored is slightly slimmer and glossier blue-black overall and the bill is also slimmer. The female Tricolored is darker overall particularly on the belly which shows little distinct streaking. There are few records of Tricolored Blackbirds in Washington.

Female red wing on cattail

Little Spokane Habitat: Red-winged Blackbirds forage in open country, particularly in agricultural areas. Their breeding territories include freshwater marshes, moist thickets, and wet fields.

World Habitat: Found throughout the United States and into southern Canada.

Male red wing chattering away

Disturbed Land Habitat

Disturbed land in the Little Spokane Watershed is difficult to describe because disturbed land is found in every habitat type. Areas more closely associated with human activities have a high amount of disturbed land. Human causes of disturbed land primarily result from human actions other than development, such as logging, road building, and agriculture. Disturbances may also be natural, such as floods, fires, high wind, and landslides. Any action that alters the land form in some way can be considered a disturbance.

The primary differences between natural and human disturbances are the scale and degree to which they occur. While natural disturbances may significantly alter a habitat on a small scale, human disturbances occur on a world-wide scale, taking place virtually anywhere that humans live, go to, or exploit.

Perhaps more important is the degree to which human disturbances occur. Often, human actions are centered on extraction, which removes vital biomass from the area. Biomass is the sum of all living and dead organic matter. Rather than being recycled back into the soil as nutrients for other organisms, the biomass is permanently removed.

Mullein stalks in a field returning to nature

Skeletonweed amidst knapweed, both are introduced noxious weeds

Inter-relationships

Some organisms are completely displaced by disturbances. Many of the species that are presently threatened or endangered fall into this category. Some of the well known representatives of this group include animal species such as grizzly bears, brown bears, and northern goshawks, and plants such as many species of the orchid family.

Large predators do better with large amounts of open territory in which to hunt for food. They often are also territorial and will not tolerate other members of the same species coming into their territory. Because of these factors, many cannot survive in areas of frequent disturbance. Grizzly bears, for example, perceive any unrecognizable animal as a potential threat. This includes humans. Before human populations were as large as they are today, the instinctual caution by grizzly bears provided a survival advantage. Today, however, it serves mainly to limit their range.

Many sensitive plants require soil that remains undisturbed for long periods of time, perhaps several years. Orchids are delicate plants whose roots are tenuously rooted in the soil and are easily killed by even small disturbances. Even walking off a trail can damage or kill such sensitive plants.

1950 A large nature area

1974 After the removal of the trees

At the other end of the spectrum are those organisms that thrive in disturbed areas. Disturbance events will often kill the vegetation in an area, thereby opening it up to new plants. Disturbed soil represents a tremendous opportunity for organisms that can first establish themselves in a newly disturbed area. Many plants thrive because they are specially adapted to rapidly occupying these newly available areas. Many of these plants also happen to be non-native plants that were introduced by immigrants to North America. A few examples are: cheatgrass, a classic indicator of overgrazing; knapweed; common mullein; St. John's wort, also known as goat weed or Klamath weed; and Dalmatian toadflax. Mullein and St. John's wort are introduced species that originated in Eurasia.

Mullein is a common plant along roadsides, especially sandy or gravelly cutbanks where the soil has been disturbed. Its tall stalk, up to 5 ft., and numerous small yellow flowers are unmistakable. St. John's wort proliferates so well in disturbed soil that it is considered to be a disturbance indicator. This means that the soil where St. John's wort is growing has recently been disturbed.

St. John's wort is a good example of what is considered to be a noxious weed. A noxious weed is one that is non-native to an area and displaces native vegetation.

St. John's wort also called goatweed, another introduced noxious weed

---

1992 A few trees along edge are coming back

Three Snapshots Spanning Forty Years

In the 1950's this nature area had an abundance of pine trees. In the north west corner the trees appear to be fairly dense.

By 1974 this area had been cleared of its native trees and native plants, becoming a disturbed habitat. Almost 20 years later, 1992, very few native trees have returned.

Perhaps this land was to be agricultural land and then was put into the Conservation Reserve Program, CRP.

In the future this may be a development site. With mature trees on the site, a development could enhance its value significantly.

Or, the few remaining nature places can be reserved, enhancing the wealth of nature for future generations.

The yellow flower of the noxious weed, toadflax

St. John's wort is very difficult to eradicate, in part because it invades overgrazed sites, and no domesticated stock will graze on it due to its bitterness. In addition, it spreads by high seed output and by creeping rhizomes, both of which are very difficult to control.

Other critters also indicate disturbed habitat. Both crow and coyote tend to be seen more frequently in disturbed areas.

Sustainability

People and Nature

Some disturbance events are an inevitable part of nature and some organisms adapt to these changes. However, humans disturb the soil to such a great extent that noxious weeds thrive more now than they ever have, some to the extent of being harmful to native species. It is extremely arrogant to continue destructive land management practices. With more adequate understanding of the cycles of nature that humans so readily alter, more sustainable land management practices are being put in place.

The continuation of destructive land management practices can have unanticipated effects that are not only harmful to wildlife habitats but can be harmful to human

Shaggy Parasol Mushroom emerging

Shaggy Parasol the next day

habitats as well. The larger repercussions of disturbance events and their creeping cumulative effects are just beginning to be understood. It is known, however, that large-scale disturbances such as some current logging and grazing practices, can have long-term effects on the ability of native species to survive, not only by direct destruction of those organisms, but also by destruction of the habitat necessary to support them.

Quality of Life Measures

There are many quality of life measures for disturbed land habitat. Here are just few.

How frequently are best management practices being used for agriculture and forestry is one measure. How often are nature corridors left intact or created between disturbed land and other habitats is another.

The number of native plants versus noxious weeds on former agricultural land and other disturbed land that is returning to native habitat is another quality of life measure.

The number of appropriate native plants planted per acre on logged forest land and former agricultural land is another measure of how restorative the land is becoming.

Mullein, knapweed and toadflax pushing out native plants

Summary of Disturbed Habitat Critters

Number of Species by Kingdom

PLANT (PLANTAE)   81

FUNGUS (EUMYCOTA)   50

ANIMAL (ANIMALIA)   54

PROTIST (PROTISTA)   8

BACTERIA & VIRUS (MONERA & VIRUS)   7

TOTAL IDENTIFIED SPECIES   200

Number of Species by Class

Moss (Bryopsida)	2
Horsetail (Equisetopsida)	2
Fern (Polypodiopsida)	1
Pine (Pinicae)	1
Magnolia (Magnoliidae)	2
Carnation (Caryophyllidae)	8
Aspen (Dilleniidae)	6
Rose (Rosidae)	16
Sunflower (Asteridae)	31
Grass (Commelinidae)	11
Lily (Liliidae)	1
Mushroom (Basidomycetes)	39
Puffball (Gastromycetes)	6
Ascomycetes (Ascomycetes)	4
To Be Determined (TBD)	1
Turbellidia (Turbellidia)	1
Spider (Arachnida)	1
Centipede (Chilopoda)	1
Millipede (Diplopoda)	1
Insect (Insecta)	23
Reptile (Reptilia)	1
Bird (Aves)	18
Mammal (Mammalia)	8
Amoeba (Rhizopoda)	1
Heliozoan (Actimpoda)	1
Foram (Forimaninifera)	1
Sporozoite (Apicomplexa)	1
Slime Mold - Cellular (Acrasiomycetes)	1
Slime Mold - Plasmodial (Myxomycetes)	1
Mildew (Oomycota)	1
Saprobe (Chytridiomycota)	1
Bacteria (Bacteria)	1
Cyanophycota (Cyanophycota)	1
Prochlorophycota (Prochlorophycota)	1
Bacteria Virus (Bacteria Virus)	1
Plant Virus (Plant Virus)	1
Vertebrate Virus (Vertebrate Virus)	1
Invertebrate Virus (Invertebrate Virus)	1

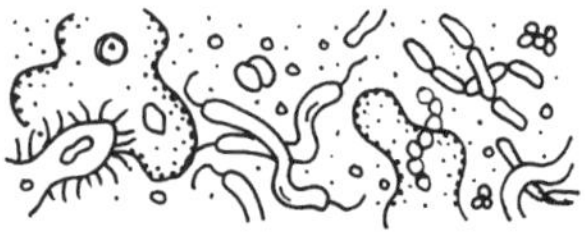

Selected Disturbed Habitat Critters

PLANT (PLANTAE)	48			
Moss (Bryopsida)	2			
Ceratodon purpureus		C		
Funaria hygrometrica		C		
Horsetail (Equisetopsida)	1			
Scouring Rush		C		
Fern (Polypodiopsida)	1			
Bracken Fern		A		
Pine (Pinicae)	1			
Ponderosa Pine		C		
Carnation (Caryophyllidae)	7			
Chickweed (A)		C	IO	
Curly Dock		C	IO	
Goose Grass		C	IO	
Goosefoot		C	IO	
Jagged Chickweed		A	IO	
Sheep Sorrel		A	IO	
Sticky Chickweed		C	IO	
Aspen (Dilleniidae)	5			
Jim Hill Mustard		A	IO	
Mustard		C	IO	
Quaking Aspen		A		
Scouler Willow		A		
Shepherd's Purse		C	IO	
Rose (Rosidae)	10			
Crane's Bill		C	IO	
Fireweed		A		
Hairy Vetch		C	IO	
Japanese Clover		C	IO	
Redstem Ceanothus		A		
Snowbrush Ceanothus		C		
White Clover		C	IO	
White Sweet Clover		A	IO	
Willow Herb		C		
Yellow Sweet Clover		A	IO	
Sunflower (Asteridae)	15			
Bull Thistle		A	IN	
Common Bugloss		A	IO	
Common Mullein		A	IN	
Common Plantain		C	IO	
Common Speedwell		A	IO	
Common Yarrow		A		
Dalmatian Toadflax		A	IN	
Goatweed		C	IO	
Gumweed (A)		C		
Honeysuckle (B)		A	IO	
Spotted Knapweed		A	IN	
Stoneseed		C	IO	
Western Coneflower		A		
White Knapweed		C	IN	
Yellow Salsify		A	IO	
Grass (Commelinidae)	5			
Bulbous Bluegrass		A	IO	
Canada Bluegrass		A	IO	
Cheatgrass		A	IO	
Japanese Brome		A	IO	
Timothy		C	IO	
Lily (Liliidae)	1			
Asparagus		A	IO	

FUNGUS (EUMYCOTA)	3			
Mushroom (Basidomycetes)	2			
Mica Cap		C		
Shaggy Mane		C		
Puffball (Gastromycetes)	1			
Lycoperdon echinatum		C		
ANIMAL (ANIMALIA)	22			
Insect (Insecta)	12			
Bumblebee spp		C		
Cabbage Butterfly		C		
Clouded Sulfur		C		
Codling Moth		A		
Colorado Potato Beetle		C		
Honeybee		C		
Lesser Migratory Grasshopper		A		
Owlet Moth		C		
Pyralid Moth		C		
Spittlebug		C		
Warrior Grasshopper		A		
Woodland Skipper		A		
Bird (Aves)	8			
American Crow		A		
American Robin		C		
Brewer's Blackbird		A		
California Quail		A		IO
Canada Goose		C		
European Starling		A		
Ring-billed Gull		C		
Ring-necked Pheasant		C		
Mammal (Mammalia)	2			
Human		C		
White-tailed Deer		C	RGM	

* The critters listed here are those identified as abundant and common .

Legend - Critters are listed by their common name followed by their abundance in the habitat. Introduced species and species at risk are indicated by type code. • **Abundance Codes: A** Abundant, **C** Common, **F** Fairly common, **U** Uncommon, **R** Rare, **V** Vagrant, **K** Known in habitat, **L** Likely in habitat, **M** Missing from habitat. • **Introduced Species Codes: IN** Introduced Noxious species, **IO** Introduced, Other than noxious species. • **At Risk Codes: MS** Missing, **ED** Endangered, **TH** Threatened, **CD** Candidate, **MN** Monitor, **RGM** Regulated Game, **RNG** Regulated Nongame, **RA** Rare, **PB** Protected Breeding Areas.

Selected Critter Descriptions

Bracken Fern

Bracken Fern *(Pteridium aquilinum)*

		Class:	Fern (Polypodiopsida)
Family:	Fern (Polypodiaceae)	**Division:**	Fern (Pterophyta)
Order:	Fern (Polypodiales)	**Kingdom:**	Plants (Plantae)

Other Name: Brake Fern
LSW Habitats: MT: U, DS: A

Relationships to Watershed: Bracken Fern is very resistant to fires and regenerates rapidly. It is poisonous to livestock if consumed in large quantities.

Description: Bracken Fern is an erect fern from 2-4 feet tall, highly rhizomatous and very clonal. The leaves are deciduous single fronds, and the blades are tripinnately compound and 1-3 feet in length. The pinnules are alternate and the edges are rolled under with a dense cluster of hairs.

Look Alikes: Bracken Fern is easily distinguished from other ferns.

Little Spokane Habitat: Bracken Fern is found on warm, dry sites at mid elevations. It is an invader and colonizer following fires, clearcutting and burning because of its ability to resist droughts.

World Habitat: Bracken Fern is widespread throughout the Pacific Northwest.

Scouler Willow *(Salix scouleriana)*

		Class:	Aspen (Dilleniidae)
Family:	Aspen (Salicaceae)	**Division:**	Flower (Magnoliophyta)
Order:	Aspen (Salicales)	**Kingdom:**	Plant (Plants)

Other Names: Pussy Willow, Willow (C)
LSW Habitats: DF; F, PP: F, RK: U, BU: U, WL: C, RP: C, DS: A

Relationships To Watershed: Scouler Willow is an early seral member that provides a cover, both hiding and thermal, for elk and deer to browse. Scouler Willow is highly palatable.

Red Clover

Description: Scouler Willow is a deciduous shrub which can reach a size from 6-30 feet tall. The new branches are gray and hairy while the older branches are brownish black in color. The buds are pointed and tightly pressed against the stem. Leaves are alternate and spatulate in form with entire margins. They are from 1-3 inches long with the widest part of the leaf occurring after the midpoint. Their upper surface is dark green and glabrous white. They are glaucous with sparse reddish hairs below. The flowers are catkins blooming March-June which appear before the leaves in spring. The female catkins (sometimes termed pussy willows) and the male catkins appear on separate plants. The fruit is a hairy capsule.

Look Alikes: Scouler Willow is easily distinguished with its spatulate leaf and its upland orientation.

Little Spokane Habitat: Scouler Willow occurs in two radically different habitats. On gravel bars and banks of mountain rivers where little soil has accumulated it occurs as a small shrub that rarely exceeds 4 feet tall. Scouler's willow also occurs on open forested slopes, beneath semi-closed forest canopies, often invading along with snowbrush. This willow reaches greatest expression following burns and clearcutting. Thriving independently of watercourses is unusual among willows.

World Habitat: Scouler Willow is widespread throughout the Pacific Northwest. Also found in Alaskan and the Yukon to California, Arizona and New Mexico.

Viper bugloss flowering stem

Viper bugloss

Redstem Ceanothus
(Ceanothus sanguineus)

		Class:	Rose (Rosidae)
Family:	Buckthorn (Rhamnaceae)	**Division:**	Flower (Magnoliophyta)
Order:	Buckthorn (Rhamnales)	**Kingdom:**	Plant (Plantae)

Other Names: Buckbrush, One Tea-tree
LSW Habitats: DF: C, PP: C, GR: C, DS: A

Relationships To Watershed: Redstem Ceanothus is an important nitrogen-fixing plant and an important browse for deer and elk.

Oblanceolate Leaf - Lance shaped leaf with the broadest part above the middle

Pinna Uni
Common Mullein
Western Prince's Pine

Mullein Flowerhead

Description: Redstem Ceanothus is an erect, loosely branched shrub that is from 3-10 feet tall and tends to form thickets. The stems are smooth and purplish-red in color. They are alternately branched. Leaves are alternate, dark green above and pale below. They are 1-4 inches long with serrated margins on a 1 inch petiole. The leaf has three main veins that branch from the leaf base. Small white flowers bloom May-June and are clustered in dense panicles.

Look Alikes: Redstem Ceanothus may be confused with the following: Snowbrush ceanothus, *Ceanothus velutinus*, which has evergreen leaves which are very shiny; Red-osier Dogwood, *Cornus stolonifera*, which has opposite leaves.

Little Spokane Habitat: Redstem Ceanothus is found in well-drained soils in openings that are a result of fires.

World Habitat: Redstem Ceanothus is a native plant that is widespread from the Cascades to the Rocky Mountains in the Pacific Northwest.

Common Mullein
(*Verbascum thapsis*)

		Class:	Sunflower (Asteridae)
Family	Foxglove (Scrophulariaceae)	**Division:**	Flower (Magnoliophyta)
Order:	Foxglove (Scrophulariales)	**Kingdom:**	Plant (Plantae)

Introduced:	Introduced Noxioius Species
Other Names:	Flannel Mullein, Mullein
LSW Habitats:	MT: F, RK: F, DS: A, HU: F

Relationships To Watershed: Common Mullein seeds provide winter food for birds.

Description: Common Mullein is a biennial herb. During the first year a basal rosette appears, in the second year an erect flowering stem forms. Yellow flowers bloom during June-August with a dense spikelike raceme. The petals of the flowers are 5-lobed, 3 of the filaments are dense yellow-hairy while the other two are longer. The anthers are orange. Basal leaves are broadly oblanceolate, 16 inches long, 5 inches wide and have entire margins. Cauline leaves are gray-green in color, numerous and

Mullein emerging

become progressively smaller up the plant. The stems are densely hairy, unbranched and up to 7 feet tall. The fruit is an ovoid capsule that is 2-celled with many small brown seeds.

Look Alikes: Common Mullein may be confused with moth mullein, *Verbascum blattaris*, whose leaves are green, not densely hairy and the filaments are covered with purple-knobbed hairs.

Little Spokane Habitat: Common Mullein can be found along roadsides, in highly disturbed dry, gravelly or sandy locations. It is also found on river bottoms.

World Habitat: Mullein is an introduced plant from Eurasia that is currently established throughout the United States.

Western Coneflower
(*Rudbecia occidentalis*)

		Class:	Sunflower (Asteridae)
Family:	Sunflower (Compositae)	**Division:**	Flower (Magnoliophyta)
Order:	Sunflower (Asterales)	**Kingdom:**	Plant (Plantae)

Other Names: Black Coneflower, Blackhead, Coneflower
LSW Habitats: MT: C, GR: U, RP: C, DS; A

Relationships To Watershed: Western Coneflower is avoided by livestock. It increases as other palatable plants are grazed out. Horses will preferentially seek the flower heads.

Description: Western Coneflower is a perennial herb from 20 inches to 6 feet tall. Flower is a dark brown to black disk elongating to cone-shape that is up to 2 inches long. It has no ray flowers and the involucral bracts are unequal. Blooming occurs June-August. Leaves are alternate, simple, broadly ovate and up to 10 inches long and 6 inches wide. The margins are entire with some teeth. The lower leaves are strongly petiolate with the

Basal Rosette - A dense radiating cluster of leaves near the base

Found On:
Common Mullein
Cheatgrass
Idaho Fescue

Involucre - A whorl of reduced or specialized leaves, bracts, below a flower cluster

Involucre

Found On:
Western Coneflower

Disk Flower - A regular flower of the sunflower family, compositae. Not a ray flower.

Found On:
Western Coneflower

upper leaves being stalkless with rounded or heart-shaped bases. Fruit is an achene.

Look Alikes: Western Coneflower is very distinguished.

Little Spokane Habitat: Western Coneflower is found on streambanks, terraces near streams and moist and dry meadows from mid to high elevations in the mountains.

World Habitat: Western Coneflower is found from Washington and Oregon to California and eastward to southwestern Montana, Wyoming, Idaho and Utah.

Butterfly on blade of grass

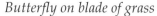

Moth on Canada thistle

Cheatgrass
(*Bromus tectorum*)

Class:		Grass (Commelinidae)
Family: Grass (Graminae)	**Division:**	Flower (Magnoliophyta)
Order: Grass (Poales)	**Kingdom:**	Plant (Plantae)

Introduced: Introduced Species
Other Name: Downy Cheat
LSW Habitats: GR: A, DS: A

Relationships To Watershed: Cheatgrass provides valuable spring forage for sheep, cattle, deer and elk. Early cheatgrass maturity in bunchgrass communities provides high flammability to fire.

Favored by frequent fires. Can outcompete bunchgrass on degraded sites in postburn stands due to high seed production, high percentage of seed viability and rapid and deep root formation. Seeds are eaten by quail, sparrows, gophers and mice. The introduced chukar partridges are dependent on annual brome seeds in winter.

Description: Cheatgrass is an introduced annual grass that is from 12-24 inches tall. Cheatgrass may be branched at the base and robust on better sites or single stemmed, shorter and with a one-sided drooping panicle on poorer sites. They are often patch forming with fibrous nonrhizomatous roots. The leaves are flat, soft, hairy and 2-4 inches long. They possess no auricle. The inflorescence is a drooping panicle that is about 2-6 inches long. Each is compact with 4 or more spikelets. The spikelets are 5-8 flowered, slender, about 1 inch long and the lemma has a straight awn that is 10-15 mm long. The inflorescence matures to orange, red or purplish in color and it flowers from April-June.

Look Alikes: Cheatgrass may be confused with the following: hairy chess, *Bromus commatatus*, and soft chess, *Bromus mollis*, which both have erect panicle branches that do not droop; rattlesnake brome, *Bromus brizaeformis*, has lemmas that are awnless.

Little Spokane Habitat: Cheatgrass is common in disturbed areas, especially in overgrazed areas. It is very common on dry rangelands where spring moisture is abundant.

World Habitat: Cheatgrass is an introduced species from Eurasia that is now widely established throughout the western United States.

Tansy

Swallowtail Butterfly

Shaggy Mane *(Coprinus Comatus)*

Family:	Gilled Dark Spores (B) (Coprinaceae)	**Class:**	Mushroom (Basidomycetes)
Order:	Gilled Mushroom (Agaricales)	**Division:**	Mushroom (Basidimycotina)
		Kingdom:	Fungus (Eumycota)

LSW Habitats: MT: L, WL: F, RP: F, DS: C, HU: C

Relationship to watershed: Shaggy Mane is a member of the inky cap family, Coprinaceae. This name comes from the inky black slime that the mushroom transforms into. It does this by producing an enzyme to auto-digest itself and thereby disperse its spores. In a mere day the fruit body can go from tall and elegant to a puddle of slime. Its name is not just descriptive; the "ink" is actually used by some artists today for paintings and in the past has been gathered for writing. It is also edible as long as two rules are followed: eat when young and fresh and never eat within 48 hours of consuming alcohol. Some members of this family of mushroom can become quite toxic in this case.

Shaggy mane just emerging

Shaggy mane just before turning into a puddle of slime

Description: Shaggy Manes are from 2 inches as a button to 12 inches fully grown in height. They are cylindric and white with shaggy white to brown scales which increasingly recurve as they mature on the cap. As they begin to auto-digest the cap margins curl out and the gills begin to blacken, the color of the spores. The stalk is more or less equal in length to the cap, smooth, white, mostly hollow, and easily separates from the cap.

Look Alikes: With a basic mushroon field guide or introduction by a more experienced mushroomer it is difficult to mistake this mushroom for another. It is one of the foolproof four and easily recognized. The only mushroom in this area that has scales, is white, and can be as large, is the Shaggy Parasol, *Lepiota Rachodes*. It can be told apart in that it is never cylindric, has a distinctive ring, white spores, and the stalk stains orange/red when cut.

Little Spokane Habitat: This large inky cap can be found as individuals or in dense clusters in hard packed soil, roadsides, grassy areas and in the middle of logging and fire roads. Sometimes it can be found breaking up through asphalt.

Human Habitat

Human habitat is simply an area that is permanently occupied by people. There is no exact number for how many people per square mile it takes to be considered human habitat, but suburban and any areas more densely populated can be considered human habitats. Even rural houses, yards, buildings, and roads can be considered human habitats, although their affects on wildlife are considerably less than more densely populated areas.

As a general guide, the following areas of human influence can be used to at least indicate the effect human habitat has on adjoining habitats. The urban areas, including airports and industrial parks can influence at least a quarter mile, about 1,300 feet, beyond the urban edge. Suburban areas can influence at least an eighth of a mile, about 700 feet, beyond the suburban edge. Rural houses, yards and buildings can influence at least 350 feet beyond their edge. Air pollution, mostly from industrial emissions and cars, can significantly extend the area affected by human habitat.

In the Little Spokane Watershed, human habitat often borders nature habitats. This does not mean however, that all wildlife is able to survive right up to the edge of human habitat. Rather, each habitat edge has an area of overlap with adjacent habitats where the habitats affect each other. Human habitat has much more of an influence on adjacent habitats than the

Swallowtail on teasel

adjacent habitats have on human habitat. In many cases the influence of the human habitat on the adjacent habitats makes the edge inhospitable to many of the adjacent habitat's critters, primarily animals.

Inter-relationships

Wildlife and Human Sites

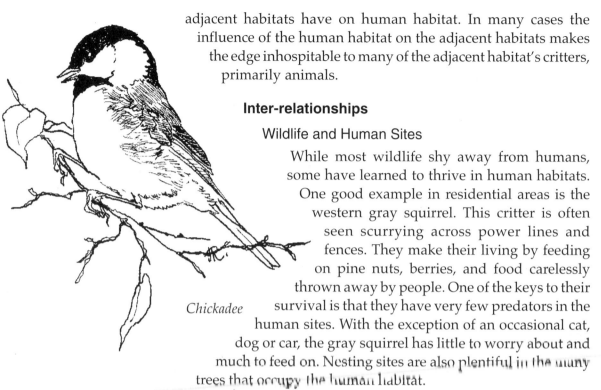

Chickadee

While most wildlife shy away from humans, some have learned to thrive in human habitats. One good example in residential areas is the western gray squirrel. This critter is often seen scurrying across power lines and fences. They make their living by feeding on pine nuts, berries, and food carelessly thrown away by people. One of the keys to their survival is that they have very few predators in the human sites. With the exception of an occasional cat, dog or car, the gray squirrel has little to worry about and much to feed on. Nesting sites are also plentiful in the many trees that occupy the human habitat.

Other common wildlife found in human habitats are insects and birds. By far, insects and birds represent the greatest diversity of wildlife in human sites. Birds flock to human areas for food including insects, protection from hawks and owls, and nesting sites. Aside from bird feeders, humans help to feed birds by planting gardens and native plants in their yards. Water also attracts birds, especially in the late summer.

Some of the more common bird species in human areas are dark-eyed juncos in the winter, house sparrows that are also called flying pigs by some bird watchers, American robins, northern flickers, red-breasted nuthatches where there are conifers, chickadees, chipping sparrows, and white-crowned sparrows.

Some birds, such as the juncos and white crowned sparrows, are migratory and may spend as a little as a month or as much as six months in the Little Spokane Watershed. Others, like the chickadees and nuthatches are year-round residents. These year-round residents are better adapted to cold winters and less able to travel long distances.

Rock doves, pigeons and violet-green swallows can be found in both urban and suburban areas. House sparrows and starlings are introduced species that compete with native species for food and nesting sites. They also do well in human habitats and increase with human numbers in suburbs.

In the winter the protection and availability of food in human habitats benefits local breeders such as juncos and wintering species such as redpolls. On the other hand, human habitats favor the proliferation of predatory bird species such as magpies and crows. Other more common critters, especially along the edge of human habitats include raccoons, skunks, an occasional coyote and every once in a while, a moose, bear, or elk.

Human-introduced species can also significantly affect adjoining nature habitats. The grasses from lawns and even some bedding plants can spread into nature habitats. Lawns, one of the largest "crops" in North America, use large amounts of water that could instead go to benefit nature. The large amount of fertilizers and biocides used on lawns can have significant affects on both people and nature. It would be considered excessive and in some cases dangerous if similar proportions of fertilizers and biocides were applied to agriculture lands.

Dalmatian toadflax, a "pretty yellow snapdragon-like flower" from the Dalmatian Coast of southern Europe spreads across disturbed fields and invades other habitats. Toadflax displaces and harms native plants which in turn can harm wildlife including bird populations. Also introduced by humans are pets, cats, dogs, bullfrogs and others, that can displace and harm native critters.

A pair of Bluebirds checking out a new home

One example of critter displacement is the introduction of the yellow iris. The yellow iris displaces cattails in wetlands. As the cattails are choked out, the birds that depended on the cattails for their food and habitat decline in numbers.

Sustainability

Unfortunately, allowing human habitat to become more restorative is not simple nor can it be done as fast as many might like. However, much can be done to reduce the needless destruction of wildlife habitat. Habitat destruction has been blamed as the single greatest cause for loss of biodiversity in the world today.

Creating continuous interconnected nature corridors throughout human habitat areas can allow the human habitat to become more sustainable. Sensible growth management planning can certainly benefit the Little Spokane Watershed by encouraging people and nature to live well together.

How new neighborhoods are designed and how older neighborhoods evolve affects human habitat sustainability. Clustered housing can be a creative way to nurture more livable and more sustainable human habitat. Clustered housing that includes neighborhood stores, schools, parks, nature areas, gardens, and places to work all within walking distance can have many benefits. The costs of roads, water and sewer, electricity, phone, heat, fire protection, schools and other infrastructure for these neighborhoods are considerably less than the infrastructure costs of excessive sprawl.

Planting native plants

This type of clustered housing can reduce the amount of traffic within and out of the neighborhood and can allow the use of bus and light rail to become more effective.

Instead of moving to the country to enjoy nature, at considerable expense to both people and nature, more nature areas can be incorporated into neighborhoods. The neighborhoods and nature areas can be linked together with pathways that provide an "out in the country" feeling and can allow neighborhoods to become more sustainable.

On an individual and neighborhood level, many more sustainable actions can be taken. Native plants can be planted in yards and neighborhoods, especially in areas with noxious weeds. The *Backyard Wildlife Sanctuary Program* sponsored by The Department of Fish and Wildlife can be participated in. The *Backyard Wildlife Sanctuary Program* recognizes individuals who are making their yards more inviting for wildlife. Some of these beneficial actions include putting up bird houses and bird boxes, planting native plants, and building ponds and other watering spots for the neighborhood wildlife.

Haven's for native plants can be created in yards for the native plants that would be destroyed during development of an area. The heavy equipment that is used to clear development areas can be used to dig up and set aside the native plants before the area is cleared. These native plants can then be moved to nearby native plant havens.

Individuals can record counts of birds and other wildlife as the critters make their annual migration cycles through an observation area. The native plants, fungi, lichens and tiny critters of an observation area can also be recorded. These records form a nature map of the area. With nature mapping, people can get a better feel for the place where they live and are better able to notice trends of the critters and nature. Early warning signs can be detected and adjustments made. Positive trends can be nurtured and celebrated.

As positive actions are taken, each neighborhood becomes more sustainable and the critters are better able to make their living too. While individual positive actions may at times seem insignificant, they do make a difference towards allowing the Little Spokane Watershed to become more healthy, thriving and restorative.

Quality of Life Measures

There are many ways cities and towns are measuring the quality of life for their city and region. Oregon produces an annual report on the progress towards a more sustainable state. Many cities and towns throughout the world are making sustainability reports.

These reports on quality of life include measurements of air and water quality, salmon runs, miles of streams meeting water quality standards, the number of good air days per year, water use per household, adult literacy skills, per capita income, children living above poverty, crimes against persons, education funds per student, health care access, fuel consumption, housing affordability and the number of miles of pathways in nature settings.

The costs of the various ways of living in human habits can be compared. When the full costs, including the all too often externalized costs, are taken into account, better decisions can be made. These costs can include the time and expense of driving to and from home, the costs for infrastructure, and the costs of house and yard maintenance.

Another quality of life measure is the number of people who are stewards of the land near where they live. The number of acres of land with native plants instead of noxious weeds in neighborhoods can be another measure. The number of neighborhood nature restoration projects is another measure. The number of gardens is another quality of life measure. The number and age of trees per acre is another measure. The number and variety of birds, native plants and other wildlife is another measure of the health of human habitat.

Robin in early spring

Summary of Human Habitat Critters

Number of Species by Kingdom

PLANT (PLANTAE)   37

FUNGUS (EUMYCOTA)   106

ANIMAL (ANIMALIA)   177

PROTIST (PROTISTA)   8

**BACTERIA & VIRUS
(MONERA & VIRUS)**   7

Number of Species by Class

Moss (Bryopsida)	2
Pine (Pinicae)	1
Carnation (Caryophyllidae)	3
Aspen (Dilleniidae)	1
Rose (Rosidae)	11
Sunflower (Asteridae)	17
Grass (Commelinidae)	2
Mushroom (Basidomycetes)	91
Puffball (Gastromycetes)	7
Ascomycetes (Ascomycetes)	6
Crusty Lichen (Crustose)	2
Turbellidia (Turbellidia)	1
Roundworm (Acari)	1
Snail (Gastropoda)	1
Earthworm (Oligocheata)	1
Spider (Arachnida)	1
Centipede (Chilopoda)	1
Millipede (Diplopoda)	1
Insect (Insecta)	58
Amphiblan (Amphibia)	2
Reptile (Reptilia)	2
Bird (Aves)	87
Mammal (Mammalia)	19
Amoeba (Rhizopoda)	1
Heliozoan (Actimpoda)	1
Foram (Forimaninifera)	1
Sporozoite (Apicomplexa)	1
Slime Mold - Cellular (Acrasiomycetes)	1
Slime Mold - Plasmodial (Myxomycetes)	1
Mildew (Oomycota)	1
Saprobe (Chytridiomycota)	1
Bacteria (Bacteria)	1
Cyanophycota (Cyanophycota)	1
Prochlorophycota (Prochlorophycota)	1
Bacteria Virus (Bacteria Virus)	1
Plant Virus (Plant Virus)	1
Vertebrate Virus (Vertebrate Virus)	1
Invertebrate Virus (Invertebrate Virus)	1

TOTAL IDENTIFIED SPECIES   335

Selected Human Habitat Critters

PLANT (PLANTAE)	22		
Moss (Bryopsida)	2		
Ceratodon purpureus		C	
Funaria hygrometrica		C	
Pine (Pinicae)	1		
Ponderosa Pine		A	
Carnation (Caryophyllidae)	3		
Goosefoot		C	IO
Mouse-ear Chickweed		C	IO
Sticky Chickweed		C	IO
Rose (Rosidae)	8		
Apple		A	IO
Crane's Bill		C	IO
Japanese Clover		C	IO
Mountain Ash (A)		C	IO
Norway Maple		A	IO
Plum		C	IO
White Clover		A	IO
Willow Herb		C	
Sunflower (Asteridae)	6		
Common Plantain		C	IO
Dalmatian Toadflax		C	IN
Honeysuckle (B)		A	IO
Spotted Knapweed		A	IN
Stoneseed		C	IO
Yellow Salsify		C	IO
Grass (Commelinidae)	2		
Bluegrass		A	
Bulbous Bluegrass		C	IO

FUNGUS (EUMYCOTA)	15	
Mushroom (Basidomycetes)	12	
Fairy Ring Mushroom		A
Fly Agaric (B)		C
Marasmius sp.		C
Mica Cap		A
Pluteus flavofuligineus		C
Poison Pie		A
Psathyrella condolleana		A
Shaggy Mane		C
Shaggy Parasol		C
Smooth Parasol		C
Spring Agrocybe		C
Velvet Foot		A
Puffball (Gastromycetes)	1	
Puffball (C)		C
Crusty Lichen (Crustose)	2	
Xanthoria elegans		C
Xanthoria polycarpa		C

ANIMAL (ANIMALIA)	42		
Roundworm (Acari)	1		
Round Worm		C	
Earthworm (Oligocheata)	1		
Oligochaeta		A	
Insect (Insecta)	20		
Aphid		A	
Aquatic Dance Fly		C	
Blow Fly		C	
Bumblebee spp		C	
Cabbage Butterfly		C	
Clothes Moth		C	
Clouded Sulfur		C	
Codling Moth		A	
Earwig		A	
Elm Leaf Beetle		A	
Flea		C	
Geometrid Moth		C	
Honeybee		C	
House Fly		C	
Leaf Bug		C	
Leafroller Moth		C	
Mountain Swallowtail		C	
Owlet Moth		C	
Pyralid Moth		C	
Syrphid Fly		C	
Reptile (Reptilia)	1		
Common Garter Snake		C	
Bird (Aves)	16		
American Crow		C	
American Robin		C	
Brewer's Blackbird		A	
California Quail		C	IO
Cliff Swallow		C	
Eastern Kingbird		C	
European Starling		A	
Great Horned Owl		C	
House Finch		C	
House Sparrow		A	
Pine Siskin		C	
Red-breasted Nuthatch		C	
Ring-billed Gull		C	
Rock Dove		A	
Tree Swallow		C	
Violet-green Swallow		A	
Mammal (Mammalia)	3		
Cat, Domestic		A	IN
Dogs, Domestic		A	IN
Human		A	

* The critters listed here are those identified as abundant and common.

Legend - Critters are listed by their common name followed by their abundance in the habitat. Introduced species and species at risk are indicated by type code. • **Abundance Codes: A** Abundant, **C** Common, **F** Fairly common, **U** Uncommon, **R** Rare, **V** Vagrant, **K** Known in habitat, **L** Likely in habitat, **M** Missing from habitat. • **Introduced Species Codes: IN** Introduced Noxious species, **IO** Introduced, Other than noxious species. • **At Risk Codes: MS** Missing, **ED** Endangered, **TH** Threatened, **CD** Candidate, **MN** Monitor, **RGM** Regulated Game, **RNG** Regulated Nongame, **RA** Rare, **PB** Protected Breeding Areas.

Selected Critter Descriptions

Mountain Swallowtail *(Papilio zelicaon)*

Sub Family: Swallowtail (Papilioninae)
Family: Swallowtail (Papilionidae)
Order: Butterfly (Lepidoptera)

Class: Insect (Insecta)
Division: Joint-legged Invertebrate (Arthropoda)
Kingdom: Animal (Animalia)

LSW Habitats: SA: U, MT: U, DF: F, PP: U, RK: U, BU: U GR: U, WL: U, RP: U, ST: U, LK: U, DS: U, HU: C

Relationships To Watershed: Mountain Swallowtail caterpillars feed on plants from the Parsley, Umbelliferae, and Citrus, Rutaceae, Families. Apparently these two very different plant families contain similar oils in their tissues that stimulate the larvae to eat.

Description: Mountain Swallowtails are large yellow and black butterflies with one or two narrow yellow stripes on each side of the abdomen. Larvae are usually green or bluish green with notched transverse bands and two black spots above each leg. Mountain Swallowtail males patrol and perch on hilltops in search of females, a behavior known as "hilltopping". Several breeding flights occur in the Pacific Northwest beginning in May.

Swallowtails gathering around moisture

Look Alikes: There are several other species of swallowtails that occur in the region.

Little Spokane Habitat: Mountain Swallowtail prefer moist to wet forests and openings in the forest.

World Habitat: Mountain Swallowtail have transitioned to Hudsonian Zone mountains, ranging from sea level to rarely above timberline.

California Quail *(Callipepia californica)*

		Class:	Birds (Aves)
Family:	Grouse (Galliformes)	**Division:**	Vertebrate (Chordata)
Order:	Thrush (Passeriformes)	**Kingdom:**	Animal (Animalia)

Introduced: Introduced Species
LSW Habitats: PP: U, BU: C, RP: U, ST: U, HU: F

Relationships To Watershed: California Quail feed on some fruits, insects, spiders and snails.

Description: California Quail are blue-gray birds with brownish wings. Their bellies have a dark, scaly appearance. Their bodies are plump and stocky. They have a short, curved, black plume, and their throats are black and framed with white while the forehead is usually buff. Their crowns are dark brown.

Look Alikes: Distinct.

Little Spokane Habitat: California Quail tolerate a relatively broad variety of climates, from arid deserts to cool, wet coast. They live in areas covered with shrubs and woodlands with patches of open ground, including suburban gardens, chaparral, and river bottoms below areas of snowfall.

World Habitat: California Quail are an introduced species, native to southern parts of Oregon on to the tip of Baja California and east barely into western Nevada. California Quail have also been introduced in other parts of the world including New Zealand.

American Robin *(Turdus migratorius)*

		Class:	Birds (Aves)
Family:	Robin (Muscicapidae)	**Division:**	Vertebrate (Chordata)
Order:	Thrush (Passeriformes)	**Kingdom:**	Animal (Animalia)

Other Name: Robin
LSW Habitats: MT: U, PP: U, BU: C, GR: C, RP: C, ST: C, LK: C, DS: C, HU: C

Relationships To Watershed: American Robins gather in large winter roosts and feed heavily on fruits and berries. They occasionally become intoxicated by fermented fruits and behave in a somewhat curious fashion.

Description: American Robin adults are dark gray above with a brick-red breast, a white lower belly, and white undertail coverts. Males have black heads, wings, and tails; females are duller. In both sexes, an incomplete, broad white spectacle frames the brown eye. The chin is streaked black and white, and the yellow bill is tipped with black.

Look Alikes: The Varied thrush closely resembles the American Robin in size and behavior but has a different song and plumage.

Little Spokane Habitat: American Robins are a widespread bird flourishing in modern, suburban areas and frequenting forest borders, woodland openings, pastures, orchards, groves, and parks.

World Habitat: American Robins are found in Northern America, Canada, Mexico, and Central America.

Young Robin looking for a snack

Measuring Watershed Quality Of Life

By measuring the Little Spokane Watershed's quality of life, progress towards allowing the watershed to become more healthy and restorative can be tracked. At one time the salmon runs on the Little Spokane were an excellent measure of the watershed's quality of life.

For thousands of years the salmon returned in great abundance to the Little Spokane Watershed. About 100 years ago the salmon were still returning, until the Spokane River dams were built without fish ladders. Then these once plentiful fish were literally locked out of their spawning grounds and soon were no longer found in the Little Spokane. By adding fish ladders to the ladderless Spokane and Columbia river dams, salmon could once again return to the Little Spokane Watershed, bringing back one measure of the watershed's quality of life.

Without measurement, slow degradation of the Little Spokane Watershed's quality of life can take place without much notice until a crisis occurs. Management by crisis can be extremely costly and have even more costly long term consequences. By establishing quality of life measures, trends can be anticipated and proactive adjustments can be made.

Birders on a winter bird count

One example of crisis management is the pollution from the Colbert landfill that is contaminating the Spokane-Rathdrum Aquifer just before it flows into the Little Spokane. This disaster has resulted in the area around the landfill being declared a superfund site. Millions of dollars have been spent trying to make the water less toxic before it pours into the Little Spokane. Each day hundreds of thousands of gallons of water are pumped out of the aquifer to have most of the toxic chemicals removed before the water goes into the Little Spokane. With better quality of life measures in place, perhaps other unsafe practices can be avoided or at least made safer before a crisis point is reached.

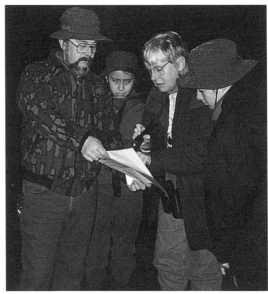

Early morning map study before starting bird count

Another crisis in the watershed continues to build. That is the significant decline in annual water flow. The average annual flow of the Little Spokane has declined by about 25 percent over the past 30 years. This is probably due to too much water being taken out of the Little Spokane. Measurements of stream flow can allow and encourage better and earlier decisions to be made.

Carrying Capacity Measures

There is only so much water, air and land available in the watershed, and only so much that can be done with the various aspects of the watershed before serious issues begin to arise. Carrying capacity is a measure of how much is available and how much can be done. By measuring the carrying capacities and current uses of the watershed, serious issues can be anticipated and work started to resolve them before a crisis occurs or before significant degradation takes place.

Carrying capacity is a measure of how much is enough. A watershed's carrying capacity is like a person's ability to eat only so much and only certain kinds of food without getting sick or seriously ill. What may be good in moderation can be deadly when taken to excess.

Going beyond the Little Spokane Watershed's carrying capacity can be done in many ways. Here are several ways the watershed's carrying capacity can be exceeded. The water can become significantly polluted. Too much of the water can be taken out of the watershed. The Little

Two elementary school classrooms on their way to plant native plants

Boxes of hundreds of native plants to be planted. Each box contains packets of ten plants ready to be planted by hand

Spokane Watershed can be loved to death by trying to allow more people to live in the watershed than the watershed can handle. The watershed's nature corridors can become seriously fragmented.

There are other carrying capacity measures that can be developed to examine how well the watershed is doing. There are also measures of how well the native plants, wildlife and their habitats are doing. These measures can encourage better decisions for the watershed.

Nature Place Diaries And Journals

Periodic written observations of critters in the Little Spokane Watershed are indispensable tools for measuring the watershed's quality of life. Each person who lives in the watershed, on a daily basis, observes their nature place of the watershed. Very few others know this nature place as well as those living there. With these daily observations individuals can gain insights into how their nature place works.

Those who are curious about specific types of critters will find using field guides invaluable. One of the best set of books in the world on plant identification happens to be *Flora of the Pacific Northwest*, by G.L. Hitchcock and A. Cronquist, University of Washington Press. Those who become interested in the Little Spokane Watershed's native plants will delight in this treasure of information.

Interviewing one of the planters

A diary or journal of nature place observations can be very helpful. For example, a written record that moose have shown up around mid June each year for the past 18 years can be invaluable, especially if the moose do not show up several years in a row or they start coming earlier or later. Noting changes in regular patterns can provide an early warning that something may have changed in the watershed. These early warnings can

Late fall planting

allow more prompt attention to small changes that may have long term consequences if not adjusted early on.

Periodic Observation Summaries

Annual summaries of diary observations can be useful to compare one year with other years. From a diary and from annual summaries much can be learned about how well the watershed is doing. Noting exceptions, especially out of the ordinary changes, can be most useful.

By writing one's observations and making annual summaries, questions about trends can be examined. Here are some questions that can be asked.

Are there significantly fewer birds this year than there were twenty years ago? Is there more knapweed in the fields that used to have native grass? Have the fish returned to the creek that was choked with silt. When do certain birds return each year? When do certain plants flower? Does one area flower earlier than others? What is the water level during the year? Are there fewer frogs croaking at night during the summer? Are more ponds drying up even in wet years? Who can better answer these questions for a particular nature place in the watershed than those who live there and who have an eye for observing the watershed and who write their observations in a nature place journal?

A fresh planting

Annual Critter Counts

Annual critter counting is another way to examine the quality of life in the watershed. By using the same date each year, rain or shine, annual counts can be an enjoyable way to see part of the watershed and can also provide useful insights on how well the watershed is doing. Counts can be done for particular types of native plants or wildlife. One example is the annual Audubon winter bird count.

Each year Spokane's Audubon Society conducts an annual winter bird count. The count is for the larger Spokane region. Several sections of the Little Spokane Watershed are included in these counts. This is an excellent opportunity to learn more about observing birds. Also, the records of the Little Spokane Watershed counts from past years can be copied and compared to see if there are any obvious trends. Just summarizing the yearly counts on one report for the Little Spokane Watershed can prove very useful.

Planting Native Plants

In addition to observing nature places, native plants can be planted to enhance and create additional nature places. The number of native plants is another measure of quality of life. Fields that are returning to nature can have noxious weeds removed and native plants can be planted. Native plants can also be planted in yards which can reduce the amount of water that yards use.

More Formal Observations

A more formal way to examine nature places in the watershed is to examine specific sites. At these sites a series of observation points can be set up or a sequence of walking lines, called transects, can be established. Observations are recorded at each observation point or while walking along the transects. The observations are systematically recorded and summarized each time the sites are studied.

There are specific procedures for establishing transects and making observations along transects that can significantly increase the usefulness of the observations. Biologists and naturalists are familiar with these procedures as well as the consequences of poorly planned observation points and transects. Biologists and naturalists can assist in developing useful transects.

Careful planting and watering

Planting begins

From time to time there are workshops for the general public to learn about techniques they can use. There are also courses at the colleges and universities that can be helpful for those interested in exploring more useful measures of qualities of life in the watershed.

Monitoring Critters

There are several common methods used to monitor critters at specific sites from the observation points or transects. Here are three methods.

Owl peeks out of a backyard bird box

Presence - Absence

Observations are made over a measured period of time. The presence and absence of critters is recorded.

Time Constraint Search

A search is made for as many critters, usually specific critters, as possible during a set period of time. This provides a relative index of the number of critters found per person hour.

Point Count Method

Consistent points are established, and observations are made from each point. The number of critters per observation time is recorded. The distance from the observation point can be estimated for each observation.

Counting Tracks In Fresh Snow

Most mammals are active during the night, nocturnal, making it difficult for day time counts to be of much use. However, a count taken 24 hours after a fresh snowfall can provide a good idea of a full day's activities for critters that move along the ground.

Before the snows fall, lines to be walked, transects, are identified for each habitat type of interest. Common transect lengths are from 300 to 1500 feet, 100 to 500 meters. For specific areas with several habitats, it is useful to make each habitat transect length in proportion to the percentage each habitat is of the specific area. For example in an area that has 60 percent ponderosa pine habitat and 40 percent grassland habitat, the pine transects could total 600 meters and the grassland transects could total 400 meters.

Just over twenty four hours after a fresh snowfall is an optimum time to count the tracks. Count the number of critters whose tracks cross or touch the transect line. Separate observations can be made of critters that are present but not on the transect line. This will give a good recording of a full day's activities on the ground.

The number of each type of critter per mile or kilometer can be calculated from the observations. This gives an idea of the species richness. The number of each type of critter per habitat can also be calculated. These numbers can be compared to estimates of what similar healthy habitat types are expected to have.

After restoration activities have taken place, these counts can be expected to begin increasing over the years, until they reach a more healthy stable state.

Backyard Wildlife Sanctuary

The Backyard Wildlife Sanctuary program sponsored by the Department of Fish and Wildlife encourages individuals to nurture their backyards for the critters of the area. Fish and Wildlife provides information on how to do this and a sign that identifies the backyard wildlife sanctuary. Appropriate native plants can be planted. Bird feeders, bird boxes and watering sites can be made.

Native Plant Havens

Native Plant Havens can be established for plants that are to be removed for development. These havens can be created by individuals or groups that can find a place to heal-in and water the plants until a permanent home can be found. Arrangements can be made, before development begins, to have the heavy equipment scoop up and move the native plants to a pick up location. Transplanting these homeless plants is another positive way to allow the watershed to become more restorative.

Nature Mapping

Nature mapping is the identification of critters in specific places and the use of this information to create maps of nature. As more information is gathered for specific places, the maps can be used to examine how healthy, thriving and restorative these places are. Schools and individuals are making nature maps of areas in their watersheds.

Nature mapping was initiated with a pilot project in 1993 by the Washington Department of Fish and Wildlife in partnership with the University of Washington's Fish and Wildlife Gap Analysis Project. The project started with 23 teachers and their students and has expanded to over 200 classrooms in just two years. A similar project, in Oregon, is now actively mapping Oregon nature places.

A long view

Washington's nature mapping project received national recognition with a Renew America Award. As more people become familiar with nature mapping, nature mapping projects are expected to become popular nationally and eventually world wide.

As nature mapping information is collected by classrooms and individuals, it is sent to the Gap Analysis Project for statewide nature mapping and analysis. Workshops, materials and equipment are being made available to help teachers and individuals collect this needed information. Landsat satellite images along with other geographic information, waterways and mountains, have been mapped for Washington. The Little Spokane Watershed Council has a copy of these maps and intends to facilitate nature mapping in the Little Spokane Watershed.

Allowing Nature Places To Become More Restorative

As more people take an active interest in the stewardship of the Little Spokane Watershed, nature places can be identified that can be allowed to become more restorative. Where appropriate, native plants can be planted. Noxious plants and other undesirable critters can be removed. Stream banks and streams that have been damaged can be reshaped so that they can reclaim their full functions and values. And other more restorative choices can be made for the Little Spokane Watershed.

As these fresh human choices are made, the habitats, their critters and their inter-relationships can become more healthy, thriving and restorative. The Little Spokane Watershed can be as magnificent as any watershed in the world.

A refreshing nature place

Photograph And Illustration Credits

Illustration Credits

Joe Guarisco
The habitat chapter graphic headings, the graphics for the life categories: Plants, Fungi, Animals, Protists, and Bacteria and Virus.

Joe Guarisco & Maurice Vial
The watershed map.

Lori Lewis
The biological illustrations.

Biological Illustrations In Alphabetic Order

Biological Term	Page	Biological Term	Page
Achene	63	Lobed Leaf	86
Aggregate Fruit	83	Oblanceolate Leaf	240
Alternate Leaves	187	Oblong Leaf	151
Awn	107	Opposite Leaves	151
Basal Leaves	65	Ovate Leaf	67
Basal Rosette	241	Palmate	104
Beak	221	Panicle Inflorescence	108
Capsule	47	Pedicel	220
Catkins Inflorescence	187	Peduncle	220
Cauline Leaves	155	Petiole	185
Cespitose	153	Pith	170
Clasping Leaves	109	Pome	105
Cordate Leaf	64	Raceme Inflorescence	155
Corymb Inflorescence	44	Ray Flower	37
Culm	153	Rhizomes	184
Cyme Inflorescence	66	Saggitale Leaf	220
Disk Flower	241	Serrated Leaf	46
Doubly Serrate or		Sessile	190
Biserrate Leaf	82	Spikelet	153
Drupe	122	Spinose	82
Elliptic Leaf	45	Spur	122
Entire Margin	64	Stolon	63
Follicle	104	Ternate	62
Hip	138	Toothed Leaf	62
Involucre	241	Truncate Leaf Base	124
Labials	157	Tuber	220
Lanceolate Leaf	108	Tubular Flower	105
Leaflet	82	Umbel Inflorescence	220
Lenticel	170	Urn-shaped	46

Photograph And Critter Drawing Credits

Page	Person	Brief Description	Page	Person	Brief Description
Cvr	Maurice Vial	Front Illustration	60	John S. Lewis	Base of red cedar tr
Cvr	John S. Lewis	Little rapids	68	Pat Dexter	Owl
Cvr	John S. Lewis	Meander	69	Ron Dexter	On branch
Cvr	John S. Lewis	Beaver hut	70	Ron Dexter	Flying squirrel goin
Cvr	John S. Lewis	Slow water, cottonwoods	71	Ron Dexter	finishing pine cone
2	John S. Lewis	Rocky portion of riv	72	John S. Lewis	Tiny falls at left,
6	Patricia Vandenhoy	Grassy clearing with	72	Ron Dexter	Pileated Woodpecker
10	Pam Kriscunas	Down stream view	73	Easy	Pathway thru Doug Fi
11	John S. Lewis	CU of one plant, thr	74	Patricia Vandenhoy	Moss on log with sur
11	Ron Dexter	Dome mushroom	75	Trish Bravo	CU of moss on dougla
11	Ron Dexter	Chipmunk	75	Pat Dexter	Golden Waxy Cap
12	John S. Lewis	Moss on rock in FG,	76	Easy	Ant mound
12	Patricia Vandenhoy	CU of slug	76	Ron Dexter	Northern Saw-whet Ow
12	Ron Dexter	Northern Pygmy Owl	77	Trish Bravo	closeup of two flowe
13	Ron Dexter	Moose in forest	80	Trish Bravo	Douglas fir cone. gr
14	John S. Lewis	Cones and needles	81	Pat Dexter	White shooting star
14	Ron Dexter	Red Squirrel on pine	81	Ron Dexter	Mushroom emerging
15	John S. Lewis	Delicate fern leaves	83	Trish Bravo	CU of cluster of thr
18	Trish Bravo	CU of one plant with	84	Patricia Vandenhoy	Spirea in flower wit
19	Patricia Vandenhoy	Moss? on forest floo	85	Patricia Vandenhoy	Closeup of flower wi
22	Joe Guarisco	LSW Map BW 3.0 eps	86	Patricia Vandenhoy	Honeysuckle and bran
23	Easy	View Across WS W to	87	Easy	Beetle CU
24	LSW Archieve	AE 92-1 Confluence N	88	Pat Dexter	White mushroom
25	Doris Allgood	Little Spokane and B	89	Patricia Vandenhoy	CU of fairy ring
26	John S. Lewis	3 pines, sunlight on	89	Trish Bravo	CU of lichen and mos
27	LSW Archieve	AE 92-1 Confluence N	89	Ron Doxter	Flat Mushroom on log
28	John S. Lewis	Overview of Painted	89	Ron Dexter	Mushroom on stump
30	John S. Lewis	Three-tiered view of	89	Pat Dexter	Brain Mushroom
31	John S. Lewis	Treeline with reflec	89	Ron Dexter	Shelf fungi
32	John S. Lewis	Large flower and clu	92	Easy	Critter hideout
32	Patricia Vandenhoy	CU of damselfly on l	93	Easy	DF, old ag, lone pin
33	John S. Lewis	Ferns and foliage ag	94	John S. Lewis	Gilia flower CU
34	John S. Lewis	Shot of river showin	94	Pam Kriscunas	Walking along trail
35	Ron Dexter	Subalpine snag	95	Trish Bravo	CU shot of plant clu
36	Ron Dexter	Subalpine Trees Hori	95	Easy	Wet Snowberry
37	Ron Dexter	Subalpine Trees & Mt	96	Patricia Vandenhoy	Young pine next to t
38	Ron Dexter	Subalpine silhouette	97	Patricia Vandenhoy	Butterfly on branch
39	Ron Dexter	Spruce & wet area	97	Pat Dexter	Grass Widow
43	Ron Dexter	Subalpine Trees	98	Patricia Vandenhoy	CU of fly on wood ro
48	John S. Lewis	Pine w/Mt. Spokane i	98	Patricia Vandenhoy	Lichen on bough with
49	John S. Lewis	Shot of falls with f	98	Easy	Field Returning Wild
50	Trish Bravo	CU in bloom, flowers	102	Trish Bravo	Cone and needle spra
50	Pam Kriscunas	Wild Rose	102	Trish Bravo	Ponderosa pine cone
51	Pat Dexter	Lupine in bloom	104	John S. Lewis	Robin feasting on se
51	Pat Dexter	White Trillium	106	Trish Bravo	Closeup of plant, se
52	Ron Dexter	Indian Peace Pipe Fu	107	Ron Dexter	Orange butterfly
53	Pat Dexter	Big yellow mushroom	110	Ron Dexter	Natterjack Toad on s
54	Ron Dexter	Sapsucker feeding on	113	Easy	Porcupine bark strip
54	Ron Dexter	Hummingbird, sapsuck	116	Easy	Gutsy Pine in rock
55	John S. Lewis	Vole in grass	117	Ron Dexter	Marmot on rock
55	Ron Dexter	Pygmy Owl with captu	118	Easy	Rockland
56	John S. Lewis	Dying tree with smok	118	Pat Dexter	skink
56	Patricia Vandenhoy	Squirrel on branch w	123	Trish Bravo	Closeup of three cas

Page	Person	Brief Description	Page	Person	Brief Description
207	Ron Dexter	Marmot on rock	252	John S. Lewis	CU of four swallowta
208	Ron Dexter	Spotted Sandpiper	252	LSW Archieve	AE 92-5 Hatchery S
208	Ron Dexter	Wood Duck pair	254	Ron Dexter	Young Robin waiting
209	John S. Lewis	View of dam with tre	255	Easy	Birders Walking
209	Ron Dexter	Cedar Waxwing	256	Easy	Line of kids, parent
210	John S. Lewis	Sandpiper on rocky b	256	Easy	Jan & Birders Map
210	Ron Dexter	Muskrat swimming	257	Easy	Planting Interview
211	Ron Dexter	on bank	257	Easy	Plants in boxes
212	John S. Lewis	Shot with hut in MG	257	Easy	Hands & boot plntg
213	John S. Lewis	River with trees in	257	Easy	Plants out of box
214	Pat Dexter	Lily pads in bloom	258	Easy	2 children planting
214	Ron Dexter	2 Turtles on log	258	Easy	Fresh planting
215	John S. Lewis	Lily pads with half	259	Easy	8 Kids planting
215	Ron Dexter	Ducklings scattering	259	Olivia Waterman	3 Kids planting
216	John S. Lewis	Duck and three duckl	260	Ron Dexter	Owl peaks out of box
217	Ron Dexter	Heron fishing	260	Easy	Birders looking
220	Pam Kriscunas	Wapato in grass	261	John S. Lewis	Iris field in foregr
221	Ron Dexter	Pond Lily in bloom	262	John S. Lewis	Falls in FG, ferns i
222	Trish Bravo	Closeup of pond lily			
223	Pat Dexter	Tiger lily			
226	John S. Lewis	CU of bullfrog in du			
226	Ron Dexter	Bull Frog menace			
227	Pam Kriscunas	Turtle			
228	Patricia Vandenhoy	Mallard female swimm			
228	Ron Dexter	Osprey feeding on fi			
229	Ron Dexter	Osprey in flight			
230	Ron Dexter	Red-wing on cattail			
230	Ron Dexter	Red-wing female eati			
231	John S. Lewis	Field of mullein wit			
232	Trish Bravo	Closeup of one plant			
232	LSW Archieve	AE 50-1 Confluence N			
232	LSW Archieve	AE 74-4 Painted Rock			
232	LSW Archieve	AE 92-3 Painted Rock			
233	Trish Bravo	Closeup of one plant			
234	Easy	Shaggy P day 1			
234	Easy	Shaggy P 2			
234	Pam Kriscunas	Toad Flax flower			
235	Patricia Vandenhoy	Mullein with trees i			
238	Patricia Vandenhoy	Clover with grass			
238	Patricia Vandenhoy	Bracken Fern			
239	John S. Lewis	CU of one plant			
239	Trish Bravo	Closeup of one plant			
240	Easy	Mullen			
242	Patricia Vandenhoy	CU of thistle groupi			
242	Trish Bravo	CU Fawn angle wing o			
243	Patricia Vandenhoy	Closeup of one plant			
243	Patricia Vandenhoy	CU of butterfly on f			
244	Ron Dexter	Shaggy Mane on way u			
244	Pat Dexter	Shaggy Mane beginnin			
245	Patricia Vandenhoy	CU of swallowtail on			
246	Jan Reynolds	Chickadee on branch			
247	Ron Dexter	Western Bluebird pai			
248	John S. Lewis	Robin perched on bra			
248	Easy	Children planting			
250	Easy	CU seedhead			

Appendix

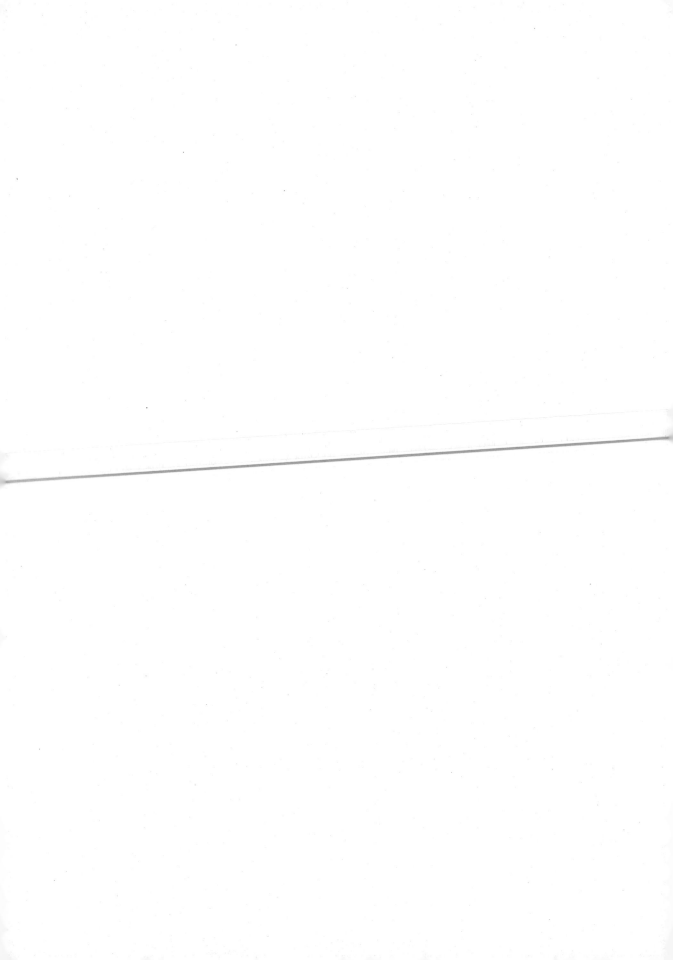

Forest Habitat Key

Forest habitats of the Little Spokane Watershed fall into the broad categories of Subalpine, Mountain, Douglas Fir and Ponderosa Pine. This Forest Habitat Key allows more specific sub-habitat identification within the broad habitat types. The decision steps of the key and their results are first presented, followed by the key.

This key is most useful in habitats that have not been very seriously disturbed in recent years. To identify habitats that have been seriously disturbed, the broad geographic location together with the position in the local vegetation are additional criteria that can be very useful.

Index

Decision Step								Habitat
								Ponderosa Pine
1	2	3	A					Ponderosa Pine – Idaho Fescue
1	2	3	B					Ponderosa Pine – Bluebunch Wheatgrass
1	2	3	C					Ponderosa Pine – Needle -and- Thread
1	2	4	A					Ponderosa Pine – Bitterbrush
1	2	4	5	A				Ponderosa Pine – Ninebark
1	2	4	5	B				Ponderosa Pine – Snowberry
								Douglas Fir
1	6	7	8	9	A			Douglas Fir – Pinegrass
1	6	7	8	9	B			Douglas Fir – Pinegrass Kinnikinnick phase
1	6	7	8	10	A			Douglas Fir – Ninebark
1	6	7	8	10	B			Douglas Fir – Snowberry
								Mountain
1	6	7	B					Grand Fir – Oregon Boxwood
1	6	11	12	13	A			Western Red Cedar – Oregon Boxwood
1	6	11	12	13	B			Western Hemlock – Oregon Boxwood
1	6	11	12	14	A			Western Red Cedar – Devil's Club
1	6	11	12	14	B			Western Red Cedar – Ladyfern
								Subalpine
1	6	11	15	A				Subalpine Fir – Oregon Boxwood
1	6	11	15	16	17	A		Mountain Hemlock – Fool's Huckleberry
1	6	11	15	16	17	B		Mountain Hemlock – Beargrass
1	6	11	15	16	18	19		Subalpine Fir – Fool's Huckleberry
1	6	11	15	16	18	20	A	Subalpine Fir – Beargrass
1	6	11	15	16	18	20	B	Subalpine Fir – Grouseberry
1	6	11	15	16	18	B		Western White Pine – Subalpine Fir

Forest Habitat Key

1. Ponderosa pine present; other conifers absent
    2. Undergrowth dominated by grasses; shrubs inconspicuous; dwarf mistletoe usually abundant
        3. Idaho fescue is principal grass
           A.   **Ponderosa Pine – Idaho Fescue Habitat**
        3. Bluebunch wheat grass the principal grass; soil usually with high stone content
           B.   **Ponderosa Pine – bluebunch Wheatgrass Habitat**
        3. Needle–and–thread the principal grass; soil conspicuously sandy
           C.   **Ponderosa Pine – Needle–And–Thread Habitat**
    2. Shrubs conspicuous in undergrowth
        4. Bitterbrush well represented; soil sandy or stony; dwarf mistletoe usually present
           A.   **Ponderosa Pine – Bitterbrush Habitat**
        4. Bitterbrush and dwarf mistletoe absent; soil a loam or stony loam
           5. Ninebark and/or ocean–spray well represented
               A.   **Ponderosa Pine – Ninebark Habitat**
           5. Ninebark and ocean–spray absent; undergrowth dominated by snowberry, wood's rose, nootka rose, shiny–leaf spiraea or chokecherry
               B.   **Ponderosa Pine – Snowberry Habitat**
1. Coniferous trees other than ponderosa pine present and reproducing
    6. Red cedar, hemlock and subalpine fir absent, or at least not reproducing
        7. Grand fir absent; undergrowth lacking, queen's cup, twinflower, wintergreen spp., Big huckleberry, and round leaved violet
           8. Pinegrass, often with much elk sedge or low northern sedge, very conspicuous in the undergrowth; shrubs other than kinnikinnick or huckleberry
               9. Kinnikinnick and huckleberry unrepresented
                  A.   **Douglas Fir – Pinegrass Habitat**
               9. Kinnikinnick present; huckleberry usually present
                  B.   **Douglas Fir – Pinegrass, Kinnikinnick Phase Habitat**
        8. Pinegrass, elk sedge and low northern sedge poorly represented, if at all present; shrubs other than kinnikinnick or huckleberry dominant
           10. Ninebark and/or ocean–spray well represented
               A.   **Douglas Fir – Ninebark Habitat**
           10. Ninebark and ocean-spray absent; snowberry and/or shiny–leaf spiraea abundantly represented
               B.   **Douglas Fir – Snowberry Habitat**
        7. Grand fir present and reproducing successfully
           A.   **Grand Fir – Oregon Boxwood Habitat**
    6. Red cedar, hemlock or subalpine present and reproducing
        11. Red cedar or mountain hemlock reproducing successfully
           12. Uplands; devil's club absent; ladyfern, if present, scarcely half a meter tall
               13. Hemlock absent; red cedar reproducing successfully
                  A.   **Western Red Cedar – Oregon Boxwood Habitat**
               13. Hemlock present and reproducing well
                  B.   **Western Hemlock – Oregon Boxwood Habitat**

12. Moist bottomlands or slopes with seepage; ladyfern usually abundant and well over half a meter tall

    14. Devil's club abundant; contiguous uplands belonging to the hemlock – boxwood habitat

        A.   **Western Red Cedar – Devil's Club Habitat**

    14. Devil's club absent; contiguous uplands usually belonging to the hemlock – boxwood habitat

        B.   **Western Red Cedar – Ladyfern Habitat**

11. Red cedar and western hemlock present as nonreproducing accidentals if at all; subalpine fir and/or mountain hemlock reproducing well

    15. Queen's cup and/or fragrant bedstraw usually present; usually with more than 14 undergrowth spp./375 m^2; moss–heather, labrador–tea and mountain–heather absent

        A   **Subalpine Fir – Oregon Boxwood Habitat**

    15. Queen's cup and bedstraw absent; usually with fewer than 14 undergrowth spp./375 m^2

        16. Mountain hemlock reproducing more vigorously than subalpine fir

            17. Undergrowth with fool's huckleberry well represented

                A.   **Mountain Hemlock – Fool's Huckleberry Habitat**

            17. Undergrowth lacking fool's huckleberry, rhododendron and labrador–tea, beargrass or big huckleberry dominant

                B.   **Mountain Hemlock – Beargrass Habitat**

        16. Mountain hemlock absent

            18 Trees tall, not wind-deformed, forming a closed forest

                19. Undergrowth with fool's huckleberry, rhododendron or smooth labrador–tea conspicuous

                    A. **Subalpine Fir – Fool's Huckleberry Habitat**

                19. Fool's huckleberry, rhododendron and labrador–tea absent

                20. Beargrass or big huckleberry dominant beneath the trees

                    A. **Subalpine Fir – Beargrass Habitat**

                20. Grouseberry dominant beneath the trees

                    B. **Subalpine Fir – Grouseberry Habitat**

        18. Trees dwarfed and wind-deformed, occurring as well separated groups or individuals

            B. **Western White Pine – Subalpine Fir Habitat**

Little Spokane Watershed Critter List

KINGDOM / Class / *Order* / FAMILY Species Name	#	At Risk	Intro	SA	MT	DF	PP	RK	BU	GR	WL	RP	ST	LK	DS	HU

Plants

KINGDOM / Class / *Order* / FAMILY Species Name	#	At Risk	Intro	SA	MT	DF	PP	RK	BU	GR	WL	RP	ST	LK	DS	HU
PLANT (PLANTAE)	**477**															
Moss (Bryopsida)	**29**															
Aluacomnium androgynum				C	C	C						C				
Aluacomnium androgynum				C	C	C						C				
Brachythecium albicans				C	C	C	C	C				C				
Brachythecium campestre				C	C	C	C	C				C				
Brachythecium salebposum				C	C	C		C				C				
Bryum pseudotriquetrum												L				
Ceratodon purpureus				C	C	C	C	C	C	C		C			C	C
Climacium dendroides												U				
Dicranum flagellare												L				
Dicranum fuscescens				C	C	C						C				
Dicranum strictum												L				
Drepanocladus aduncus											C	L				
Fissidens grandifrons												U				
Funaria hygrometrica				C	C	C	C	C	C	C		C			C	C
Grimmia apocarpa								F								
Grimmia montana								C								
Homalothecium nevadense				C	C	C	C					C				
Mniaceae spp.											C	L				
Orthrotrichum speciosum												L				
Orthrotricum anomalum												L				
Pohlia nutans				F	F	F	F					F				
Plagiomnium insigne											C					
Polytrichum juniperum				A	A	A	A	A	A	A	A	A				
Polytrichum piliferum				A	A	A	A	A				A				
Racomitrium hetrostichum				C	C	C	C	C								
Rhacomitrium canescens				C	C	C		C								
Rhytidiadelphus triquetrus												L				
Tortula princeps					F							L				
Torula ruralis				C	C	C	C									
Nornwort (Authocerotae)	**4**															
Anthoceros sp.				R												
Conocephalum conicum												F				
Marchantia polymorpha				F	F	F						L				
Porella cordaeana												L				
Club Moss (Isoetopsida)	**1**															
Selaginella								C								
Horsetail (Equisetopsida)	**3**															
Field Horsetail											F					
Scouring Rush				A	-	-	-	-	-	-	C	C	-	-	C	-
Smooth Horsetail											C			L		
Fern (Polypodiopsida)	**9**															
Bracken Fern				-	U	-									A	
Brittle Bladder Fern						U										
Lady Fern												F				
Licorice-Root Fern								F								
Malefern								R								
Oakfern					C											
Rocky Mountain Woodsia								C								
Spreading Woodfern								L								
Sword Fern					F							-				
Pine (Pinicae)	**13**															
Douglas Fir				-	A	A	U	-	-	-	-	-	-	-	-	-
Engelmann Spruce				C	F	-	-	-	-	-	-	-	-	-	-	-
Grand Fir				-	A	F	F	-	-	-	-	-	-	-	-	-
Lodgepole Pine				F	A	A	F	-	-	-	-	-	-	-	-	-
Pacific Hemlock				F	A	C	-	-	-	-	-	-	-	-	-	-
Pacific Yew				-	U	-	-	-	-	-	-	-	-	-	-	-
Ponderosa Pine				-	U	U	A	A	F	U	-	C	-	-	C	A
Rocky Mountain Juniper												U				
Subalpine Fir				A	-	-	-	-	-	-	-	-	-	-	-	-
Tamarack				U	F	F	-	U	-	-	-	-	-	-	-	-
Western Juniper							U			U						
Western Red Cedar					C	U	U									
Western White Pine					F											
Magnolia (Magnoliidae)	**22**															
Wild Ginger (Aristolochiales)	**1**															
Wild Ginger					U											

KEY: Risk – At Risk Codes: MS Missing, **ED** Endangered, **TH** Threatened, **CD** Candidate, **MN** Monitor, **RGM** Regulated Game, **RNG** Regulated Nongame, **RA** Rare, **PB** Protected Breeding Areas. • **Intro – Introduced Species Codes: IN** Introduced Noxious species, **IO** Introduced, Other than noxious species. • **Habitat Types: SA** Subalpine, **MT** Mountain, **DF** Douglas Fir , **PP** Ponderosa Pine , **RK** Rocklands, **BU** Bushy areas, **GR** Grassland, **WL** Wetlands, **RP** Riparian, **ST** Streams, **LK** Lakes & Ponds, **DS** Disturbed Soil, **HU** Near Human Habitation. • **Habitat Frequency Codes: A** Abundant, **C** Common, **F** Fairly common, **U** Uncommon, **R** Rare, **V** Vagrant, **K** Known in habitat, **L** Likely in habitat, **M** Missing from habitat.

Species Name	#	Risk	Intro	SA	MT	DF	PP	RK	BU	GR	WL	RP	ST	LK	DS	HU
Water Lily (Nymphaeales)	1												F	F		
Indian Pond Lily													F	F		
Buttercup (Ranunculales)	20															
Baneberry (B)						L										
Blue Clematis						F			F							
Buttercup (B)											F					
Columbian Monkshood					F						F					
Columbine															L	
False Bugbane				A	A	-	-	-	-	-	U	C	-	-	-	-
Idaho Goldthread					F	F										
Larkspur (A)											U					
Mancoun's Buttercup											U					
Meadow Larkspur										A						
Mousetail											U			-		
Oregon Grape					-				F		-					
Piper's Anemone					F	F										
Sagebrush Buttercup							A			A						
Small Oregon Grape				-	C	A	C	F	-	-	-	-	-	C	-	-
Spearwort											U			C		
Water Buttercup														C		
Western Baneberry												U				
Western Meadowrue				-	A	-	-	-	F	F	-	-	-	-	U	-
Western Virgin's Bower									F							
Birch (Hamamelidae)	3															
Oak (Fagales)	3															
Mountain Alder				-	F	-	-	-	-	-	A	A	-	-	-	-
Paper Birch				-	F	-	-	-	-	-	F	C	-	-	-	-
River Birch												A				
Carnation (Caryophyllidae)	35															
Carnation (Caryophyllales)	26															
Bigleaf Sandwort						L										
Bitterroot (B)								U								
Bluntleaf Sandwort					F						C	F				
Broad-leaved Montia					C							C				
Capitate Sandwort						F	F	R		F						
Chickweed (A)			IO									F			C	
Douglas Silene					-	-	F			-						
Field Chickweed					F	F	F	F								
Field Dodder									U		U					
Goosefoot			IO												C	C
Grass Pink			IO							R						
Jagged Chickweed			IO				C			C					A	
Long-stalked Starwort											U	F				
Longstem Chickweed											C	C				
Menzies' Silene											C					
Miner's Lettuce					C		F									
Mouse-ear Chickweed			IO													C
Narrow-leaved Spring Beauty						F				C						
Red Spurry			IO		F										U	
Sandwort (C)					C											
Scouler Silene												R				
Shining Chickweed										F						
Sleepy Catchfly										F						
Sticky Chickweed			IO								C	C			C	C
Western Spring Beauty						-	F			C	-					
Wild Pink										F						
Buckwheat (Polygonales)	9															
Canyon Heather								F								
Colored Smartweed														C		
Curly Dock			IO												C	
Golden Dock														U		
Goose Grass			IO												C	
Knotweed							C									
Sheep Sorrel			IO				C								A	
Subalpine Sulfur Buckwheat				C	C											
Wyeth Buckwheat										C						
Aspen (Dilleniidae)	44															
Nettle (Urticales)	2															
Siberian Elm			IO												U	
Stinging Nettle												C	C			
Violet (Violales)	4															
Blue Violet						F										
Pioneer Violet					C							C				
Round-leaved Violet				C	C	F	-	-	-	-	-	-	-	-	-	-
Stickleaf										R						
Aspen (Salicales)	7															
Black Cottonwood				-	U	-	-	-	-	-	C	A	A	A	-	-
Pacific Willow				-	-	-	F	F	-	-	A	A	-	F	-	-
Peach Willow														F		
Quaking Aspen				-	A	-	-	-	-	-	-	A	A	A	A	-
Scouler Willow				-	-	F	F	U	U	-	C	C	-	-	A	-
Slender Willow													F			
Willow (B)														F		
Mustard (Capparales)	11															
Elegant Rockcress							F			F						
Geyer's Twinpod							F						F			
Holboellis Rockcress								C								
Jim Hill Mustard			IO												A	
Mustard			IO												C	
Pepperpod								R								
Shepherd's Purse			IO												C	
Watercress														C		

Species Name	#	Risk	Intro	SA	MT	DF	PP	RK	BU	GR	WL	RP	ST	LK	DS	HU
Western Wallflower							U			U				–		
Western Yellowcress															U	
Whitlow Grass						A				A						
Heath (Ericales)	**15**															
Common Pink Wintergreen				C	C	-			F	F		-	-	-		-
Dwarf Huckleberry						U	U									
Fool's Huckleberry (A)				C	F	-						–	F			
Globe Huckleberry				F												
Green Pyrola					F											
Green Wintergreen					F											
Grouse Huckleberry				F	F	-										
Huckleberry (A)					C											
Kinnikinnick				-	F	F	C	C	-	-	-	-	-	-	-	F
Little Prince's Pine				-	C	-	-									
Pinedrops							F									
Sidebells Pyrola					F											
Western Prince's Pine				F	F	-										
Whiteveined Pyrola					F											
Wintergreen (C)										L						
Primrose (Primulales)	**5**															
Fringed Loosestrife											U			U		
Shooting Star (A)										A	F					
Shooting Star (B)						A				A				F		
Tufted Loosestrife														U		
Western Starflower										L						
Rose (Rosidae)	**95**															
Rose (Rosales)	**43**															
Alumroot								C								
Apple			IO							–						A
Bitter Cherry								F	F							
Bitterbrush				-	-	-	A	A	C	U		-	-	-	-	-
Blackcap						F		U				U				
Burnet															U	
Ceanothus							C		C							
Chokecherry				-	-	U	A	F	-	C		-	-	C	-	-
Cinquefoil							C			C						
Coolwort Foamflower				F	C	U							C			
Douglas Hawthorn								R					C			
Golden Currant									F							
Laceflower					C											
Mahaleb Cherry			IO						R							
Mallow Ninebark				-	-	C	A	U	A							
Mitrewort															L	
Mock Orange							A	C								
Mountain Ash (A)			IO													C
Mountain Ash (B)					C				C							
Mountain Sweet-Cicely					C											
Nootka Rose				-	C	C	C	-	A	-		-	-	-	-	-
Ocean Spray				-	A	A	-		A	-		-	-	-	-	-
Old Man's Whiskers (A)										C						
Pale Cinquefoil							C			C						
Pink Spiraea					C											
Plum			IO							C						C
Saxifrage (A)										L						
Serviceberry (B)										L						
Silverweed														U		
Small-flowered Fringecup							C			C						
Smooth Fringecup							C			C						
Spiraea														U		
Sticky Currant					F											
Swamp Gooseberry				C	F	-		-	F	-		C	-	-	-	-
Thimbleberry				-	A	A	-	U	-	-		C	-	-	-	-
Wax Currant				U		-	C		F	-		-				
Western Saxifrage								F								
Western Serviceberry				-	-		A	R	-	-		-	-	-	-	-
White Spiraea				-		-	C	-	-	C		-	-	-	-	-
Wild Strawberry						C	C			–						
Woodland Rose				-	F	F	-									
Woods Rose				-	-	C	C	-	-	C		C	-	-	-	-
Woods Strawberry					C											
Pea (Fabales)	**17**															
Alsike Clover			IO												U	F
American Vetch						U										
Big Leaf Lupine					C											
Blue Lupine							C			A						
Canada Vetch						U						U				
Cup Clover										F	F					
Hairy Vetch		•	IO							C					C	
Japanese Clover			IO			–				C					C	C
Nevada Deervetch										C						
Red Clover			IO							–					U	U
Small Hop Clover			IO												U	U
Small-bead Clover							F				F	C				
Spanish Clover										C						
White Clover			IO												C	A
White Sweet Clover			IO												A	

KEY: Risk – At Risk Codes: MS Missing, **ED** Endangered, **TH** Threatened, **CD** Candidate, **MN** Monitor, **RGM** Regulated Game, **RNG** Regulated Nongame, **RA** Rare, **PB** Protected Breeding Areas. • **Intro – Introduced Species Codes: IN** Introduced Noxious species, **IO** Introduced, Other than noxious species. • **Habitat Types: SA** Subalpine, **MT** Mountain, **DF** Douglas Fir , **PP** Ponderosa Pine , **RK** Rocklands, **BU** Bushy areas, **GR** Grassland, **WL** Wetlands, **RP** Riparian, **ST** Streams, **LK** Lakes & Ponds, **DS** Disturbed Soil, **HU** Near Human Habitation. • **Habitat Frequency Codes: A** Abundant, **C** Common, **F** Fairly common, **U** Uncommon, **R** Rare, **V** Vagrant, **K** Known in habitat, **L** Likely in habitat, **M** Missing from habitat.

Species Name	#	Risk	Intro	SA	MT	DF	PP	RK	BU	GR	WL	RP	ST	LK	DS	HU
White-leaf Lupine										F						
Yellow Sweet Clover			IO												A	
Myrtle (Myrtales)	6															
Cottonweed						L										
Enchanter's Nightshade					C											
Evening Primrose												U				
Fireweed					A	F									A	
Purple Loosestrife			IN										A			
Willow Herb						U				–					C	C
Dogwood (Cornales)	2															
Douglas Maple					C							C				
Red Osier Dogwood					C							C	C	C		
Sandalwood (Santalales)	1															
Dwarf Mistletoe							C									
Holly (Celastrales)	1															
Pachistima		–			*A*	*C*	–	*F*	–	·	–	·	–		–	–
Buckthorn (Rhamnales)	3															
Buckthorn						–	U					R				
Redstem Ceanothus				–	–	C	C	–	–	C	–	–	–	–	A	–
Snowbrush Ceanothus				–	C	C	C	–	A	–				–	C	–
Maple (Sapindales)	4															
Mountain Maple				–	F	F	–	–	–	–	–	C	–	–	–	–
Norway Maple			IO													A
Poison Ivy				–	–	–	–	F	–	–						–
Western Sumac									F	F						
Geranium (Geraniales)	4															
Crane's Bill			IO							C					C	C
Geranium							U								F	
Sticky Geranium							C	–		C	U					
Touch-me-not											F	F	F			
Parsley (Umbellales)	14															
Canby Licoriceroot					C											
Cow Parsnip (A)												F				
Cow Parsnip (B)											–	L				
Gray's Lomatium										C						
Large-fruit Lomation										C						
Lovage					C											
Nine-leaved Lomatium				–	–	–	–	–	–	C	–	–	–	–	–	–
Pepper and Salt							U			C						
Roundleaf Alumroot (B)								F	–							
Stonecrop								A								
Swale Desert Parsley								F		F						
Sweet Cicely					C											
Water Parsnip														C		
Yampah						U	F				F					
Sunflower (Asteridae)	140															
Gentian (Gentianales)	5															
Blue Gentian						U					U					
Frasera albicaulis										U						
Indian Hemp												U			–	
Milkweed										F						
Spreading Dogbane				U	U	U	A	–	–	A	–	–	–	–	–	–
Phlox (Polemoniales)	23															
Bittersweet			IO									U				U
Blue Phacelia										F						
Bluebells										F						
Common Bugloss			IO												A	
Forget-me-not										F						
Lemonweed										C						
Littlebells Polemonium										F					U	
Longleaf Phlox										F						
Microsteris							A			A						
Mountain Bluebells					A											
Narrow-leaved Collomia						C				C						
Needle-leaf Navarretia												C	C			
Panicle Bluebells					C											
Prickly Phlox							–		C	C						
Salmon Collomia						C				C						
Scarlet Gilia										F						
Scouler's Popcorn Flower										F						
Showy Phlox										F						
Slender Popcorn Flower										F						
Stoneseed			IO												C	C
Tar Weed										F					F	
Torrey's Cryptantha										F					F	F
Whiteleaf Phacelia										C						
Mint (Lamiales)	7															
Catnip															F	
Marsh Scullcap														C		
Narrow-leaved Scullcap								U		U						
Peppermint															U	
Self-heal						F						C				
Western Germander														R		
Wild Mint													C	C		
Plantain (Plantaginales)	2															
Common Plantain			IO												C	C
Wooly Plantain										C						
Foxglove (Scrophulariales)	20															
American Brooklime														C		
Annual Paintbrush											F				–	
Bladderwort															U	
Blue Lips					U		C	R		C						

Species Name	#	Risk	Intro	SA	MT	DF	PP	RK	BU	GR	WL	RP	ST	LK	DS	HU
Cancerroot								R								
Common Mullein			IN	-	F	-	-	F	-						A	F
Common Speedwell			IO							U					A	
Dalmatian Toadflax			IN				F	R		F					A	C
Figwort					R							–			–	
Indian Paintbrush						F						C	C			
Kitten Tail										F						
Lousewort					F											
Marsh Speedwell											F			–		
Moth Mullein			IN							–					U	
Musk Flower												U	U			
Owl's Clover										R	F					
White Beardtongue								U								
Yellow Beardtongue							C	C		C						
Yellow Indian Paintbrush								C		C						
Yellow Monkeyflower					U									U		
Bellflower (Campanulales)	3															
Bellflower								C		C	U					
Heterocodon											C	C				
Howellia														R		
Gardenia (Rubiales)	4															
Bedstraw											C					
Northern Bedstraw						F										
Small Bedstraw					F									U		
Sweetscented Bedstraw					F											
Teasel (Dipsacales)	12															
Black Elderberry					F											
Blue Elderberry				-	C					-	F	F			-	-
Common Snowberry				-	-	C	R	A	F	-	-			-	-	-
Highbush Cranberry														R		
Honeysuckle (B)			IO			C						R			A	A
Longhorn Plectritis												F				
Orange Honeysuckle						C										
Oregon Boxwood					F	C										
Red Twinberry				C	A	F	-	-	-	-	-			-	-	-
Sitka Valerian					U											
Teasel															F	F
Western Twinflower					C	C										
Sunflower (Asterales)	64															
Annual Agoseris										F						
Arrowleaf Balsamroot							U			A						
Arrowleaf Groundsel				F	C	C	C	-	F	F	-	C	-	-	F	-
Beggartick														F		
Big Sagebrush										A						
Blanket Flower							U			C						
Bride's Bouquet								R		F						
Broadleaf Arnica										F						
Brown-eyed Susan							U			C						
Bull Thistle			IN												A	
Bushy Goldenrod												R				
Canada Thistle															F	F
Cocklebur															F	F
Common Tansy			IN												F	F
Common Tarweed							F			F						
Common Yarrow				F	F	C	C	C	-	C	-	-	-	-	A	-
Cudweed												F				U
Cut-leaf Daisy							A	C		A						
Daisy Fleabane															U	
Fennel			IO												U	U
Fleabane										C						
Goatweed			IO				F			F					C	
Golden Aster							U			F						
Goldenweed										C						
Gumweed (A)															C	
Hairy Albert					F		F			C						
Heartleaf Arnica					C	F										
Horseweed														–	F	F
Indian Blanket							C			C						
Large-flowered Agoseris										F						
Long-leaved Hawksbeard										F						
Low Fleabane						C				C						
Low Pussytoes										C						
Montana Goldenrod							C			C						
Mule's Ears						U	U				F					
Narrow-leaved Skeletonweed								U								
Nodding Microseris										F						
Oregon Fleabane							F			F						
Oysterplant			IO							L					L	L
Pathfinder					C	C										
Pearly Everlasting					C	C										
Plains Thistle										F						
Raceme Pussytoes					F	F										
Ragwort					C	C										
Rosy Pussy-toes										F						
Showy Aster					F											
Skeletonweed (A)			IN												F	-

KEY: Risk – At Risk Codes: MS Missing, **ED** Endangered, **TH** Threatened, **CD** Candidate, **MN** Monitor, **RGM** Regulated Game, **RNG** Regulated Nongame, **RA** Rare, **PB** Protected Breeding Areas. • **Intro – Introduced Species Codes: IN** Introduced Noxious species, **IO** Introduced, Other than noxious species. • **Habitat Types: SA** Subalpine, **MT** Mountain, **DF** Douglas Fir , **PP** Ponderosa Pine , **RK** Rocklands, **BU** Bushy areas, **GR** Grassland, **WL** Wetlands, **RP** Riparian, **ST** Streams, **LK** Lakes & Ponds, **DS** Disturbed Soil, **HU** Near Human Habitation. • **Habitat Frequency Codes: A** Abundant, **C** Common, **F** Fairly common, **U** Uncommon, **R** Rare, **V** Vagrant, **K** Known in habitat, **L** Likely in habitat, **M** Missing from habitat.

Species Name	#	Risk	Intro	SA	MT	DF	PP	RK	BU	GR	WL	RP	ST	LK	DS	HU
Slender Hawksbeard										F						
Spotted Knapweed			IN												A	A
Tall Pussytoes						F	—			F						
Tarweed (A)							F			F						
Tarweed (B)							F			F						
Twin Arnica										C						
Western Coneflower				-	C	-	-	-	-	C	-	C	-	-	A	-
Western Hawkweed				F	F	C	U	-	-	U					-	-
White Hawkweed (C)					F		F			-						
White Knapweed			IN												C	
White-flowered Hawkweed					F	F										
Wild Aster						C	A	A			-					
Woodrush Pussytoes										F						
Wooly Groundsel								F		U						
Wreath Aster										F						
Yellow Fleabane										F						
Yellow Salsify			IO							U					A	C
Water Plantain (Alismatidae)	3															
Water Plantain (Alismatales)	2															
Wapato				-						-	F	-	-	F	-	-
Water Plantain														F		
Water Hawthorn (Najadales)	1															
Pondweed														F		
Grass (Commelinidae)	42															
Grass (Poales)	32															
Barren Fescue			IO				F			F						
Bentgrass			IN												U	
Big Bluegrass										F						
Bluebunch Wheatgrass				-		-	C	C	-	A					-	-
Bluegrass															F	A
Bulbous Bluegrass			IO							A				A	A	C
California Oatgrass										C						
Canada Bluegrass			IO							A					A	
Cheatgrass			IO							A					A	
Columbia Brome										U						
Foxtail			IO							F						
Green Fescue										L						
Idaho Fescue				-		-	F	-		A					-	
Japanese Brome			IO							C					A	
Junegrass										C						
Lemmon's Needlegrass																
Mannagrass										F	F					
Needlegrass										A						
One-spike Oatgrass			IO							A						
Panic Grass										F		F		F	U	
Pinegrass				-	F	C	C	-	-	-					F	-
Quackgrass															L	
Red Three-awn										U						
Redtop			IO								C					
Reed Canary Grass			IO								A					
Rough Fescue			IO							F						
Rye Grass										C						
Short-awn Foxtail											F			C		
Small Fescue							C			C						
Thurber's Needlegrass										F						
Timber Danthonia							U									
Timothy			IO								C				C	
Rush (Juncales)	3															
Bulrush (C)										C						
Parry's Rush															L	
Woodrush										U						
Sedge (Cyperales)	5															
Bulrush (A)														F		
Elk Sedge				F	C	A	-	-	-	-	-	-	-	-	-	-
Inflated Sedge														L		
Spike Rush														C		
Tule														A		
Cattail (Typhales)	2															
Bur-reed														U		
Common Cattail				-						-	C	C	A	A	-	-
Duckweed (Arecidae)	2															
Duckweed (Arales)	2															
Duckweed														A		
Skunk Cabbage				-						-	C	C	U	-	-	-
Lily (Liliidae)	32															
Lily (Liliales)	25															
Asparagus			IO							-	R				A	
Beargrass				A	A											
California Falsehellebore											U					
Camas											C					
Claspleaf Twisted Stalk						-					F					
Death Camas				-		-	-	U	C	C	-	-	-	-	-	-
Fairy Bells (A)											L					
Fairy Bells (B)											L					
False Hellebore										-	U					
Glacier Lily				A	A	C	C			A						
Grass Widow					R	A	C			C						
Mariposa Lily						C										
Purple Trillium												F				
Queencup					C											
Starry False Solomon's Seal				F	-	-	-	-	-	-					-	-
Tiger Lily														F	F	

Species Name	#	Risk	Intro	SA	MT	DF	PP	RK	BU	GR	WL	RP	ST	LK	DS	HU
Western Blue Flag											C					
Western False Solomon's Seal			U	F	F		C	F	-	F	-	C	-	-	-	-
White Trillum					C											
Wild Hyacinth										F						
Wild Onion (A)							C			C						
Wild Onion (B)												C				
Wild Onion (C)							C			C	-					
Yellow Flag Iris			IN										A			
Yellowbell							C			C						
Orchid (Orchidales)	7															
Bog Orchid						F	-				-					
Coralroot					U	F										
Fairy Slipper					U	F										
Habenaria												L				
Listera					F											
Rattlesnake Plantain						F										
Spotted Coralroot					U							U				
TOTAL PLANTS	**477**															

Fungi

Species Name	#	Risk	Intro	SA	MT	DF	PP	RK	BU	GR	WL	RP	ST	LK	DS	HU
FUNGUS (EUMYCOTA)	**452**															
Mushroom (Basidomycetes)	**343**															
GILLED WHITE SPORES(A) (AMANITACEAE)	12															
Amanita alba						L		L	L							L
Amanita porphyria					L											
Amanita solitaria						L		L	L						L	L
Amanita sp.						L										
Death Angel				K	L											
Fly Agaric (A)				L												
Fly Agaric (B)				F	L	C						U				C
Gemmod Amanita				K	F	F										
Grisette				L												
Panther Amanita				L	L	U	U								L	F
Western Yellow Veil				L	L											
Western Grisette				C	C											
LEPIOTACEAE (LEPIOTACEAE)	6															
Flower Pot Lepiota																F
Lepiota sp.														L		F
Malodorous Lepiota				C	C				F							F
Shaggy Parasol														L		C
Shaggy-stalked Lepiota				F	F											
Smooth Parasol											U					C
BRITTLE MUSHROOM (RUSSULACEAE)	33															
Delicious Milk Cap				C	U	C						C				
Delicious Milkcap				C	U	U										
Emetic Russula				K	U	L										
Lactarius aurantiacus				L												
Lactarius barrowsii						L										
Lactarius circellatus				L												
Lactarius fallax				L												
Lactarius glyciosmus				L												
Lactarius kaufmanii				L												
Lactarius olympianus				K		L										
Lactarius pallescens				L												
Lactarius pseudomucidus				L												
Lactarius subdulcis				L												
Lactarius uvidus				L												
Pink-fringed Milky				C		C	F									
Purple-bloom Russula				K	L											
Rosy Russula				L												
Russula abietina				K	L											
Russula aeruginia				L												
Russula albonigra				L												
Russula cascadensis				L												
Russula decolorans				L												
Russula foetens				L		U	U									
Russula integra				L												
Russula lepida				K	L											
Russula occidentalis				L												
Russula olivacea				C								C				
Russula paludosa				L												
Russula sp.				L												
Russula vesca				L												
Short Stemmed Russula				A	A	A										

KEY: Risk – At Risk Codes: MS Missing, **ED** Endangered, **TH** Threatened, **CD** Candidate, **MN** Monitor, **RGM** Regulated Game, **RNG** Regulated Nongame, **RA** Rare, **PB** Protected Breeding Areas. • **Intro – Introduced Species Codes: IN** Introduced Noxious species, **IO** Introduced, Other than noxious species. • **Habitat Types: SA** Subalpine, **MT** Mountain, **DF** Douglas Fir , **PP** Ponderosa Pine , **RK** Rocklands, **BU** Bushy areas, **GR** Grassland, **WL** Wetlands, **RP** Riparian, **ST** Streams, **LK** Lakes & Ponds, **DS** Disturbed Soil, **HU** Near Human Habitation. • **Habitat Frequency Codes: A** Abundant, **C** Common, **F** Fairly common, **U** Uncommon, **R** Rare, **V** Vagrant, **K** Known in habitat, **L** Likely in habitat, **M** Missing from habitat.

Species Name	#	Risk	Intro	SA	MT	DF	PP	RK	BU	GR	WL	RP	ST	LK	DS	HU
Spotted-stalked Milky					C	C										
Willow Milky					L											
WAXY CAP (HYGROPHORACEAE)	16															
Bitter Brown Hygrophorus					L											
Brown Almond Smelling Waxy					A	A						C				
Fading Scarlet Waxy Cap					C	C										
Glutinous Waxy Cap					F		A									
Golden Waxy Cap					L											
Golden-spotted Waxy Cap					A	A						C				
Hygrophorus borealis					L	K										
Hygrophorus fuscoalboides					L											
Hygrophorus ponderatus					L											
Hygrophorus purpurascens					L											
Hygrophorus pusillus					L											
Larch Waxy Cap					A	F										
Meadow Waxy Cap					L											
Olive Brown Waxy					U	C	A									
Subalpine Waxy Cap					U	U	U									
GILLED WHITE SPORES (B) (TRICHOLOMATACEAE)	81															
Witch's Hat					C	C	U									K
Alkaline Mycena							L									L
Baeospora myriodophylla					L	U	U									
Bitter Brown Leucopaxillus					F	F	L									
Blewit					L											L
Calocybe carnea									L	L					L	U
Clitocybe albirhiza					K											
Clitocybe deceptiva									L	L					L	L
Clitocybe ectypoides					L	K										
Clitocybe inversa					L	U	U									
Clitocybe irina							L									
Clitocybe (Lepista) irina					L	U	U									
Clitocybe rhizophora					L											
Clitocybe rivularis																L
Clustered Collybia							L		L							
Collybia abundans					L											
Collybia conigenoides					L											
Collybia dryophila						K				L					L	L
Collybia maculata							L									
Cystoderma amianthinum					K	K	K								L	L
Cystoderma fallax					C	C	K			−					−	−
Cystoderma granulocum					L	K				K					U	
Fairy Ring Mushroom										L					L	A
Fetid Armillaria					A	A	I					F				
Funnel Clitocybe					F				K	K					L	L
Giant Clitocybe					K					K					L	L
Hohenbuehelia petaloides					L										L	K
Honey Mushroom					A	A	L					A				
Horsehair Fungus							L									
Laccaria amethestina					F	U	U									
Laccaria laccata					C	C	L									
Lepista brunneocephala																L
Lepista (Clitocybe) subconnexa																L
Lepista sp.																L
Lepista subconnexa																L
Leptoglossum retirugum					L	U	U									
Lilac Mycena					C	U	L									
Lyophyllum atratum					U											
Lyophyllum atratum					K		C									
Lyophyllum decastes					U	U	U					U			L	L
Lyophyllum montanum					U											
Lyophyllum sp.					U	U	U									
Man On horseback					F	F	C									
Marasmiellus candidus									L	L					L	L
Marasmius androsaceous									L	L					L	L
Marasmius copelandi									L							L
Marasmius rotula					K	L										
Marasmius sp.					L											C
Matsutake					F	C										
Melanoleuca melaleuca					K	L									K	F
Melanoleuca sp.					L											
Mouse Tricholoma					F	F	L									
Mycena adonis					L	K										
Mycena metata						U	U									L
Mycena murina					−	U	K									L
Mycena overholzii					L	U	U		L							
Mycena sp.					C											
Myxomphalia maura					U											
Omphalina ericetorum						U	U									
Omphalina griseopallida					L											L
Omphalina luteicolor					K											
Oyster Mushroom					F	U					U	F			L	K
Phyllotopsis nidulans					K											
Pleurotus geogenius					K											
Pleurotus (Hypsizygu) elongatipes					R							R				
Pleurotus ulmarius																L
Separating Trich					U	U	U									
Shaggy-stalked Armillaria					F	F	R									
Soapy Trich					C	C	L									
Strobilurus albipilatus						L	L									
Strobilurus kemptonae						L	L									

Species Name	#	Risk	Intro	SA	MT	DF	PP	RK	BU	GR	WL	RP	ST	LK	DS	HU
Sweat Producing Clitocybe					K					K					F	F
Swollen-stalked Cat					L											
Tiger Trich					C	C	L									
Train Wrecker																K
Tricholoma atroviolaceum					L											
Tricholoma imbricatum					U	U						U				
Tricholoma vaccinum					F	F	L									
Tricholomopsis decora					L											
Tricholomopsis rutilans					L											
Velvet Foot					U		K			L		C				A
Xeromphalina campanella					L											
GILLED PINK SPORES (ENTOLOMATACEAE)	12															
Alboleptonia sericella						L										
Clitopilus prunulus					L											
Entoloma rhodopolium					L											L
Entoloma sp.					K											
Fawn Mushroom															L	L
Leptonia gracilis					L	L										L
Livid Entoloma					L											
Pluteus flavofuligineus					L							L				C
Rhodocybe nitellina					L											
Rhodophyllus sp.					L											
Silky Nolanea						L				L						L
Springtime Nolanea					L	K	L							L		L
VOLVARIELLA (VOLVARIELLA)	2															
Common Volvariella														L		K
Volvariella volvacea																L
PAXCILLIUS (PAXCILLIUS)	3															
Paxillus atrotomentosis					L											
Paxillus panuoides					L											
Poison Paxillus										U						F
AGARICACEAE (AGARICACEAE)	9															
Agaricus crocodilinus															L	
Agaricus nivescens																L
Agaricus rodmani															L	
Agaricus sp.																L
Meadow Mushroom										L					L	K
Prairie Agaric										K						K
The Prince					K	L										K
Wood Agaric					K	K	L									K
Yellow Staining Agaricus						L										
GILLED BROWN SPORES (CORTINARIACEAE)	51															
Belted Slimy Cortinarius					L											
Big Laughing Mushroom						L										
Brown Cortinarius						L										
Cortinarius alutinus					L											
Cortinarius camphoratus					L											
Cortinarius cinnabarinus						L										
Cortinarius cinnamomeus					L											
Cortinarius croceofolius					L	K	L									
Cortinarius delibutus					L											
Cortinarius fulgens					L											
Cortinarius fulvocrassens					L											
Cortinarius pinetorum					L											
Cortinarius renidens					L											
Cortinarius repetitus					L											
Cortinarius, sec. phlegmacium: 2 spp.					L											
Cortinarius subfoetidus					L											
Cortinarius trivialis					L											
Cortinarius varius					L											
Cortintarius, sec. dermocybe: 4 spp.					L											
Crepidotus versutus					L											
Dermocybe crocea					L											
Fragrant Cortinarius					L											
Galerina cerina																L
Galerina heterocystis					K	K										L
Galerina marginata					L											
Gymnopilus penetrans																L
Gypsy Mushroom					L											
Hebeloma sinapizans																L
Hebeloma sinuosum					L											
Inocybe flocculosa					L	K										
Inocybe geophylla					L											
Inocybe lanuginosa					L	K	L									
Inocybe maculata							L									L
Inocybe sp. (A) (chestnut-brown)					L											
Inocybe sp. (B) (cinnamon brown)					L											
Inocybe sp. (C) (gray-brown)					L											
Inocybe sp. (D) (light brown-yellow-brown)						L										
Inocybe sp. (E) (white-yellow-brown)					L											
Inocybe sp. (F) (yellow-brown)					L											
Lilac Conifer Cortinarius					L											
Little Brown Cortinarius				L	L												
Poison Pie																A
Pungent Fiber Head					L											

KEY: Risk – At Risk Codes: MS Missing, **ED** Endangered, **TH** Threatened, **CD** Candidate, **MN** Monitor, **RGM** Regulated Game, **RNG** Regulated Nongame, **RA** Rare, **PB** Protected Breeding Areas. • **Intro – Introduced Species Codes: IN** Introduced Noxious species, **IO** Introduced, Other than noxious species. • **Habitat Types: SA** Subalpine, **MT** Mountain, **DF** Douglas Fir , **PP** Ponderosa Pine , **RK** Rocklands, **BU** Bushy areas, **GR** Grassland, **WL** Wetlands, **RP** Riparian, **ST** Streams, **LK** Lakes & Ponds, **DS** Disturbed Soil, **HU** Near Human Habitation. • **Habitat Frequency Codes: A** Abundant, **C** Common, **F** Fairly common, **U** Uncommon, **R** Rare, **V** Vagrant, **K** Known in habitat, **L** Likely in habitat, **M** Missing from habitat.

Species Name	#	Risk	Intro	SA	MT	DF	PP	RK	BU	GR	WL	RP	ST	LK	DS	HU
Purple Staining Cortinarius					L											
Scaly Cortinarius							L									
Sooty-Olive Cortinarius					L											
Straw-colored Fiber Head					L	K									L	L
Torn Fiber Head															L	
Tubaria furfuracea																L
Veiled Hebeloma															L	L
Violet Cortinarius					L											
BOLBITIACEAE (BOLBITIACEAE)	10															
Agrocybe dura															L	L
Bolbitius vitellinus																L
Common Agrocybe															L	L
Conocybe filaris																L
Conocybe lactea																L
Conocybe tenera																L
Dung Loving Bolbitius									L	L					L	L
Maple Agrocybe																L
Maple Agrocybe																L
Spring Agrocybe					–					L					F	C
GILLED DARK SPORES (A) (STROPHARIACEAE)	18															
Bell-shaped Panaeolus																L
Conifer Tuft					K	L										
Dispersed Naematoloma					L											
Garland Stropharia																L
Haymakers Panaeolus																L
Lacerated Stropharia					L	K										
Lubricous Pholiota					L											
Pholiota decorata					L											
Pholiota limonella						L										
Pholiota sp. (terrestrial)					L											
Pholiota subangularis					L											
Psilocybe sp.																L
Scaly Pholiota					F	C										L
Slender Pholiota					L											
Sulfur Tuft					F	L									K	F
Terrestrial Pholiota																L
Woodlover					L											
Yellow Pholiota					L											
GILLED DARK SPORES (B) (COPRINACEAE)	10															
Coprinus lagopus															L	
Coprinus plicatilis							U									
Inky Cap					L										L	F
Japanese Umbrella Inky					L	K										L
Mica Cap						L			L						C	A
Psathyrella carbonicola					L											
Psathyrella condolleana																A
Psathyrella sp.					L											
Psathyrella velutina					L											
Shaggy Mane					L							F	F			C	C
GOMPHIDIACEAE (GOMPHIDIACEAE)	3															
Brownish Chroogomphus					L											
Slimy gomphidius						L										
Woolly Chroogomphus					L											
PORED MUSHROOM (BOLETACEAE)	24															
Admirable Bolete					K	K										
Blue-Staining Slippery Jack						L										L
Boletus coniferarum					L											
Boletus smithii					L											
Gastroboletus turbinatus					K											
Grayish Larch Bolete					L	L	L									
Hollow-stalked Larch Suillus					K	L										
King Bolete Pinicola					F	F										
Larch Suillus					L	L										
Leccinum aurantiacum					L											L
Leccinum insigne					L	L						F					
Leccinum scabrum													U				
Leccinum sp.					L											
Rosy Larch bolete					C	C	L									
Suillus albivelatus							L										K
Suillus brevipes							L										
Suillus pseudobrevipes							L										L
Suillus punctatipes					K	L										
Suillus sibiricus					L											
Suillus subaureus					L	L										
Suillus subolivaceous					K	L	L									
Suillus tomentosus					L											
Western Painted Suillus					L	K	L									
Yellow-cracked Bolete					L											
POLYPORE FUNGI (POLYPORACEAE)	32															
Albatrellus ellisii					L											
Albatrellus fletii					L											
Albatrellus ovinus					L											K
Bjerkandera adusta										L						
Boletopsis griseus					L											
Chicken Of The Woods					L											
Coltrichia cinnamomeus					K											

Species Name	#	Risk	Intro	SA	MT	DF	PP	RK	BU	GR	WL	RP	ST	LK	DS	HU
Coltrichia perennis					K	L										
Cotylidia diaphana															L	L
Fomes fomentarius					L											
Fomes pinicola					L											
Ganoderma applanatum									L			L				
Ganoderma tsugae					K	L										
Hershioporus abietinus						L										
Inonotus tomentosus					L											
Ischoderma resinosum					L											
Merulius tremellosa									L							
Merulius tremellosus									L							
Oldman's Whiskers					L											
Phaelous schweinitzii					L											
Phaeolus albaluteus					K											
Polyporus cinnabarinus									L							
Polyporus elegans					L											
Polyporus melanopus					L											
Polyporus picipes					K	L										
Polyporus squamosus									L							
Stereum burtianum																L
Trametes hirsuta									L							
Turkey Tail					L											
Tyromyces chioneus					L											
Tyromyces fragilis					L											
Tyromyces mollis					L											
TEETH FUNGI (HYDNACEAE)	7															
Auriscalpium vulagre					L											
Conifer Coral Hericium					L											
Dentinum umbilicatum					L											
Hydnellum aurantiacum					L											
Hydnum imbricatum					L											
Indian Paint Conk					K	K										
Toothed Mushroom					K	K										
CHANTERELLE (CANTHARELLACEAE)	6															
Cantharellus infundibuliformia					L											
Golden Chanterelle				-	L	C	-	-	-	-	-	U		-	-	-
Pigs Ear					K											
Scaly Chanterelle					K											
White Chanterelle						U										
CORAL FUNGI (CLAVARIACEAE)	8															
Cauliflower Mushroom					L	U										
Clavaria cristata					L	C										
Clavaria crocea						L	L									
Clavariadelphus ligula						L	L									
Clavariopsis laeticolor					L											
Common Club Coral					K								K				
Ramaria stricta					K	L										
Yellow Corn					K	L										
DACRYMYCES (DACRYMYCES)	1															
Witches Butter				L	K											
Puffball (Gastromycetes)	22															
STINKHORN (PHALLALES)	2															
Mutinus caninus					L											
Stink Horn															L	L
BIRD'SNEST FUNGUS (NIDULARIALES)	2															
Crucibulum vulgare						L										
Nidula candida					L											
EARTHSTAR FUNGUS (LYCOPERDALES (A))	2															
Earth Star					L					R						
Geastrum limbatum					L											
TRUE PUFFBALL (LYCOPERDALES (B))	16															
Astraeus sp.																L
Bovista pila															L	L
Bovista plumbea							L									
Calvatia booniana					K		L								L	L
Calvatia sp.					K										L	
Common Puffball					L				L							
Lycoperdon echinatum					K	L									C	
Lycoperdon gemmata							L									
Lycoperdon marginatum					K	L										
Puffball (B)							C			C						
Puffball (C)					K		C			C						C
Puffball (D)					K	L										L
Puffball (E)															L	
Purple-spored Puffball					L											
Rhizopogon roseolus					L											
Sculptured Puffball					K	L										L
Phragmobasidiomycetes																

KEY: Risk – At Risk Codes: MS Missing, **ED** Endangered, **TH** Threatened, **CD** Candidate, **MN** Monitor, **RGM** Regulated Game, **RNG** Regulated Nongame, **RA** Rare, **PB** Protected Breeding Areas. • **Intro – Introduced Species Codes: IN** Introduced Noxious species, **IO** Introduced, Other than noxious species. • **Habitat Types: SA** Subalpine, **MT** Mountain, **DF** Douglas Fir , **PP** Ponderosa Pine , **RK** Rocklands, **BU** Bushy areas, **GR** Grassland, **WL** Wetlands, **RP** Riparian, **ST** Streams, **LK** Lakes & Ponds, **DS** Disturbed Soil, **HU** Near Human Habitation. • **Habitat Frequency Codes: A** Abundant, **C** Common, **F** Fairly common, **U** Uncommon, **R** Rare, **V** Vagrant, **K** Known in habitat, **L** Likely in habitat, **M** Missing from habitat.

Species Name	#	Risk	Intro	SA	MT	DF	PP	RK	BU	GR	WL	RP	ST	LK	DS	HU
(Phragmobasidiomycetes)	3															
JELLY FUNGI (B)																
(TREMELLALES)	3															
Christiansenia mycetophila							L		L							
Gum Drop				K	A	A	L									
Wood Ear					A	L										
Ascomycetes (Ascomycetes)	35															'
TRUE MORE																
(MORCHELLACEAE)	3															
Black Morel					L	L	L									U
Black Morel (Narrow)					F	F	F							K		U
Morchella esculenta					K	K	L									F
																U
FALSE MOREL																
(HELVELLACEAE)	12															
Brain Mushroom (A)					C	C	L									
Brain Mushroom (B)					F											
Brown Elfin Saddle					L											
Discina ancilis					L											
Elfin Cup							L									
Gyromitra infula					L											
Helvella esculenta					L											
Helvella infula					L	K	L									
Helvella lacunosa							L								L	K
Helvella leucomelaena							L									
Helvella queletii					L											
Jew's Ear					K	K	K									
CUP FUNGUS (PEZIZACEAE)	14															
Aleuria aurantia					K	L										
Caloscypha fulgens				L	K										L	
Geopyxis sp.					L											
Peziza aria					L											
Peziza badia					L											
Peziza sp. 1 (blue-black)					L	L										
Peziza sp. 2 (small brown)					L	L										
Peziza sylvestris															L	
Plectania sp.							L									
Plicaria endocarpoides					L											
Plicaria sp.					L											
Pulvinula					l											
Spreading Cup					L											L
Wood Cup					L	K	K									
EARTH TONGUE (LEOTIACEAE)	1															
Cudonia grisea					K											
PYRENOMYCETE																
(PYRENOMYCETE)	4															
Cordyceps ophioglossoides					L											
Cordyceps washingtonensis																L
Hypomyces chrysospermum							L									
Hypomyces luteovirens					L											
TUBERACEAE (TUBERACEAE)	1															
Sepultaria arenicola															L	
TO BE DETERMINED (TBD)	10															
Bisporella citrina							L									
Chlorociboria aeruginascens					K	K										
Cotylidea diaphana					L											
Cudonia sp.							L									
Earth Fan							L									
Endoptychum agaricoides															L	
Mythicomyces corneipes					L											
Nectria cinnabarina									L							
Thallophyta					L											
Xerampalina campanella					L											
Lichen (lichen)	39															
CRUSTY LICHEN (CRUSTOSE)	14															
Acarospora chlorophana							L	F								
Calcium viride							L									
Candelariella vitellina							F	F								
Diploschistes scruposus							L	F								
Evernia mesomorpha							A									
Evernia prunastri							L									
Hypocenomyce (Lecidea) scalaris							L	C								
Lecanora rupicola								C								
Lecidea fuscoatra								L								
Lecidea tessellata								L								
Rhizocarpon geographicum								L	C							
Usnea spp						C										
Xanthoria elegans								C								C
Xanthoria polycarpa									C							C
LEAFY LICHEN (FOLIOSE)	16															
Cetraria candensis							C									
Cetraria merrillii							L									
Cetraria plotyphylla							L									
Hypogymnia enteromorpha							A									
Hypogymnia imsaugii							C									
Hypogymnia physodes					A	A	A									
Parmelia saxatilis								C								
Parmelia sulcata					A	A	A	C	C							
Parmeliopsis ambigua								L								
Peltigera aphthosa						F		L								
Peltigera horizontalis						F		L								

Species Name	#	Risk	Intro	SA	MT	DF	PP	RK	BU	GR	WL	RP	ST	LK	DS	HU
Peltigera membranacea								L								
Peltigera polydactyla								L								
Peltigera venosa						U										
Platismatia glauca					C	C	C									
Umbilicaria spp.								C		F						
FRUITY LICHEN (FRUTICOSE)	9															
Bryoria capillaria							L									
Bryoria fremontii							L									
Cladonia bacillaris							L									
Cladonia chlorophana							L									
Cladonia spp.							L									
Goatbeard Lichen (A)					A											
Goatbeard Lichen (B)					A											
Letharea vulpina							A									
Letharia columbiana							F	L								
TOTAL FUNGI	**452**															

Animals

Species Name	#	Risk	Intro	SA	MT	DF	PP	RK	BU	GR	WL	RP	ST	LK	DS	HU
ANIMAL (ANIMALIA)	**753**															
Hydrozoa (Hydrozoa)	**2**															
Hydra sp.												F		F		
Hydroida														F		
Turbellidia (Turbellidia)	**2**															
Planariidae				L	L	L	L	L	L	L	L	L		L	L	L
Tricladidae													F			
Roundworm (Acari)	**1**															
Round Worm														C		C
Clam (Pelecypoda)	**1**															
Clam												F		F		
Snail (Gastropoda)	**5**															
Gastropoda					F	F								C		
Lymnea auriculais													F			
Lymnoa stagnalis													F			
Pisidium sp.													F			
Slug						F										F
Earthworm (Oligocheata)	**4**															
Haplotaxida (Haplotaxida)	*2*															
Naididae													F			
Oligochaeta												U				A
Lumbriculida (Lumbriculida)	*2*															
Lumbriculida										C						
Lumbriculidae													F			
Leech (Hirudinea)	**2**															
Rhynchobdellida (Rhynchobdellida)	*2*															
Hirudinea														F		
Piscicola sp.													F			
Crustacean (Crustacea)	**17**															
Scud (Amphipoda)	*3*															
Gammarces lacustris													F			
Gammaridae													F			
Talitridae													F			
Eucopepoda (Eucopepoda)	*4*															
Calanoid													F			
Copepoda														A		
Cyclopoid													F			
Harpacticoid													F			
Crayfish (Decapoda)	*3*															
Crayfish														C		
Decapoda														C		
Pacifastacus sp.													F			
Water Flea (Cladocera)	*7*															
Alona sp.													L			
Chrodoridae													L			
Cyclops														A		
Daphnia														A		
Daphnia galeata mendotae													L			
Eurycercus lamaellatas													L			
Seed Shrimp														A		
Spider (Arachnida)	**4**															
Funnel Weaver Spider						F										F
Jumping Spider																F
Orb Weaver Spider																F
Tick				L	L	L	L	F	L	L	L			L		

KEY: **Risk – At Risk Codes:** **MS** Missing, **ED** Endangered, **TH** Threatened, **CD** Candidate, **MN** Monitor, **RGM** Regulated Game, **RNG** Regulated Nongame, **RA** Rare, **PB** Protected Breeding Areas. • **Intro – Introduced Species Codes:** **IN** Introduced Noxious species, **IO** Introduced, Other than noxious species. • **Habitat Types:** **SA** Subalpine, **MT** Mountain, **DF** Douglas Fir , **PP** Ponderosa Pine , **RK** Rocklands, **BU** Bushy areas, **GR** Grassland, **WL** Wetlands, **RP** Riparian, **ST** Streams, **LK** Lakes & Ponds, **DS** Disturbed Soil, **HU** Near Human Habitation. • **Habitat Frequency Codes:** **A** Abundant, **C** Common, **F** Fairly common, **U** Uncommon, **R** Rare, **V** Vagrant, **K** Known in habitat, **L** Likely in habitat, **M** Missing from habitat.

Species Name	#	Risk	Intro	SA	MT	DF	PP	RK	BU	GR	WL	RP	ST	LK	DS	HU
Centipede (Chilopoda)	1															
Centipede				L	L	L	L	L	L	L	L	L	L	L	L	L
Millipede (Diplopoda)	1															
Millipede				L	L	L	L	L	L	L	L	L	L	L	L	L
Insect (Insecta)	358															
Mayfly (Ephemeroptera)	22															
Attenella margarita													F			
Baetidae													L			
Cinygmula sp.													F			
Drunella flavilinea													F			
Drunella grandis													F			
Epeorus albertae													F			
Epeorus longimanus													F			
Epeorus tricaudatus													F			
Ephemerella inermis-infrequens													F			
Ephemerella verruca													F			
Ephemerellidae													L			
Heptageniidae													L			
Leptophlebiidae													L			
Paraleptophlebia bicornutus													F			
Paraleptophlebia memorialis													F			
Parameletus columbiae													F			
Rithrogena morrisoni													F			
Seratella tibialis													F			
Siphlonuridae													L			
Stenacron sp.													F			
Tricorythidae													L			
Tricorythodes minutus													F			
Dragonfly (Odonata)	8															
Aeshna sp.													F			
Aeshnidae														A		
Clubtail														L		
Damselfly												A				
Darner														L		
Dragon Fly												A				F
Omphiogomphus sp.													F			
Skimmer												A				
Grasshopper (Orthoptera)	19															
Band-winged Grasshopper (A)							F			F						
Band-winged Grasshopper (B)						F	F			F						
Bush Katydid									II							
Carolina Locust										F						
Cave Cricket					F											
Chorthippus curtiponnis										R						
Field Cricket									F							
German Cockroach																F
Jerusalem Cricket										R						
Lesser Migratory Grasshopper										A					A	
Mantid						-				U						
Meadow Grasshopper												A				
Pseudopomala brachyptera										R						
Red-winged Grasshopper										F						
Redlegged Grasshopper											C					
Sand Cricket							F			-						
Snowy Tree Cricket									F							
Two-striped Grasshopper						-				L						
Warrior Grasshopper										A					A	
Stonefly (Plecoptera)	22															
Alloperla sp.													F			
Amphineura sp.													F			
Amphipoda														F		
Calineura californica nymphs													F			
Chloroperla sp.													F			
Despaxia augusta													F			
Diura knowltoni													F			
Isoperla fulva													F			
Isoperla mormoni													F			
Malenka sp.													F			
Megarcys sp.													F			
Nemoura sp.													F			
Paraleuctra sp.													F			
Perlodidae													L			
Pteronarcyidae													L			
Skwalia parallela													F			
Stonefly													A			
Suwallia pallidula													A			
Sweltsia coloradensis													F			
Tiger Moth												A				
Triznaka sp.													F			
Zapata cinctipes													F			
Earwig (Dermaptera)	1															
Earwig																A
Barklice (Psocoptera)	1															
Barklice						U										
Chewing Lice (Mallophaga)	1															
Chewing Lice												-		L		
Thrip (Thysanoptera)	1															
Thrip																F
True Bug (Hemiptera)	21															
Ambush Bug												-			R	
Assassin Bug												-		L		
Backswimmer												-		C		

Species Name	#	Risk	Intro	SA	MT	DF	PP	RK	BU	GR	WL	RP	ST	LK	DS	HU
Bed Bug												−				U
Box Elder Bug																F
Damsel Bug												A				
Gerris sp.													F			
Giant Water Bug												−		U		
Lace Bug												F				
Leaf Bug												A				
Leaf-footed Bug						U						−				C
Megaloptera													L			F
Seed Bug												−				
Shield-backed Bug												A				
Stink Bug												F			F	
Trepobates sp.													F			
Trichorixa sp.													F			
Water Boatman														A		
Water Measurer Bug												−		U		
Waterscorpion														U		
Whirligig Beetle (A)												L		L		
Aphid (Homoptera)	**6**															
Aphid										F		F				A
Leafhopper												A				
Spittlebug												F			C	
Spruce Aphid												L				
Treehopper												F				
Wax Scale												−				U
Ant Lion (Neuroptera)	**8**															
Antlion						U					−					
Brown Lacewing																R
Green Lacewing					−							U				F
Lacewing												L				
Lacewing Fly					−							L				
Sialis sp													L			
Sialis sp. larvae													F			
Snakefly												L				
Beetle (Coleoptera)	**44**															
Bark Beetle					C	O	C					−				
Blister Beetle											C					
Brychius sp.													F			
Carrion Beetle											U	−				
Checkered Beetle						U						A				
Click Beetle												−	L			
Colorado Potato Beetle												−			C	R
Convergent Lady Beetle												A				F
Coptomus sp.													F			
Darkling Beetle											F	−				
Dermestid Beetle																U
Diving Beetle													F			
Elm Leaf Beetle																A
Elmidae												L	F			
Elodea sp.													F			
Flat Bark Beetle												L				
Glow-worm												−				
Ground Beetle												A				
Haliplidae													L			
Haliplus sp.													F			
Heterlimnius sp.													F			
Hydrophiliidae													L			
Hydrophilus sp.												−		F		
Hydrovatus sp.													F			
Hygrotus sp.													F			
Lady Beetle												L				
Ladybird Beetle												−	L			
Lara sp.													F			
Long-horned Beetle					F	F	F									
Metallic Wood-boring Beetle					C							A				
Net-winged Beetle												L				
Optioservus quadrimaculatus													F			
Peltodytes sp.													F			
Rove Beetle													C			
Scarab Beetle						U									F	
Scirtidae												L				
Snout Beetle												L				
Soldier Beetle												L				
Stenus sp.													F			
Tiger Beetle											C	C				
Tropisternus sp.												−		F		
Tumbling Flower Beetle											C					
Whirligig Beetle (B)												L		A		
Zaitzevia parvulus													F			
Scorpionfly (Mecoptera)	**2**															
Scolytidae												−	L			
Snow Scorpion												−	L			
Caddisfly (Trichoptera)	**34**															
Agapetus sp													L			
Allocosmoecus sp.													F			
Amphicosmoecus canax												F	F			

KEY: Risk – At Risk Codes: MS Missing, **ED** Endangered, **TH** Threatened, **CD** Candidate, **MN** Monitor, **RGM** Regulated Game, **RNG** Regulated Nongame, **RA** Rare, **PB** Protected Breeding Areas. • **Intro – Introduced Species Codes: IN** Introduced Noxious species, **IO** Introduced, Other than noxious species. • **Habitat Types: SA** Subalpine, **MT** Mountain, **DF** Douglas Fir , **PP** Ponderosa Pine , **RK** Rocklands, **BU** Bushy areas, **GR** Grassland, **WL** Wetlands, **RP** Riparian, **ST** Streams, **LK** Lakes & Ponds, **DS** Disturbed Soil, **HU** Near Human Habitation. • **Habitat Frequency Codes: A** Abundant, **C** Common, **F** Fairly common, **U** Uncommon, **R** Rare, **V** Vagrant, **K** Known in habitat, **L** Likely in habitat, **M** Missing from habitat.

Species Name	#	Risk	Intro	SA	MT	DF	PP	RK	BU	GR	WL	RP	ST	LK	DS	HU
Anabolia bimaculata													F			
Apatania sp.													F			
Asynarchus aldinus													F			
Brachycentrus sp													L			
Ceratopsychae oslari													L			
Ceratopsyche cockerelli													L			
Ceratopsyche oslari													L			
Cheumatopsyche sp													L			
Dicosmoecus gilvipes													L			
Ecclisomyia sp.													F			
Glossosoma sp													L			
Helicopsyche borealis													L			
Helicopsychew borealis													L			
Hydropsyche occidentalis													L			
Hydropsychidae													L			
Hydroptilidae													L			
Limnephilidae													L			
Micrasema bactro													L			
Neophylax sp.													F			
Onocosmoecus sp.													L			
Parapsyche almota													L			
Philopotamidae													L			
Protoptila sp													L			
Psycholglypha sp.													F			
Psychomyiidae													F			
Rhyacophila acropedes													L			
Rhyacophila arnoudi													F			
Rhyacophilidae													F			
Small instars													L			
Tinodes sp.													L			
Wormaldia sp.													F			
Butterfly (Lepidoptera)	79															
Alexandria Sulfur						U										
Arrowhead Blue							U									
Becker's White										U						
Brown Elfin						F	F									U
Butler's Alpine						U						U				
Cabbage Butterfly															C	C
California Hairstreak							I									
California Tortoiseshell						F		F								
Clear-winged Moth															U	U
Clothes Moth												—				C
Clouded Sulfur				—		—									C	A
Codling Moth																A
Common Checkered Skipper										F						F
Common Sooty Wing																U
Compton's Tortoiseshell					R							R				
Creamy Marble Wing										U		L				
Cutworm												A				
Dreamy Dusky Wing					F					F		A				
Geometrid Moth												A				
Giant Silkworm Moth																
Gray Hairstreak						F	F		—		F					
Great Spangled Fritillary						F										
Hawk Moth												U				U
Isabella Tigermoth												F				
Juba Skipper							F			F		F				
Large Wood Nymph							F			F						
Lawn Moth												L				
Leaf Blotch Miner																F
Leafroller Moth																C
Least Wood Nymph							C			C						
Lorquin's Admiral						C						C				R
Milbert's Tortoiseshell				F								F				R
Monarch Butterfly												R				
Mountain Swallowtail				U	U	F	U	U	U	U	U	U	U	U	U	C
Mourning Cloak			IO	-	-	-	-	-	-	-	-	C	-	-	-	U
Mylitta Crescentspot						—	—					F				
Northern Blue					U											
Northern Cloudy Wing										U						
Ochre Ringlet							C			C						
Olethreutid Moth												L				
Orange Sulfur										U					U	U
Orange-bordered Blue							F			F						
Owlet Moth												—			C	C
Painted Lady												C			F	F
Pale Checkerspot						—										
Pale Tiger Swallowtail					F											
Pearly Crescentspot						C	C									
Persius' Dusky Wing										U						
Phoebus Parnassian				F								—				R
Plume Moth														L		
Polyphemus Moth												—			U	U
Prominent Moth												F				
Purplish Copper						F	F					—			C	C
Pyralid Moth												U				
Red Admiral						—				F						
Ringed Blue										F						
Roadside Skipper								R								
Russet Hairstreak					F				F							
Sara's Orange Tip						—	F									
Satyr Anglewing						C						C				

Species Name	#	Risk	Intro	SA	MT	DF	PP	RK	BU	GR	WL	RP	ST	LK	DS	HU
Silver-spotted Skipper																U
Silver-studded Blue																
Silvery Blue									–	U						
Spring Blue										F		A				
Tailed Blue												U				
Tent Caterpillar												A				
The Early Elfin							F									
Thicket Hairstreak							R									
Tomato Hornworm																U
Tussock Moth						A										
Veined White					F							F				
Western Pine Elfin							F									
Western Tiger Swallowtail				–	–	C	–	–	C	–	–	–	–	–	–	F
Western White					C					C						
White Pine Butterfly							F									
White Skipper										R						
Woodland Skipper							F								A	F
Zephyr Anglewing					C	U										
Zerene Fritillary						C						C				
Fly (Diptera)	61															
Anthomyiid Fly															L	
Anthomyzid Fly													L			
Antocha sp.													F			
Apple Maggot																L
Aquatic Dance Fly												A				C
Aquatic Longlegged Fly												A				
Athericidae													L			
Atherix sp.													F			
Bee fly						–				C						
Bezzia sp.													F			
Biting Midge												A				
Black Fly				A	A											
Blephariceridae sp.													L			
Blow Fly						F	F									C
Chelifera sp.													F			
Chironomidae													–	L		
Clinocera sp.													F			
Cnophia sp.													F			
Crane Fly												F				F
Deer Fly				C												
Dicranata sp.													F			
Dixid Midge													F	C		
Ephydra sp.													F			
Euparyphus sp.													F			
Flesh Fly																U
Fruit Fly												L				U
Fungus Gnat						F										
Gall Gnat									–			F	F			
Glutops sp.													F			
Gyraulis sp.													F			
Hemerodromia sp.													F			
Hexatoma sp.													F			
Horse Bot Fly															U	
Horse Fly				C												
House Fly																C
Limnophila sp.													F			
Limnophora aequifrons													F			
Louse Fly						R						–				
March Fly												A				
Midge														A		
Mosquito				A	A							A		C		
Moth Fly												A				
Pedicia sp.													F			
Pelecorhynchidae												A				
Pericoma sp.													F			
Physa nuttali													F			
Pomace Fly												L				
Primitive Crane Fly												A				
Prosimulium sp.													F			
Protanyderus sp. larvae													F			
Pteronarcys californicus													F			
Pteronarcys princeps													F			
Robber fly						C				C						
Shore Fly												A				
Simulium sp.													F			
Soldier Fly												L				
Syrphid Fly												A				C
Tabanus sp.				C												
Tachinid Fly						F	F									
Tipula sp.													F			
Trypetidae												L				
Flea (Siphonaptera)	1															
Flea																C
Ant & Bee (Hymenoptera)	27															
Andrenid Bee												–	L			
Ant						C	C									U

KEY: Risk – At Risk Codes: MS Missing, **ED** Endangered, **TH** Threatened, **CD** Candidate, **MN** Monitor, **RGM** Regulated Game, **RNG** Regulated Nongame, **RA** Rare, **PB** Protected Breeding Areas. • **Intro – Introduced Species Codes: IN** Introduced Noxious species, **IO** Introduced, Other than noxious species. • **Habitat Types: SA** Subalpine, **MT** Mountain, **DF** Douglas Fir , **PP** Ponderosa Pine , **RK** Rocklands, **BU** Bushy areas, **GR** Grassland, **WL** Wetlands, **RP** Riparian, **ST** Streams, **LK** Lakes & Ponds, **DS** Disturbed Soil, **HU** Near Human Habitation. • **Habitat Frequency Codes: A** Abundant, **C** Common, **F** Fairly common, **U** Uncommon, **R** Rare, **V** Vagrant, **K** Known in habitat, **L** Likely in habitat, **M** Missing from habitat.

Species Name	#	Risk	Intro	SA	MT	DF	PP	RK	BU	GR	WL	RP	ST	LK	DS	HU
Argid Sawfly					F							−				
Braconid										U		−				
Bumblebee						C	C									
Bumblebee spp						C	C								C	C
Chalcidids												L				
Cimbicid Sawfly												F				
Gall Wasp												A				
Golden Digger Wasp						−	U									
Halictid Bee												−	L			
Homoptera spp												L				
Honeybee															C	C
Hornet						F	F									
Hymenoptera												L				
Ichneumon												F				F
Leafcutting Bee												U				U
Mud Dauber Wasp											−					U
Sawfly					F		C				F		C			
Sphecid Wasp						F	F						F			
Spider Wasp												L				
Terrestrial												L				
Thysanura												L				
Velvet Ant										R						
Xyelid Sawfly												−	L			
Yellow Jacket					C	C	C						C	L			
Yellow-faced Bee												−	L			F
Eel, Lamprey (Cyclostomata)	2															
Eel (A)												L				
Eel (B)												L				
Bony Fish (Osteichthyes)	46															
Sturgeon (Acipenseriformes)	1															
White Sturgeon													L	L		
Salmon (Salmoniformes)	11															
Brook Trout			IO										L	L		
Brown Trout			IO										L	L		
Chinook Salmon		MS											M	M		
Coho Salmon		MS											M	M		
Cutthroat Trout			IO										L	L		
Dolly Varden													L	L		
Eulachon														M		
Kokanee Salmon		HA											U	M		
Lake Trout			IO										L	L		
Mountain Whitefish													L	C		
Rainbow Trout		RGM		-	-	-	-	-	-	-	-	-	F	C	-	-
Bridgelip Sucker				-	-	-	-	-	-	-	-	-	F	-		
Carp (Cypriniformes)	15															
Carp			IO	-	-	-	-	-	-	-	-	-	C	C	-	
Chiselmouth													L	L		
Goldfish			IO										L	L		
Lake Chub													L	L		
Largescale Sucker													L	L		
Leopard Dace													L	L		
Longnose Dace													L	L		
Longnose Sucker													L	L		
Mountain Sucker													L	L		
Northern Squawfish													L	L		
Peamouth													L	L		
Redside shiner													L	L		
Speckled Dace													L	L		
Tench			IO										L	L		
Catfish (Siluriformes)	2															
Brown Bullhead			IO										L	L		
Channel Catfish			IO	-	-	-	-	-	-	-	-	-	-	C	-	-
Trout Perch (Percopsiformes)	1															
Sand Roller													L	L		
Cod (Gadiformes)	1															
Burbot													L	L		
Perch (Perciformes)	9															
Black Crappie			IO										L	L		
Bluegill			IO										L	L		
Green Sunfish			IO										L	L		
Largemouth Bass			IO										L	L		
Pumpkinseed			IO										L	F		
Smallmouth Bass			IO	-	-	-	-	-	-	-	-	-	F	F	-	-
Walleye			IO	-	-	-	-	-	-	-	-	-	C	C	-	-
White Crappie			IO	-	-	-	-	-	-	-	-	-	F	-	-	-
Yellow Perch			IO										L	L		
Sculpin (Scorpaeniformes)	5															
Mottled Sculpin													L	L		
Piute Sculpin													L	L		
Shorthead Sculpin													L	L		
Slimy Sculpin													L	L		
Torrent Sculpin													L	L		
Herring (Clupeiformes)	1															
American Shad			IO										L	L		
Amphibian (Amphibia)	10															
Salamander (Caudata)	2															
Long-toed Salamander				-	U	U	U	-	-	-	−	−	-	F	-	-
Tiger Salamander														F		
Frog (Anura)	8															
Bull Frog			IN	-	-	-	-	-	-	-	-	-	F	F	-	-

Species Name	#	At Risk	Intro	SA	MT	DF	PP	RK	BU	GR	WL	RP	ST	LK	DS	HU	Sp	Su	F	W
Great Basin Spadefoot												L								
Northern Leopard Frog																				
Pacific Tree Frog		CD		-	-	-	U	-	R	R	U	U	U	U	-	R				
Pacific Treefrog							R		U	R		U		C						
Spotted Frog		CD												L						
Tailed Toad					U								U							
Western Toad					R	U	C	-	U	-	U	-	-	-	-	F				
Reptile (Reptilia)	14																			
Turtle (Testudines)	3																			
Mud Turtle												-	L	L						
Water Turtle												L								
Western Painted Turtle		RNG		-	-	-	-	-	-	-	-	-	F	C	-	-				
Snake (Squamata)	11																			
Anguid Lizard								L												
Common Garter Snake				-	-	U	U	-	-	C	-	U	U	-	-	C				
Gopher Snake				-	-	U	U	-	-	U	-	R	-	-	-	-				
Iguanid Lizard								L												
Northern Alligator Lizard								L				-								
Pygmy Short-Horned Lizard								L												
Rubber Boa				-	-	R	R	R	-	-	-	R	-	-	-	-				
Western Racer				-	-	R	U	-	R	U	-	-	-	-	-	-				
Western Rattlesnake				-	-	-	-	F	-	U	-	-	-	-	U	U				
Western Skink				-	-	-	F	F	-	U	-	-	-	-						
Western Terrestrial Garter Snake												U		-						
Bird (Aves)	215																			
Grebe (Podicipediformes)	6																			
GREBE (PODICIPEDIDAE)	6																			
Common Loon		CD											-	U			U	R	U	R
Eared Grebe		PB												C			C	U	U	
Horned Grebe		MN												R	R		R	R	U	-
Pied-billed Grebe		PB											U	F			F	F	F	U
Red-necked Grebe		MN											U	U			U	C	U	
Western Grebe		MN												U			U	C	U	-
Pelican (Pelecaniformes)	1																			
CORMORANT (PHALACROCORACIDAE)	1																			
Double Crested Cormorant											V						V			
Heron (Ciconiiformes)	3																			
HERON (ARDEIDAE)	3																			
American Bittern											U		U			R	U	R	-
Great Blue Heron		MN		-	-	-	-	-	-	-	F	F	F	C	*	-	F	F	F	R
Great Egret											V	V	V	V			V			
Waterfowl (Anseriformes)	26																			
WATERFOWL (ANATIDAE)	26																			
American Wigeon											U		U	F			F	F	U	F
Barrow's Goldeneye														F			F	U	F	F
Blue-winged Teal									F				F	F			U	F	U	-
Bufflehead		RGM							U				F	F			F	-	F	U
Canada Goose										C			F	C	C		C	U	F	U
Canvasback													U	U			U	U	U	R
Cinnamon Teal									U				F	C			F	C	U	
Common Goldeneye													F	F			C	-	F	C
Common Merganser													C	C			C	C	C	
Eurasian Widgeon													R	U			U	-	-	U
Gadwall													U	U			C	C	F	R
Green-winged Teal													F	F			F	U	F	U
Harlequin Duck													R				R	R	R	-
Hooded Merganser		RGM											U	U			U	R	U	C
Lesser Scaup													C	F			C	U	U	C
Mallard				-	-	-	-	-	-	-	C	-	C	C	-	-	A	A	A	C
Northern Pintail											-	U	F	F	-		A	U	F	R
Northern Shoveler													R	F			F	F	F	R
Red-breasted Merganser													-	R			R	-	R	-
Redhead													U	U			U	U	U	U
Ring-necked Duck													U	U			U	U	U	R
Ruddy Duck									U				-	U			C	C	U	R
Snow Goose									U	R			-	U			U	-	U	R
Trumpeter Swan											C						R	-	R	R
Tundra Swan											C		-	C			C	-	C	R
Wood Duck		RGM										U	U	U			U	U	U	U
Hawk (Falconiformes)	15																			
VULTURE (CATHARTIDAE)	1																			
Turkey Vulture				-	-	-	U	-	U	-	-	-	-	-	-	-	U	U	R	-
HAWK (ACCIPITRIDAE)	10																			
Bald Eagle		TH										U	U	U			U	-	U	F
Cooper's Hawk					U	U											U	R	U	U
Golden Eagle		CD			U	U	U		U							R	R	R	R	
Goshawk		RNG			U	U	U										U	R	R	R
Northern Harrier											F	C					U	U	U	U
Osprey		MN		-	-	-	-	-	-	-	-	C	-	U	C	-	F	F	U	C
Red-tailed Hawk		RNG			U	-	F	-	-	F	-	-	-	-			C	C	C	C
Rough-legged Hawk		RNG					F			U							U	-	U	F
Sharp-shinned Hawk						U	U						U			U	U	R	U	U
Swainson's Hawk											V						V			
FALCON (FALCONIDAE)	4																			

KEY: Risk – At Risk Codes: **MS** Missing, **ED** Endangered, **TH** Threatened, **CD** Candidate, **MN** Monitor, **RGM** Regulated Game, **RNG** Regulated Nongame, **RA** Rare, **PB** Protected Breeding Areas. • **Intro – Introduced Species Codes: IN** Introduced Noxious species, **IO** Introduced, Other than noxious species. • **Habitat Types: SA** Subalpine, **MT** Mountain, **DF** Douglas Fir , **PP** Ponderosa Pine , **RK** Rocklands, **BU** Bushy areas, **GR** Grassland, **WL** Wetlands, **RP** Riparian, **ST** Streams, **LK** Lakes & Ponds, **DS** Disturbed Soil, **HU** Near Human Habitation. • **Habitat Frequency Codes: A** Abundant, **C** Common, **F** Fairly common, **U** Uncommon, **R** Rare, **V** Vagrant, **K** Known in habitat, **L** Likely in habitat, **M** Missing from habitat.

Species Name	#	At Risk	Intro	SA	MT	DF	PP	RK	BU	GR	WL	RP	ST	LK	DS	HU	Sp	Su	F	W
American Kestrel							U			F					U		R	R	U	U
Merlin		MN			U					F						U	U	R	U	U
Peregrine Falcon							U			F					-		R	-	R	-
Prairie Falcon							U			U					-		U	R	R	U
Grouse (Galliformes)	6																			
GROUSE (PHASIANIDAE)	6																			
Blue Grouse		RGM				F			U	U							U	U	U	U
California Quail			IO	-	-	-	U	-	C	U	-	U	U	-	A	C	F	F	F	F
Ring-necked Pheasant									U	C					C	U	U	U	U	U
Ruffed Grouse		RGM		-	-	U	-		U	-	-	U	-	-			U	U	U	U
Sharptailed Grouse		MS								M							M	M	M	M
Wild Turkey						U	U			U							U	U	U	U
Rail (Gruiformes)	3																			
RAIL (RALLIDAE)	3																			
American Coot													F	A			C	C	C	U
Sora											U						U	U	U	-
Virginia Rail											U						U	U	R	R
Sandpiper (Charadriiformes)	20																			
PLOVER (CHARADRIIDAE)	2																			
Killdeer										F		C		C	U		F	F	F	R
Semi-palmated Plover											U			U			U	-	R	-
SANDPIPER (SCOLOPACIDAE)	11																			
Common Snipe											U						F	F	F	R
Greater Yellowlegs													F	F			F	-	F	-
Least Sandpiper														F			U	-	U	-
Lesser Yellowlegs														F			F	-	F	-
Long-billed Curlew											U						-	R	-	-
Long-billed Dowitcher														F			F	-	C	-
Pectoral Sandpiper														F			R	-	U	-
Semipalmated Sandpiper														F			U	-	U	-
Solitary Sandpiper														U			R	-	U	-
Spotted Sandpiper													F	F			F	F	R	-
Western Sandpiper														F			R	-	U	-
PHALAROPE (PHALAROPODIDAE)	2																			
Red-necked Phalarope														R			R	-	R	-
Wilson's Phalarope											U			U			U	U	R	-
GULL (LARIDAE)	5												F		F			R	-	R	-
Black Tern													F		F			R	-	R	-
Bonaparte Gull											U							R	-	R	-
California Gull															R			-	R	-	R
Herring Gull															R	R		-	-	-	R
Ring-billed Gull											U				F	C	C	A	A	A	C
Pigeon (Columbiformes)	2																			
PIGEON (COLUMBIDAE)	2																			
Mourning Dove							U		U	C						F	C	C	C	U
Rock Dove								R					R				A	F	C	F	R
Owl (Strigiformes)	10																			
OWL (STRIGIDAE)	10																			
Barn Owl								R		R	R	R					R	R	R	R
Barred Owl					U	U											R	R	R	R
Flammulated Owl						R	R			F							R	-	R	-
Great Horned Owl				-	U	C	C	C	C	F	F	C	C	-	F	C	C	C	C	C
Long-eared Owl										R	R	U					R	R	R	R
Northern Pygmy Owl					U	F	F					R					R	F	F	F
Northern Saw-whet Owl						R	R	R									R	R	R	R
Short-eared Owl										R							R	R	R	R
Snowy Owl										R							-	-	-	R
Western Screech Owl						U										U	U	U	U	R
Nighthawk (Caprimulgiformes)	2																			
NIGHTHAWK (CAPRIMULGIDAE)	2																			
Common Nighthawk							U			F							R	U	R	-
Common Poorwill							R			R							R	R	R	-
Swift (Apodiformes)	8																			
SWIFT (APODIDAE)	3																			
Vaux's Swift		CD			U	U											U	U	U	-
White Throated Swift		CD					U									U	U	U	-	-
Yellow-throat							U				F					R	F	F	U	-
HUMMINGBIRD (TROCHILIDAE)	5																			
Anna's Humming Bird				-				R								R	-	-	-	R
Black-chinned Hummingbird								R	U							U	F	F	U	-
Broad-tailed Humming Bird										V							F	F	U	-
Calliope Hummingbird							R		F			U				F	F	F	U	-
Rufous Humming Bird				F			R		R			U				F	F	R	C	-
Kingfisher (Coraciiformes)	1																			
KINGFISHER (ALCEDINIDAE)	1																			
Belted Kingfisher												U	U			U	C	C	U
Woodpecker (Piciformes)	8																			
WOODPECKER (PICIDAE)	8																			
Black-backed Woodpecker		MN				U	U	R									-	R	-	-
Downy Woodpecker						U	C					U				U	F	C	U	U
Hairy Woodpecker					U	U	U					U				F	C	U	U
Northern Flicker					U	U	U					U			F	F	C	C	C	F
Pileated Woodpecker		CD			U	U	U									F	F	F	U
Red-naped Sapsucker						U						U			U	F	F	U	-
White-headed Woodpecker							R									R	R	R	R
Williamson's Sapsucker					R	R										U	U	S	-
Thrush (Passeriformes)	104																			
TYRANT FLYCATCHER (TYRANNIDAE)	10																			

Species Name	#	At Risk	Intro	SA	MT	DF	PP	RK	BU	GR	WL	RP	ST	LK	DS	HU	Sp	Su	F	W
Dusky Flycatcher						F	F		U							-	F	F	R	-
Eastern Kingbird								F	F	F			C			F	C	-	C	U	-
Hammond's Flycatcher					U		U					R				-	C	C	R	-
Least Flycatcher								R		-		R					-	-	-	-	-
Olive-sided Flycatcher					U		U									-	-	U	-	-
Say's Phoebe									U	U		-				R	C	U	R	-
Western Flycatcher						R	R		U	U		R				R	F	F	R	-
Western Kingbird						-	-	U		U		U				U	U	U	R	-
Western Wood-Pewee					U		F					F				R	F	F	U	-
Willow Flycatcher												F	C				?	?	?	?
PIPIT (MOTICILLIDAE)	2																			
American Pipit							-		U	U						R	U	-	C	-
Horned Lark							F		U	C						R	F	F	C	C
SWALLOW (HIRUNDINDAE)	6																			
Bank Swallow								A				A	A	A			U	U	U	-
Barn Swallow										F	C	A		C		F	C	C	C	-
Cliff Swallow								A			C		F	C		C	C	A	U	-
Northern Rough-winged Swallow								U			C			C		C	U	U	U	-
Tree Swallow											C			C		C	-	C	U	-
Violet-green Swallow											U		A	A		A	-	A	U	-
CROW (CORVIDAE)	7									C							C	C	C	C
American Crow										C					A	C	C	C	C	C
Black-billed Magpie						F			C							R	V	V	V	V
Blue Jay					R	R										R	U	U	U	U
Clark's Nutcracker				F	F		F										U	U	U	U
Common Raven					F	C	C	F		F		C				-	C	C	C	C
Gray Jay				F	U	U	F									-	U	U	U	U
Steller's Jay					F	F										U	U	U	U	U
CHICKADEE (PARIDAE)	3																			
Black-capped Chickadee						U	C					C				F	C	C	C	C
Chestnut-backed Chickadee				F	U	U	C									R	F	U	U	U
Mountain Chickadee				U	F	F	F		F			C	C			F	F	F	F	F
NUTHATCH (SITTIDAE)	3																			
Pygmy Nuthatch					C	C	C										F	F	F	F
Red-breasted Nuthatch					F	F	C					C				C	F	F	F	F
White-breasted Nuthatch							U			U						R	U	U	U	U
CREEPER (CERTHIIDAE)	1																			
Brown Creeper					U	U	U									R	U	U	U	U
WREN (TROGLODYTIDAE)	6																			
Bewick's Wren L												R				R	R	R	R	R
Canyon Wren								U				F				U	U	U	U	U
House Wren						F			C							U	F	F	U	-
Marsh Wren											F			F		U	F	F	U	R
Rock Wren				U	U			U								U	U	U	U	R
Winter Wren					C	C	-	-				C	C			U	C	U	U	U
DIPPER (CINDIDAE)	1																			
American Dipper					F							U	F			U	U	U	U	U
ROBIN (MUSCICAPIDAE)	11																			
American Robin				-	U	-	U	-	C	C	-	C	C	C	C	C	C	C	C	C
Golden-crowned Kinglet					C	C		-				U				R	C	U	U	C
Hermit Thrush					F	C	U					C				R	F	F	U	-
Mountain Bluebird					F		F		C							R	U	F	F	R
Northern Waterthrush												F	F			R	-	F	R	-
Ruby-crowned Kinglet					F	F			C			F				R	U	F	F	-
Swainson's Thrush					C	C						U				R	U	F	F	-
Townsend's Solitaire					U	U	U		U	-		U				R	U	U	U	U
Varied Thrush					F								F			U	U	F	F	U
Veery									R	-	U	U	U	U	-	U	R	F	U	-
Western Bluebird		CD					F			F						U	F	U	U	R
MIMIC THRUSH (MIMIDAE)	1																			
Gray Catbird									U			U	F	U		U	U	U	U	-
WAXWING (BOMBYCILLIDAE)	2																			
Bohemian Waxwing					-				U							U	-	-	-	U
Cedar Waxwing									C		C	U	C	C		U	U	C	C	U
SHRIKE (LANIIDAE)	2																			
Loggerhead Shrike								R	R						R	-	-	R	-	-
Northern Shrike								U	U							R	-	-	-	U
STARLING (STURNIDAE)	1																			
European Starling										-	-	-			A	A	A	A	A	A
VIREO (VIREONIDAE)	3																			
Red-eyed Vireo									U			F	U	U		U	R	F	R	-
Solitary Vireo					U	F	U		U			U				U	U	U	U	-
Warbling Vireo					C	C	C		C			C				R	R	C	R	-
WARBLER (EMBERIZIDAE)	34																			
American Redstart											R	R					R	R	R	-
American Tree Sparrow											U									U
Black-headed Grosbeak						F			F			F	U			F	F	F	R	-
Bobolink										R						U	U	U	-	-
Brewer's Blackbird										A		A			A	A	A	A	A	R
Brown-headed Cowbird					R	F	-	-		-					-	U	U	C	U	-
Chipping Sparrow				-		C	C	-	C	U					-	C	C	C	C	-
Common Yellowthroat											C		F	F		F	F	F	R	-
Dark-eyed Junco				C	C	C			C							R	C	C	C	C
Fox Sparrow				-	U	U			-			U	R	R		R	U	U	U	R
Golden-crowned Sparrow									U			U				R	R	-	R	-

KEY: Risk – At Risk Codes: **MS** Missing, **ED** Endangered, **TH** Threatened, **CD** Candidate, **MN** Monitor, **RGM** Regulated Game, **RNG** Regulated Nongame, **RA** Rare, **PB** Protected Breeding Areas. • **Intro – Introduced Species Codes: IN** Introduced Noxious species, **IO** Introduced, Other than noxious species. • **Habitat Types: SA** Subalpine, **MT** Mountain, **DF** Douglas Fir, **PP** Ponderosa Pine, **RK** Rocklands, **BU** Bushy areas, **GR** Grassland, **WL** Wetlands, **RP** Riparian, **ST** Streams, **LK** Lakes & Ponds, **DS** Disturbed Soil, **HU** Near Human Habitation. • **Habitat Frequency Codes: A** Abundant, **C** Common, **F** Fairly common, **U** Uncommon, **R** Rare, **V** Vagrant, **K** Known in habitat, **L** Likely in habitat, **M** Missing from habitat.

Species Name	#	At Risk	Intro	SA	MT	DF	PP	RK	BU	GR	WL	RP	ST	LK	DS	HU	Sp	Su	F	W
		Risk	**Intro**																	
Grasshopper sparrow										U							U	U	U	–
Harris Sparrow										R								R		–
Lark Sparrow										U							U	U	U	–
Lazuli Bunting									U				C	U	U		R	R	F	R	–
Lincoln's Sparrow					–	U	U				–	–	F					R	U	U	–
MacGillivray's Warbler					F	F	F						F					R	F	R	–
Nashville Warbler					U	U			U		–	–	F				U	F	F	S	–
Northern Oriole										–	–	F	F	F		U	F	F	R	–	
Orange-crowned Warbler									F				F				R	R	R	U	–
Red-winged Blackbird							U					A			A		R	C	A	A	U
Savannah Sparrow										C							R	R	C	R	–
Song Sparrow					F				U			C	C	C		F	F	F	F	F	
Spotted Towhee									F			F	F			R	F	F	U	R	
Townsend's Warbler					F	F	U									R	F	F	U	–	
Vesper Sparrow										C						R	R	C	U	–	
Western Meadowlark									F	C						U	C	C	C	R	
Western Tanager					C	C	U					F					U	C	U	–	
White-crowned Sparrow					C				C							R	A	R	A	U	
Wilson's Warbler					F				U							R	F	R	F	–	
Yellow Warbler												C	F			U	C	C	U	–	
Yellow-breasted Chat									U		U	C					R	U	R	–	
Yellow-headed Blackbird											C			C			C	C	U	–	
Yellow-rumped Warbler					C	F	F									R	C	C	C	R	
FINCH (FRINGILLIDAE)	10																			
American Goldfinch									F					C	U	U	F	C	F	U	
Cassin's Finch					F	F	F									R	F	F	U	U	
Common Redpoll					R							U	U			R	–	–	–	R	
Evening Grosbeak					C	C	C									R	C	U	C	U	
House Finch							C		C			F		C		C	C	C	C	C	
Pine Grosbeak			U		U	U	U									C	U	U	U	R	
Pine Siskin					A	A	U					F				C	C	C	C	U	
Purple Finch					V	V	V									V	V	V	V	V	
White-winged Crossbill					R	–	–										–	R	R	R	
Red Crossbill					C	C	C		U							U	F	F	F	F	
WEAVER (PASSERIDAE)	1																			
House Sparrow																A	A	A	A	A	
Mammal (Mammalia)	68																			
Insect Eater (Insectivora)	5																			
Dusky Shrew							U				C										
Masked Shrew					U	U	U		C		–	C									
Merriam Shrew						U	U														
Northern Water Shrew														U	U						
Vagrant Shrew							U					C									
Rabbit (Lagomorpha)	3																			
Common Pika				U																	
Nuttall's Cottontail						U	U														
Snowshoe Hare				-	F	F	-	-	R	-	-	U	-	-	-	-				
Rodent (Rodentia)	24																			
Beaver				-	-	-	-	-	-	-	-	-	U	U	-	-				
Black Rat																L				
Boreal Red-backed Vole					L															
Columbian Ground Squirrel										F										
Eastern Gray Squirrel																F				
Golden Mantled Squirrel					L															
House Mouse															U	U				
Marmota monax								L								U				
Meadow Vole					K															
Mountain Phenacomys					L															
Mountain Vole					L															
Muskrat				-	-	-	-	-	-	-	-	F	U	F	–	F				
Neotoma cinerea					U				U											
Neotoma fuscipes									L											
Northern Flying Squirrel					U															
Northern Pocket Gopher				-	F	F					U				F	U				
Norway Rat												–				U				
Pigmy Shrew		CD			L															
Porcupine					F	U	F	-	U	-	-	-	-	-	-	-				
Red Squirrel					F	F	F													
Richardson's Vole					L															
Western Jumping Mouse					A	A	A				A									
Yellow Pine Chipmunk				-	F	F	F	F	F	-	-	-	-	-	U	-				
Yellow-bellied Marmot				U	-	-	-	F	F		U				-	F				
Bat (Chiroptera)	14																			
Big Brown Bat							U	U												
California Myotis								U												
Fringed Myotis																U				
Hoary Bat					U	U	U													
Little Brown Myotis				-	–	R	–	–	–	–	–	U	–	U	U	–				
Long-legged Myotis									U							R				
Northern Long-eared Myotis							U									R				
Pallid Bat							U	R								R				
Silver-haired Bat					U	R														
Townshend's Big-eared Bat							R									R				
Western Long-eared Myotis							U									U				
Western Red Bat							L													
Western Small-footed Myotis							R	U												
Yuma Myotis							R	U												
Primate (Primate)	1																			
Human				R	U	F	C	R	C	C	U	U	U	U	C	A				
Carnivore (Carnivora)	16																			

Species Name	#	Risk	Intro	SA	MT	DF	PP	RK	BU	GR	WL	RP	ST	LK	DS	HU
Badger										F						
Black Bear				R	U	U	U			-		-			-	-
Bobcat				-	R	-	-	U	-	-	-	U		-	–	-
Cat, Domestic			IN									U			F	A
Cougar					U	U	R									
Coyote				F	F	F	F	F	F	F	F	F	-	-	F	R
Dogs, Domestic			IN			R	R									A
Grizzly Bear		MS		M	M											
Long-tailed Weasel					–	U	U		U	U		U				
Marten		RGM			U											
Mink													F			
Raccoon				-	R	U	U	-	F	-	-	F	F	F	-	-
River Otter													U	U		
Short-tailed Weasel													L			
Striped Skunk				-	-	U	U	-	F	-	F	C	-	-	U	U
Wolf		MS			M											
Deer (Artiodactyla)	5															
Buffalo		MS					M			M						
Elk		RGM		–	F	F	U	-		–	R	-	-	-	-	-
Moose		RGM			U	-	-	-	-	-	-	U	U	U	-	-
Mule Deer		RGM			F		R		F							
White-tailed Deer		RGM		-	F	C	C	-	C	–		C	-	-	C	U

TOTAL ANIMALS 753

Protists

PROTIST (PROTISTA)	17
Amoeba (Rhizopoda)	1
Heliozoan (Actimpoda)	1
Foram (Forimaninifera)	1
Sporozoite (Apicomplexa)	1
Zooflagellate (Zoomastigophera)	1
Ciliate (Ciliophora)	1
Dinoflagellates (Dinoflagellata)	1
Golden Algae (Chrysophyta)	1
Diatom (Bacillumiophyta)	1
Euglena (Euglenopphyta)	1
Green Algae (Chlorophyta)	1
Brown Algae (Phaeophyta)	1
Red Algae (Rhodophyta)	1
Slime Mold - Cellular (Acrasiomycetes)	1
Slime Mold - Plasmodial (Myxomycetes)	1
Mildew (Oomycota)	1
Saprobe (Chytridiomycota)	1

Bacteria & Virus

BACTERIA & VIRUS (MONERA & VIRUS)	7
Bacteria (Bacteria)	1
Cyanophycota (Cyanophycota)	1
Prochlorophycota (Prochlorophycota)	1
Bacteria Virus (Bacteria Virus)	1
Plant Virus (Plant Virus)	1
Vertebrate Virus (Vertebrate Virus)	1
Invertebrate Virus (Invertebrate Virus)	1

KEY: Risk – At Risk Codes: MS Missing, **ED** Endangered, **TH** Threatened, **CD** Candidate, **MN** Monitor, **RGM** Regulated Game, **RNG** Regulated Nongame, **RA** Rare, **PB** Protected Breeding Areas. • **Intro – Introduced Species Codes: IN** Introduced Noxious species, **IO** Introduced, Other than noxious species. • **Habitat Types: SA** Subalpine, **MT** Mountain, **DF** Douglas Fir , **PP** Ponderosa Pine , **RK** Rocklands, **BU** Bushy areas, **GR** Grassland, **WL** Wetlands, **RP** Riparian, **ST** Streams, **LK** Lakes & Ponds, **DS** Disturbed Soil, **HU** Near Human Habitation. • **Habitat Frequency Codes: A** Abundant, **C** Common, **F** Fairly common, **U** Uncommon, **R** Rare, **V** Vagrant, **K** Known in habitat, **L** Likely in habitation, **M** Missing from habitat.

Plant Common Names

There are 991 common names catalogued for the 477 plants identified in the Little Spokane Watershed. The following is an alphabetic list of these common names. Following each common name is the primary common name that is used in this book.

Common Name	Primary Name	Common Name	Primary Name	Common Name	Primary Name
Alaska Rein-orchid	Bog Orchid	Blooming Sally	Fireweed	Canyon Heather	Canyon Heather
Alder	Mountain Alder	Blue Bead	Queencup	Capitate Sandwort	Capitate Sandwort
Alkanet	Common Bugloss	Blue Bunchgrass	Idaho Fescue	Carolina Geranium	Geranium
All-heal	Self-heal	Blue Clematis	Blue Clematis	Cascara	Buckthorn
Alpine Fir	Subalpine Fir	Blue Elderberry	Blue Elderberry	Cat Mint	Catnip
Alpine Pyrola	Common Pink Wintergr	Blue Flag Iris	Western Blue Flag	Catch-fly	Douglas Silene
Alsike Clover	Alsike Clover	Blue Gentian	Blue Gentian	Catnip	Catnip
Aluacomnium androgyn	Aluacomnium androgyn	Blue Lips	Blue Lips	Cattail	Common Cattail
Alumroot	Alumroot	Blue Lupine	Blue Lupine	Ceanothus	Ceanothus
American Brooklime	American Brooklime	Blue Mustard	Mustard	Cedar	Western Red Cedar
American Great Bulru	Tule	Blue Phacelia	Blue Phacelia	Ceratodon purpureus	Ceratodon purpureus
American Vetch	American Vetch	Blue Scorpion Grass	Forget-me-not	Cheatgrass	Cheatgrass
American Water Plant	Yellow Flag Iris	Blue Violet	Blue Violet	Chickweed (A)	Chickweed (A)
Annual Agoseris	Annual Agoseris	Bluebells	Bluebells	Chickweed (B)	Longstem Chickweed
Annual Paintbrush	Annual Paintbrush	Bluebind Weed	Bittersweet	Chickweed (C)	Mouse-ear Chickweed
Antelope Brush	Bitterbrush	Bluebunch Wheatgrass	Bluebunch Wheatgrass	Chickweed (E)	Sticky Chickweed
Anthoceros sp.	Anthoceros sp.	Bluegrass	Bluegrass	Chittambark	Buckthorn
Apple	Apple	Bluntleaf Sandwort	Bluntleaf Sandwort	Chokecherry	Chokecherry
Arrowhead	Wapato	Bog Orchid	Bog Orchid	Christmas Fern	Sword Fern
Arrowleaf Balsamroot	Arrowleaf Balsamroot	Brachythecium albica	Brachythecium albica	Cinquefoil	Cinquefoil
Arrowleaf Groundsel	Arrowleaf Groundsel	Brachythecium campes	Brachythecium campes	Claspleaf Twisted St	Claspleaf Twisted St
Arumleaf Arrowhead	Wapato	Brachythecium salebp	Brachythecium salebp	Cleavers	Bedstraw
Asparagus	Asparagus	Bracken Fern	Bracken Fern	Clematis (A)	Blue Clematis
Aspen	Quaking Aspen	Brake Fern	Bracken Fern	Clematis (B)	Western Virgin's Bow
Aster	Wild Aster	Branching Daisy	Daisy Fleabane	Climacium dendroides	Climacium dendroides
Autumn Willow Herb	Willow Herb	Bride's Bonnet	Queencup	Climbing Nightshade	Bittersweet
Baldhip Rose	Woodland Rose	Bride's Bouquet	Bride's Bouquet	Clover (A)	Cup Clover
Ballhead Sandwort	Capitate Sandwort	Brittle Bladder Fern	Brittle Bladder Fern	Clover (B)	Small-bead Clover
Balsam Fir	Grand Fir	Broad-leaved Montia	Broad-leaved Montia	Clover (C)	Japanese Clover
Balsam Fir	Subalpine Fir	Broadleaf Arnica	Broadleaf Arnica	Clover (D)	Red Clover
Balsamroot	Arrowleaf Balsamroot	Brooklime	American Brooklime	Clover (E)	Small Hop Clover
Baneberry (A)	Western Baneberry	Brown-eyed Susan	Brown-eyed Susan	Clover (F)	Spanish Clover
Baneberry (B)	Baneberry (B)	Bryum pseudotriquetr	Bryum pseudotriquetr	Clover (G)	White Clover
Barren Fescue	Barren Fescue	Buckbrush	Redstem Ceanothus	Clover (H)	White Sweet Clover
Bearberry	Kinnikinnick	Buckbrush	Snowbrush Ceanothus	Clumped Phlox (A)	Showy Phlox
Beardtongue	Yellow Beardtongue	Buckthorn	Buckthorn	Clumped Phlox (B)	Prickly Phlox
Beargrass	Beargrass	Buckwheat 1	Wyeth Buckwheat	Cluster Tarweed	Common Tarweed
Bedstraw	Bedstraw	Buckwheat 2	Knotweed	Coast Pine	Lodgepole Pine
Beggartick	Beggartick	Buffalo Bunchgrass	Rough Fescue	Cocklebur	Cocklebur
Bellflower	Bellflower	Bugloss	Common Bugloss	Codwort	Laceflower
Bentgrass	Bentgrass	Bulbous Bluegrass	Bulbous Bluegrass	Colored Smartweed	Colored Smartweed
Big Bluegrass	Big Bluegrass	Bull Pine	Ponderosa Pine	Columbia Brome	Columbia Brome
Big Huckleberry	Huckleberry (A)	Bull Thistle	Bull Thistle	Columbia Clematis	Blue Clematis
Big Leaf Lupine	Big Leaf Lupine	Bulrush (A)	Bulrush (A)	Columbia Goldenweed	Goldenweed
Big Sagebrush	Big Sagebrush	Bulrush (B)	Tule	Columbia Lily	Tiger Lily
Big-leaved Lanatium	Big Leaf Lupine	Bulrush (C)	Bulrush (C)	Columbia Poccoon	Lemonweed
Bigleaf Maple	Norway Maple	Bur-reed	Bur-reed	Columbia Virgins-bow	Blue Clematis
Bigleaf Sandwort	Bigleaf Sandwort	Burdock	Cocklebur	Columbian Monkshood	Columbian Monkshood
Birch (A)	Paper Birch	Burke's Larkspur	Meadow Larkspur	Columbian Spruce	Engelmann Spruce
Birch (B)	River Birch	Burnet	Burnet	Columbine	Columbine
Birdbill	Shooting Star (B)	Bush Wirelettuce	Narrow-leaved Skelet	Common Bugloss	Common Bugloss
Birdbill Shooting St	Shooting Star (A)	Bushy Goldenrod	Bushy Goldenrod	Common Cattail	Common Cattail
Biscuitroot 2	Swale Desert Parsley	Bushy Knapweed	White Knapweed	Common Dogbane	Indian Hemp
Biscuitroot 3	Large-fruit Lomation	Bushy Mentzelia	Stickleaf	Common Mullein	Common Mullein
Biscuitroot 4	Gray's Lomatium	Buttercup (A)	Mancoun's Buttercup	Common Pink Wintergr	Common Pink Wintergr
Biscuitroot (A)	Nine-leaved Lomatium	Buttercup (B)	Buttercup (B)	Common Plantain	Common Plantain
Bitter Cherry	Bitter Cherry	Buttercup (C)	Sagebrush Buttercup	Common Snowberry	Common Snowberry
Bitterbrush	Bitterbrush	Buttercup (D)	Spearwort	Common Speedwell	Common Speedwell
Bitterroot (B)	Bitterroot (B)	Buttercup (E)	Water Buttercup	Common Tansy	Common Tansy
Bittersweet	Bittersweet	California Danthonia	California Oatgrass	Common Tarweed	Common Tarweed
Black Coneflower	Western Coneflower	California Falsehell	California Falsehell	Common Yarrow	Common Yarrow
Black Cottonwood	Black Cottonwood	California Hellebore	False Hellebore	Coneflower	Western Coneflower
Black Elderberry	Black Elderberry	California Oatgrass	California Oatgrass	Conocephalum conicum	Conocephalum conicum
Black Hawthorn	Douglas Hawthorn	Camas	Camas	Coolwort Foamflower	Coolwort Foamflower
Black Medic	Japanese Clover	Campion	Douglas Silene	Coralroot	Coralroot
Black Raspberry	Blackcap	Canada Bluegrass	Canada Bluegrass	Corn Gromwell	Stoneseed
Black Scrub Pine	Lodgepole Pine	Canada Thistle	Canada Thistle	Corn Mint	Wild Mint
Blackcap	Blackcap	Canada Vetch	Canada Vetch	Cottonweed	Cottonweed
Blackhead	Western Coneflower	Canadian Fleabane	Horseweed	Cottonwood	Black Cottonwood
Blackjack Pine	Ponderosa Pine	Canadian Thistle	Canada Thistle	Cow Parsnip (A)	Cow Parsnip (A)
Bladderwort	Bladderwort	Canby Licoriceroot	Canby Licoriceroot	Cow Parsnip (B)	Cow Parsnip (B)
Blanket Flower	Blanket Flower	Cancerroot	Cancerroot	Cow Sorrel	Sheep Sorrel

Common Name	Primary Name	Common Name	Primary Name	Common Name	Primary Name
Cranberry Tree	Highbush Cranberry	Foxtail	Foxtail	Huckleberry (B)	Grouse Huckleberry
Crane's Bill	Crane's Bill	Foxtail Barley	Foxtail	Huckleberry (C)	Fool's Huckleberry
Creambrush Ocean Spr	Ocean Spray	Fragrant Goldenrod	Bushy Goldenrod	Idaho Fescue	Idaho Fescue
Creek Dogwood	Red Osier Dogwood	Fragrent Bedstraw	Sweetscented Bedstra	Idaho Goldthread	Idaho Goldthread
Creeping Buttercup	Spearwort	Frasera albicaulis	Frasera albicaulis	Indian Arrowwood	Ocean Spray
Creeping Oregon Grap	Small Oregon Grape	Fringe Cup 1	Smooth Fringecup	Indian Basketgrass	Asparagus
Cudweed	Cudweed	Fringe Cup 2	Small-flowered Fring	Indian Blanket	Indian Blanket
Cup Clover	Cup Clover	Fringed Loosestrife	Fringed Loosestrife	Indian Hemp	Indian Hemp
Curly Dock	Curly Dock	Fritillary Lily	Yellowbell	Indian Paintbrush	Indian Paintbrush
Cut-leaf Daisy	Cut-leaf Daisy	Funaria hygrometrica	Funaria hygrometrica	Indian Pond Lily	Indian Pond Lily
Daisy Fleabane	Daisy Fleabane	Gaillardia	Indian Blanket	Indian Wheat	Wooly Plantain
Dalmatian Toadflax	Dalmatian Toadflax	Gairdner's Yampa	Yampah	Inflated Sedge	Inflated Sedge
Dark Throated Shooti	Shooting Star (B)	Geranium	Geranium	Iris (A)	Western Blue Flag
Deadly Zigadenus	Death Camas	Geyer's Onion	Wild Onion (C)	Jagged Chickweed	Jagged Chickweed
Death Camas	Death Camas	Geyer's Twinpod	Geyer's Twinpod	Japanese Brome	Japanese Brome
Deptford Pink	Grass Pink	Glacier Lily	Glacier Lily	Japanese Choat	Japanese Brome
Desert Shooting Star	Shooting Star (A)	Glandular Cinquefoil	Pale Cinquefoil	Japanese Clover	Japanese Clover
Desert Yellow Daisy	Yellow Fleabane	Globe Huckleberry	Globe Huckleberry	Jim Hill Mustard	Jim Hill Mustard
Dicranum flagellare	Dicranum flagellare	Goatweed	Goatweed	Junegrass	Junegrass
Dicranum fuscescens	Dicranum fuscescens	Golden Aster	Golden Aster	Juniper (B)	Western Juniper
Dicranum strictum	Dicranum strictum	Golden Currant	Golden Currant	Juniper (C)	Rocky Mountain Junip
Dodder	Field Dodder	Golden Dock	Golden Dock	Kinnikinnick	Kinnikinnick
Dogbane (B)	Indian Hemp	Goldenrod 1	Bushy Goldenrod	Kitten Tail	Kitten Tail
Douglas' Brodiaea	Wild Hyacinth	Goldenrod 2	Montana Goldenrod	Klamath Weed	Goatweed
Douglas Fir	Douglas Fir	Goldenweed	Goldenweed	Knapweed (B)	Spotted Knapweed
Douglas Hawthorn	Douglas Hawthorn	Goldthread	Idaho Goldthread	Knapweed (C)	White Knapweed
Douglas Maple	Douglas Maple	Goose Grass	Goose Grass	Knotweed	Knotweed
Douglas' Onion	Wild Onion (B)	Goosefoot	Goosefoot	Koeler's Grass	Junegrass
Douglas Silene	Douglas Silene	Goosegrass	Bedstraw	Laceflower	Laceflower
Douglas' Spiraea	Pink Spiraea	Gorman's Desert Pars	Pepper and Salt	Lady Fern	Lady Fern
Downy Cheat	Cheatgrass	Gorman's Lomatium	Pepper and Salt	Lady's Thimble	Bellflower
Drepanocladus aduncu	Drepanocladus aduncu	Grand Fir	Grand Fir	Lamb's Quarters	Goosefoot
Duckweed	Duckweed	Grass Pink	Grass Pink	Lance-leaf Figwort	Figwort
Dutch Clover	White Clover	Grass Widow	Grass Widow	Lanceleaf Spring Bea	Western Spring Beaut
Dutch Rush	Scouring Rush	Grass-leaved Speedwe	Marsh Speedwell	Larch	Tamarack
Dwarf Bilberry	Dwarf Huckleberry	Grassy Death Camas	Death Camas	Large-flowered Agose	Large-flowered Agose
Dwarf Huckleberry	Dwarf Huckleberry	Gray's Desert-parsle	Gray's Lomatium	Large-flowered Coolo	Salmon Collomia
Dwarf Mistletoe	Dwarf Mistletoe	Gray's Lomatium	Gray's Lomatium	Large-flowered Golde	Goldenweed
Dwarf Mountain Heab	Cut-leaf Daisy	Greek Milkweed	Milkweed	Large-fruit Desert P	Large-fruit Lomation
Early Blue Violet	Blue Violet	Green Fescue	Green Fescue	Large-fruit Lomation	Large-fruit Lomation
Elderberry ?	Black Elderberry	Green Pyrola	Green Pyrola	Large-leaved Lanatiu	Big Leaf Lupine
Elderberry (A)	Blue Elderberry	Green Wintergreen	Green Wintergreen	Large-leaved Lupine	Big Leaf Lupine
Elegant Rockcress	Elegant Rockcress	Green-barded Star-tu	Mariposa Lily	Larkspur (A)	Larkspur (A)
Elk Sedge	Elk Sedge	Grimmia apocarpa	Grimmia apocarpa	Larkspur (B)	Meadow Larkspur
Enchanter's Nightsha	Enchanter's Nightsha	Grimmia montana	Grimmia montana	Lava Alumroot	Alumroot
Engelmann Spruce	Engelmann Spruce	Groundsel	Ragwort	Leafy Beggarticks	Beggartick
European Mountain As	Mountain Ash (B)	Grouse Huckleberry	Grouse Huckleberry	Leafy Lousewort	Lousewort
Evening Primrose	Evening Primrose	Grouse Whortleberry	Grouse Huckleberry	Leafy Sticktight	Beggartick
Evergreen Ceanothus	Snowbrush Ceanothus	Grouseberry	Grouse Huckleberry	Least Hop Clover	Small Hop Clover
Everlasting	Rosy Pussy-toes	Gumweed 2	Common Tarweed	Lemmon's Needlegrass	Lemmon's Needlegrass
Fairy Bells (A)	Fairy Bells (A)	Gumweed (A)	Gumweed (A)	Lemonweed	Lemonweed
Fairy Bells (B)	Fairy Bells (B)	Habenaria	Habenaria	Licorice Root	Lovage
Fairy Slipper	Fairy Slipper	Hairy Albert	Hairy Albert	Licorice-Root Fern	Licorice-Root Fern
False Buckwheat	Wyeth Buckwheat	Hairy Owl-clover	Owl's Clover	Line-leaf Fleabane	Yellow Fleabane
False Bugbane	False Bugbane	Hairy Vetch	Hairy Vetch	Line-leaf Indian Let	Narrow-leaved Spring
False Dandelion 1	Large-flowered Agose	Harebell Bellflower	Bellflower	Listera	Listera
False Dandelion 2	Annual Agoseris	Hawksbeard 1	Long-leaved Hawksbea	Little Buttercup	Buttercup (B)
False Hellebore	False Hellebore	Hawksbeard 2	Slender Hawksbeard	Little Meadow Foxtai	Short-awn Foxtail
False Huckleberry	Fool's Huckleberry (	Hawkweed (A)	Western Hawkweed	Little Pipsissewa	Little Prince's Pine
False Solomon's Seal	Western False Solomo	Hawkweed (B)	White-flowered Hawkw	Little Prince's Pine	Little Prince's Pine
False Spikenard	Starry False Solomon	Hawthorn (A)	Douglas Hawthorn	Little Tarweed	Common Tarweed
Felonwort	Bittersweet	Heartleaf Arnica	Heartleaf Arnica	Little Wild Rose	Woodland Rose
Fennel	Fennel	Heath-leaved Aster	Wreath Aster	Littlebells Polemoni	Littlebells Polemoni
Fescue 1	Barren Fescue	Hemlock	Pacific Hemlock	Liverleaf Wintergree	Common Pink Wintergr
Fescue 2	Small Fescue	Hemlock Water Parsni	Water Parsnip	Lodgepole Pine	Lodgepole Pine
Fescue 3	Green Fescue	Hemp Dogbane	Indian Hemp	Long-flowered Bluebe	Bluebells
Fescue 5	Rough Fescue	Heterocodon	Heterocodon	Long-leaf Fleabane	Cut-leaf Daisy
Fescue (D)	Idaho Fescue	Highbush Cranberry	Highbush Cranberry	Long-leaved Hawksbea	Long-leaved Hawksbea
Few Flowered Shootin	Shooting Star (B)	Hoary Chaenactis	Bride's Bouquet	Long-purples	Purple Loosestrife
Few-flowered Wild Oa	One-spike Oatgrass	Hoary False Yarrow	Bride's Bouquet	Long-stalked Starwor	Long-stalked Starwor
Field Chickweed	Field Chickweed	Holboellis Rockcress	Holboellis Rockcress	Longhorn Plectritis	Longhorn Plectritis
Field Dodder	Field Dodder	Holly Fern	Sword Fern	Longleaf Phlox	Longleaf Phlox
Field Horsetail	Field Horsetail	Homalothecium nevade	Homalothecium nevade	Longstem Chickweed	Longstem Chickweed
Field Mint	Wild Mint	Honeysuckle (A)	Orange Honeysuckle	Loosestrife	Purple Loosestrife
Figwort	Figwort	Honeysuckle (B)	Honeysuckle (B)	Lousewort	Lousewort
Fir (A)	Douglas Fir	Honeysuckle (C)	Red Twinberry	Lovage	Lovage
Fir (B)	Grand Fir	Hooded Coralroot	Coralroot	Low Dogbane	Spreading Dogbane
Fir (C)	Subalpine Fir	Hook Violet	Blue Violet	Low Fleabane	Low Fleabane
Fireweed	Fireweed	Hooker Fairybells 1	Fairy Bells (B)	Low Gumweed	Gumweed (A)
Fissidens grandifron	Fissidens grandifron	Hooker Fairybells 2	Fairy Bells (B)	Low Pussytoes	Low Pussytoes
Five-angled Dodder	Field Dodder	Hooker Onion	Wild Onion (C)	Lowland Cudweed	Cudweed
Flannel Mullein	Common Mullein	Hop Clover	Japanese Clover	Lowland Fir	Grand Fir
Flattop Spiraea	White Spiraea	Horse Sorrel	Sheep Sorrel	Lowland Hemlock	Pacific Hemlock
Fleabane	Fleabane	Horseweed	Horseweed	Lowland White Fir	Grand Fir
Fool's Huckleberry	Fool's Huckleberry	Hot-rock Penslemon	White Beardtongue	Lupine	Big Leaf Lupine
Foothill Daisy	Cut-leaf Daisy	Howellia	Howellia	Mahaleb Cherry	Mahaleb Cherry
Forget-me-not	Forget-me-not	Huckleberry (A)	Huckleberry (A)	Malefern	Malefern

Common Name	Primary Name	Common Name	Primary Name	Common Name	Primary Name
Mallow Ninebark	Mallow Ninebark	Owl's Clover	Owl's Clover	Red Osier Dogwood	Red Osier Dogwood
Mancoun's Buttercup	Mancoun's Buttercup	Oysterplant	Oysterplant	Red Sorrel	Sheep Sorrel
Mannagrass	Mannagrass	P Pine	Ponderosa Pine	Red Spurry	Red Spurry
Many-leaved Lanatium	Big Leaf Lupine	Pachistima	Pachistima	Red Three-awn	Red Three-awn
Many-leaved Lupine	Big Leaf Lupine	Pacific Coralroot	Spotted Coralroot	Red Twinberry	Red Twinberry
Marchantia polymorph	Marchantia polymorph	Pacific Hemlock	Pacific Hemlock	Red Willow	Pacific Willow
Mariposa Lily	Mariposa Lily	Pacific Willow	Pacific Willow	Redstem Ceanothus	Redstem Ceanothus
Marsh Scullcap	Marsh Scullcap	Pacific Yew	Pacific Yew	Redtop	Redtop
Marsh Speedwell	Marsh Speedwell	Pale Cinquefoil	Pale Cinquefoil	Redwool Saxifrage	Western Saxifrage
Mayweed Chamomile	Fennel	Pale Dogtooth Violet	Glacier Lily	Reed Canary Grass	Reed Canary Grass
Meadow Death Camas	Death Camas	Pale Fawn-lily	Glacier Lily	Rhacomitrium canesce	Rhacomitrium canesce
Meadow Larkspur	Meadow Larkspur	Palouse Knotweed	Knotweed	Rhytidiadelphus triq	Rhytidiadelphus triq
Meadowrue	Western Meadowrue	Pan Bluebells	Bluebells	River Birch	River Birch
Menzies' Silene	Menzies' Silene	Panic Grass	Panic Grass	Rock Clematis	Western Virgin's Bow
Microsteris	Microsteris	Panicle Bluebells	Panicle Bluebells	Rocky Mountain Junip	Rocky Mountain Junip
Milfoil	Common Yarrow	Paper Birch	Paper Birch	Rocky Mountain Maple	Mountain Maple
Milk-vetch	Canada Vetch	Parry's Rush	Parry's Rush	Rocky Mountain Woods	Rocky Mountain Woods
Milkweed	Milkweed	Pathfinder	Pathfinder	Rose (A)	Nootka Rose
Miner's Lettuce	Miner's Lettuce	Peach Willow	Peach Willow	Rose (B)	Woodland Rose
Mitrewort	Mitrewort	Peach-leaf Willow	Peach Willow	Rose (C)	Woods Rose
Mniaceae spp.	Mniaceae spp.	Pearly Everlasting	Pearly Everlasting	Rosy Pussy-toes	Rosy Pussy-toes
Mock Azalea	Fool's Huckleberry	Penslemon	Yellow Beardtongue	Rough Fescue	Rough Fescue
Mock Orange	Mock Orange	Pepper and Salt	Pepper and Salt	Round-leaved Violet	Round-leaved Violet
Monkshood	Columbian Monkshood	Peppermint	Peppermint	Roundleaf Alumroot 1	Alumroot
Montana Goldenrod	Montana Goldenrod	Pepperpod	Pepperpod	Roundleaf Alumroot	Roundleaf Alumroot
Moth Mullein	Moth Mullein	Petioled Wake-robin	Purple Trillium	Rowan Tree	Mountain Ash (B)
Mountain Alder	Mountain Alder	Phlox (A)	Showy Phlox	Rush	Bulrush (C)
Mountain Ash (A)	Mountain Ash (A)	Phlox (B)	Prickly Phlox	Rusty Menziesia	Fool's Huckleberry
Mountain Ash (B)	Mountain Ash (B)	Pholia nutans	Pholia nutans	Rusty-leaf	Fool's Huckleberry
Mountain Bluebells	Mountain Bluebells	Pinedrops	Pinedrops	Rye Grass	Rye Grass
Mountain Box	Oregon Boxwood	Pinegrass	Pinegrass	Sagebrush Buttercup	Sagebrush Buttercup
Mountain Field Sorre	Sheep Sorrel	Pink Spiraea	Pink Spiraea	Sagebrush Mariposa L	Mariposa Lily
Mountain Hemlock	Pacific Hemlock	Pink Wintergreen	Common Pink Wintergr	Salmon Collomia	Salmon Collomia
Mountain Lover	Oregon Boxwood	Pioneer Violet	Pioneer Violet	Salsify	Oysterplant
Mountain Maple	Mountain Maple	Piper's Anemone	Piper's Anemone	Sand Spurry	Red Spurry
Mountain Spray	Ocean Spray	Piper's Windflower	Piper's Anemone	Sandberry	Kinnikinnick
Mountain Spruce	Engelmann Spruce	Pipsissewa	Western Prince's Pin	Sandwort 1	Capitate Sandwort
Mountain Sweet-Cicel	Mountain Sweet-Cicel	Plagiomnium insigne	Plagiomnium insigne	Sandwort 2	Bluntleaf Sandwort
Mountain Tarweed	Common Tarweed	Plains Thistle	Plains Thistle	Sandwort (C)	Sandwort (C)
Mouse-ear Chickweed	Mouse-ear Chickweed	Plantain (A)	Common Plantain	Saskatoon Serviceber	Western Serviceberry
Mousetail	Mousetail	Plantain (B)	Wooly Plantain	Saxifrage 2	Western Saxifrage
Mule's Ears	Mule's Ears	Plantain (C)	Rattlesnake Plantain	Saxifrage (A)	Saxifrage (A)
Mullein	Common Mullein	Plantain (D)	Water Plantain	Scarlet Gilia	Scarlet Gilia
Musk Flower	Musk Flower	Plantain (E)	Yellow Flag Iris	Scarlet Paintbrush	Indian Paintbrush
Muskplant	Musk Flower	Pleated Gentian	Blue Gentian	Scotch Bellflower	Bellflower
Mustard	Mustard	Plum	Plum	Scouler Silene	Scouler Silene
Myrtle Boxwood	Oregon Boxwood	Poison Ivy	Poison Ivy	Scouler Willow	Scouler Willow
Naked Broom-rape	Cancerroot	Poison Oak	Poison Ivy	Scouler's Popcorn Fl	Scouler's Popcorn Fl
Narrow-leaved Collom	Narrow-leaved Collom	Polytrichum juniperi	Polytrichum juniperi	Scouring Rush	Scouring Rush
Narrow-leaved Hawkwe	Western Hawkweed	Polytrichum piliferu	Polytrichum piliferu	Seaside Dock	Golden Dock
Narrow-leaved Montia	Narrow-leaved Spring	Ponderosa Pine	Ponderosa Pine	Sedge 1	Inflated Sedge
Narrow-leaved Scullc	Narrow-leaved Scullc	Pondosa Pine	Ponderosa Pine	Sego Lily	Mariposa Lily
Narrow-leaved Skelet	Narrow-leaved Skelet	Pondweed	Pondweed	Selaginella	Selaginella
Narrow-leaved Spring	Narrow-leaved Spring	Popcorn Flower 1	Scouler's Popcorn Fl	Self-heal	Self-heal
Needle-leaf Navarret	Needle-leaf Navarret	Popcorn Flower 2	Slender Popcorn Flow	Serviceberry (A)	Western Serviceberry
Needlegrass	Needlegrass	Porella cordaeana	Porella cordaeana	Serviceberry (B)	Serviceberry (B)
Nettle	Stinging Nettle	Prairie Gentian	Blue Gentian	Shaggy Fleabane	Low Fleabane
Nevada Bluegrass	Big Bluegrass	Prairie Junegrass	Junegrass	Sheep Sorrel	Sheep Sorrel
Nevada Deervetch	Nevada Deervetch	Prairie Smoke	Old Man's Whiskers	Shepherd's Purse	Shepherd's Purse
Nine-leaved Lomatium	Nine-leaved Lomatium	Prairiestar	Small-flowered Fring	Shining Chickweed	Shining Chickweed
Ninebark	Mallow Ninebark	Prickly Gooseberry	Swamp Gooseberry	Shining Oregon Grape	Oregon Grape
Nippleseed Plantain	Common Plantain	Prickly Phlox	Prickly Phlox	Shiny-leaf Spiraea	White Spiraea
Nodding Cerastium	Longstem Chickweed	Prince's Pine	Western Prince's Pin	Shooting Star (A)	Shooting Star (A)
Nodding Chickweed	Longstem Chickweed	Prostrate Knotweed	Goose Grass	Shooting Star (B)	Shooting Star (B)
Nodding Microseris	Nodding Microseris	Puccoon	Lemonweed	Shore Pine	Lodgepole Pine
Nootka Rose	Nootka Rose	Purple Loosestrife	Purple Loosestrife	Short-awn Foxtail	Short-awn Foxtail
Northern Bedstraw	Northern Bedstraw	Purple Trillium	Purple Trillium	Showy Aster	Showy Aster
Northern Wyethia	Mule's Ears	Purple-eyed Grass	Grass Widow	Showy Milkweed	Milkweed
Northwest Trumpet	Orange Honeysuckle	Pussytoes 1	Low Pussytoes	Showy Phlox	Showy Phlox
Norway Maple	Norway Maple	Pussytoes 2	Woodrush Pussytoes	Siberian Elm	Siberian Elm
Oakfern	Oakfern	Pussytoes 3	Raceme Pussytoes	Sickletop Lousewort	Lousewort
Ocean Spray	Ocean Spray	Pussytoes 4	Rosy Pussy-toes	Sidebells Pyrola	Sidebells Pyrola
Old Man's Whiskers	Old Man's Whiskers	Pussytoes 5	Tall Pussytoes	Sierra Fairybell	Fairy Bells (B)
One Tea-tree	Redstem Ceanothus	Pussywillow	Scouler Willow	Sierra Juniper	Western Juniper
One-spike Danthonia	One-spike Oatgrass	Pyramid Spiraea	Spiraea	Silene	Douglas Silene
One-spike Oatgrass	One-spike Oatgrass	Quackgrass	Quackgrass	Silky Lupine	Blue Lupine
One-stemmed Butterwe	Ragwort	Quaking Aspen	Quaking Aspen	Silver Fir	Grand Fir
Orange Balsam	Touch-me-not	Queencup	Queencup	Silver Spruce	Engelmann Spruce
Orange Honeysuckle	Orange Honeysuckle	Queens Cup Beadlily	Queencup	Silverleaf Phacelia	Whiteleaf Phacelia
Oregon Boxwood	Oregon Boxwood	Raceme Pussytoes	Raceme Pussytoes	Silverweed	Silverweed
Oregon Fleabane	Oregon Fleabane	Racomitrium hetrosti	Racomitrium hetrosti	Sitka Mountain Ash	Mountain Ash (B)
Oregon Grape	Oregon Grape	Ragwort	Ragwort	Sitka Valerian	Sitka Valerian
Oregon Grape (A)	Oregon Grape	Rattlesnake Plantain	Rattlesnake Plantain	Six-weeks Fescue	Barren Fescue
Oregon Grape (B)	Small Oregon Grape	Red Baneberry	Western Baneberry	Skeletonweed (A)	Skeletonweed (A)
Oregon Lily	Tiger Lily	Red Besseya	Kitten Tail	Skeletonweed (B)	Narrow-leaved Skelet
Orthrotrichum specio	Orthrotrichum specio	Red Birch	River Birch	Skullcap 1	Narrow-leaved Scullc
Orthrotricum anomalu	Orthrotricum anomalu	Red Clover	Red Clover	Skullcap 2	Marsh Scullcap

Common Name	Primary Name	Common Name	Primary Name	Common Name	Primary Name
Skullcap Speedwell	Marsh Speedwell	Tall Bluebells	Bluebells	Western Wallflower	Western Wallflower
Skunk Cabbage	Skunk Cabbage	Tall Cinquefoil	Pale Cinquefoil	Western White Pine	Western White Pine
Skyrocket Gilia	Scarlet Gilia	Tall Oregon Grape	Oregon Grape	Western Yellow Pine	Ponderosa Pine
Sleepy Catchfly	Sleepy Catchfly	Tall Pussytoes	Tall Pussytoes	Western Yellowcress	Western Yellowcress
Slender Hawksbeard	Slender Hawksbeard	Tamarack	Tamarack	Wheatgrass	Quackgrass
Slender Popcorn Flow	Slender Popcorn Flow	Tamarack Pine	Lodgepole Pine	White Balsam Fir	Subalpine Fir
Slender Tarweed	Common Tarweed	Tansy	Common Tansy	White Beardtongue	White Beardtongue
Slender Willow	Slender Willow	Taper Tip Onion	Wild Onion (B)	White Clover	White Clover
Slimpod Shooting Sta	Shooting Star (A)	Tapertip Hawksbeard	Long-leaved Hawksbea	White Hawkweed (B)	White-flowered Hawkw
Small Bedstraw	Small Bedstraw	Tar Weed	Tar Weed	White Hawkweed (C)	White Hawkweed (C)
Small Bluebells	Bluebells	Tarweed (A)	Tarweed (A)	White Knapweed	White Knapweed
Small Cleavers	Small Bedstraw	Tarweed (B)	Tarweed (B)	White Plectritis	Longhorn Plectritis
Small Fescue	Small Fescue	Tarweed (C)	Common Tarweed	White Spiraea	White Spiraea
Small Hop Clover	Small Hop Clover	Teasel	Teasel	White Spruce	Engelmann Spruce
Small Oregon Grape	Small Oregon Grape	Thimbleberry	Thimbleberry	White Sweet Clover	White Sweet Clover
Small-bead Clover	Small-bead Clover	Thin-leaved Blueberr	Huckleberry (A)	White Trillum	White Trillum
Small-flowered Blue-	Blue Lips	Thinleaf Alder	Mountain Alder	White Water Buttercu	Water Buttercup
Small-flowered Bulru	Bulrush (A)	Thistle	Bull Thistle	White-flowered Hawkw	White-flowered Hawkw
Small-flowered Fring	Small-flowered Fring	Threadleaf Phacelia	Blue Phacelia	White-leaf Lupine	White-leaf Lupine
Small-flowered Mentz	Stickleaf	Thurber's Needlegras	Thurber's Needlegras	Whiteleaf Phacelia	Whiteleaf Phacelia
Small-fruit Bulrush	Bulrush (A)	Tiger Lily	Tiger Lily	Whiteveined Pyrola	Whiteveined Pyrola
Small-head Clover	Cup Clover	Timber Danthonia	Timber Danthonia	Whitlow Grass	Whitlow Grass
Smoot Sumac	Western Sumac	Timothy	Timothy	Wild Aster	Wild Aster
Smooth Aster	Wild Aster	Toadflax	Dalmatian Toadflax	Wild Dill	Nine-leaved Lomatium
Smooth Fringecup	Smooth Fringecup	Torrey's Cryptantha	Torrey's Cryptantha	Wild Ginger	Wild Ginger
Smooth Horsetail	Smooth Horsetail	Tortula princeps	Tortula princeps	Wild Guelder-rose	Highbush Cranberry
Smooth Prairiestar	Smooth Fringecup	Torula ruralis	Torula ruralis	Wild Hyacinth	Wild Hyacinth
Smooth Scouring Rush	Smooth Horsetail	Touch-me-not	Touch-me-not	Wild Mint	Wild Mint
Smooth Woodlandstar	Smooth Fringecup	Trail-plant	Pathfinder	Wild Onion (A)	Wild Onion (A)
Snow Buckwheat	Canyon Heather	Trembling Aspen	Quaking Aspen	Wild Onion (B)	Wild Onion (B)
Snowball	Highbush Cranberry	Tufted Loosestrife	Tufted Loosestrife	Wild Onion (C)	Wild Onion (C)
Snowberry	Common Snowberry	Tufted Phlox	Prickly Phlox	Wild Pink	Wild Pink
Snowbrush	Snowbrush Ceanothus	Tufted White Prairie	Wreath Aster	Wild Strawberry	Wild Strawberry
Snowbrush Ceanothus	Snowbrush Ceanothus	Tule	Tule	Willow (A)	Slender Willow
Snowy Fleabane	Oregon Fleabane	Tule Potato	Wapato	Willow (B)	Willow (B)
Softstem Bulrush	Tule	Tumble Knapweed	White Knapweed	Willow (C)	Scouler Willow
Sour Cherry	Plum	Tumble Mustard	Jim Hill Mustard	Willow (D)	Pacific Willow
Sour Dock	Curly Dock	Twin Arnica	Twin Arnica	Willow Herb	Willow Herb
Sourweed	Sheep Sorrel	Twinflower	Western Twinflower	Willow Weed Scullcap	Marsh Scullcap
Spanish Clover	Spanish Clover	Upland Larkspur	Meadow Larkspur	Winter Vetch	Hairy Vetch
Spear Thistle	Bull Thistle	Utah Honeysuckle (A)	Red Twinberry	Wintergreen 2	Green Wintergreen
Spearwort	Spearwort	Valley Cinquefoil	Pale Cinquefoil	Wintergreen (A)	Common Pink Wintergr
Speedwell	Common Speedwell	Velvet Lupine	White-leaf Lupine	Wintergreen (C)	Wintergreen (C)
Spike Rush	Spike Rush	Viper Bugloss	Common Bugloss	Wiry Knotweed	Knotweed
Spiked Willow-herb	Purple Loosestrife	Wooly Groundsel	Wooly Groundsel	Witchgrass	Panic Grass
Spiraea	Spiraea	Wakas	Indian Pond Lily	Woodland Pinedrops	Pinedrops
Spotted Coralroot	Spotted Coralroot	Wall Speedwell	Common Speedwell	Woodland Rose	Woodland Rose
Spotted Knapweed	Spotted Knapweed	Wallace's Selaginell	Selaginella	Woodlandstar	Small-flowered Fring
Spreading Dogbane	Spreading Dogbane	Wapato	Wapato	Woodrush	Woodrush
Spreading Woodfern	Spreading Woodfern	Wartberry Fairybell	Fairy Bells (B)	Woodrush Pussytoes	Woodrush Pussytoes
Spring Beauty 1	Narrow-leaved Spring	Water Birch	River Birch	Woods Rose	Woods Rose
Spring Beauty 2	Western Spring Beaut	Water Buttercup	Water Buttercup	Woods Strawberry	Woods Strawberry
Spring Beauty 4	Broad-leaved Montia	Water Crowfoot	Water Buttercup	Wooly Clover	Small-bead Clover
Spring Birch	River Birch	Water Parsnip	Water Parsnip	Wooly Groundsel	Wooly Groundsel
Spruce	Engelmann Spruce	Water Plantain	Water Plantain	Wooly Plantain	Wooly Plantain
Squaw Currant	Wax Currant	Water Smartweed	Colored Smartweed	Wooly Vetch	Hairy Vetch
Squirrel-tail	Foxtail	Watercress	Watercress	Wormleaf Stonecrop	Stonecrop
St. Johns-wort	Goatweed	Wavy-leaved Thistle	Plains Thistle	Wreath Aster	Wreath Aster
Star Solomon's Seal	Starry False Solomon	Wax Currant	Wax Currant	Wyeth Buckwheat	Wyeth Buckwheat
Star-flowered Solomo	Starry False Solomon	Western Baneberry	Western Baneberry	Yampah	Yampah
Starry False Solomon	Starry False Solomon	Western Blue Flag	Western Blue Flag	Yarrow	Blue Elderberry
Starry Solomon-plume	Starry False Solomon	Western Clematis	Western Virgin's Bow	Yellow Beardtongue	Yellow Beardtongue
Stickleaf	Stickleaf	Western Coneflower	Western Coneflower	Yellow Dock	Curly Dock
Sticky Cerastium	Longstem Chickweed	Western Dwarf Mistle	Dwarf Mistletoe	Yellow Fawn-lily	Glacier Lily
Sticky Chickweed	Sticky Chickweed	Western False Solomo	Western False Solomo	Yellow Flag Iris	Yellow Flag Iris
Sticky Currant	Sticky Currant	Western Germander	Western Germander	Yellow Fleabane	Yellow Fleabane
Sticky Geranium	Sticky Geranium	Western Goldthread	Idaho Goldthread	Yellow Indian Paintb	Yellow Indian Paintb
Sticky Purple Gerani	Sticky Geranium	Western Gromwell	Lemonweed	Yellow Iris	Yellow Flag Iris
Stinging Nettle	Stinging Nettle	Western Gromwell 2	Lemonweed	Yellow Monkeyflower	Yellow Monkeyflower
Stinking Mayweed	Fennel	Western Hawkweed	Western Hawkweed	Yellow Penstemon	Yellow Beardtongue
Stonecrop	Stonecrop	Western Hemlock	Pacific Hemlock	Yellow Pine	Ponderosa Pine
Stoneseed	Stoneseed	Western Juniper	Western Juniper	Yellow Pond Lily	Indian Pond Lily
Striped Coralroot	Coralroot	Western Larch	Tamarack	Yellow Pondosa Pine	Ponderosa Pine
Subalpine Fir	Subalpine Fir	Western Meadowrue	Western Meadowrue	Yellow Salsify	Yellow Salsify
Subalpine Sulfur Buc	Subalpine Sulfur Buc	Western Prince's Pin	Western Prince's Pin	Yellow Sweet Clover	Yellow Sweet Clover
Suckling Clover	Small Hop Clover	Western Red Cedar	Western Red Cedar	Yellow Water Lily	Indian Pond Lily
Sumac	Western Sumac	Western Saxifrage	Western Saxifrage	Yellowbell	Yellowbell
Swale Desert Parsley	Swale Desert Parsley	Western Serviceberry	Western Serviceberry	Yellowish Buffalo	Yellow Indian Paintb
Swamp Black	Swamp Gooseberry	Western Shadbush	Western Serviceberry	Yew	Pacific Yew
Swamp Gooseberry	Swamp Gooseberry	Western Solomon-plum	Starry False Solomon		
Swamp Saxifrage	Western Saxifrage	Western Spring Beaut	Western Spring Beaut		
Sweet Cicely	Sweet Cicely	Western Starflower	Western Starflower		
Sweetscented Bedstra	Sweetscented Bedstra	Western Sumac	Western Sumac		
Sword Fern	Sword Fern	Western Trillium	White Trillum		
Syringa	Mock Orange	Western Twinflower	Western Twinflower		
Tall Annual Willow H	Willow Herb	Western Virgin's Bow	Western Virgin's Bow		
Tall Bilberry	Huckleberry (A)	Western Wake-Robin	White Trillum		

References

Excellent Introductory Books and Materials

_____ *A Correlated History Of Earth* - Poster, Pan Terra (1-800-216-8130), 1994

_____ *Butterflies and Moths of the USA and Canada* - Poster, Pan Terra (1-800-216-8130), 1995

_____ *Smithsonian Chart Of Animal Evolution*, Smithsonian Institution Press, 1991

_____ *Trees Of Washington*, Extension Bulletin No. 440, Cooperative Extension, Washington State University, 1982

Marshall Community Coalition, *A Property Owners Guide To Enhancing Or Restoring Rivers, Streams and Wetlands Using Native Plants*, phone: 509.448.1254, 1995

Reynolds, Jan and Cassidy, Heather Hastings, *The Little Spokane River Journal*, Spokane County Conservation District and Spokane Falls Community College, 1984

Tekiela, Stan and Shanberg, Karen, *Nature Smart - A Family Guide To Nature* (Midwest and Eastern U.S.), Adventure Publications (1-800-678-7006), 1995

Little Spokane Watershed Studies And Materials

_____ *Cavity Nester Habitat Enhancement Program for Nine Mile Reservoir and Little Spokane River Natural Area 5-Year Report 1989-1993*, Washington Water Power Company, 1994

_____ *Birds of the Inland Empire*, Spokane Audubon Society, 1986

_____ Colbert Landfill Superfund Site Cleanup Documents

_____ *A Resource Inventory for the Little Spokane Scenic River Area*, Urban and Regional Planning Department, Eastern Washington University

_____ *Washington State Parks Natural Forest Inventory: Mount Spokane*, Washington State Parks

Gill, Dale C., *Checklist of Lichens for the Little Spokane River Natural Area*

Gill, Dale C., *Checklist of Mosses and Ferns for the Little Spokane River Natural Area*

Gill, Dale C., *Common Mosses of Turnbull National Wildlife Refuge*

Jones, Grant R. *Study Documenting the Recreational and Resource Value of the Lower Reach of the Little Spokane River*, Jones and Jones, 1975

Resources Northwest, Inc., *Wintering Bald Eagles in the Spokane River Corridor 1989-92*, Washington Water Power Company, 1995

Rogers, Thomas H., *Plants of the Little Spokane River State Park and Deep Creek Canyon, Preliminary List*

Rogers, Thomas H., *Plants of Mount Spokane*

Schwab, Suzanne, Margaret O'Connell and Easy, *Little Spokane River Natural Area Base Line Plant Community and Wildlife Report*, 1995

Simms, Horace R., *Some Lichens of Turnbull National Wildlife Refuge*

_____ Spokane Aquifer Documents

Other Studies And Materials Related To The Little Spokane Watershed

_____ *Summer Wildflowers Of North Idaho*, Idaho Panhandle National Forests, R1-92-36

_____ *Vascular Plants, Turnbull National Wildlife Refuge*, U.S. Fish and Wildlife Service, 1991

_____ *Colville National Forest Plant Count Survey - 967 Species Identified*, Colville National Forest, 1976

Burke, T. and J. Nisbet, *Birds Of The Colville National Forest*, Colville National Forest, 1979

Burke, T., *Mammals Of The Colville National Forest*, Colville National Forest, 1976

Burke, T., *Reptiles And Amphibians Of The Colville National Forest*, Colville National Forest, 1976

O'Laughlin, Kate, Barber, Michael R., Scholz, Allan T., Gibson, Flash and Weinand, Marie, *An Instream Flow (IFIM) Analysis of Benthic Macroinvertebrates in Chamokane Creek, Spokane Indian Reservation*, Upper Columbia United Tribes Fisheries Center, 1988

Rogers, Thomas H., *Butterflies of the Dishman Hills – Tower Mountain Area, Spokane, Washington*, Dishman Hills Natural Area Association, 1987

Rogers, Thomas H., *Birds, Mammals, Reptiles and Amphibians of the Dishman Hills – Tower Mountain Area, Spokane, Washington*, Dishman Hills Natural Area Association, 1987

Rogers, Thomas H., *Fungi of the Dishman Hills – Tower Mountain Area, Spokane, Washington*, Dishman Hills Natural Area Association, 1987

Rogers, Thomas H., *Plants and Animals Recorded at Larry Barnes' Place, Springdale-Cemetery Road, Washington, July 9, 1981*

Rogers, Thomas H., *Three Springs Natural Area Plants List*

Rogers, Thomas H., *Vascular Plants of the Dishman Hills, Spokane, Washington*, Dishman Hills Natural Area Association

Rogers, Thomas H., *Wildlife Species Impacted by Urban Development , 1991*

Scholz, Allan T.; Barber, Michael R., O'Laughlin, Kate, Whalen, John, Peone, Tim, Uehara, Jim and Geist, Dave, *Brown Trout, Rainbow Trout, Brook Trout, Mountain Whitefish, Piute Sculpin, and Torrent Sculpin Population and Production Estimates in Chamokane Creek, Spokane Indian Reservation: 1986 and 1987*, Upper Columbia United Tribes Fisheries Center, 1988

Teel, Darci, Bradburn, Steve and Schultz, Tim, *Selected Noxious Weeds of Eastern Washington*, Spokane County Noxious Weed Control Board

Van Pelt, Roger, *Washington Big Tree Program*, College of Forest Resources, University of Washington, 1994

Wheeler, Ralph A., *Undesirable Weeds of Idaho Forest Lands*, State of Idaho, Department of Agriculture

Historic Sources

Allen, John Eliot, Burns, Marjorie and Sargent, Samuel C., *Cataclysms on the Columbia: A Layman's Guide to the Features Produced by the Catastrophic Bretz Floods in the Pacific Northwest*, Timber Press, 1986

Anderson, Alice Racer, ed., *Plant Life of Washington Territory: Northern Pacific Railroad Survey, Botanical Report. 1853-1861*, Washington Native Plant Society, 1994

Durham, N.W., *The History of the City of Spokane and Spokane Country Washington, From Its Earliest Settlement to the Present Time*, 1912

Caywood, Louis R., *Archeological Excavations at Fort Spokane: 1951*, United States Department of the Interior National Park Service, 1952

Combes, John D., *Excavations at Spokane House – Fort Spokane Historic Site: 1962-1963*, Washington State University, 1964

Ewing, Russell C., *Report on Field Investigation of Spokane House, Washington Region IV*

Schalk, Randall, Ed., *Cultural Resources Reconnaissance in Washington State Parks Biennial Summary for 1987-1989*, Center for Northwest Anthropology, Washington State University, 1990

Critters

Comprehensive Guides

_____ The Peterson Field Guide Series, Houghton Mifflin, includes field guides for Western Birds, Bird Nests, Western Reptiles and Amphibians, Mammals, Animal Sign, etc.

Algae

Prescott, G.W., *How to Know the Fresh Water Algae*, William C. Brown Co., Dubuque Iowa, 1954

Amphibians

Leonard, W.P., H.A. Brown, L. L. C. Jones, K. R. McAllister, and R.M. Storm. *Amphibians of Washington and Oregon*. Seattle Audubon Society; The Trailside Series, Seattle, WA, phone: 206.523.4483. 1993

Nussbaum, Ronald A., Brodie, Edmund D., Jr. and Storm, Robert M., *Amphibians and Reptiles of the Pacific Northwest*, University of Idaho Press, 1983

Stebbins, Robert C., *A Field Guide to Western Reptiles and Amphibians*, Houghton Mifflin Co., Boston, 1966

Birds

Audubon Society, *The Audubon Society Master Guide to Birding*, (Books 1, 2 and 3), Alfred A. Knopf, Inc., 1983

Carey, A. B. et al., *Training Guide For Bird Identification In Pacific Northwest Douglas Fir Forests*. U.S.D.A. Forest Service. General Technical Report, PNW-GTR-260. Gives descriptions of bird calls. 1990

Dobkin, D. S., *Conservation and Management of Neotropical Migrant Landbirds*, University of Idaho Press, Moscow, ID. 1994

Ehrlich, Paul R., Dobkin, David S. and Wheye, Darryl, *The Birder's Handbook*, Simon & Schuster, Inc., 1988

Houston, Mark and Vial, Maurice, *Birds of the Channeled Scablands of Eastern Washington*, Spokane District - Bureau of Land Management, 1995

Prichard, Don, *Peterson Field Guide to Western Birds*. Houghton Mifflin Co., New York. A very comprehensive field guide that includes habitats and excellent illustrations, 1994.

Fish

Wydoski, Richard S. and Whitney, Richard R., *Inland Fishes of Washington*, University of Washington Press, 1979

Fungi

Arora, David, *Mushrooms Demystified*, Ten Speed Press, Berkeley, 1986. This book is a very thorough field guide and reference for all levels of skill. It is filled with useful information and amusing comments.

Kendrick, Bryce, *The Fifth Kingdom- Second Edition*, University of Waterloo, 1992. This book is used as a college textbook. It's extensive information may be more than the average person is interested in. But, for those that want to learn about fungi the book is quite good.

Miller, Orson K. Jr., *Mushrooms of North America*, Chanticleer Press, E. P. Dutton

Philips, Roger, *Mushrooms of North America*, Little, Brown and Company, 1991. Though this field guide and reference book's descriptions and explanations are short and scarce, the book has a good representation of north American fungi, and a comprehensive collection of color photos.

Smith, Alexander H., *A Field Guide to Western Mushrooms*, University of Michigan Press, 1975

McKenny, Margaret & Daniel E. Stutz, *The Savory Wild Mushroom*, University of Washington Press, 1971

Insects

Borror, Donald J. and DeLong, Dwight M., A*n Introduction to the Study of Insects*, Third Edition, Holt, Rinehart and Winston, Inc., 1964

Borror, Donald J. and White, Richard E., *A Field Guide to the Insects*, Houghton Mifflin Co., Boston, 1970

Ehrlich, Paul R. and Ehrlich, Anne H., *How to Know Butterflies*, William C. Brown Co., Dubuque, Iowa, 1961

McCafferty, W. Patrick, *Aquatic Entomology*, Jones & Bartlett Publishers, London, 1981

Merritt, Richard W. and Cummins, Kenneth W., Eds. *Introduction to the Aquatic Insects of North America*, Kendall/Hunt Publishing Co., Dubuque, Iowa, 1978

Neill, W.A. and Hepburn, D.J. *Butterflies Afield in the Pacific Northwest*, Pacific Search Books, 1976

Lichens

Hale, Mason E., *How to Know the Lichens*, William C. Brown Co., Dubuque, Iowa, 1969

Vitt, Dale H., et. al., *Mosses, Lichens & Ferns of Northwest North America*

Mammals

_____ American Society Of Mammologists publishes a series of species accounts entitled: *Mammalian Species.*

Burt, William H., and Grossenheider, Richard P., *Peterson Field Guide to Mammals*, Houghton Mifflin Co., New York. The authoritative field guide for mammals; a comprehensive listing of mammals, habits, habitats, and excellent illustrations, 1980

Chapman, J. A. and G. A. Feldhamer, *Wild Mammals Of North America*, Johns Hopkins University Press, Baltimore, MD. 1982.

Christensen, James, R. and Larrison, Earl J., *Mammals of the Pacific Northwest*, University Press of Idaho, 1982

Hall, E. R., *Mammals Of North America*, John Wiley & Sons, New York, NY. 1980.

Haley, Delphine, *Pacific Search*, Sleek & Savage, 1975.

Jones, J.K., Jr., and Manning, R. W., *Illustrated Key To Skulls Of Genera Of North American Land Mammals*, Texas Tech University Press, Lubbock, TX. 1992.

Kritzman, Ellen B., *Little Mammals of the Pacific Northwest*, Pacific Search Press, 1977

Larrison, Earl J., *Mammals of the Northwest*, Seattle Audubon Society, 1976

Nagorsen, David W. and Brigham, Mark R., *Bats of British Columbia*, Royal British Columbia Museum, 1993

Novak, M., J. A. Baken, M.E. Obbard, B. Malloch, *Wild Furbearer And Management And Conservation In North America*, Ministry Of Natural Resources, Ontario, Canada. 1987.

van Zyll de Jong, G.G., *Handbook Of Canadian Mammals*. Seven Volumes. National Museums of Canada, Ottawa, Canada. 1983

Mosses

Conard, Henry S., *How to Know the Mosses and Liverworts*, William C. Brown Co., Dubuque, Iowa, 1956

Crum, Howard A., *Mosses of the Great Lakes Forest*, University of Michigan, 1976

Crum, Howard A. and Anderson, Lewis E., *Mosses of Eastern North America Volume 1 and 2*, University of Michigan, 1981

Flowers, Seville, *Mosses: Utah and the West*, University of Utah, 1973

Grout, A. J., *Moss Flora of North America Volumes 1-3*, 1929-1934, Reprint 1972

Grout, A. J., *Mosses with a Hand Lens and Microscope*

Lawton, Elva, *Moss Flora of the Pacific Northwest*, University of Washington, 1971

Vitt, Dale H., et. al., *Mosses Lichens & Ferns of Northwest North America*, Lone Pine Press, 1988

Plants

Arno, S. F. and R. P. Hammerly, *Northwest Trees*, The Mountaineers, Seattle. 1979

Bailey, L.H., *How Plants Get Their Names*, Dover Publications, 1963

Craighead, Craighead and Davis, *Field Guide to Rocky Mountain Wildflowers*, Houghton Mifflin, 1963

Harrington, H.D. and Durrell, L.W. *How to Identify Plants*, First Swallow Press/Ohio University Press, 1957

Harris, James G. & Woolf, Melinda Harris *Plant Identification Terminology*, Spring Lake Publishing, 1954

Hart, Jeff *Montana - Native Plants and Early Peoples*, The Montana Historical Society, 1976

Hitchcock, A. S. *Manual Of The Grasses Of The United States*, Dover Publications, NY. 1971

Hitchcock, C. Leo and Arthus Cronquist *Flora of the Pacific Northwest*, University of Washington Press, Seattle, 1973

Larrison, E. J., G.W. Patrick, W. H. Baker, and J. A. Yaich. *Washington Wildflowers*. Seattle Audubon Society, Seattle. 1977

Johnson, Charles Grier, Jr., *Common Plants of the Inland Pacific Northwest*, U.S.D.A. Forest Service General Technical Report R6-ERW-TP051-93. A good field guide to common plants; provides excellent pictures and brief descriptions of plant and habitat. 1993

Jones, J. Knox Jr., Armstrong, David M & Chote, Jerry R., University of Nebraska Press, 1985

Kirk, Donald R. *Wild Edible Plants Of Western North America, Naturegraph Publishers,* 1975

Kozloff, Eugene N. *Plants and Animals of the Pacific Northwest*, University of Washington Press, 1976

Larrison, Earl J. *Washington Wildflowers*, Seattle Audubon Society, Seattle, 1974

Martin, Alexander C., Zim, Herbert S. and Nelson, Arnold L. *American Wildlife and Plants: A Guide to Wildlife Food Habits*, Dover Publications, New York, 1951

Mathews, Daniel, *Cascade - Olympic Natural History; A Trailside Reference*. Raven Editions, Portland. An excellent book that provides readable descriptions of many natural processes as well as descriptions, illustrations, and photographs. 1990

Niehaus, Theodore F. and Ripper, Charles, A *Field Guide to Pacific States Wildflowers*, Houghton Mifflin Company, 1976

Patterson, Patricia A., Neiman, Kenneth E., Tonn, Jonalea R., Fie*ld Guide To Forest Plants Of Northern Idaho, General Technical Report INT-180*, U.S. Forest Service. A good field guide with habitat references; includes illustrations, 1985

Pfeiffer, Ehrenfried E. *Weeds and What They Tell*

Pojar, Jim and MacKinnon, Andy *Plants of the Pacific Northwest Coast*, Lone Pine Publishing, 1994

Porsild, A.E. *Rocky Mountain Wildflowers*, National Museum of Natural Sciences/National Museum of Canada, 1979

Randall, Warren R., Keniston, Robert F., Bever, Dale N. and Jensen, Edward C. *Manual of Oregon Trees and Shrubs*, Oregon State University, 1988

Roche´, Ben F. and Roche´, Cindy Talbott *Pacific Northwest Weeds*, Washington State University Cooperative Extension, 1991

Taylor, R. J. *Northwest Weeds*, Mountain Press, Missoula. 1990

Taylor, R. J. *Sagebrush Country: A Wildflower Sanctuary*, Mountain Press, Missoula. 1990

Spellenberg, Richard, *The Audubon Society Field Guide to North American Wildflowers (Western Region)*, Chanticleer Press, Alfred A. Knopf, 1979

Strickler, Dee, Ph.D. *Forest Wildflowers*, The Flower Press, 1988

Strickler, Dee, Ph.D. *Prairie Wildflowers*, The Flower Press, 1986

Reptiles

Leonard, W.P., H.A. Brown, L. L. C. Jones, K. R. McAllister, and R.M. Storm, *Amphibians of Washington and Oregon.*, Seattle Audubon Society; The Trailside Series, Seattle, WA, phone: 206.523.4483. 1993

Gregory, Patrick T. and Campbell, R. Wayne, *The Reptiles of British Columbia*, British Columbia Provincial Museum, Victoria, 1944

Stebbins, Robert C., *A Field Guide to Western Reptiles and Amphibians*, Houghton Mifflin Co., Boston, 1966

Habitats

_____ *Riparian Area Management; Process for Assessing Proper Functioning Condition for Lentic-Riparian Wetland Areas*. U.S. Department of the Interior Technical Reference 1737-11 Rodgers, C. Leland, and Rex E. Kerstetter. 1974

_____ *The Ecosphere; Organisms, Habitats, and Disturbances*, Harper and Row, New York. An introductory book that covers a broad range of topics; sections have become outdated; look for a recent edition.

Benyus, Janine M., *The Field Guide to Wildlife Habitats of the Western United States*. Simon and Schuster, New York. An excellent introduction to broad habitat types with emphasis on a number of interesting animals, 1989

Borror, Donald J. and White, Richard E., *A Field Guide to the Insects*, Houghton Mifflin Co., Boston, 1970

Burt, William H., and Richard P. Grossenheider, *Peterson Field Guide to Mammals* Houghton Mifflin Co., New York. The authoritative field guide for mammals; a comprehensive listing of mammals, habits, habitats, and excellent illustrations.1980

Campbell, Neil A. *Biology*, Third Edition Benjamin/Cummings Publishing Co., Redwood City, CA. Designed to be a text to introductory college biology, but is very readable and covers a wealth of information. 1993.

Conard, Henry S., *How to Know the Mosses and Liverworts*, William C. Brown Co., Dubuque, Iowa, 1956

Cooper, S. V., K. E. Neiman and D. W. Roberts, *Forest Habitat Types Of Northern Idaho: A Second Approximation* US Forest Service Intermountain Research Station Technical Report INT-236. Ogden, UT, 1991

Cooperrider, Allen Y., et al., *Inventory And Monitoring of Wildlife Habitat* U.S. Department of Interior, Bureau of Land Management. 858 pp.,1986.

Daubenmire, R., *Steppe Vegetation Of Washington*. Washington Agricultural Experiment Station Technical Bulletin 62, Washington State University, Pullman. 1970.

Ehrlich, Paul R. and Ehrlich, Anne H., *How to Know Butterflies*, William C. Brown Co., Dubuque, Iowa, 1961

Franklin, J. F. and C. T. Dyrness, *Natural Vegetation Of Oregon And Washington*, Oregon State University Press, Corvallis. 1973

Hale, Mason E. *How to Know the Lichens*, William C. Brown Co., Dubuque, Iowa, 1969

Heyer, W.R., M. A. Donnelly, R. W. McDiarmid, L. C. Hayek, and M.S. Foster, *Measuring And Monitoring Biological Diversity: Standard Methods For Amphibians*, Smithsonian Institution Press, Washington, DC, 1994

Hitchcock, C. Leo and Cronquist, Arthur, *Flora of the Pacific Northwest*, University of Washington Press, Seattle, 1973

Johnson, Charles Grier, Jr., *Common Plants of the Inland Pacific Northwest. U.S.D.A. Forest Service General Technical Report R6-ERW-TP051-93*. A good field guide to common plants; provides excellent pictures and brief descriptions of plant and habitat, 1993

Kozloff, Eugene N., *Plants and Animals of the Pacific Northwest*, University of Washington Press, 1976

Larrison, Earl J., *Washington Wildflowers*, Seattle Audubon Society, Seattle, 1974

Martin, Alexander C., Zim, Herbert S. and Nelson, Arnold L., *American Wildlife and Plants: A Guide to Wildlife Food Habits*, Dover Publications, New York, 1951

Mathews, Daniel, *Cascade - Olympic Natural History; A Trailside Reference*. Raven Editions, Portland. An excellent book that provides readable descriptions of many natural processes as well as descriptions, illustrations, and photographs, 1990

Merritt, Richard W. and Cummins, Kenneth W., Eds. *Introduction to the Aquatic Insects of North America*, Kendall/Hunt Publishing Co., Dubuque, Iowa, 1978

Nussbaum, Ronald A., Edmund D. Brodie, Jr. and Storm, Robert M., *Amphibians and Reptiles of the Pacific Northwest*. University of Idaho Press, Moscow. A very comprehensive field guide that provides much information on amphibians and reptiles and their habitat types. 1983

Patterson, Patricia A., Neiman, Kenneth E., Tonn, Jonalea R., *Field Guide To Forest Plants Of Northern Idaho, General Technical Report INT-180*, U.S. Forest Service. A good field guide with habitat references; includes illustrations, 1985

Prichard, Don, *Peterson Field Guide to Western Birds*, Houghton Mifflin Co., New York. A very comprehensive field guide that includes habitats and excellent illustrations, 1994

Prescott, G.W., *How to Know the Fresh Water Algae*, William C. Brown Co., Dubuque Iowa, 1954

Pyle, Robert Michael, *Watching Washington Butterflies*, Seattle Audubon Society, Seattle, 1974

Scheminitz, S. D., editor, *Wildlife Management Techniques Manual - Fourth Edition*, The Wildlife Society, Washington, DC. 1980

Stebbins, Robert C., *A Field Guide to Western Reptiles and Amphibians*, Houghton Mifflin Co., Boston, 1966

Index

Little Spokane Watershed Council

Purpose

The Little Spokane Watershed Council is a volunteer group of individuals who care about the health and well-being of the Little Spokane Watershed. The Council's purpose is to nurture the stewardship of the Little Spokane Watershed. The Council is intended to be a place for sharing success stories and visions and to be a resource center for the watershed.

The Council's goal is to foster attitudes, of the people living in and involved with the Little Spokane Watershed, that work toward the stewardship of the Little Spokane Watershed. This is no small project and not an unworthy goal.

Leadership

The Little Spokane Watershed Council works on various projects nurturing the health of the watershed and allowing the watershed to become more restorative. Each specific project has its own active participants who are responsible for the project. Project ideas and project volunteers are most welcome.

Newsletter

Current, the Council's newsletter, provides a forum for individuals, groups, and organizations working for the stewardship of the Little Spokane Watershed. Photographs, drawings, stories, articles, humor, and examples of what works and what can work are most welcome; especially those that show stewardship of the Little Spokane Watershed.

Little Spokane Watershed Council

P.O. Box 413, Spokane, WA 99210
Phone: 509.747.5738, Fax: 509.838.5155
Email: Easy@ieplc.desktop.org